Book of Tarnogrod;
in Memory of the Destroyed Jewish Community
(Tarnogród, Poland)

Translation of
Sefer Tarnogrod;
le-zikaron ha-kehila ha-yehudit she-nehreva

Original Book Edited by: Sh. Kanc

Originally published in Tel Aviv 1966

A Publication of JewishGen, INC
Edmond J. Safra Plaza, 36 Battery Place, New York, NY 10280
646.494.5972 | info@JewishGen.org | www.jewishgen.org

Book of Tarnogrod; in Memory of the Destroyed Jewish Community (Tarnogród, Poland)
Translation of *Sefer Tarnogrod; le-zikaron ha-kehila ha-yehudit she-nehreva*

Copyright © 2023 by JewishGen, INC All rights reserved.
First Printing: July 2023, Av 5783
Editor of Original Yizkor Book: S. Kanc
Project Coordinator: Tom Merolla
Cover Design: Irv Osterer
Layout: Jonathan Wind
Name Indexing: Stefanie Holzman

Printed in the United States of America by Lightning Source, Inc.

Library of Congress Control Number (LCCN): 2023931948

ISBN: 978-1-954176-72-0 (hard cover: 460 pages, alk. paper)

About JewishGen.org

JewishGen, an affiliate of the Museum of Jewish Heritage - A Living Memorial to the Holocaust, serves as the global home for Jewish genealogy.

Featuring unparalleled access to 30+ million records, it offers unique search tools, along with opportunities for researchers to connect with others who share similar interests. Award winning resources such as the Family Finder, Discussion Groups, and ViewMate, are relied upon by thousands each day.

In addition, JewishGen's extensive informational, educational and historical offerings, such as the Jewish Communities Database, Yizkor Book translations, InfoFiles, Family Tree of the Jewish People, and KehilaLinks, provide critical insights, first-hand accounts, and context about Jewish communal and familial life throughout the world.

Offered as a free resource, JewishGen.org has facilitated thousands of family connections and success stories, and is currently engaged in an intensive expansion effort that will bring many more records, tools, and resources to its collections.

Please visit https://www.jewishgen.org/ to learn more.

Executive Director: Avraham Groll

About the JewishGen Yizkor Book Project

Yizkor Books (Memorial Books) were traditionally written to memorialize the names of departed family and martyrs during holiday services in the synagogue (a practice that still exists in many synagogues today).

Over the centuries, as a result of countless persecutions and horrific atrocities committed against the Jews, Yizkor Books (Sefer Zikaron in Hebrew) were expanded to include more historical information, such as biographical sketches of famous personalities and descriptions of daily town life.

Following the Holocaust, the idea of remembrance and learning took on an urgent and crucial importance. Survivors of the Holocaust sought out other surviving residents of their former towns to memorialize and document the names and way of life of those who were ruthlessly murdered by the Nazis. These remembrances were documented in Yizkor Books, hundreds of which were published in the first decades after the Holocaust.

Most of these books were published privately, or through Landsmanshaftn (social organizations comprised of members originating from the same European town or region) that still existed, and were often distributed free of charge. Sadly, the languages used to document these crucial histories and links to our past, Yiddish and Hebrew, are no longer commonly understood by a significant percentage of Jews today. As a result, JewishGen has undertaken the sacred responsibility of translating these books into English so that the culture and way of life of these communities will be preserved and transmitted to future generations.

In 1986, a group of farsighted JewishGenners started a project to pool their efforts together in groups based upon their ancestors from each town and donate money to get the Yizkor books of their ancestral towns translated into English. As the translated material became available, it was made accessible for free at www.JewishGen.org/Yizkor. Hardcover copies can be purchased by visiting https://www.jewishgen.org/Yizkor/ybip.html (see below).

It is our hope that the translation of these books into English (and other languages) will assist the countless Jewish family researchers who are so desperately seeking to forge a connection with their heritage.

Director of JewishGen Yizkor Book Project: Lance Ackerfeld

About JewishGen Press

JewishGen Press (formerly the Yizkor Books-in-Print Project) is the publishing division of JewishGen.org, and provides a venue for the publication of non-fiction books pertaining to Jewish genealogy, history, culture, and heritage.

In addition to the Yizkor Book category, publications in the Other Non-Fiction category include Shoah memoirs and research, genealogical research, collections of genealogical and historical materials, biographies, diaries and letters, studies of Jewish experience and cultural life in the past, academic theses, and other books of interest to the Jewish community.

Please visit https://www.jewishgen.org/Yizkor/ybip.html to learn more.

Director of JewishGen Press: Joel Alpert
Managing Editor - Jessica Feinstein
Publications Manager - Susan Rosin

Dedications

In memory of Yitzhak and Mali Rosengarten, who perished in the Shoah. In memory of Louis Rosengarten, son of Yitzhak and Mali, who immigrated to America in 1913. In memory of Alan Rosengarten, son of Louis, who presented Sefer Tarnogrod to his children, encouraging its translation and publication so the perished would not be forgotten.

Lorraine Rosengarten
Florida, 2023

In memory of Louis and Hannah Strassberg, born in Tarnogrod, married there, who left to start a new life in America. In memory of their daughter Ruth Strassberg Rosenbloom and with thanks to my wife Nancy who started me on the journey to remember Tarnogrod and the people who lived and died there.

Tom Merolla
New Jersey, 2023

Acknowledgement

I would like to thank Lance Ackerfeld, long time Director of the JewishGen Yizkor Book Project for his invaluable help in all stages of the project going back 14 years. Thanks to the JewishGen publishing team led by Susan Rosin, Publications Manager; Jonathan Wind, Layout, Stefanie Holzman, Indexing and Irv Osterer Cover Design.

Very special thanks to Lorraine Rosengarten who started this project, donated her time to scan Sefer Tarnogrod, as well as extensive transliteration, editing, formatting, and donating the resources necessary to hire the translators who converted the Yiddish and Hebrew texts into English.

Thanks to Jewish Records Indexing – Poland, especially Stanley Diamond, Robin Magid and Shelley Pollero for their excellent work making available Polish, Jewish Vital Records to the public.

I want to acknowledge our translators including Sara Mages, Martin Jacobs, Tina Lunson and Zvika Welgreen and especially Miriam Leberstein, who become an honorary Tarnogroder during this project.

Special thanks to Joseph Schorer and his family, especially his son Sheldon. Joseph survived the Holocaust in Tarnogrod and returned years later to erect memorials to those who lived and died there.

I would like to thank those who manage and contribute to the Tarnogroder Facebook Page, Tarnohotzkies, especially Jadwiga Zmuda, Helene Roumani and Nadiv Schorer.

In memory of Morris Gradel, translator of the Tarnogrod chapter of Pinkas Hakehillot Polin, who died in 2010 and Kristen Gradel who "volunteered" me to take on the role of JRI-Poland Volunteer Coordinator for Tarnogrod.

Tom Merolla
New Jersey, 2023

Sefer Tarnogrod – Introduction

"Mormons study their genealogy, and by extension, everybody's genealogy, in order to identify their ancestors and gain salvation for them. That may sound like a silly superstition. And yet, each time I have uncovered the name of one of my long-forgotten ancestors I have been filled with the mystical feeling that I was indeed rescuing that ancestor, not from hellfire, perhaps, but from oblivion. They did walk the earth, our ancestors, once upon a time, and they are still out there somewhere. There is much they can teach us even now, if we can find them."

Dan Rottenberg
Finding Our Fathers, A Guidebook to Jewish Genealogy
Copyright 1977, 1985

Genealogy, for the first 40 years of my life meant little. My grandparents, parents, aunts and uncles and cousins all lived within a short drive of our house in Queens, NY. Then my Uncle Dan handed me a copy of a family tree program. "Why don't you work on a family tree for your dad's family"? I started slowly, finding the names of my dad's grandparents and the town they left behind when they came to America early in the 20th Century. Once the word spread that I was researching Dad's family, his cousin sent me a handwritten family tree going back to the first quarter of the 19th Century. A friend introduced me to the Mormon "Family History Centers" and I was able to obtain copies of vital records from the town my grandparents were born in going back to 1809. I was hooked.

My wife Nancy knew very little about her roots. Her maternal grandparents died before she was born. She lost contact with aunts, uncles and cousins. One day at a gathering of my wife's family I explained the research I was doing on my dad's family and asked my mother-in-law Ruth Strassberg Rosenbloom, about her family. She revealed her parents were uncle and niece, they were born in Tarnogrod, and they left there for New York in the early 20th Century. As anyone who has travelled this path knows these small details can lead to a journey of discovery. Thanks to immigration records, Ancestry and the Family History Centers I began constructing the Strassberg family tree and to learn about the city of Tarnogrod.

Finding copies of Louis Strassberg's birth and marriage records was exciting. Understanding the hand-written Cyrillic was a challenge. Doing research led me to the amazing repository of information that is JewishGen and the wonderful team of researchers and administrators who manage JRI-Poland. While current vital records for Tarnogrod only go back to 1870, I was able to unlock more secrets. Since the JRI volunteer position for Tarnogrod was vacant I was asked to fill the position. It was in this role I was approached by Lorraine Rosengarten to see if we could add Sefer Tarnogrod to the JewishGen Yizkor Book project. Sefer Tarnogrod was given to Lorraine by her father-in-law, Alan Rosengarten, with the request the book be translated into English for those who cannot read Yiddish or Hebrew. That was 14 years ago. We persevered and the result is the book you are holding today.

Tarnogrod was like many other shtetls in Eastern Europe. A mixture of Jews and Christians living and working in a small town. By the 1680s there were enough Jewish people to erect an attractive stone synagogue. By the 1760, there were more than 1600 poll tax paying Jews in Tarnogrod and the surrounding villages. There were rabbis and schools of Jewish learning. By the threshold of WWII about half of all Tarnogrod residents were Jewish. Six years later there were none. Yet some survived, exiles in Russia or living in local forests in family camps. When the war ended the survivors relocated to Israel, Canada, South America, the UK, the United States, and other countries around the world. The memories of the Tarnogrod they knew led a group to document their stories resulting in the publishing of Sefer Tarnogrod in 1966 in Tel Aviv. Through their collective knowledge they convey the history of the town, the customs, the people, interesting stories, poems, old photographs, and drawings. And they tell the story of what happened to their town starting in September 1939. The executions and the rounding up of those who still lived in Tarnogrod in 1942 to be sent to the death camp at Belzec. At the end of the book there is a Necrology, a list of those who died, documented by those who remembered them and did not want their memory to die when they did.

After the translation of the original text there is an appendix with photographs, additional reading materials, useful Internet links and additional information about Tarnogrod.

Today there are descendants of Tarnogroders around the world. I have been able to meet some of them, in person and in telephone calls and emails. The Synagogue has been refurbished and today is the beautiful Tarnogrod library, complete with the remains of the ark. Through the efforts of people like Joseph Schorer, memorials have been built in Tarnogrod and headstones from the desecrated Jewish Cemetery have partially been recovered and re-erected as another memorial.

As you read this book, remember that in addition to learning the history of Tarnogrod, you will be meeting the Tarnogroders who came before you, "they did walk the earth, our ancestors, once upon a time, and they are still out there somewhere. There is much they can teach us even now, if we can find them."

Tom Merolla
June 2023
Hillsborough, NJ, USA

Photo Credits

Front Cover:

Reproduction of the original Yizkor Book cover – Irv Osterer

Back Cover:

Clockwise from top left:

Joseph Schorer standing in front of the Tarnogrod Synagogue, circa 1984, *photograph courtesy of Sheldon Schorer*

Tarnogrod Library, former Synagogue, 2023, *photograph courtesy of Jadwiga Zmuda*

Recovered Headstones from the Tarnogrod Jewish Cemetery, *photograph courtesy of Sheldon Schorer*

The Tarnogrod Cemetery, circa 1939/1949, *photograph by Marcel Weise, used by permission of his family*

Geopolitical Information

Tanogród, Poland is located at 50°22' N 22°45' E and 151 miles SSE of Warsaw

	Town	District	Province	Country
Before WWI (c. 1900):	Tarnogród	Biłgoraj	Lublin	Russian Empire
Between the wars (c. 1930):	Tarnogród	Biłgoraj	Lublin	Poland
After WWII (c. 1950):	Tarnogród			Poland
Today (c. 2000):	Tarnogród			Poland

Alternate Names for the Town:

Tarnogród [Pol], Tarnogrud [Rus, Yid]

Nearby Jewish Communities:

Łukowa 9 miles E

Cewków 10 miles SSE

Cieplice 10 miles SSW

Dzików Stary 11 miles SE

Biłgoraj 13 miles N

Ułazów 13 miles ESE

Kuryłówka 13 miles WSW

Józefów 14 miles ENE

Sieniawa 15 miles SSW

Leżajsk 16 miles WSW

Krzeszów 18 miles W

Oleszyce 19 miles SE

Grodzisko Dolne 19 miles SW

Zwierzyniec 19 miles NNE

Cieszanów 19 miles ESE

Lubaczów 22 miles SE

Frampol 22 miles N

Rudnik nad Sanem 22 miles W

Wola Żarczycka 23 miles WSW

Ulanów 23 miles WNW

Przeworsk 23 miles SSW

Krasnobród 24 miles ENE

Żołynia 24 miles SW

Jarosław 24 miles S

Goraj 24 miles N

Szczebrzeszyn 25 miles NNE

Narol 25 miles E

Lipsko 26 miles E

Jeżowe 26 miles W

Kamień 27 miles W

Janów Lubelski 28 miles NNW

Nisko 29 miles WNW

Radymno 29 miles S

Chrzanów 29 miles NNW

Sokołów Małopolski 29 miles WSW

Tomaszów Lubelski 30 miles ENE

Wielkie Oczy 30 miles SE

Horyniec 30 miles ESE

Skołoszów 30 miles S

Bełżec 30 miles E

Kańczuga 30 miles SSW

Pysznica 30 miles WNW

Jewish Population: 1,673 (in 1857), 2,238 (in 1921)

Map of Poland showing the location of **Tarnogród**

Table of Contents

III   Death and Destruction

IV   Heroism

Book of Tarnogrod;
in Memory of the Destroyed Jewish Community
(Tarnogród, Poland)

50° 22' / 22° 45'

Translation of
Sefer Tarnogrod; le-zikaron ha-kehila ha-yehudit she-nehreva

Edited by: Sh. Kanc

Published in Tel Aviv 1966

Acknowledgments

Project Coordinator:

Tom Merolla

**With thanks to Lorraine Rosengarten who started this project, donated her time to scan
Sefer Tarnogrod, as well as extensive transliterating, editing and formatting.**

**In memory of Louis Rosengarten, son of Yitzhak and Mali, who immigrated to America in 1913.
In memory of Alan Rosengarten, son of Louis, who presented Sefer Tarnogrod to his children,
encouraging its translation and publication so the perished would not be forgotten.**

**In memory of Louis and Hannah Strassberg, born in Tarnogrod, married there in 1904,
who left to start a new life in America; and with thanks to their daughter Ruth who started
me on my efforts to remember Tarnogrod and the people who lived and died there.**

In memory of Morris Gradel, translator of the Tarnogrod chapter of *Pinkas* Hakehillot Polin, who died in 2010

This is a translation from: Sefer Tarnogrod; le-zikaron ha-kehila ha-yehudit she-nehreva
Book of Tarnogrod; in memory of the destroyed Jewish community, Editor: Sh. Kanc,
Organization of Former Residents of Tarnogrod and Vicinity in Israel, United States and England, Tel Aviv
1966 (592 pages H,Y)

BOOK OF TARNOGROD - YIZKOR BOOK

In Memory of the Destroyed Jewish Community

Editor: Shimon KANC

Editorial Board: M. Ringer, N. Krymerkopf, M. Shprung, J. Hering, M. Bornstein, Sh. Futer, Sh. Fefer

Published: Tel Aviv 1966

Organization of Former Residents of Tarnogrod and Vicinity in Israel, United States and England

Synagogue in Tarnogrod   Artist: Yakov Muterperl

Map Tarnogrod

Translated by Lorraine Rosengarten **and** Zvika Welgreen

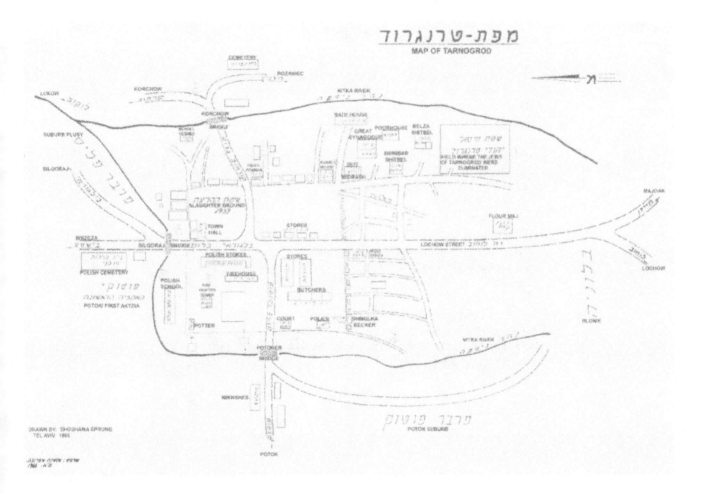

[Page 9]

Kaddish

by B. Mordechai

Translated by Sara Mages

Wind, gather your wings, your wrath on the crisis is over!
It has been a long time since darkness raged over graves
My voice emerges, and if there is no one to hear and if there is:
Yitgadal v'yitkadash! [Magnified and sanctified!]

And if there is no exploration into the abyss and no escape to the lost –
This time, too, I will stand and not collapse,
And in a broken voice I will wrestle with the storm:
Yitgadal v'yitkadash!

And if there is no limit to pain and no limit to grief
And a shipwreck in the depths will anchor,
And the darkness is deep and the day is late –
Yitgadal v'yitkadash!

I hold the wind and with the storm I descend.
My weakness has passed, also this time I am not lost,
And from the depths of the abyss I will ascend and be renewed:
Yitgadal v'yitkadash!

[Page 10]

We Will Remember

by K. Shimon

Translated by Sara Mages

We will remember the souls of millions of brothers and sisters who were cut off from the land of the living, all the Jewish people who were led to the slaughter and their ashes were scattered all over the world; the tortured and the heroes, those who fell in battles, those who raised the standard of revolt and consecrated the name of the Jewish people when they fought and fell within the walls of the burning ghetto, among the ranks of the partisan battalions, in the forests and on the battlefronts all over Europe, and in their hearts the vision of immigration to the homeland, faith in humanity and the redemption of the Jewish people.

We will remember the simple Jews and the scholars, the glory of humanity, from the old to the young, the righteous and the precious, those who gave charity and benevolence, love of humanity and total devotion.

We will remember all the brilliant talents, the dreams, the hopes and desires, the lofty aspirations, the love for the Jewish people and the love for *Eretz Yisrael*, faith and heroism in the face of death.

We will remember the synagogues and *Beit HaMidrash*, the institutions of charity and mercy, the libraries and the houses that were dedicated to the work of the people and the country.

We will remember all those who were destroyed and cut off by all sorts of worthless evil people: some by fire and some by water, some by starvation and some by thirst, some by the sword, some were buried alive and some in the gas chambers, all those who were tortured and uprooted gave their lives for the sanctification of God's name.

We will remember and eulogize you in all twenty–four letters in which your lips sang songs of hope.

We will remember – we will not forget!

[Pages 11-14]

Our Gathering at the Chamber of the Holocaust on the Mountain of Remembrance[1]

by K. Shimon

Translated by Miriam Leberstein

Mr. Meir Ringer delivers a speech to the assembled Tarnogrod Jews at the unveiling of the memorial for the martyrs of Tarnogrod who will remain engraved in the hearts and memories of the survivors forever

Iser Stockman from London speaking at the memorial about the life and death of the Jews of Tarnogrod, their spiritual courage and faith, their heroic struggle and martyrdom

When you ascend the hundred stairs that lead to the top of Mount Zion, the echo of your feet striking the stone steps evokes a flood of memories about the past. You hear voices, words fluttering with anxiety and despair. You see faces, tortured and dead, in the land that fell into Nazi hands. In deep silence you cross the threshold into the Chamber of the Holocaust, a memorial for those who died, where there have been gathered the remains of what was. You are engulfed by feelings for which human language has never before had words to express, thoughts that you still cannot fathom. Yet you can feel the greatness of the place.

The rebbetzin, widow of the Zamech rabbi, son of the Tarnogrod rabbi,
Mordechai Tsvi Teicher, light the candle at the memorial on Mount Zion

You walk through dark, narrow passageways paved with massive stones. You enter niches that look like they were hacked out of rock, you stand momentarily in deep silence; your eyes and your limbs absorb the horror and the sanctity of the place. This is the Chamber of the Holocaust.

Old stone buildings with yellowed walls on the outside; inside, the vaulted ceilings are painted black. The hundreds of candles attached to the walls and ceiling do little to alleviate the sorrowful darkness that reigns in these rooms.

It seems as if the souls of the millions of dead are fluttering around the candle flames and you feel as if blood is dripping, flowing, freezing and seething unseen between the stone walls.

Generation after generation will come here, feel the seething of their own blood, relive the Holocaust by silently contemplating the fate of their people.

The Chamber of the Holocaust, the memorial to 6 million brothers killed at the hands of the most horrific murderers in human history, a chamber of ashes.

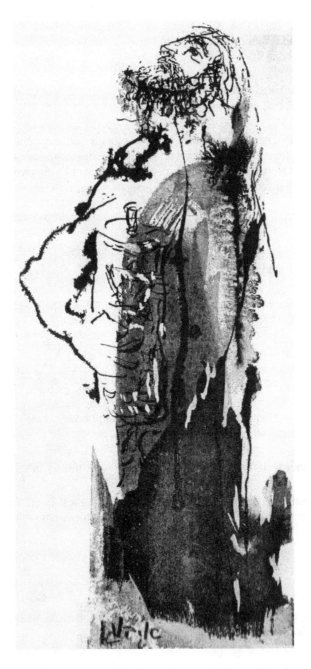

In giant earthen vessels lie torn parchments, pieces of holy scrolls, remainders of the destroyed communities. Large black letters call out:

"Our Father our King, do it for the sake of those who went through fire and water for the sanctification of thy name."
[From the prayer *Avinu Malkeinu*]

And then your eyes fall upon on words that proclaim:

"Earth, do not cover my blood, may my cry find no resting place." [Job 16:18]

One large glass case holds earthenware vessels marked with white, blue and black stripes, like the uniforms worn in the death camps, each holding the ashes of murdered Jews.

Soon your eyes encounter other items that exude horror. A simple glass jar holds Zyklon gas, used to murder our families. Here are pieces of yellow soap made from the fat, milk and blood of the murdered, labeled, "Soap for washing, manufactured in Munich" and "Best soap for shaving."

Another jar holds poison gas marked with a skull and cross bones. Death, the breath of mass murder swirls in this room, filling the air between the vaulted black ceiling and the stone walls.

More earthenware containers hold parchment scrolls, covered with the curtains from Torah Arks, and prayer shawls spotted with blood. The walls are covered from ceiling to floor with plaques naming communities of which they remain the only trace. You approach and read them with feverish eyes: "In memory of the martyrs of Lyubavichi, Pinsk, Minsk, Oswiecim, Tshizheva, Plotzk, Karlin, Loshitz" -- room after room.

Now we see the plaque for our town – Tarnogrod.

Let us walk through the rooms again and absorb the horror of the past. Here is a Torah scroll in a glass case, splattered with the blood of the old rabbi who was holding it when he was shot.

Here is a curtain for a Torah ark, rescued from a death camp. Dozens of the prisoners had brought with them pieces of such curtains and later lovingly sewed the pieces together.

Another glass case holds a holy Torah cover, this one sewn together by the Nazis. They liked to torment the Jews by mocking their holy practices. It's odd to bend down and read, *Ki Sovo* [When you will come], the *parsha* [weekly Torah portion] of Toykekher, the 50th *sedre* [verse] of the Torah.

Here are the yellow Stars of David, with their inscription of shame and pride, "*Jude*" – a symbol of isolation and annihilation which today is the symbol of our national rebirth.

Here are pieces of yellow paper with the inscription "Jews Only" – the money of the ghetto.

You continued with measured steps to the small synagogue on the highest floor. The curtain for the Torah ark is woven with words from the Torah, covered with thousands of inscriptions by visitors from various cities in Israel and the entire world.

Translator's footnote:

1.   *Martef HaShoa*, [lit. Cellar of the Holocaust, commonly translated as Chamber of the Holocaust], is a small Holocaust museum located on Mt. Zion in Jerusalem

[Pages 15-16]

The memorial plaque in Martef HaShoah [Chamber of the Holocaust] on Mount Zion in the capital city of Israel, Jerusalem

El Maleh Rachamim

K. Shimon

Translated by Sara Mages

God, full of Mercy defender of widows and father of orphans
Be not be silent or restrained regarding the blood of the Jews
Which was spilt like water, grant proper rest beneath the wings
Of Your Presence in the great heights of the holy and the pure
Who like the brilliance of the heavens gives light
And shines for the souls of the martyrs of

Tarnogrod and the vicinity

Men, women, boys and girls who were killed
And slaughtered, burnt and drowned, suffocated
And buried alive, all of them are holy and pure.

Earth, do not cover their blood!

[Page 17]

I Shall Take Up Weeping and Lamentation

K. Shimon

Translated by Sara Mages

Tarnogrod my town,
I will carry with lamentation and weeping for you,
For your Jews because they are gone,
For their destruction and loss.

I am silent, suffocating a sigh all my life,
But the shouts of pain were not silenced,
The pure shouted from generation to generation;
We will remember them forever.

In their sacred memory
We will dedicate our memories,
We will pray Kaddish
And dedicate our memories.

[Pages 18-20]

> "These I will remember and pour out my soul within me
> for wicked people have swallowed us, like a cake, unturned."

The beginning of *piyyut*[i] "Aseret Harugei Malchut"
["The Ten Martyrs"[ii]] for Yom Kippur

Those I Shall Remember

K. Shimon

Translated by Sara Mages

It's impossible to describe in words the destruction of the Jewish people over the years 5700-5705.

It is impossible to find an adequate expression to the magnitude of our grief for the loss of the six million Jews, holy and pure, who were murdered during the terrible destruction of the Jews of Europe.

It is impossible to find anyone who can lament this destruction.

We can do nothing now for these martyrs.

It is not even possible to erect a tombstone on their grave, because the accursed villains, who murdered them, burned their bodies and it is not known where their ashes are.

But we cannot forget them!

Although we cannot erect a stone monument on their graves, we can erect a spiritual monument for them.

This monument – the history of the town and the memories of its people – is a candle in their memory, so that they may live forever.

And we will end with a prayer that is also the end of *piyyut "Aseret Harugei Malchut"* for Yom Kippur:

> "Gracious One! Look down from Heaven, at the
> spilled blood of the righteous, and their life blood.
> Look from the place of Your holy Presence and remove all
> stains, Almighty, King, Who sits upon a throne of mercy."

Translator's footnotes:

i.   *Piyyut* – a Jewish liturcal poem, usually designated to be sung, chanted or recited during religious services.
ii.   "The Ten Martyrs" were ten rabbis living during the era of the *Mishnah* who were martyred by the Roman Empire in the period after the destruction of the Second Temple. Their story is detailed in Midrash Eleh Ezkerah – Those I shall remember.

[Pages 21-22]

On The Threshold

by The Book Committee

Translated by Sara Mages

We do not pretend to erect a full memorial to the ancient Jewish settlement in our city. Tarnogrod deserves a more perfect monument. In this book before us we seclude ourselves with the sacred memory of our beloved townspeople, who were annihilated in such a terrible and terrifying way that there are no words in the human mouth to describe it and call it by name.

We made sure to contain, mostly, the material on Tarnogrod when it was alive, and unfortunately - is no more. Our ambition was to describe and commemorate the Tarnogrod that is still lives in us, that is still our bones and flesh.

Jewish Tarnogrod was and is no more. Together with its Jews it was wiped off the face of the earth without a trace, and it is not possible to unveil all its past.

This is what the enemies intended and to a large extent their plot succeeded.

The only source that enabled us to write, to the proper extent, the chapters of our recent past, is the power of human memory. Therefore, we endeavored to draw from this spring, to weave chapters from the life of the town, life of toil and creation, life of matter and spirit, vibrant life in all its forms and periods.

The next generations will find in this book, as in all the books of remembrance for the victims of the Holocaust, evidence of what was in the Diaspora of Europe, before the great destruction and before any trace of Jewish life there was erased.

And we found in this work a kind of consolation in our grief and the preservation of the past so that it wouldn't be forgotten from the heart of generations to come.

This is not the time for our generation, who saw the Holocaust in its terrible form, to write long chapters. But, within the chapters that mention the intensity of our disaster and the intensity of the evil of our malicious murderers, this memory will also rise in the book, this monument to our town Ternogrod.

And if anyone will ask about the ruined Ternogrod community, if it still has a name and memory in the hearts of its sons, the preacher will tell him: on the contrary, open this book and read it.

After all, as you go through a broken heart, you also go through the pages of this book, in which hearts beat and cling to the generations of our patriarchs and the vision of the landscapes.

Read and see that the grace of the town is on its sons and is fixed in our hearts like a seal.

Since it lives in the heart of its sons, it is a sign that it deserves an eternal life in the history of our people.

Sacred is the Jewish suffering and sacred is the shed blood, it cries out to us and the sound of its cry will not be silenced.

May the "Book of Tarnogrod" be a kind of bridge between the past that has been so cruelly interrupted, and between the future whose sun rises before our eyes, It will remind us what we must take from yesterday and deliver to tomorrow.

May the book be a monument and everlasting memory!

Yitgadal v'yitkadash…

[Pages 23-28]

"Remember What Amalek Did to You"[1]

by Shimon Kanc

Translated by Miriam Leberstein

Tarnogrod, like hundreds of other Jewish small towns in Poland, is today a world of the past, and this Yizkor Book is a memorial for the beautiful Jewish life that was led there for centuries. This is a nostalgic book, a book of attachment and longing, of the bitterness of scores of orphaned sons and daughters of the destroyed Jewish community.

Like all of Jewish history, the history of the Jews in Tarnogrod is interwoven with oppressive laws, false accusations, persecution and martyrdom. They weren't heroes or world conquerors, but a community of the suffering and oppressed. Yet out of the sorrow and darkness of their lives they produced human gems, pure and great Jewish hearts.

The Jewish community grew larger and stronger. Private, social and economic life were accompanied by sorrows and joys, gloomy and sunny days, dark and light spots, until the outbreak of the brown plague [Nazis] that brought total annihilation.

We were witnesses to great wonders, romantic and heroic. The town frequently experienced fires and destruction, hunger and epidemics, but also miracles, awakenings, an ascent through thousands of pitfalls and struggles, to a better, more beautiful life.

It is clear and understandable that in the majority of the accounts in this book one hears the sorrow of the bereaved. Every memoir will sound like a eulogy, an elegy, a lamentation. For those who participated in producing this Yizkor Book, a memorial for the annihilated Jewish community, the Holocaust, the general tragedy for European Jews, is entwined with personal tragedy and eternal sorrow over the loss of loved ones.

For that reason, there are repetitious descriptions and accounts of the same topics, events and people. But each one complements the others and helps to create a complete picture of an entire way of life, from disappointments to achievements. Everything taken together tells how much we have lost, how immense and actually immeasurable the loss is.

A common characteristic of the entries in this book is the warmth with which they are told. It is the special warmth of Tarnogrod Jews, experienced by the refugees who passed through our town during World War I. It made such a profound impression on them that they spoke of it with great affection in later years when they encountered Jews from Tarnogrod in the Siberian taiga or the Kazakhstan steppes.

This warmth is preserved by Tarnogrod Jews living in the most distant lands, who treasure it along with the longing for the lost world of the former Jewish way of life. It inspired simple ordinary people who had never dreamed of being writers or historians. It was only their shocking suffering that made them eloquent.

Let us here mention some of the most active, hardworking representatives of Tarnogrod Jews, who so devotedly helped to produce this book.

Nuchum Krymerkopf, whose contributions constitute the vast majority of the book. Without his passion and energy, the Yizkor Book would never have happened. Everything he has written exudes a love for the town, its many institutions, its people. You can feel his deep attachment to the life of the town.

When you learn more about Nuchum Krymerkopf's work for the community, back when he was Secretary for the Tarnogrod library, you conclude that there are traditions that stubbornly persist even through difficult experiences. In his work for the Yizkor Book he revealed the extent of his sense of responsibility. In addition to all of his writing, he put enormous effort into raising money for its publication. This was an arduous task. But he was blessed with deep conviction and had the strength to instill that conviction in others. He conducted his fundraising both in Israel, where he also worked to put up the memorial in the Chamber of the Holocaust on Mount Zion, as well as in America, where he put great effort into realizing his dream of publishing the Yizkor Book.

Meir Ringer, the chairman of the Tarnogrod Landsmanshaft in Israel and the soul of the book committee, was born for important missions and highly responsible tasks. While still in Tarnogrod, he was the leader of the Zionist youth movement and then was one of the first pioneers who made *aliya*. In his work on behalf of the Yizkor Book, he distinguished himself with his native intelligence. Also blessed with the analytical intelligence of a *lamden* [religious scholar] and with a steady temperament, his contributions at the consultations, meetings and private conversations about the book were very significant and a blessing for those who worked with him.

Shmuel Khefer (Fefer), Moyshe Shprung, Shmuel Puter, Khaim Borenshtein, Tsvi Ben Efrem (Yehiel Hering). Each of these deserves special appreciation and praise. Their communal activity, their hearty friendship and idealism are key to their devotion to their work on the Yizkor Book, for their impeccable execution of the tasks which each voluntarily undertook.

First row, from right to left: Shmuel Khefer, Meir Ringer, Nachum Krymerkopf
Second row: Shmuel Puter, Tsvi Ben Efrem (Yehiel Hering), M. Shprung, Kh. Borenshtein

These men, who represent the Association of Tarnogroders in Israel, put all their effort into the work of organizing and raising funds for the Yizkor Book and enthusiastically overcame internal and external difficulties. Committed to the activities, dedicated to the sacred work of keeping alive the memory of the martyrs.

Zahava Shprung, whose work on behalf of the Yizkor Book is even more impressive because she herself was not from Tarnogrod, but participated as the wife of the energetic Moyshe Shprung, who was one of the initiators of the first memorial to the Tarnogrod martyrs. He came to Israel as a soldier in General Anders' army and remained in Tel Aviv, where he met Zahava. She came to Israel from Drobnik, near Plotsk, in 1936 and settled in Givatayim, which was then still a *moshav* [agricultural cooperative village]. Since their marriage, she has shared her husband's deep interest in everything related to keeping alive the memory of the dead of Tarnogrod.

At every meeting at their home, the participants felt the warmth of this woman, who became so close to the world of Tarnogrod Jews. She worked to establish the memorial, to see to it that it honored the dead with the greatest respect, and that the Yizkor Book should have the requisite appearance and contents. She must certainly see in the book a reward for her great efforts.

I want to express deep appreciation to all of these people who did everything in their power to see that the book would be as beautiful and complete as possible, so that it could serve as a worthy monument. Special thanks to them for the tremendous interest they exhibited in the daily work and for their understanding of all my demands during the various phases of the work on the book. Their contribution was especially great in the last section of the book – the list of names [of those who died], which they assembled with great effort and respect. May the quality and comprehensiveness of Sefer Tarnogrod served as the reward for their effort.

This is the reward for the survivors, for those who had the privilege of emerging from the great conflagration and constantly see before them the words of the ancient law that is inscribed in letters of blood and fire: "Remember what Amalek did to you" -- the Amalek of the twentieth century.

This is actually the role and purpose of this book. Not just memoirs of the distant and near past, not only a memorial candle for the pure souls who were so brutally murdered. In recording their memories, Tarnogrod Jews felt the need to express the nobility of the ordinary people of the town. May it impart to future generations some notion of the beauty that was destroyed.

May this Yizkor Book be a constant reminder for future generations, who will see in it a document and a reflection of a way of life that no longer exists.

May the cry that rises from this book never be silenced and never cease to serve as a reminder.
"Yiskadal v'yiskadash" [First words of the Yizkor prayer for the dead], Jewish Tarnogrod, and "Live in spite of your blood" [Ezekial 16:6].

Translator's footnote:

1.   Amalek is the name of a nation which in Biblical times sought to destroy the Jews. It is also used to denote enemies of the Jews at any time in history. The words "Remember what Amalek did to you" is God's command to the Jews cited twice in the Bible, in Exodus and Deuteronomy.

[Pages 29-30]

Once there was a Tarnogrod Community

by Meir Ringer

Translated by Sara Mages

In reverence we approach the work of erecting a monument and commemorating the memory of our martyrs, the martyrs of the city of Tarnogrod, the Lublin District in Poland, and in my mouth a silent prayer: may we not fail, that we may succeed in discovering the source of beauty and purity, the moral power, thanks to which we have been able to stand, for all generations, against every wave of malice that came to swallow us, and thanks to them they demonstrated devotion and courage in days of panic and confusion, and sanctified the name of Israel in public.

Throughout the generations that our ancestors lived in the Diaspora, they worked hard, created something out of nothing, and made a living from their hard work, set up homes, various businesses and magnificent institutions. They participated in the country's life, and donated their money and their blood for the benefit of the country. As honest citizens they fulfilled all the duties of the country, and with all this the nations, in which they lived, saw them as strangers to everything and the exploiters of the people and the state, and therefore also our brothers lived there in fear of false accusations and the pogroms, which have become a normal phenomena in their lives. From time to time their lives were subjected to ridicule and mockery, to murder, robbery and looting, until the rage erupted on them and everything they labored and created for all generations was destroyed in one day, young to old perished in all sorts of deaths by the German evil regime and their helpers, may their names be blotted out.

According to our concepts there are two types of heroism: A) Physical heroism, like the one who lifts weights or heavy loads, or the one who bends iron bars with his hands. B) Mental heroism, such as a war hero, or the kind that the *Mishnah* teaches us, "Who is the hero? One who conquers his impulse to evil," of course, in all sorts of situations. But the heroism shown by the Jewish families while living in the forest with their children and infants, who fled there from the Nazi murderers during the extermination period, such heroism has not yet been written and no one thought to describe it.

With all these, the Jews, who sought refuge to save their lives, chose the forest, to live there under the open sky, and even there they lived in constant fear, not only from the cruel enemy from which they fled, or from the animals of the forest, or from the cold of the snow and the rain, or from the hunger that constantly bothered them, or because they were torn, worn and barefoot, but also from those who were called partisans, who also fled to the forest from the same cruel enemy in order to fight it, also these partisans harassed, attacked and shed the blood of the Jews, their neighbors to the forest and brothers to trouble.

And here we read the manuscript in the diary *Ud Mutzal MeEsh* [Survivor], written by two families, Haler and Ephraim Lumerman, from the village of Lukowa, on everything they and their families, went through before they fled to the forest, and later about the life in the forest of two families, Holler and Ephraim, with their children and infants. About their terrible sufferings and also about the miracles that happened to them every day and every hour, and later, when the war ended, when they tried to start a new life, their Polish neighbors did not let them build their ruined nests, their lives were in danger again and there were also cases of murder. A hand of horrors was wrapped around them like a giant vise-grip and with no choice they left their city.

They escaped from Tarnogrod, and escaped from Poland.

Not a single Jew remained in Tarnogrod. Also those who returned from Russia didn't find a place in their country of origin. Some survivors found shelter in North and South America and also in Western Europe, and most turned to the gate of aliya [immigration].

Most of the survivors from Tarnogrod were absorbed in Israel. They found their home in the independent State of Israel, which gives them a feeling of freedom and national human independence, and they participate in all areas of life of the state, in the city, in the village and in the acts of development.

They arrived beaten and devastated, torn and worn, and became partners in the day-to-day responsibilities of an established and developing country. They willingly accepted all the duties and hardships, and tied their lives and future with the people and to their country.

The few survivors who immigrated to Israel feel the duty imposed on them, to remind and tell the future generations about the beloved and precious who were murdered, about the history of the town and its destruction.

May these few rows be like a stone in the monument for our town Tarnogrod.

Once there was a Tarnogrod community and is no more.

It was cut down from the multi-branched tree trunk of the Polish Jewry by the German murderers.

Its memory remains in the hearts of its dozens of survivors who are scattered all over the world, most of whom were absorbed in the homeland, in the State of Israel.

[Pages 31-32]

There Once Was a Jewish Community in Tarnogrod

by Meir Ringer

Translated by Miriam Leberstein

We approach the task of creating this book with reverence and apprehension, aiming to establish a monument to eternalize the memory of the holy martyrs of Tarnogrod. We whisper a prayer, "May it be God's will," that we shall not stumble that we will succeed in uncapping the well of pure beauty, of moral strength and persistence that helped us to endure, over the course of centuries, despite the waves of evil and hostility that threatened to inundate us. In the worst times of panic and horror we evinced boldness, devotion and willingness to sacrifice ourselves for our faith.

In the course of the many years that our forebears lived in the diaspora, they worked hard and created, out of nothing, buildings, businesses and social institutions; participated in the economic and social life of the country; were good and loyal citizens. Yet the people among whom they lived regarded them as strangers, as parasites. That was what led to the libels and pogroms that became common events in their lives. From time to time they were subjected to jeering and mockery, robbery and murder, until the wrath of [their enemies] engulfed them and everything that they had created in the course of generations was destroyed, young and old suffered all kinds of horrific deaths at the hands of the Germans and their helpers.

There are two kinds of strength: One, physical strength which manifests itself in unusual feats like lifting heavy weights or breaking iron with one's hands and two, psychic strength, which manifests itself in fighting, under various circumstances. But the strength that the Jews exhibited in those times has not yet been described. We do not yet have the words capable of describing it. The Jews fought in the ghetto and in the forests where they lived in constant fear, more of the Nazis than of the wild animals or the cold and rain and hunger.

The Tarnogrod Jews who fled to the forest also had to watch out for the Polish partisans, who were being pursued by the same Nazi enemy. In this book we will read the diary of Avraham Haler, which describes the experiences of his and other Jewish families who hid in the forest, their frightful suffering, as well as the miracles that occurred every hour of every day. When the war ended and they returned to Tarnogrod, hoping to begin a new life, they faced new dangers. Their Polish neighbors threatened them and even killed some until they had to flee the town. They fled Tarnogrod, they fled Poland. The majority of the surviving Tarnogrod Jews settled in Israel. Broken and depressed and mourning their loved ones, they found a home in Israel, became partners in the daily task of developing the land, binding their fates to that of the country and the Jewish people.

We all feel the obligations to future generations to tell about the life and death of the Jewish community of Tarnogrod. Its memory will live forever in our hearts.

[Page 33]

I

<u>Town History</u>

[Page 34]

Translated by Joseph Lipner

...as long as my heart beats,
As long as I know how and why
Whatever happens,
I will not forget,
I will not want to forget!...

D. Shimoni

[Pages 42-50 Yiddish] [Pages 35-41 Hebrew]

The History of the Town

by Shimon Kanc

Translated by Tina Lunson

In the history of Poland, Tarnogrod is well known: a town near Bilgoraj along the road that leads to Lublin. As early as 1241 there were bitter battles in the area against the Tatars. Indeed, the town was a fortress against the Tatar invaders but in those days Tarnogrod was not yet a town.

In pre-Christian times the area of Tarnogrod was covered with thick forests, surrounded with valleys, rivers and swamps. In later times wanderers from Mazowsze (Mazovia), Kujawa and Pomorze (Pomerania) settled in those same areas. The Slavs drew upon the abundance of animal life and the fruitful earth. Over time, Jews from Silesia and Poland also settled there.

Jews in Tarnogrod are mentioned for the first time in a document from the year 1455. The reports from that era are vague. We learn from the Lublin and Krakow *pinkus* [Jewish community record of important events] books that there were periods when Tarnogrod Jews went off to Lublin. In the year 1555 the borders of the Jewish quarter of Lublin were enlarged significantly. King Zygmunt August confirmed the gift-decree of the Krakow *voivode* [local ruler or govenor] and Lublin *starosta* [royal official], Stanisław Tęczyński, for about three places that were given to the Lublin Jewish community. Two years later the same *starosta* gave as a gift to the well-known Lublin doctor, Yitzhak Maj, a place with a lake and the right to construct a building there. The gift decree was approved by the king in 1566 and on that place was built the *MaHaRaSHaL* [Solomon Luria (1510 – 1574)] Synagogue, the yeshiva and other structures. Among those who prayed in that *shul* was a Tarnogrod Jew by the name of Azriel.

Thanks to the rights that Jews had received in those years, the Jewish quarter in Lublin was enlarged at a rapid pace. Individual families arrived from settlements near and far, and among them were Jews from Tarnogrod.

Lublin occupied an important place in Polish trade even in the 15th century, when the city was a central point in the intersection of the trade routes that led from the west to the north and southeast. In hindsight, its importance was no less than that of Lvov and it is no wonder that the famous fairs in the era of their blossoming (in the 16th century until the middle of the 17th century) were a meeting place for the Jewish merchants of all the towns and trade centers in the Poland of that time, among whom could be found Tarnogrod Jews who bought imported goods at the Lublin fairs and brought to them woven fabric of their own production and also furs.

In the second half of the 15th century, the Poles in the city began a war against Jewish trade. Krakow – which had in 1485, through extortion, already forced the head of the Jewish community to sign an agreement that restricted Jewish trade to a selected list of families and certain Jewish workshops in tailoring and hat-making – gave the signal. The Krakow merchant's slogan was soon picked up by their Polish comrades in Posen, Kuzmir, Plotsk, Lublin, and by 1521 there was effectively a tight bond among the larger Polish cities in a war against Jewish trade. On the 30th of December 1521 the King issued a decree in the parliament in Pietrokov (Piotrków Trybunalski) that forbade Jewish shopkeepers from buying the grain that the peasants brought into town. That prohibition also brought a series of limitations for the Tarnogrod Jews, limitations whose goal was to liquidate Jewish retail trade. The unraveling economic situation of the community stopped the further influx of Jews.

In the stormy period from 1648 to 1660, Tarnogrod was turned over from one government to another. Merchants and craftsmen were impoverished, the trade routes were erased. In 1672 the misfortune of the Tatar invasion was visited upon Tarnogrod and the town was completely destroyed.

Over a short period of time it was built up anew, and then, it seems, the war against the Jews was quieted. Besides trade, the Tarnogrod Jews occupied themselves with artisanry. Old historical sources mention Jewish tailors, a baker, a butcher, a shoemaker, a leather strap maker, a barber-surgeon, and a blacksmith. In those times, artisanry was tied to trade and the Jewish artisans were thus also occupied in selling the products of their labor. The population then did not hate the Jews and in a certain sense the atmosphere was comfortable for the Jews. The Jews also lived in the nearby villages. The main livelihood of the village Jews was inn keeping, estate managing and brokering for those who owned farmlands. There were also shop-keepers, from whom the village population bought the products that they could not make themselves, such as salt, fuel oil, an axe, a plow blade and so on. No doubt that the Jewish livelihoods in the towns were not much different from the livelihoods in the villages.

We have no systematic material regarding the Jewish population and occupations in Tarnogrod and their economic role in relation to the Christians. But there are clear indications that the Tarnogrod Jews dealt with Krakow and Lublin, and in several villages some Jewish families were engaged in agriculture.

The geographic situation gave the town some economic advantages that strengthened the competitive capability with Bilgoraj, which in those days was independent from Tarnogrod. But the development of the town did not go on for long because of the heavy taxation.

From the documents of the *Vaad Arba Aratzot* [Council of the Four Lands], the central governing institution of Polish Jewry, from the end of first century one can draw the conclusion that the Tarnogrod Jews helped in the fight that the leaders of Polish Jewry conducted against their persecutors.

These documents also deal with the running payments to the *Vaad Arba Aratzot* that concentrated in their hands the payments from all the Jewish communities. Their significance does not consist of their showing the exact calculation of the sum, because not even the yearly norm that the Tarnogrod community had to pay to the Vaad can be determined from the documents – something that would help to determine the relative size of the community. Their importance consists in that they present a clear indication that Tarnogrod paid the taxes directly to the *Vaad Arba Aratzot* and not through the intermediary of a larger community. From that one can make the inference that Tarnogord was an erstwhile town at the time, with its own competence that could even take smaller Jewish communities, like Bilgoraj and others, under its protection.

Disregarding the fact that we do not have any details about the process that Tarnogrod went through until it arrived at that position, one could learn much from it about the development of the Jewish communities in Poland – a development that in that time was almost unique in the land.

Among the documents from the *Vaad Arba Aratzot* there is a document from the year 1665 in which Avraham ben Yitzhak from Tarnogrod is among the participants in the meeting and of those who signed the obligatory note: "We acknowledge in this obligatory deed ... that we have received from our advocate Kazimierz Kawalkowski, Secretary to His Royal Majesty and Signer for the King's Treasury, who has aided us in our most difficult situation, in our need and under pressure from the military, which has in its hands promissory notes to the King's Treasury from us and from the entire Jewish congregation in the Polish kingdom, and who have accepted on account our debt of not only our possessions but also our bodies and our soul. The representative Mr. Kawalkowski, the Secretary to His Royal Majesty, has rescued us, our soul and our possessions, from our most difficult need, having paid for us Jews, who live in the Polish kingdom, from the King's Treasury the sum of 26,000 gilden. Having received such great help ... we obligate ourselves in our names, in the names of all the leaders and in the names of the entire Jewish society in the Polish Kingdom ... that we will pay the above-mentioned sum of 26,000 *gilden* to the representative Mr. Kawalkowski or to him who brings this obligatory deed ... installments, namely the 12th of May 1667 (18 *Iyer* 5427) 3,250 gilden. The 12th of May 1668 (2 *Sivan* 5428) 3,350 gilden, the 12th of May 1669 (11 *Oder* 5429) 3250 gilden, the 12th of May 1670 (22 5430) 1,250 *gilden* . If we are not able to meet our commitment to the end and in the stated place ... the representative Mr. Kawalkowski or he who brings this deed is permitted to rob us, arrest us, capture us and put us in jail, both in public and in private, us and all Jews ... who are located in the Polish Kingdom. This applies to fairs, markets, on the roads and in our houses. In addition (it would be permissible) to confiscate all of our merchandise ... in any place, close our shuls [synagogues], take ... the houses and install Christians or whoever else in them and hold them (the houses) until the debt is paid .... This is agreed upon in Yaroslav, the 3rd of January 1666.

Following are the signatures of those who signed, written in the language of Yisrael."

This is the language of the document, and it is worth turning our attention to the announcement from the 16th of November 1663 (16 Cheshvan 5424), in which the Polish king Jan Kazimierz warns the Jews, men and women, that they must pay the head tax that has been assessed on them by the last parliaments. If not, he was permitted to confiscate all their merchandise that is found in the customs houses, on the roads, in the towns and villages and also to arrest Jews themselves, rich and poor, and hold them in jail until the tax is paid (according to the archive in Lvov).

From this document can be drawn a picture of social life against the background of the circumstances of that time, and from that we can see that the Tarnogrod Jews were interested in the protection of their rights exactly as were the residents of the big towns. Those rights ensured the Jews the proper conditions for their existence.

One of the key factors that made possible the enclosure of the Jewish settlement in Tarnogrod in that era was their comfortable position regarding their rights, as expressed also in the comfortable living conditions, more so than in many of the Polish towns. The main document that teachers us about the rights position is the decision from the *Vaad Arba Aratzot* which requires that the institutional leaders of the Krakow province come to judgment before the Tarnogrod *Vaad*, which would deal with the unjust conduct of the Krakow leaders, who had to take upon themselves the sentence that the *Vaad* decreed.

The decision was given in the year 5427 at the Gromnitzer fair, a Christian holiday during which the fair in Lublin also occurred and when the *Vaad Arba Aratzot* also convened. The fair began on the 2nd of February and lasted for seven days. Jews also called it the Oder fair.

In 1685 during the reign of King Jan Sobieski, the Vaad met in Yaroslav and among the decisions made was the agreement of the *rabbonim* [rabbi, plural] to publish the book "*Nakhlat Azriel*" [Azriel's Legacy] by *Rav* [Rabbi] Azriel Halevi, who was the head of the *beit-din* [Rabbinical court] in Tarnogrod. It says:

"We are presented with remarkable things from the great and preeminent Rav, our teacher and rabbi, Azriel Halevi, may his holy memory be for a blessing, who was head of the beit-din and leader of the holy congregation of Tarnogrod, may his rock and redeemer protect him, and who wrote new commentaries on the Torah, the Poskim [Rabbinic authorities and literature on questions of Jewish law], *Gemara* [300 years of rabbis' legal and ethical commentaries on the *Mishnah*], *Perush Rashi* [Rashi Commentaries], *Tosafot* [Supplements and additions – 12th to 14th century commentaries on Talmud] which were sweeter than honey; knowing and understanding him as a great Talmud scholar, large in Torah and in good works, spreading Torah among the Jews of several communities; and as soon as the news reached our ears that it was the will of the community leaders to bring his marvels to print to the merit of the community, to the use of his soul and for his good remembrance, and so as the Sages have said: 'What are the achievements of a person – Torah and good deeds', those are the generations of that Talmud scholar, for he left no children behind him, and therefore even though there is a statute against the printing of any new treatises we have abolished the statute for the above-mentioned book for the honor of the *Rav* and for the spiritual pleasure of his pure soul."

Among the *rabbonim* who gathered at the conference of the *Vaad Arba Aratzot* and gave his approval for the book was the name of *Rav* Natan-Nata bar Yakov, the current *rav* of Tarnogrod, who signed "Natan-Nata of Lublin, leader of the holy congregation of Tarnogrod". We assume from this that the Tarnogrod *rav* took part in the gathering of the *Vaad Arba Aratzot*.

The document from the year 1717 (2nd of *Heshven* [October-November] 5478), leaves no doubt that Tarnogrod was already outstanding, that its representatives came from an independent province in the Vaad. The document from the *Vaad* Arba *Aratzot* deals with (p. 275) the conflict between the Jewish community in Pshemishl and the local rav, who "was afraid of being taken by his debtors" and the Vaad ruled: "…there shall no kind of harm and no kind of persecution befall him from any debtor or from any person in the world … and the Jewish institutional leaders shall also swear a firm oath here in the presence of the *Vaad Arba Aratzot*, that they will implement this … and all the previous writings and the court ruling having to do with these debtors…"

Among the participants in that meeting and those who signed the court ruling was Shlomo, son of Rabbi Shimshon from Tarnogrod and Aizik from the holy congregation of Tarnogrod, whose names are also among the participants in other meetings of the *Vaad Arba Aratzot*.

It can also be seen that those *rabbonim* who were great minds of Torah study attended the meetings on the merit of their importance, but this also gives witness to the importance and esteem of the town that was able to invite such Torah greats as these *rabbonim*.

An even clearer indication, although from a later time, is in a Polish source, in the lists dealing with the *Vaad Arba Aratzot* and its composition, from which it is clear that the Tarnogrod *rabbonim* in certain time periods belonged to the Vaad.

Tarnogrod is also proud of one of the pillars of Hasidism, Rabbi Levi Yitzchak, "The Berditchever *Rav*", who on his mother Sosha-Dvora's side, was from the R. Samuel Eliezer ben Judah Levi Edels' family and of the Gaon [honorific title for eminent scholar] *Rav* Moshe Margoliot, head of the beit din in Tarnogrod…

Although the town was never a big *Hasidic* center, the spiritual situation there was like that of a large city that had a big *Hasidic* center, with the same enthusiasm for doing *mitzvot*, for dance and for nigunim [wordless melody; tune. Often used when referring to prayer melody], that occupied an important place in Hasidism. Tarnogrod Jews stayed true to the core principles of Hasidism in the various eras until the horrible destruction of Polish Jewry.

So the Tarnogrod Jews understood the honor and importance of having Rabbi Avraham Yehoshua Heschel, "The Apter *Rav*", whose name was associated with the Tarnogrod rav, *Rav* Shimshon, in whom the greatest *rabbonim* of the time took pride, a son-in-law of *Rav* Feivish, son of the great *Gaon Rav* Moshe, head of the *beit din* and head of the yeshiva of the community of Tarnogrod.

During the 200 years of its existence the influence of the *Vaad Arba Aratzot* was huge in the whole Diaspora and so the honorable relations that the *Vaad* had to the Tarnogrod *rabbonim*, placed the town among the most esteemed communities in Poland.

The unusual times that were to befall Poland in the coming eras left their deep mark on the position of the Tarnogrod community as well and in particular on its future development. The disrupted political situation whose alarm was the partition of Poland and the loss of its political independence, the wars and rebellions that came as a result of the national awakening, all caused the instability and undermining of the previous blossoming, and laid a new yoke on the Jewish community and disallowed its further development. And its position as a trade center for the area was destroyed. In time the surrounding towns developed and began to compete with Tarnogrod and after a while, it seems, pushed Tarnogrod into a corner and Bilgoraj began to take its place.

These changes are the reason that Tarnogrod remained stalled in place, both the town in general and the Jewish community. Yet it must be emphasized that this was not a uniform process, and that the activity of the Tarnogrod Jews showed that the community had not settled for its situation and continued to struggle with new aspirations.

*

We have assembled a small part of the history of Tarnogrod. There remain many chapters of other eras, for which not so much material has been preserved. But even the modest material gives witness to the important role that Tarnogrod played among the Jewish communities in Poland; but new times came, new events, new circumstances, that did not allow the Jewish community in Tarnogrod to plant its glorious traditions.

[Pages 51-63]

The Jewish Community in Tarnogrod

by Nachum Krymerkopf

Translated by Miriam Leberstein

Dedicated to the sacred memory of my parents, Chaim and Khana-Lea, my wife Mindil, and my children Pesia, Kopl and Malka, who were killed by the Nazi murderers, Cheshvan [October-November], 1942.

The town of Tarnogrod was located in Lublin *gubernie* [province], in the *rayon* [district] of Zamosc, near Bilgoraj. Set on a low mountain, the town is at a higher elevation than the nearby towns of Jozefow, Sieniawa, Krzeszow, and the many surrounding villages. Because of this higher elevation the town suffered from a shortage of water. It had no river, and there were few wells, and these wells did not all supply potable water.

The wells that were located on the streets where Jews lived were called by Jewish names, like Avrahamele Kofi's well in Lakhower Street, which in later days, before World War II, was called Shmuel Zeis' well; Matyas Beker's well, with its salty water; Leibish Baritche's well. The well on the rampart past the Christian houses was called *shteyn* [stone].

Not far from the houses where the butchers lived was a well called Moshe-Hillel's *stak* [well]. Its water came from the surrounding hills and was very tasty, especially when it was used to make tea. Jews drew water for cooking and drinking from that well day and night.

There were also Jews who earned a living by carrying water to the prosperous households. Among the water carriers were Moshe-Elchanan, Yekl Getz, Moshe Mayfie, and Mendele-Ketsele. Their entire lives they carried on their shoulders a frame from which hung two full pails of water. Before the last war people still paid 10 groschen for two full pails.

Jewish water carriers also drew water from wells owned by Christians. One such well outside the town was called Zhadil. Because it was so far away, Shimon David Stockman and Mordechai Treger transported the water in a barrel on a horse drawn wagon. Every water carrier had his own customers. They were paid on Friday for the entire week, and also received as a bonus a white bread roll for the Sabbath.

The bakers hired the water carriers by the week. Each baker had a large barrel and the water carrier had to see to it that it was always full. Because the majority of women baked at home on Friday for the entire week, only some bakers baked every day. There were also bakers who baked only for the fairs held every Tuesday and Friday. On those two days the bakers set up their stalls at the marketplace and sold the baked goods from straw baskets.

The Tarnogrod marketplace was ringed by low-rise buildings that housed the Jewish shops. Behind these were the shops of the Jewish butchers. Later, many Polish stores appeared and competition grew. The Christians were supported by the town government, which installed small wooden shops in the middle of the marketplace and rented them to Jews, evicting those who could not pay the rent.

Widows and other women would set up shops which sold various kinds of merchandise, fruits and vegetables. These shops consisted of long wooden benches on which sat shallow woven baskets.

Until the outbreak of World War I in 1914, Tarnogrod was under Russian rule. In those days, the Jews there were able to make a living, and Tarnogrod was renowned for having wealthier rich people than other towns in the area. This was because the town was situated close to the Austrian border, where both legal and illegal business was conducted.

On Both Sides of the Border

The border was located past the Lakhower Forest, in the village of Majdan, 7 kilometers from Tarnogrod. On the Russian side, soldiers called obyeshtshikes [mounted patrol officers] guarded the border. On the Austrian side, there were no soldiers, just a few officials who collected payment for goods transported from Tarnogrod to Sieniawa.

Tarnogrod Jews encountered no difficulties in crossing the border. They needed only to obtain a certificate costing one-half Russian *ruble* from the communal authority. This certificate was valid for a whole month, during which one could cross the border as frequently as one wished. In other towns it was much more difficult to cross the border legally and so people often had to sneak across, risking their lives to do so.

The barracks for the Russian military near Tarnogrod were owned by the Tarnogrod Jew Mendl Silberzweig who was called Mendele Bishtsher, and he collected rent for them. The colonel and his entire general staff rented quarters in Mordechai.Mantl's building in the Bilgoraj City Gate.

There were Jewish contractors who provided goods to the military, such as hay and oats for the army horses. One such contractor was Naftali Wakslicht (Yokter), who lived on the marketplace, near Yosl Rupa (Struzer).

Tarnogrod Jews traded with Germany and Austria in flax, linen, grain and various other products. This business was legal, but there was also a black market, which smuggled horses, fabric, and various alcoholic drinks. Most of the illegal business was conducted by Christians, but Jews participated as well. Many smugglers paid for it with their lives.

The peasants from nearby villages brought their agricultural products to sell to the Jews and later used the proceeds to buy various goods in the Jewish shops. The fairs held on Tuesday were renowned throughout the region and Jews from surrounding towns would come to Tarnogrod to sell their goods and to buy agricultural products from the peasants.

Among the great merchants in Tarnogrod were Yosef Moynis and Moshe Moynis (Feingold) wholesalers of raw goods, who brought from smaller-scale merchants what they had accumulated during the week. Among the great grain merchants were Israel-Avraham Itches (Krumpenholz). There were also big flour warehouses in Tarnogrod.

In those days Jews in Tarnogrod did not have to endure a heavy tax burden, as they did later under Polish rule.

Village Jews

Jews lived in almost all the villages around Tarnogrod. These village Jews excelled in the practice of *hakhnasat-orchim* [providing hospitality and shelter to guests, especially the poor or strangers]. They did not distinguish between rich and poor, but treated everyone equally with the same hearty warmth, providing food and drink and a bed to sleep in. The townspeople who came to the villages to buy raw materials, like the tailors who sewed fur winter coats for the Christians, always stayed over as guests of the Jewish villagers, who never asked for money for room and board.

The life of the village Jews was similar to that of the [Christian] peasants. They owned fields, horses, and cows and worked the land along with the peasants, plowing, sowing and reaping.

There were also Jewish villagers who did not own any land, possessed only one or two cows, and made their living from small shops where women did the selling. They lived all week on dairy foods made from the milk of their own cows, eating meat only on the Sabbath. *Shochets* [ritual slaughters] would come from town on Thursday to slaughter poultry or a calf or sheep. If the road was in bad condition and the *shochet* didn't come, the village Jew had to do without meat and observe the Sabbath with a dairy meal.

Very few village Jews could read religious texts or write a letter. They would hire teachers to instruct their children in the village. There weren't any *baal-tefillot* [leaders of prayers]. Each man prayed alone and on Sabbath they would gather in a *minyan* [quorum] at one of the respectable homes that had a sufficiently large room where they could pray together. They borrowed a Torah scroll from a *besmedresh* [house of study, also used for worship] in town. For the High Holy Days they came to town to pray. In the last years before world War II they would hire a *baal-tefillah* from town and pray in their own *minyansin* the village.

Jewish Landholders

Many of the large agricultural estates, called *"heyf"* [literally courtyards] around Tarnogrod were occupied by Jews who held them on *arende* [lease], granted by the *poritz* [Polish landowner]. The estate at Razhnits was ruled by the Jewish *poritz Reb* [respectful term of address] Elyele Shochets, a pious Jew and very learned man, son of a shochet.

At Zamosc, the *arende* was held by Nachmiele, who was also considered a great scholar and upstanding man. Sobol held the estate at Absher and Arish Weintraub the estate at Fils. By the last years before the Second World War, only one Jewish *poritz* remained, in the village of Shariuvke, Yakov Ritzer, who was called Yankl Shariavker.

People would also talk about other Jewish leaseholders, telling various stories about their wealth, their industriousness, and their piety. I didn't know all of them and many of their names are gone from my memory. But I do remember Shmuel Weltcher, from Lipen; his son Avraham Weltcher from the Patiker estate; Avremele Nutels (Fabrikant) from the Lakhover estate. The latter also held the lease on the Lakhover forest, where bakers and other townspeople bought wood for fuel.

The Jewish estate holders gave a lot of money to the town's poor and institutions. Before a holiday they would send to town wagons full of potatoes and other agricultural products. Avremele Fabrikant would send enough wood to heat the *besmedresh* for an entire winter. Other wagons brought free wood for the poor. Shmuel Weltcher and his son sent potatoes and straw to the poor for Passover.

Both Jewish and Christian landholders had Jewish agents and merchants who bought grain from them and made a living from selling it. They also engaged Jewish tenant farmers who would collect milk from the estates. They were often given a house to live in, with a cellar where they could keep the milk so it wouldn't spoil. They were also allowed to pasture their horses or cows on the estate fields.

The tenant farmers, as well as orchardists from town, also rented fruit orchards from the estate. But they never neglected to bring milk, butter and cheese in their own horse and wagon to town, where each one had his own concession and always took the same spot in the marketplace. The tenant farmers sold the milk by the quarter in tin containers. The butter was prepared in nicely shaped wooden molds, and sold by the quarter or half-quarter.

The wives of the tenant farmers drove into town with them to help sell the dairy products, which they kept on the wagon where they sat, measuring and doling out the requested amounts.

There were days, especially the "nine days" at the end of the "three weeks" of mourning for the destruction of the Temple [Tisha b'Av] during the summer, when it was forbidden to eat meat, and dairy foods were in short supply. On those days, Jews would get up very early and go to the marketplace with pots and bowls to buy the only permitted food.

After World War I, when Tarnogrod belonged to Poland, there were very few Jewish estate holders, and Christians took over the dairy trade.

The Economic Conditions of Tarnogrod Jews Before World War I.

The 700 Jewish families that lived in Tarnogrod fell into three economic categories: 40% considered themselves wealthy by small-town standards; 50% middle class; and 10% poor, but not, God forbid, so poor they had to rely on charity. They were poor because it was so hard to eke out a living. Aside from the merchants, the retailers, and the small-scale dealers in agricultural products, there were also artisans who sold their wares in the marketplace – tailors who sewed cheap, ready to wear clothing, weavers who made their own linen cloth, and bakers and cobblers. There were also people who dealt in *kroples* [alcoholic drink], an illegal trade. The consumers were Christian peasants. The main supplier was Avraham Kagan (Rosenfeld).

The Tarnogrod Jews excelled in the practice of *hakhnasat-orchim*. Poor people, wanderers, would come to Tarnogrod from towns near and far. On the Sabbath, each home hosted a guest or two at the Sabbath meal. In many homes the poor were also invited to sleep over. David Yoel Shuster and his son Yeshayahu Leib were especially known for their hospitality. They prepared special beds for their guests and tried to make them comfortable. After David Yoel's death his son continued with this *mitzvah* [commandment or good deed].

It is the tragedy of Jewish fate that the garden of these fine, generous people, which served as a place of respite for the poor and for strangers, was turned by the Nazis into a mass grave for hundreds of Jewish families.

Shortly after the First World War Moshe Walfish, brother of Shaye-Leib, came from America to visit Tarnogrod. Before he left, he gave his brother money to build a new house with a separate room where poor people could lodge overnight. Shaye-Leib built a larger house, devoting the largest room for guests, whom he also provided with comfortable beds and new straw mattresses and blankets.

Tarnogrod Jews lived in low wooden houses. There were only two stone houses in the town, one owned by Mordechai Mantl and the other by Leib Shimshon (Weintraub). After World War I, a two-story stone building housing the post office was built by Yosl Shprung, Wolwish Melamed's son in law, on Lakhover Street. Several stone buildings were also built around the marketplace. After a fire occurred, the Polish authorities no longer permitted the construction of wooden buildings.

Streets and lanes led to and from the marketplace – Lakhover, Royshnitser, the Bilgoraj city gate, Patiker and Karkhever. Many streets were called by the Jewish names of the people who lived there. Lakhover Street was long, extending to the Shiniaver Road at the Austrian border. Jews lived on this street as far as Moshe Kalikstein's house. On Royzhnitser Street, Jews lived as far as Leibush Kovel's house. The side streets and lanes, as well as the city gates, were inhabited solely by Jews. They were very crowded and so fights often broke out. A dispute over a bit of space would be brought to rabbinical and civil courts.

Most Jews owned their own small houses, but there were some who rented. The living conditions were generally difficult. Even a rich person would have only one all-purpose room and an alcove. Only the rare, very rich people had several rooms. The poor water carriers and flour porters and poor tradesmen lived in single rooms which held beds arranged in the form of the [Hebrew letter] "*daled*," [i.e. at a ninety degree angle] and a bench-bed [bench that converted to a bed] for the children. The cradle stood by the mother's bed. If it was a big family with a lot of children -- like those of Yekl Potshter (Wertman); Itsik-Leib; Naftali Mindeshes (Ringler); and others -- four children slept on the bench-bed, two at the head and two at the foot, and the other children slept on a plank. The children slept covered by the father's overcoat and the mother's shawl.

The children were fed all week on *kasha* [porridge] and beans, or millet and honey. At the end of the week, when the bread had grown stale, the mother would buy two or three bagels from Berish the Yakhlekhe, or hot chickpeas from Matish Beker.

Tarnogrod Jews had large families. When a boy turned three, his father brought him to *heder* [religious school for young children] wrapped in a prayer shawl, and distributed sweets to the pupils.

Women gave birth at home. For 8 days after the birth, until the *bris* [circumcision], the mother and the newborn lay behind a sheet hung like a curtain. Attached to the sheet and the walls were copies of the *Shir Hamayles* [Psalm 121] to drive away evil spirits.

If the newborn was a boy, the youngest children from the *heder* were brought to the home by the *belfer* [teacher's assistant] to recite the *Sh'ma Yisroel* prayer every evening until the *bris*. The day before the bris, the *mohel* [who performs the circumcision] came to see if the child was healthy and he would leave behind the circumcision knife as a charm against demons.

The *bris* took place in the synagogue, even in the coldest weather. In the synagogue there stood a throne-like chair that was called the *kise shel eliyohu*, [throne of the Prophet Elijah], which it was meant to resemble. On this chair sat the *sandek* [one who holds the child during the circumcision]. Near the chair stood a footstool.

When the child was brought in, the *hazzen* [cantor] or the *shammes* [synagogue caretaker] called out "Welcome." He took the child from the *kvatar* [godfather] while reciting several verses from the Torah, then handed the child to the *sandek*, the rabbi *Reb* Leibele Teicher. The mohel – *Reb* Yeshayahule Khona Pinkhases or ChaimYechiel Shochet or Moshele dem Rebs – carried out the *mitzvah* with great concentration.

In the last years before World War II, the *brises* were no longer performed in the synagogue, but at home. The mohel then was Moshele Shochet (Kenigsberg) who lives today in Israel.

Heders and *Melameds* [teachers]

A Jewish boy began *heder* when he turned three. The education of girls was not considered important; they only needed to learn to pray. But a boy attended *heder* daily from morning to night.

If a *melamed* lived in a house that had an alcove in addition to the one all-purpose room, the beds stood in the alcove and the *heder* was conducted in the one room. If he had only one room without an alcove, the beds were lined up against the wall, concealed by a hanging sheet. At the window stood a big table with long benches.

Every melamed who taught the youngest children had two *belfers* – one a senior assistant, a grown youth, the second an under-assistant. Each day they came to the children's homes, washed and dressed them, and led them in reciting the "*moyde-ani*" [prayer said upon waking], then brought them to *heder*. In winter, when there was a lot of snow or deep mud, the *belfers* would carry the children to school on their backs.

Not all the children could fit on the benches and some sat on the floor playing with buttons or other playthings.

The under-assistant spent his time bringing the children food from their homes. The senior *belfer* helped with teaching, using a special pointer to indicate the big letters in the prayer books, the pages of which were yellowed with age and with the tears of children.

The *melamed* had a hard life. A father would complain that his child knew nothing. He wanted the child to have learned the Torah by heart in a few days. The *melamed* took out his anger on the children. A whip with 7 leather straps was always on the table. Fear of the whip destroyed any desire to go to school and the *belfer* often had to forcibly drag a child. All the way to school, the child would scream and cry and struggle to escape.

In school, the boys especially dreaded the terrible punishment called a "*pak*." The sinning child would have his face blackened with soot and be forced to wear an old, wrinkled hat. He had to hold a broom and stand in a corner near the kitchen. For an entire hour the children would shout at him, "Moshele, or Shloymele" or whatever his name might be, "Vivat [hurrah]!" If the *melamed* wanted to, he would lower the child's pants and beat him with the whip. A child who underwent such punishment would no longer dare to rebel.

On Friday nights in summer the *melamed* and the *belfers* brought the boys to *kabale shabes* [ceremony to welcome the Sabbath] in the synagogue. The children repeated the Sabbath blessing after the cantor and the *shammes* would gave them sweet raisin wine. On Saturday morning the *belfers* brought the children to synagogue where their shrill voices resounded. Each *belfer* sat with his pupils at a designated place on the synagogue's long benches.

The *melameds* also suffered persecution by the Russian government. The police would inspect the *heders*, draw up official reports, and send the children home. The teachers would alert each other about the police raids. As soon as a policeman showed up, the pupil knew that he had to run to the next *heder* and tell the teacher, "They're after us!" The *melamed* knew what that meant and he would send the children away.

The boys eagerly awaited such days, when they would run off to various places to play. When these police raids began to become more frequent, the teachers decided that something had to be done and they began to pay regular bribes to the police.

Before World War I the *melameds* who taught the youngest children were Chaim Tsibalkerles (Kreitner), Shmuel Zeis, Leibush Barishtsh (Grosman), Leibush Melamed (Fefer). There were many others who taught the more advanced classes.

In those days, the streets had no lighting. In winter the teachers did not have time to complete their lessons while it was still light. They sent the children who were still beginners home before dark. The older, more advanced students stayed after dark, until the teacher returned from evening and night prayers. Each child had a lantern lit by a candle to see his way home at night. Some boys decorated their lanterns with colored glass. The streets would be covered in mud, so the boys had to wear heavy boots.

Fathers would send their sons to various *heders* until they turned 13. Later, when a boy already knew how to study the Talmud, he would continue his religious studies in the *besmedresh* on his own, until he became a learned man.

[Pages 63-73]

Legend and Reality

Nuchim Krymerkopf

Translated by Miriam Leberstein

Reb Koppel Likover and the Tzadik of Krzeszow

Jews of the older generation used to tell stories that they had heard from their parents about the olden days in Tarnogrod, about remarkable people who once lived there and who were buried in the Tarnogrod cemetery.

In my day, Tarnogrod belonged to the district of Bilgoraj, and the town of Bilgoraj was the district capital. But things were different many years ago, when Tarnogrod was the district capital and Bilgoraj, along with the other towns in the area, belonged to the Tarnogrod district.

The cemetery was located about 300 meters outside the town on the left side of the Rozhenistser Road. There were two societies responsible for carrying out the burials: the *khevre kedushe* [burial society], which prepared the body, and the khevre *noysim* [pallbearers], who carried the body to the cemetery on a *mita* [bier] borne on their shoulders. Hearses were not used to transport the body.

The members of the *khevre kedushe* were the more prosperous Jews, Hasidim. Their last *gabbai* [administrator] was Shmuelke Stockman. The members of the *khevre noysim* were tradesmen – shoemakers and tailors. Their last *gabbai* was Avraham Lipeles (Schwetzer). Once a year the two societies would get together on Sabbath for *Kiddush* [blessing over wine] and drink together.

Tarnogrod produced brilliant religious scholars like *Reb* Chaim Sanzer [Chaim Halberstam, 1797-1876], the author of "*Divrei Chaim*" [book of commentary]. He was born and raised and studied in Tarnogrod. After he was married, he became the first Sanzer Rabbi and his dynasty extends to the present day.

Buried in the Tarnogrod cemetery is the *mekubl* [mystic, Kabbalist] *Reb* Koppel Likover, who lived in the village of Lukowa, 14 kilometers from Tarnogrod. When Tarnogrod Jews visited the village they would proudly point out the place where *Reb* Koppel Likover's inn once stood. They would tell how he had been a great miracle worker. On holidays he would leave Lukowa for Tarnogrod with his family. Once, before Passover, when he wanted to (temporarily) sell his tavern and liquor to a non-Jew for the duration of the holiday, all the Christians got together and refused to buy it, so that the liquor would belong to no one, and the peasants could steal it.

Having no choice, *Reb* Koppel abandoned the tavern and travelled to Tarnogrod. On the night of Passover, the peasants took sacks and baskets and set off to loot the tavern. As soon as they entered and reached for the bottles, their arms froze in the air and stayed there as if petrified. They began to cry and scream, as an invisible hand beat them about their heads and shoulders. Bloodied, they fled the inn and as long as they lived never found out who had beaten them. When *Reb* Koppel returned home after Passover, he found the tavern's doors and windows open, but nothing was missing.

Since that time 200 years have passed and the stories about him and about the Kabbalistic works he wrote continued until recent years. One of his grandchildren was the *Chozeh* [Seer] of Lublin [Hasidic Rabbi Yakov Yitshak Horowitz, cir.1745-1815]. The last rabbi of Tarnogrod, *Reb* Leibele Teicher, also considered himself a grandson of *Reb* Koppel Likover.

People also recounted that 100 years ago when they had finished building the Great Synagogue in Tarnogrod, there lived another grandson, the Kreshover Tzadik, who was rabbi there for many years and is buried there. It was the custom in Tarnogrod, on Tish b'Av, after the saying of Lamentations, to go to the cemetery and scatter garlic on the graves of family and friends. Everyone would also scatter garlic on the grave of *Reb* Koppel Likover. His tombstone was large, with a deep and wide inscription that had been eroded by time. Around the tombstone were rotted pieces of wood, probably all that remained of a wooden *ohel* [monument built over a grave].

In the *ohel* of the Kreshover Tzadik lights were always burning. There was also a receptacle to collect money for charity. The Kreshover Tzadik had one son, *Reb* Saul, who did not become a rabbi. He lived on Razhenitser Street, near the garden of Shlomele Marshalek.

The Religious Way of Life

The Jews of Tarnogrod distinguished themselves with their piety. They also produced great religious scholars. Morning and night, men gathered in the *besmedresh* to pray and study the Talmud. People wore long *hasidic* clothing – kaftans during the week and silk cloaks on the Sabbath and holidays. On the Sabbath they exchanged their black cloth caps for silk or velvet ones. The rabbi wore a *shtrayml* or a *spodek* [large fur hat].

The young unmarried men didn't cut or shave their beards. People got married young. An unmarried boy or girl over 20 was considered old. By the time a young man entered the army at the age of 21, he already had a wife and a child or two.

Right after the wedding they would cut off the bride's hair. All married women covered their heads with wigs or scarves and observed the *mitzvot* [religious obligations] of *khale-nemen* ["challah-taking" burning or discarding a portion of dough when baking, as symbolic offering to God], lighting the Sabbath candles, and immersing themselves in the *mikveh* [ritual bath.]

In some homes, the husband would stay at home and study and the wife would be the breadwinner. She joyfully accepted her fate to serve as footstool to her pious husband in heaven.

The Sabbath before the wedding, the groom's parents and in-laws would lead him to the synagogue for the *aufruf* ceremony [pre-wedding service]. He was given the *aliyah mafter* [privilege of reading the last part of the Torah portion] and when the prayers were concluded, everyone accompanied the groom at the Kiddush. At the same time, the bride held a pre-wedding celebration for her girlfriends. Weddings were never held on Sunday or Monday. The reason for this is not known.

There were no *klezmorim* [musicians] in Tarnogrod; they had to be brought in from Bilgoraj. Gimpel and his band were well known, as was the *badkhan* [wedding jester/ master of ceremonies] who was called Shlomele Marshalek. There was no such thing as a quiet wedding. Music was mandatory. The wedding ceremony was always held outdoors, outside the synagogue. The cantor Itsik-Yeshaya sang the blessings and the rabbi conducted the ceremony. After the ceremony the *klezmorim* played as they accompanied the newlyweds home.

After the wedding feast the in-laws danced the traditional *mitzvah*-dance with the bride, taking turns at leading her by a handkerchief in a circle. The last one to lead the bride was the groom and as he did so, the others joined in and led the couple to a separate room to sleep.

In those days it was considered a grave sin for a boy and girl to take a stroll together, and if they were discovered, there would be serious consequences. In later years, after World War I, the stricter religious practice gradually faded. One often saw boys and girls walking together and young people would form romantic friendships that led to marriage. Their walks took place in the fields along the road to Bartshashik's mill, and at the well at the suburb of Plusy. It was said of this well that its waters could heal illnesses of the eye. In any case, it provided good drinking water and it refreshed the lovesick couples on hot days.

The main place where people took their strolls was the Bilgoraj city gate on the Bishtsher road, which led to three wells outside the (non-Jewish) cemetery. These were shallow wells from which you could scoop up water with your hands. Just before World War I they erected a brick cross with a small opening through which the water constantly flowed.

The Place of the Mass Execution.

Outside the (non-Jewish) cemetery, to the left of the mountain, was the second mass grave of our Tarnogrod martyrs. In the month of *Tammuz* [June-July], 1945, I stood for hours at this grave, unable to suppress my weeping over the horrific deaths of my family and friends. A Polish village magistrate told me how the murders were carried out. There lay Moshele the Rabbi's son (Teicher) with his extended family of nearly 100 souls. There too lay Khaneke Shtruzer and her child, members of my own family.

Magistrate Skare told me how he stood and watched the Germans shoot the victims, who fell directly into a huge grave. When I asked him how he could stand to watch this horrifying scene, he said that as magistrate he was forced by the Germans to attend the mass execution. He added that he hoped to be of help to the surviving Jews who would return here after the war, by being able to show them where the bodies of their loved ones were buried.

There was no train line running through Tarnogrod. When people wanted to travel to Warsaw they had to first travel the long distance to the train station in Lublin by wagon, which took two days and nights. There were several Jewish wagon drivers in Tarnogrod. Usually, wagons carrying passengers and merchandise left for Lublin Saturday night or Sunday morning, and would return on Friday at midday.

On the way to Lublin you had to drive through several towns –Bilgoraj, Zwierzyniec, Szczebrzeszyn, Zamosc, Izbica, Krasnystaw and Piasek. The road was not entirely paved. In winter, the wagons coming back on Fridays would sometimes get stuck several kilometers outside town. Twilight would approach and there was no possibility of arriving in time for Sabbath.

In order not to violate the Sabbath, they would remain in the middle of the road the entire Sabbath. The wagon drivers were strict Sabbath observers and for the entire time they would stay by their wagons loaded with goods, for which they were responsible.

The Synagogue, the Besmedresh and the two *Hasidic Shtibls* [small house of prayer]

In addition to the synagogue and *besmedresh* there were also two *Hasidic shtibls*, one for the *Belzer* [sect] and the other for the *Shiniaver* sect. All these places of worship were on the east side of town. The *besmedresh* stood at the beginning of Razhinitser Street, near the market place. To the right of the entrance to the *besmedresh* there was the "tailors little synagogue," where tailors and other artisans prayed on Sabbath and holidays. The *gabbai* of the little synagogue was *Reb* Yoel Schneider (Magram). Opposite the tailors' synagogue, on the left side, there was a hidden exit, which looked like a small room, where they kept wood to heat the oven in the *besmedresh* in winter. Inside, right at the entrance, on the left side, was a basin for washing hands before praying. Nearby stood the oven for heating, and a long bench where the older men sat and warmed their backs.

To the right of the door there was a niche where an eternal flame burned. Near the door, where there was a long towel for drying one's hands, there was a wide table with a top that opened, in which the *shames* [beadle] kept the tablecloths and towels. On the south side stood two long tables with long benches where young men sat and studied by the light of kerosene lamps that hung by wires from the ceiling.

In the middle of the eastern wall, at the top of several steps, stood the Holy Ark that held the Torah scrolls. Nearby stood the pulpit where the *bal tfile* [rabbi, cantor or other prayer leader] recited the prayers. In the very center of the *besmedresh* stood the crooked lectern from which the Torah was read. Along the sides were benches for sitting.

The women's section had a separate entrance and was at the top of a flight of stairs. On winter nights Moshe Shames would sell cookies and herring to supplement his wages. After his death, Kalmen Shames [Lerner] took over his position.

The walls were lined with shelves packed with religious books, old and new, dusty and yellowed or well kept, with leather bindings. Every Friday afternoon, one of the boys who studied in the *besmedresh* would circulate among the worshippers and collect money for repairing the books.

From Reb Itsik to Reb Yentche Melamed

In addition to the permanent students who sat in the *besmedresh* entire days and nights, there were others who studied in groups. One study group, Ein Yaakov, was led by Yokl Shmetsh (Bas). Itsik Melamed led a group that met every Sabbath in the little synagogue to study the Bible along with Rashi's commentary. When Itsik Melamed and his wife left for *Eretz Yisroel*, where he died in Safad, others took on this role, the last of whom was Yentche Melamed. A group studying *Mishnah* [part of Talmud] was led by Volvish Melamed (Blitman). There was also a group that studied psalms.

There was also a society for providing housing for the indigent and a society for visiting and caring for the sick. The *gabbai* Leibish Margulies (Klein), the bath attendant at the town baths, belonged to both societies. In later years there was also a society founded by Chava Galis (Zeis) and other women that visited the homes of the prosperous on Friday night to collect *challot* and bread to distribute to poor families. There were also women who took responsibility for providing poor brides with a trousseau.

The Festive Sabbath Dinners in the Little Synagogue of the Weavers

Behind the *besmedresh* was the synagogue. To the right, off the anteroom, was a little synagogue which was called the "*shkotsher* [weavers] little synagogue," where the hand weavers sometimes prayed. In the old days, approximately 40% of the Jews in Tarnogrod were employed in producing canvas for sacks, which they sold in Lublin or Warsaw to the big agricultural estates. On Saturday, in this little synagogue they would hold festive dinners for the third Sabbath meal at twilight. These were paid for by Matish Beker (Arbesfeld) --and later by his son, Moshe --who had the exclusive right to perform this mitzvah. He did it even in later times, before World War II, when he had already become quite impoverished and actually went hungry himself.

The synagogue had two large gates that were locked when it wasn't being used for worship. The *shammes* Nachum Trib held the keys. Over the gate to the anteroom an inscription in large letters read "How awesome is this place! This is none other than the house of God, and this is the gate of Heaven." [Genesis 28:17]

To get to the synagogue one had to go up several steps.

In the middle of the synagogue stood four thick stone pillars. The walls were like those in a fortress. Each wall had four long rectangular windows and the upper panes were of stained glass. The ceiling was round and vaulted and from it hung very bright oil lamps and chandeliers with dozens of brass tubes where candles would be inserted. Along the walls were long benches and lecterns where the prosperous men purchased their places. The prayers were recited in the Ashkenazic manner.

Two sets of stairs led to the *balemer* [raised desk from which Torah is read] that stood in the middle of the synagogue, one on the north and one on the south. Along the walls near the lectern were benches where the gabbais sat. By the railings across from the lectern was a long bench where people sat with the Torah scrolls before they were returned to the Holy Ark, which was built into the Eastern wall, at the top of a long staircase. Over the Ark were two carved golden lions and over the lions a metal eagle hung by ropes.

The lectern, which stood to the right, was made of plain wood. The "*shevisi*" [inscription from Psalms 16:8, "I place God in front of me always."] glittered over the brass candleholder. On the table to the right of the lectern was a large brass menorah.

Reb Leibele's Unforgettable Yom Kippur

In the mid-18th century *Reb* Leibele Rozenfeld was cantor in Tarnogrod. People told a story about the time when he became very sick after Rosh Hashanah, and another cantor was hired to replace him for Yom Kippur. But at the last minute, just before Kol Nidre, *Reb* Leibele ordered them to wait for him before starting to pray. The choir members dressed him in his robe and prayer shawl, carried him in a chair to the synagogue and set him down in front of the cantor's pulpit. From there he led the entire Yom Kippur service until late at night, when they carried him back home and put him to bed. The same thing happened the next day. He glowed like fire and his praying was more fervent and heartfelt than ever before.

My father's father, *Reb* Benyamin Krymerkopf, was a member of *Reb* Leibele's choir for many years. When they brought the cantor home after services and put him to bed, he asked the cantor, "Tell me the truth; how did you manage to pray and sing more forcefully today than ever before?"

Reb Leibele looked around the room and having assured himself no one could hear him, he answered: "I swear to you on my life, Benyamin, but you must tell no one the secret I am about to tell you. You know how sick I am. I couldn't even get out of bed. But when I said the evening prayer before Yom Kippur in my bed the Prophet Elijah appeared to me and ordered me to lead the prayers from my pulpit, telling me he would give me the strength to conduct the services. So I prayed the entire service with the strength of Elijah."

Reb Leibele died in the winter of that same year. After his death Benyamin told everyone the big secret. *Reb* Leibele's grave is by the wall of the Kreshever Tzadik's *ohel*.

The Blessing of Reb Itsik-Yeshayaby the Old Trisker Magid

After *Reb* Leibele died, his son Yisraelish served as cantor for several years. *Reb* Leibele left behind a large extended family, most of who were killed by the Nazis. One great-grandson, Avraham Kagan, lives now in Israel.

Before World War I, Itsik-Yeshaya served as cantor for a long time. With his extraordinarily strong voice and beautiful way of chanting the prayers, he enchanted his listeners and brought down the house. Chaim Trib, a man of 96 who now lives in America, told me that a man named Goldman came to Tarnogrod and wanted to pay Itsik-Yeshaya $5000 to come to America just one time to lead the High Holy Day prayers. Itsik-Yeshaya turned him down. He didn't want to abandon Tarnogrod and leave the Jews there without a cantor for the High Holy Days. It was his habit to lead the prayers in the synagogue on the first night of Rosh Hashanah. He would recite the *Musaf* prayer in the *besmedresh* while the rabbi led the *Musaf* prayer in the synagogue. On the second day of Rosh Hashanah they switched places. On Yom Kippur, Itsik Yeshaya sang Kol Nidre and *Musaf* in the synagogue and the rabbi in the *besmedresh*.

Itsik-Yeshaya never became hoarse. When he was over 70, his voice was as strong as in his youth and he chanted with the same fervor that thrilled his congregation. The Jews of Tarnogrod said that the Magid of Trisk had given him a blessing, so that his voice would remain young and would never become hoarse.

The night of Kol Nidre is deeply engraved in my memory. The synagogue was packed with worshippers, dressed in white *kitls* [long robes] with black sashes, their prayer shawls covering their heads, and holding their prayer books and reciting the *tefillah zaka* [prayer of confession]. Some wept silently, others aloud. From the women's section came a lamentation that broke your heart. Everyone was shoeless, their feet in socks only. The floor was spread with hay, which the children would pile up under the tables and benches and burrow into.

After the *tefillah zaka* Itsik-Yeshaya and his choir sang Kol Nidre. There were Christians who would come to the synagogue just to hear his wonderful melodies. After prayers were over, many people remained in the synagogue the entire night, not sleeping, chanting various hymns and prayers.

The interior walls of the synagogue were not painted or whitewashed, because the rabbi forbade that, saying that the walls had absorbed so many tears and so many prayers that they should remain bare.

[Pages 74-84]

Prayer Leaders of the Period Between the Two World Wars

by Nuchim Krymerkopf

Translated by Miriam Leberstein

Itsik-Yeshaya died in the summer two months before the outbreak of World War I. After his death there was not a full-time cantor in Tarnogrod. During the war no one thought to hire a new cantor, and after the war the impoverished town no longer had the means to support one year-round. There were various prayer leaders. For several years Abish Roizes (Akerman) led the prayers. Later, Yitzshak Shlomoles (Leder) was prayer leader for several years; he had been a member of Itsik Yeshaya's choir. He then went to Tomaszów Lubelski, where they hired him year-round.

Once, a week before the first *Selichot* [penitential prayers preceding High Holy Days], the *omed* [cantor's pulpit] caught fire from a *yahrzeit* candle that burned late into the night. The *omed* and a nearby table were burned along with a part of the floor where the cantor stood, but the fire didn't spread any further and went out all by itself. The next morning, I entered the synagogue along with several other men and we all gazed in amazement at this wonder.

After that event, the *ba'al tefillah* was Moshele Shohet (Kenigsberg) who had also long been a member of Itsik Yeshaya's choir. He led the *Musaf* prayers [recited on Sabbath and holidays] in the synagogue until World War II. He lives today in Haifa. His grandfather Leib Itsik Shohet led the *Shacharit* [morning] prayers for many years. After Moshele Shohet died, David Inalers (Elboim) succeeded him and served until the final destruction of the community.

The Synagogue that Fire Could Not Destroy

Within weeks of invading Tarnogrod, the Germans twice set fire to the synagogue and each time the fire extinguished itself. So, the synagogue stands there to this day, orphaned and alone, without its faithful congregation.

Many legends about the synagogue were passed on from generation to generation. Parents told their children about the souls [of the dead] that came to pray in the synagogue in the middle of the night. On dark nights, the children were afraid to walk alone on Synagogue Street.

Behind the synagogue, down the hill, stood the municipal baths with two *mikvahs*, one heated, one not. This was a large bathhouse with two sets of benches, banked like steps, so that you could climb up to where the heat was highest and have a good sweat. Every Sabbath and holiday the bath was well heated; the only Sabbath that it was not heated was, *Shabbat Chazon* the Sabbath before Tisha b'Av, when people had to make do with just the *mikvah*. The *mikvah* was heated twice a week, Monday and Thursday.

The bath attendants were just as pious and refined as the other highly respected Jews, like the ritual slaughterers, cantors and rabbis. Until the fire that destroyed half of the bathhouse, the longtime bath attendant was Shlomo Leib Silberzweig, along with his son Yisroelke, an upstanding Jew, a good *baal korei* [one who reads aloud from the Torah] and a religious scholar. After them various other men took care of the baths. The last two were brothers-in-law, Leibish Margolis (Klein) and Dan Dvokeles (Elboim).

To the right of the synagogue were two *shtibls* [small *Hasidic* house of worship]. To get from the *shtibl* of the Shiniaver sect to that of the Beldzer sect you had to go along a narrow lane where Leibish Melamed lived. Every *Hasidic shtibl* had a women's section. In later years, when there were few [older] boys who engaged in religious studies fulltime, they were concentrated in the Beldzer *shtibl*, which was bigger than that of the Shiniaver.

Hasidim and their *Rebes* [*Hasidic* spiritual leaders]

There were other *Hasidic* groups in Tarnogrod in addition to the Beldzer and Shiniaver, including the Trisker, Razvadover, and Kuzmirer. The tradesmen were followers of the Tarbiner *rebe*; they jokingly called him the proletarian rebe.

The *Hasidic* rebes would often come to Tarnogrod on the Sabbath to be with their followers. There were hardly any Jews in Tarnogrod who were *mitnagdim* [opponents of Hasidism]. Everyone believed the rebe had special powers, that with his prayers he could intercede with God on their behalf. They were happy to go to the *rebe* with their *kvitlekh* [written requests], which were accompanied by a monetary gift. In the *kvitlekh* people poured out their hearts, pleading for help, a cure for an illness, advice on how to handle a business problem or a family quarrel. The *rebe's* word was sacred, his approval or opposition decided everything, starting with sending a child to *heder*, then yeshiva, learning a trade, or making a marriage match.

Sometimes, a son or daughter needed to go to America. The father would go to see the *rebe* for advice, but the rebe always shook his head, "no," saying that America was an unkosher land where they violated the Sabbath. That was enough for the young boy or girl to have to abandon the plan to emigrate, because they could no longer rely on their parents' permission and to act against their parents' wishes was impossible, since they had not saved any money of their own.

The same thing happened when parents sought advice from the *rebe* about sending a child to Eretz Yisroel. Certain *rebes* saw it as a land of heretics where boys and girls lead a sinful life, and stubbornly opposed emigration from Poland to Eretz Yisroel, telling them to wait for the Messiah, who would take all Jews there. Deferential but confused, these parents would take leave of the *rebe* unsure whether to oppose their own children, who struggled to free the Holy Land and live a free and healthy life there.

The Last of the Tarnogrod Rabbis

The rabbi, *Reb* [respectful term of address] Leibele Teicher, lived near the *besmedresh* [house of study also used for worship] in a stone house. The rabbi lived on one side of the house, his son *Reb* Hershele and his family lived on the other side.

The Reb Rabbi Aryeh Lieb and Family

Our rabbi, *Reb* Leibele Teicher, treated everyone with love and devotion. His piety reflected his boundless love for the creator and his creatures. His devotion to the Jewish people was paired with a pure and unblemished faith. His chief characteristic was honesty toward others and himself, which he passed on to his children.

Reb Hershele died in Russia during the Second World War. His wife and children live today in Israel. His son Moshele lived upstairs. *Reb* Moshele was the last rabbi of Tarnogrod.

It is not entirely clear how long *Reb* Leibele Teicher held the rabbinical seat. I remember only the date of his death, at the age of 96, a Saturday in the month of Av, in 1935. His funeral was attended not only by all the Jews in Tarnogrod, but also those from Bilgoraj and surrounding villages. Pursuant to his wish he was buried in the *oyel* [small structure serving as a memorial] near the Kreshever *tsadik* [saintly man].

Customs

Until the outbreak of World War I the Jews of Tarnogrod followed the custom of summoning people to morning prayer by knocking on their shutters. I remember the small man with a short gray beard called Zanvele Shul-Klapper [one who summons people to prayer by knocking]. He lived in an alley in a dark little house, as a tenant of Yoylish Schneider.

Every day at dawn Zanvele *Shul-Klapper* would walk through the town with a wooden hammer resembling a *shofar* [ram's horn] banging it on the shutters of Jewish homes, calling out, "Get up to pray to God!" The banging woke up everyone in the house. The husband would leave to go to pray, the wife began to prepare breakfast and the children got dressed to go to *heder*. The older boys went to the *besmedresh* to study.

After returning from prayers, the husband would eat breakfast and go to his shop. If he was a tradesman, he would set about his work.

Zanvele *Shul-Klapper* had his own rhythm for banging the hammer. He used another, special rhythm on the days when the *Selichot* prayers were said, before the High Holy Days. On those days he would get up an hour earlier than usual. In the dark, heavy fog, in pouring rain, he would slink through the muddy streets with a lantern in his left hand and the hammer in his right hand, and would bang on the shutters, calling people to go to synagogue to say *Selichot*.

Every Friday evening, a half-hour before the lighting of the Sabbath candles, he would bang out the call to go to synagogue. At this signal the women would begin to prepare for candle lighting and the men changed into their Sabbath attire.

On Friday, Zanvele would visit Jewish homes with a basket and collect candles to be used in the *yahrzeit* prayers for rabbis held in the *besmedreshes*. His income consisted of the several *kopeks* he was given each week in each home. It sometimes happened that by accident or on purpose he failed to bang on someone's shutters, and that person would complain and demand an explanation for the omission.

The Sabbath and holidays were the only days Zanvele did not bang on the shutters. On those days, the *shamosim* [sing *shames* -- caretaker] of the synagogue and *besmedresh* would go around the town and summon people to pray with the traditional religious melody. Nuchim, the synagogue shames, made the rounds of the houses in the marketplace; Moshe, the *shames* of the *besmedresh*, went around the back streets. On the non-sacred intermediate days of the Passover holiday, the *shamosim* visited the houses with baskets to collect eggs, willingly donated by every woman.

When Moshe the *shames* died, Kalman Lerner took his place. When Zanvele *Shul-Klapper* died, Kalman took over his job as well. After World War I the custom of *shul-klapping* disappeared, possibly because people then had alarm clocks to awaken them. The only custom that remained was the summons to prayer on the Sabbath by the shames. This continued until the last Sabbath preceding the complete destruction of the Jewish community.

Nuchim the *shul shames* died several years before World War I, at the age of 97. He was succeeded by Aharon Dovid Tryb, who was called the *Magid* [preacher-storyteller], who held the post until the end, killed along with the rest of the Jewish community.

The Poorhouse

The poorhouse was in an old abandoned wooden building that had a vestibule without a floor. Under the threshold there were holes made by feral cats. By a sidewall stood the equipment used by the burial society for preparing corpses for burial – the tare board [on which the body was laid], and a pot to heat water for washing the body.

The poorhouse was the permanent home for the poor and abandoned. The walls were always black with dust and dirt. Spider webs hung from the corners of the ceiling. Bottles and broken glass stood on the cracked windowsills. Rags were stuffed into the spaces left by missing windowpanes.

In the main room there was a small alcove, set off by a hanging sheet, where the keeper of the poorhouse lived with his family. His name was Aharon, but people called him Kuni Leml [a character in a play by A. Goldfaden, synonomous with a comic fool]. He was his 60's, had a broad, burly face with a big snarled beard that, like his nostrils, was stained by the tobacco, which he stuffed into his nose all day long. On the Sabbath and holidays he wore the same greasy long coarse coat that he wore all week. In that coat, bound by a broad sash, he would sit up overnight with the corpses awaiting burial. In winter and summer he wore thick boots with wide bootlegs. The soil-stiffened skirts of his coat banged against the bootlegs with a tinny sound.

He earned his living by working for the burial society. He sat up with every dead body and carried the board and pot of water for washing the corpse.

His wife Shifra bore him two sons in the poorhouse. One, Leibush, entered the Russian army in 1914 and never returned from the war. The second son, Gedalia, at the age of 16, was in the attic of the poorhouse when its rotted ceiling fell down and killed him.

An investigative commission then ordered that the neglected poorhouse be torn down. Sometime later, the town began to build a new poorhouse behind the synagogue, on the road to the bath, but it was never completed. Under Polish rule [i.e., after the establishment of Independent Poland in 1920] the Jews of Tarnogrod became increasingly impoverished and no longer had the means to build this institution.

Shifra, the wife of the poorhouse keeper, was like her husband Kuni Leml very pious and just like him sniffed tobacco. On her shaven head she wore a scarf. She very rarely went out into the street; only during the two weeks before Passover would she go out the matzo bakery to help roll out the dough. All year long she would sit in the little alcove with her prayer book, praying and reciting psalms. In her 50's she became blind in both eyes. She would sit near the oven by the window, reciting prayers and psalms from memory. She knew by heart the entire liturgy for the HIgh Holy Days. And so she lived on, blind and silent, for several years until death liberated her from her impoverished and unhappy life.

Jewish Holidays:

Purim

It is impossible to describe the merriment that began with the feast held on Purim eve. The prosperous sat at tables covered with all kinds of delicacies –*kreplach* and *hamantashen* – and distributed money to the Purim-*shpilers* [amateur actors who performed traditional Purim play] as well as alms-seekers that solicited contributions, some for themselves, others on behalf of the needy. Children distributed *shalekh mones* [gifts of food and drink] on plates covered with pretty napkins.

Right after Purim, people began to whitewash their houses [in preparation for Passover]. Peasants delivered wagonloads of potatoes and beets, which Jews bought several weeks before the holiday. Women peeled and sliced the beets and put them in big pots and small barrels to make Passover borsht. The potatoes were put in the attic to keep them from being contaminated with *hametz* [leavening].

But much earlier, as far back as Hanukkah-time, the women had already started to prepare *shmaltz* to use in preparing the Passover dishes. Even the poor would save up for a farm-raised goose to use for *schmaltz*. Right after Shabbat Shirah [the Sabbath on which the Torah portion Beshalach is read] people brought wheat for baking matzo to the rabbi for inspection. That wheat was very expensive because it carried a special tax designed to raise money to provide the poor with matzo. The rabbi inspected it to assure that it was kosher and received a fee for that service. The wheat was then brought to a mill for grinding. The rabbi strictly required that it be ground in a mill with grindstones, not rollers, and that it be sifted so it had a finer appearance than ordinary coarse flour. Because Tarnogrod didn't have such a mill, the wheat had to be brought to Bilgoraj for milling. After World War I Ben Tzion Weinrib and his brother-in- law Itche Silberzweig built a mill on the *blonye* [pasture land] that met the requirements and it was no longer necessary to bring the wheat to Bilgoraj for milling.

Ready-made matzo was not available for purchase in Tarnogrod, as it was in other towns. Everyone had to go the warehouse to buy the amount of flour needed for his family from the people who had bought wheat and had it ground. The *redler* [person who perforates the matzo] then delivered the flour to the matzo baker, where each customer had already obtained the right to have his matzo baked.

The matzo bakers started their preparations before Purim. They bought dry wood and sought out women to hire to help in rolling out the dough, kneading and perforating it, and shoveling it into the oven. The baking began on the first day of [the month of] *Nisan* and went on for two weeks until the eve of Passover. On the very eve of Passover the bakeries were occupied by Hasidim who baked their own *shmure* matzo [made under especially strict rules]. They didn't want women rolling out the dough. They themselves did the rolling, kneading, piercing, and insertion in the oven, singing psalms the entire time.

In the days before Passover there was a rush of women coming to the rabbi with questions about how to make their utensils kosher for the holiday, especially those from families that didn't have sufficient pots for exclusive use on Passover. They had to kosher their regular pots, which were tainted by hametz. The iron pots had to be put in a burning hot oven, all the openings of which had been sealed with clay.

Several days before they went to have their matzo baked, people washed their cupboards with boiling water, and scoured the boards with sand with a special stone that had been immersed in flames.

For two weeks before Passover, the matzo bakers could be seen everywhere carrying baskets of matzo on their backs to deliver to their well-off customers.

If the weather permitted, cupboards, tables and benches were brought outdoors where the Christian women [servants] cleaned and washed them. Their husbands would whitewash the interior walls. On the rubbish heaps lay the old broken straw that had been used to stuff the mattresses.

The people who worked the hardest on the eve of Passover were the bakers, because they had to get rid of their hametz before 9 AM., by selling or giving it or giving it away to non-Jews. Then, not having slept much and very tired, they had to get ready for the holiday. They had to do in one day what others had had two or three weeks to accomplish.

At night, at the seder, when the father returned home from synagogue with the children, with a beaming holiday greeting, the table was waiting with its fresh, white tablecloth, the plates of matzo and *charoses*, raisin wine in the big carafe and in the sparkling goblets, which had belonged to their grandfathers and great-grandfathers. The candles in the silver candleholders shone with a holy joy. In most families they lit a candle for each family member. They also used an oil lamp set to its highest flame and even though Tarnogrod did not have electricity at this time; the room was flooded with light. The home was filled with the aroma of delicious food. The children, scrubbed from head to toe, sat around the table impatiently waiting to ask the four questions.

Father wore his pure white *kitel* [special robe] and reclined on the special upholstered chair like an angel, reciting the *haggadah*. The wife served the *kneydlekh* and all the other delicious Passover dishes. And so, the two Passover nights passed with worldly pleasure and spiritual exaltation.

[Pages 84-95]

Chol Hamoed[1]

by Nuchim Krymerkopf

Translated by Miriam Leberstein

The *chol hamoed* days were a mix of holiday and weekday. People travelled and did business and yet there was a festive feeling. The tradesmen did not work, but strolled around in the market place dressed in new work smocks, met up with friends and family, and chatted in groups about various topics. The shopkeepers were also dressed in a semi-holiday, semi-workday fashion. The grain merchants were a bit aggrieved during Passover, since they weren't allowed to buy grain, and like the bakers they slept all day and rested up.

The matchmakers were especially active during these days, setting up meetings between prospective matches and their families. At tables bedecked with *khremzlekh* [matzo meal pancakes] the boys presented the girls with presents, and the girls did the same when the boys were invited to their homes. In the meantime, the parents discussed the wedding arrangements.

During *chol hamoed* the bakers went house to house to collect the money owed them for baking the matzo. In the prosperous homes they were treated to *khremzlekh* and slivovitz [plum brandy] and Passover *vishnik* [cherry liquor].

Among the matzo bakers whom I recall were Moshe and Grafs (Lipiner); my father Chaim Krymerkopf; Itsik-Hersh Fefer, who was partners with Meir Leibeles; Khaye Beile-Rechl; Berger; Yekutiel Honik and his wife.

On the Sabbath and holiday they conducted the prayers in the *besmedresh* with great enthusiasm. All kinds of good food were prepared at home, even among the poor. The parents derived joy from the sweet voices of their children, who joined in singing the *zemirot* [melodies]. Every boy who went to *heder* wished that Passover lasted several months. Classes ended several days before the holiday, because the rebe had to get ready.

In the pleasant *chol hamoed* days the *heder* boys were busy making whistles from tree twigs and playing games with nuts. Even before Purim, the prosperous parents had bought their children new clothing and shoes for Passover. The tailors and shoemakers had no time to finish orders for the poor children; they were too overwhelmed with work for the children of the rich and postponed the orders for the poor until after the holiday. The children of the poor cried in shame, but still ran out to play in their old clothes and forgot about their troubles.

During these days the *melameds* would visit the parents of their pupils and entreat them not to remove their children and send them to another teacher. They collected payment for the tuition that was owed them and at the same time took the occasion to recruit new pupils. The *belfers* [teacher's assistants] also went around to collect the money owed them for whole year of washing the children, helping them with their morning prayers and polishing their shoes.

It was a delight during *chol hamoed* to go outside to the large Tarnogrod market place, where the warm spring sun had already dried up the mud. Everything had a semi-holiday appearance. Yankl Getz (Spielsinger), the water carrier, went around with his water cans on his shoulders singing a song about half-holidays, half-matzos, half-eggs, and half-potatoes, mixed in with verses from Psalms.

On the other [sacred] days of the holiday, the Jews felt exalted and in good spirits. These days were spent praying, eating the festive meals, taking an afternoon nap and then going back to the *besmedresh* to study and recite psalms.

The last day of Passover the *shmirenikes* [ultra-observant], who during the holiday refrained from eating *kneidlach* [matzo balls] and other delicacies made with matzo meal, indulged themselves and made up for the entire holiday by eating in one day all the foods which they had been eyeing with great appetite, but had not eaten.

The *khevre kedushe* had a custom of holding a feast for its members on the last day of Passover, to which they also invited the members of the *khevre noysim*.

When the holiday ended, it felt as if something precious had been lost. The mood was sad. People began counting the days of the *Omer* [the 49-day period between the end of Passover and *Shavuot*], waiting impatiently for the arrival of the holiday of *Shavuot*. During this period people did not hold weddings, sew new clothing, or cut their hair.

Shavuot

On the day of *Shavuot* eve boys visited the houses of the prosperous with bunches of wild iris to sell. The flowers grew along the Zheke, where this small stream flowed far from the town, and the boys went there to pick them. They would make whistles from the stems. The women spread the flowers over the floor and on windowsills.

There were also families who sent each other these flowers as an expression of friendship. Thus, when a Jewish woman wanted to say that she and another woman didn't get along, she would use the expression, "Well, so she won't send me flowers on *Shavuot*."

While the women saw to it that there were flowers at *Shavuot*, the men took care to supply the household with *Shavuot* trees. The tree boughs were hung on nails that had been hammered into the walls, in the corners, on the ceiling around the chandeliers. No one in town knew the correct name of the trees, which grew outside the town and behind the synagogue. They called them *Shavuot* trees because every year they cut the branches of those trees to use to decorate the houses for *Shavuot*.

Heder boys pasted special colorful paper decorations on the windowpanes in the shape of flowers, which were called hag *hashvueslekh*.

In the synagogues and *besmedreshes* the tables, altar, pulpit, lectern and Torah ark were decorated with tree boughs, and these houses of worship, just like the homes, looked like fragrant gardens.

The first day of *Shavuot*, before reading the Torah, they recited the *Akdamut* prayer. On the second day, they read the *Megilla* of Ruth. In the synagogue, where they prayed in the Ashkenazic manner, they recited *yotzros* [liturical poems] every Sabbath from after Passover until *Shavuot*.

On the first day after *Shavuot*, there was an *Isru Chag* [half-holiday] and the tradesmen did not begin work until noon.

Orchardists

Then came the days and weeks of summer. Everyone was busy with their weekday work, some in commerce, others in their workshops. On hot days, doors and windows stood open. At some houses ducks and chickens wandered about. Children ran around barefoot; the youngest wore only shirts. People ate mostly dairy foods. When the berries ripened they cooked them into compote. On Friday the mothers prepared baked goods with the berries especially for the children, but grown-ups didn't mind eating them as well. The children's mouths were constantly smeared and blackened from eating berries. The mothers put up big jars of berry preserves.

After berry season came the season of fruit – cherries, sour cherries and all other fruits that grew in orchards around Tarnogrod. In the month of Av, when the sour cherries were harvested, they started to make *vishnik* for Passover.

There were Jewish orchardists in Tarnogrod who rented orchards with fruit trees outside the town or in the surrounding villages from estate owners and peasants. When the fruit ripened, they picked them and brought them to town, keeping them in cellars, and in this way supported themselves for the entire year.

In the month of *Av* the orchardists would travel to the orchards with their wives and children, taking with them their prayer shawls and *tefillin*, and some pots to cook with. The family lived together in a hut that they built, cooking on a fire lit in the middle of the orchard.

The huts were made from poles covered with straw. Inside there was more straw, on which the family slept. The huts were so cleverly constructed, under the protection of the trees, that they could withstand the strongest winds and torrential rains.

The orchard keepers lived in the orchards from the beginning of *Av* until Rosh Hashanah. If the harvest was late, they would stay there through the High Holy Days and Sukkot, and would erect a *sukkah* in the orchard.

The orchardists whose orchards were in the villages would pray with the village Jews in their *minyans* on the Sabbath and holidays. The Tarnogrod orchardists would not pick up fruit that fell on the ground on the Sabbath.

The well-off orchardists who had wholesale businesses hired peasants with wagons to transport the fruit to sell in the nearby towns: Jozefow, Bilgoraj, Sieniawa, Lezajsk, where there were no orchards. In the last years before the war there were already orchard keepers who owned their own horses and wagons and transported the fruit to town themselves.

The wives of the smaller-scale orchardists would sit in the market place near the fabric shops, with piles of fruit which they sold year-round. In winter they sat with a fire-pot at their feet and sold by the kilo. A frozen apple was considered a desirable delicacy in Tarnogrod.

It was harder to make a living in summer than in winter. Most of the customers were peasants, who in summer were busy in the fields and rarely came into town. The big fairs were also less busy in the summer.

Business didn't pick up until the month of *Elul*, when the peasants had already harvested the grain from the fields. The well-off Jews began to buy wood, so it would be dry in time for winter. The poor got ready by buying potatoes, beets and carrots. Wood was too expensive for them, and only when the cold weather approached did they buy a small wagonload of pine branches, which were wet and did not burn well, filling the house with smoke.

High Holy Days

The day of Rosh Hashanah eve, before the *slikhes* prayers, the women began baking for the holiday and the entire week following. They baked special challahs that looked different from the regular Sabbath challahs, called "*radishen*" When people returned home from the *slikhes* prayers, the smell of sugar pears drying in the ovens after the challah was baked emanated from many houses.

It was considered a *mitzvah* to buy a living carp or other fish on Rosh Hashanah, as a charm for another year of life. Two partners, Zisman Fink and Zalman Weintraub, sold live fish for many years until World War II. They bought the fish from estate owners who raised them in the lakes on their estates. They transported the live fish in barrels filled with water to other towns.

Many years before World War I, the practice was that on the day of Rosh Hashanah eve, just as on Friday, the bathhouse was reserved for women until noon. After noon, Moshele Tsvaniak went through the streets ringing a bell to signal that the bath was now available to the men. For this service he was paid a few *groshen* by the bath attendant. When Moshele Tsvaniak died Hetish Wassertreger, the mute, took over the job of ringing the bell.

On the first night of Rosh Hashanah prayers began a bit earlier than on an ordinary Sabbath eve, and ended much later. On their way home, people wished each other a good year – *leshone tova tikateyvu.*

All of the next day was spent in prayer and reciting psalms. For the ceremony of *tashlekh* people went to the Zheke, where it flowed under the bridge at the Bilgoraj gate. The entire way back the worshippers, along with the rabbi, sang various *nigunim* [religious melodies].

During the 10-day period of repentance between Rosh Hashanah and Yom Kippur everyone was very serious, fearful of the approaching Day of Judgment. On Yom Kippur eve, by order of the rabbi, the bath was not heated and people had to make do with the heated *mikve*.

During *Mincha* [afternoon prayers], they performed the *malkus* ceremony [symbolic whipping]. Two men stood at the torah ark to administer the lashes. The person who was to receive the lashes lay face down on the floor, which was covered in hay. With a wide leather belt, the beater slowly counted out forty strokes, while the person receiving the blows struck himself in the chest and confessed his sins. People paid three *kopeks* in advance to undergo the *malkus* ceremony. In addition, people donated money for the poor who stood at the door to the synagogue, and to communal charitable institutions, which had laid out plates on a table for that purpose. That is how things were done until World War I; after that, the custom was abandoned.

After the *seudah hamafsekes* [final meal before the Yom Kippur fast] and the candle lighting at home, you would hear weeping from parents and children. Relatives and friends would drop in to wish each other a good year, meanwhile shedding copious tears. Teary-eyed, people went off to the synagogues and *besmedreshes* to pray, and did not leave until late in the night. Many did not go home to sleep, but studied and recited psalms all night. The same occurred the entire day of Yom Kippur; prayers lasted all day, until people left to bless the new moon. They took with them the stubs of candles that had been burning for 24 hours. They had made sure that a piece of candle remained to be used in the ceremony of *Hoshana Rabbah* [7th day of Sukkot] when the *Hoshanot* prayer is recited.

Sukkot

It was an old tradition to begin building the *sukkah* immediately after the first meal after the Yom Kippur fast had ended. There were *sukkah*s for individual families, and *sukkahs* that were shared, with several families eating together.

During World War I Tarnogrod and Bilgoraj shared a single *esrog* [citron used in religious ritual on Sukkot]. The Tarnogrod Jews had to delay the ritual requiring the *esrog* until 2 o'clock in the afternoon, when a Christian boy rode in from Bilgoraj, 21 kilometers away, and delivered the fruit.

Chol hamoed Sukkot was similar to Passover. Matchmakers came to propose marriage matches; prospective brides and grooms arranged to meet and invited each other to their parent's homes. But the *chol hamoed* days of *Sukkot* lacked the joy of the renewal of nature felt at Passover. The approaching chill of winter was already in the air.

On *Hoshana Rabbah*, people spent the day in prayer, reciting psalms and study. The Rabbi went around collecting alms for the hidden poor [people who concealed their poverty] and other charitable causes. On the night of *Shimini Atzeret* the Jews who followed Sephardic tradition carried the Torah around, as on Simchat Torah. Those who followed the Ashkenazi tradition did this only on Simchat Torah, after the conclusion of prayers.

Simchat Torah was a joyous holiday. After prayers people would visit the gabbais of the *besmedresh* for Kiddush that included *kreplach* [filled dumplings]. Relatives and good friends would visit back and forth, so people spent the whole day in a state of intoxication. People didn't sleep during the day, as on other holidays, but caroused until late into the night.

1914 – A New Era

Until World War I Tarnogrod was under Russian rule. In my childhood old people told stories about how the Russian "*khappers*" sent away two poor boys from the town to become *kantonists* in the Russian army, where they served 25 years.[i]

Moshe Klug, who came from the village Rozaniec, near Tarnogrod, served 15 years in the Russian army, in a unit stationed in Moscow. His wife stayed in Moscow the entire time. He returned to his village and lived to be very old, until one night a peasant burnt down his home, with him in it.

Tarnogrod Jews lived through all the wars fought by Russia. Jews remembered participating in the Russo-Turkish War [1877-78] and the Russo-Japanese war of 1904, in which several Tarnogrod Jews died. There were several Jews who fled to America [to avoid military service] and returned to Tarnogrod when the war was over; others remained in America and brought over their families.

After the war with Japan, when life in Russia returned to normal, Jewish life in Tarnogrod was quiet and peaceful until war broke out in 1914. The First World War broke out on *Tisha b'Av* 1914. There was a mobilization in the entire country, and Jews from Tarnogrod were drafted into the Russian army. The impact of the war was strongly felt from the first day. The town was close to the Austrian border and immediately became the front line.

The border military, called *obietshikes*, penetrated deeper into the country. The Austrian army crossed the border and invaded Tarnogrod. That day, there were still several Russian border patrol soldiers on the Folwark, near the Bilgoraj gate. When they spotted an Austrian cavalry patrol, the Russian soldiers ran toward it with rifles in hand, positioning themselves behind Mordechai Mantl's stone building, and began shooting. One rider was wounded, another fell off his horse, dead, and the rest retreated. Having accomplished this bit of work, the Russians went off in the direction of Bilgoraj.

A half-hour after this incident, the town was quiet. There wasn't a soldier to be seen anywhere in town, except for the dead Austrian cavalryman who lay in the middle of the market place near the water pump. After a quiet pause, the Austrian army began marching in, without encountering any resistance. The military regiments passed through the town, continuing further on all of the roads that led deeper into Poland.

A military authority was established in Tarnogrod. The dead cavalryman was quickly removed from the market place. A Pole arrived and told how he had seen Chaim Maler (Blinderman) kick the body of the dead man. Chaim was arrested and sentenced to death by a military court. Twenty-four hours later, he was shot in the Jewish cemetery. He had no children, just a wife who was left a widow.

During the short pause before the soldiers marched in, the horse of the dead cavalryman ran around the market place. Hersh Adler, the 16 year-old son of Meir Wolf Katsev, a horse-dealer, caught the horse and brought it back to his stable. When the Austrian soldiers found the horse, they arrested Hersh. He, too, was in danger of being sentenced to death, but was saved because he was a minor. He was sentenced to an internment camp where he remained until 1918. Today Hersh Adler, now an old man, lives in Mexico.

In the villages and in Tarnogrod there were Russian peasants who shot at the Austrian soldiers as they marched through. This happened in Plusy, on the road to Bilgoraj. The Austrian military command arrested the village peasants along with every civilian they encountered on the roads. In this way several Tarnogrod Jews were arrested just for walking on the street. Among those arrested were: Meir Wolf Katsev, Yeshaye Mendak (Fisher), my father, Chaim Krymerkopf, who was arrested in his orchard, where he was praying in his prayer shawl and tefillin. All of the arrestees were sent to a prison camp where they remained until the end of the war.

The Austrians commandeered all the agricultural products and manufactured goods, issued ration cards for food, and forbade any private commerce conducted without special permission from the military authority. The Austrian military also took all the newly harvested grain and all food stores found in the villages. As a result, there were no longer any market days or fairs. The rich peasants were afraid to sell even the products that they had been allowed to keep after the military had confiscated their required amount.

Accordingly, people began to deal in smuggled goods, which entailed many problems, arrests and confiscations.

Money lost its previous value. The cost of living rose and hunger afflicted many Jewish homes. Tradesmen went idle, with no prospect of work. In the course of the war, our town changed hands twice, but it wasn't subjected to heavy shooting as was the neighboring town of Krzeszow, which was completely destroyed by fire. Sieniawa experienced the same fate, under heavy attack by Russian cannons. Jews from Sieniawa fled their destroyed homes for Tarnogrod where they received a warm welcome. Every Jew took in a burned-out family from Sieniawa and provided them with necessities.

Poverty grew greater every day. Jews went out to work on repairing the roads that had been damaged by the military. The town authorities paid very little for this work. Prices for food and materials rose daily. A piece of black bread was a great treat; no one baked challahs for the Sabbath. People wore clothes made from the dyed homespun woven by the peasants.

Tarnogrod, like the entire region of Lublin, was occupied by Austria twice: the first time, at the beginning of the war, from the month of *Av* to *Tishri* [1914]; the second time, from the month of *Tammuz* in 1915 until *Kislev* 1918, when Independent Poland was established.

Translator's Footnote:

1.   Intermediate days of the 8-day holidays of Passover and *Sukkot*

Original Footnote:

i.   During the reign of Tsar Nicholas I (1825-55) young Jewish boys were conscripted into long years of pre-military service under oppressive conditions after which they entered the military, where they served 25 years. They were called kantonists. They were often rounded up by force by *khappers*, lit. "catchers" or kidnappers.

[Pages 95-99]

The *Shvartse Khupe* at the Cemetery[1]

by Nuchim Krymerkopf

Translated by Miriam Leberstein

In the month of Tishrei, 1914, the Russians succeeded in pushing out the Austrians, chasing them back to the Carpathian Mountains. The battlefront was established outside Krakow. Conditions in Tarnogrod improved. Fresh supplies -- flour, sugar, tea, and chocolate – began to flow in and warehouses reopened, full of goods.

Tarnogrod Jews resumed doing business with the Austrian towns now occupied by the Russian army. Avraham Kagan (Rosenfeld) brought large shipments of flour, sugar and tea to Rzeszow, Tarnow and other towns close to the battlefront.

The economic situation in town greatly improved. Yet people still feared the Russian army, especially the Cossacks, who marched through the town on their way to the battlefront. At those times, Jewish girls didn't dare go out into the street.

After the defeat of the Russian army in the Carpathians, the Austrians again occupied Tarnogrod. All of the food reserves that the Russian army had left behind in their rush to retreat were confiscated by the Austrians, who also seized food supplies from private homes. Once again life was marked by anxiety and hunger was the norm.

During the Russian retreat a relentless battle took place 7 kilometers from Tarnogrod at the bridge over the Tanew River. The Russians mounted a rigorous resistance. The Jews of Tarnogrod rushed to the big stone synagogue seeking the protection of its thick walls. Those who could not fit into the fully packed synagogue ran to find hiding places outside of town. A Jew from Krezeszow was hit by shrapnel and fell dead in the priest's garden, where his body remained. Not one house was damaged by the shooting.

In the summer of 1916 there came reports that an illness affecting children was raging in nearby towns, and that it was being transmitted to adults. This was cholera. Young and old died. In Bilgoraj there were 30 deaths a day. The same happened in Jozefow, and soon the disease spread to Tarnogrod.

It was a horrific epidemic. People died within hours of falling ill. It began with cramps in the arms or legs and a few hours later, the person was dead. Tarnogrod had fewer victims than other towns because people realized early on that it was unacceptable to sit by and do nothing and they organized a committee of young volunteers – called the Sanitorer Committee --to fight the plague. Still, many Jews there died of cholera and there were houses where two or three family members were lost.

The members of the committee that had undertaken the mission to fight the epidemic threw themselves into their work with body and soul. Among them were: Moshe Firsht, Hersh-Meir Zychler, Faiwel Bas, Simcha Tarbiner, Shimon Schorer, Shimon Fluk, Moshele Shohet, etc. etc.

The committee was based in the home of Faiwel Bas. There they kept a whole pharmacy's worth of remedies –various ointments and bottles of medicine. In particular they amassed bottles of pure alcohol which they applied to the body parts where the patients were experiencing cramps.

People could not understand why the disease spread in the Jewish towns but barely touched the villages. The disease was especially virulent during the hot summer months of *Tammuz* and Av.

The committee members worked with tremendous dedication. I remember how an 8-year-old boy, Avraham Batsh, while sitting on a bench on Razhnitser Street, was seized by cramps and began writhing in convulsions. His mother Chana-Lea immediately ran to the committee offices and Moshele Shohet and Moshe Firsht responded to the scene in their white aprons. At the Batsh family home, they put a sugar cube saturated with a yellow liquid into the boy's mouth and he immediately opened his eyes. They rubbed his entire body with alcohol, put him to bed, well covered, and the boy recovered within a few hours.

Those members of the committee who did not directly treat the sick were tasked with regularly visiting the homes of those who had recovered, monitoring their condition and reporting to the committee.

During the summer of 1916 our rabbi *Reb* Leibele Teicher worked tirelessly on the rescue effort. He and his sons Moshele, Hershele and Shayele studied day and night, researching religious books that talked about terrible epidemics and gave instructions on remedies that had been used to fight them. He summoned the *shameses* of the synagogues and *besmedreshes* and ordered them to announce during prayers that the rabbi had decreed that fasting was not permitted on Tisha b'Av; that after reciting the Lamentations people should go home, eat, and drink as much whiskey as possible, since it was probably whiskey drinking that had helped the villages to evade the epidemic.

The epidemic continued to rage and the rabbi began to look for a prospective bride and groom who would be married under a black *khupe* at the cemetery. It was an old custom among Jews to do this as a remedy against a plague.

Among the Jews who had fled to Tarnogrod from Sieniawa there was an old, poor bachelor named Skhariye, who had a hunchback, and an old maid Taybele Tam [simpleton] -- two friendless people who lived in the poorhouse and slept on its decrepit floor. They were designated to get married under the black *khupe*, thereby stopping the plague in town. When they went to ask the prospective bride if she wanted to marry Skhariye, she merely lowered her eyes and said nothing. The same thing occurred with the prospective groom.

Having no choice the rabbi sent the *shames* to summon the couple to his rabbinical court. The rabbi himself assumed the role of the matchmaker, carried out the formalities, and the date for the wedding was set for the same week.

A bed and a bench-bed were purchased and set up in a corner of the poor house run by Kuni-Leml, and curtains were hung [to provide privacy]. On the day of the wedding, the *shames* announced in the *besmedresh* that Skhariye and Taybele would get married that day and that the ceremony would take place in the cemetery [traditional site for a black *khupe*].

At noon, the *shames* went around town banging on doors to summon people to prayers and at the same time inviting everyone to come to the wedding ceremony. The shopkeepers shut their stores, tradesmen set aside their work and everyone came to the cemetery. Moshele the rabbi's son and his wife Malkale accompanied one of the wedding couple to the *khupe*, and Simchale Zetzer and his wife Tshipele accompanied the other one. Shlomole Marshalek and Mulye Schleiser were the wedding musicians.

The ceremony of *badekns* [placing the veil on the bride] took place in the rabbi's court and the couple was then escorted to the cemetery. Along the entire way the musicians played and everyone held burning candles as they walked. Little boys carried the poles of the *khupe*. The rabbi *Reb* Leibele conducted the marriage ceremony.

People danced the traditional *mitzvah* dance with the bride and drank a lot of whiskey.

After the ceremony they escorted the couple to their corner in the poorhouse. It's true that the cholera epidemic did not end as a result of the ceremony but I do remember that afterwards, everyone felt relieved.

Finally the epidemic gradually began to ease. People calmed down and life returned to normal. But that didn't last long. Soon after the cholera disappeared, a typhus epidemic broke out. It was much less severe than the cholera. There were some fatalities, but in large part the illness was repelled, until it disappeared entirely.

Translator's Footnote:

1.   The Yiddish word *khupe* denotes both the Jewish wedding canopy and the wedding ceremony itself. It was a traditional belief that holding a *shvartse khupe*, or black wedding, between two orphans was a way to put an end to an epidemic in the shtetl.

[Pages 99-118]

The Origins of the Polish State

by Nuchim Krymerkopf

Translated by Miriam Leberstein

Autumn, 1918

The First World War brought about radical changes in the economic conditions of Jews in Tarnogrod. People became newly rich or newly impoverished. There were war profiteers who made fortunes by smuggling and illegal trading, risking their lives to do so. There were formerly wealthy merchants who could not follow such a path and were forced to live on their reserves, which exhausted their capital and often became ordinary poor folk. Especially hard hit were those merchants who were owed money by Christian peasants in the villages. It was a rare peasant who remembered the debt that he still owed to a Jew. Even if an honest Christian did pay off an old debt, the money no longer had its previous value. The most devalued currency was the Russian *ruble*. The Austrian crown was still in circulation.

The economic conditions for Jews worsened day to day. There were households where they didn't have a scrap of meat to eat, even on the Sabbath. Things got even worse when the government banned the slaughter of cattle, because the lingering war had depleted all the cattle to feed the soldiers.

The Christian population did not feel the effects of poor economic conditions as strongly as the Jews. The Austrian regime did not force the occupied populace to serve in the army, although it did impose forced labor for which people were paid a negligible wage.

The Austrian authorities had a police station in town manned by several police officers. One fine clear morning, several young Poles approached an Austrian police officer and ripped off his belt and rifle, as well as the insignia designating his military rank. The policeman did not resist and seemed to accept this as a natural thing.

The Jews were in an uproar. They could not understand the meaning of this episode. They did not receive newspapers; no one was interested. People were busy in the pursuit of a livelihood and mourning their children and parents who died in the epidemic. Each person interpreted this unusual event in their own way.

But after a while we began to see Christian civilians walking around the market place with rifles on their shoulders and rumors quickly spread that a Polish state had been reestablished, one which included parts of Galicia and Germany as well. In a word – a cataclysm!

The Jews immediately felt the effects of this huge event, the reestablishment of Polish independence. First of all, Austrian currency became worthless. The new regime issued a new Polish mark, made of paper; even the smallest unit of currency, the groshen, was made of paper. Those Jews who didn't have a reserve store of merchandise suddenly became poor and couldn't afford to buy a piece of bread; they had no prospects at all for a way to support themselves.

The First World War had ended. In Russia the revolution was still being fought. Soldiers began to return from the front, and prisoners of war from captivity, bringing joy to many homes. But there were other homes that were revisited by grief, where they had hoped for the return of a son or father but now realized that they had fallen in battle or died in captivity. Among those who did not return were: Daniel Aharon Wassertreger, Yekl Moshe Khanes, Leibush Kuni Lemels, Hersh Dovid Yoels (Walfish), Bunim der Shegekhes (Agert), Avraham Honik, Pinkes, Kozak's son in law, and many others whose names I have forgotten.

We should mention here the support that Tarnogrod's Jews received from relatives in America. The Tarnogrod Society in America sent money for poor people to buy what they needed to celebrate Passover. The money from America was tremendously important in improving the quality of life. The dollar was very valuable, worth incomparably more than Polish currency. You needed hundreds of thousands, even millions, of Polish paper currency to buy anything. Purchases were made by the "packet," with a packet consisting of 100,000 marks. When you had to pay half million marks, that was called "five packets." Everything was calculated with reference to the dollar, the value of which was constantly rising. It got to the point that a dollar was worth 11 million marks.

In Poland the war with the Bolsheviks flared up. There was a military draft which included the Jews. The Polish army was dominated by anti-Semitism. Especially threatening to Jews were the forces of [General Josef] Haller. Luckily the Hallerites did not pass through Tarnogrod, although the Jews there suffered from sheer terror, since we had heard of the horrific acts these bands had carried out. Especially terrifying was the pogrom the Polish army carried out against Jews in Lvov in 1918, after driving out the Ukrainians.

The Zionist Movement

Along with economic changes came changes in the intellectual and cultural life of the Jews of Tarnogrod. New winds began to blow. Cautiously and gradually young people began to take an interest in what was happening in the outside world. The religious *besmedresh* student sitting over his *Gemara* was also holding a concealed newspaper or secular book.

The historic Balfour Declaration evoked a great stir. When news of the Declaration reached Tarnogrod it caused tremendous joy, especially among young people, who saw before them the possibility of realizing the 2000-year-old dream of national redemption. On the street, in the *besmedresh* they exchanged mazel-tovs. At prayers they recited *Hallel* [Psalms 113-118] in praise of God to express their great enthusiasm for this historic event.

There were debates in the *besmedresh*. Certain religious Jews held that it was not appropriate to say *Hallel* over the Balfour Declaration, that the recognition of the rights of Jews to *Eretz Yisroel* did not constitute a true deliverance, which required the coming of Messiah and the rebuilding of the Temple. But the majority of religious Jews were carried away with the enthusiasm of the young people and recited the psalms along with them in honor of the great event.

Enthusiasm among the young grew. They began to organize clandestine groups. They were afraid not only of the police but also their own parents who opposed the new political movements and who didn't want their children to put aside their religious studies and take up reading heretical [i.e.secular] books. There were fights at home. Boys and girls became insolent, fighting their unenlightened religious parents who wouldn't permit them to join a Zionist organization.

There were fathers who in their hearts understood their children's ideas but who concealed their feelings because that would subject them to harassment from the extreme fanatics. Berish Ringer's bakery was boycotted because his son Meir became a Zionist.

The young increasingly oriented themselves in the ideological struggle between right and left. Revolutionary [i.e. socialist] circles were formed, but the young were mostly in the thrall of Zionism. Every movement or idea that arose among Polish Jewry received a warm response in Tarngorod. The boys who studied in the *besmedresh* found their way to the sources of Hebrew literature. Moshe Lemer's home became an intellectual meeting place for progressive young men. Moshe Lemer had gotten married during the war and for a short time lived with his father in law Yekl Trinker in the village Rozaniec.

Trinker was a large landowner and supported his son in law so he could engage in religious studies. He bought him a large Talmud and other religious books. Several years later, when Moshe Lemer abandoned his religious studies and was drawn into Zionist activity he donated the books to the *besmedresh*.

Moshe Lemer continued to live in the village, but spent the entire week in town, staying with his parents and earning a living from a small soda water factory. On the Sabbath he would return to his family in Rozaniec. Several years later he relocated his family to Tarnogrod. There, they lived communally with his parents, sisters and brothers, paying for expenses and purchases from a single purse. When times were bad, they all shared the hardship.

When times were good and their situation improved, everyone shared the income.

Many *besmedresh* students took their first steps toward Zionism in the Lemer home. Every day they would gather there in their free time and discuss Zionism and other cultural issues. *Eretz Yisroel* was the center of every discussion. Everyone worked to learn the Hebrew language, but Yiddish literature also took up a lot of their time.

This communal beginning helped to activate young people as well as a certain part of the older Jewish population. The young people led the *shtetl* out of the stagnation and generations-old quiet that characterized pre-war Tarnogrod. People decided to establish a library, which was actually the first Tarnogrod had ever had.

Cultural Activity

Cultural activities began in the library. Young people of every social and economic sector who yearned to read a Yiddish or Hebrew book came there. They elected a board of directors whose task it was to buy new books and collect books from individual book owners. Bazhe Bank was designated chairman. He and his parents had come to Tarnogrod from Sieniawa. One of his assets was his knowledge of Hebrew that he spoke more fluently than anyone else. Moshe Lemer was selected to be vice-chairman and Meir Ringer was the librarian. I was assigned the job of secretary. Shortly after, Chaim Apteker took over as secretary; he kept the minutes of our activities in Hebrew.

The group was on a high cultural level.

They threw themselves into the work body and soul. They bought a large number of books and obtained some as gifts or loans from private parties. Gitele Wachnachter from the village of Biszcza loaned out all of her books, but she never asked for them to be returned. Itche-Ber Adler donated several books by Mendele Moykher Sforim and Sholem Aleichem when he came to Tarnogrod on a visit from America.

That was what the Zionist movement [in Tarnogrod] looked like at the time when it did not yet have an official name or charter.

Thanks to the systematic educational work the number of members of the Zionist movement increased and the Zionist ideal spread among broader circles of the Tarnogrod population. The Jews, especially young people, every day became more convinced in the correctness of Dr. Herzl's words: "Zionism is the return to the Jewish people even before the return to the Jewish land." And so they constantly increased their Zionist activity, raising the younger generation in the national spirit and encouraging in them love for the Hebrew language, even though among themselves they spoke Yiddish most of the time.

As regards to national ideology, the Jews in Tarnogrod were pro-Zionist although of course there were a sufficient number who didn't understand what that designation meant and opposed it. But even among the opponents there was a love for Israel and yearning for national liberation.

Tzeriei Agudat Israel

There were also other ideologies. Many people sympathized with *Agudath Israel* [ultra-orthodox, conservative, anti-Zionist organization]. There were also young people with leftist leanings. But these were not many and they did not engage in any public activity in accord with their ideologies and certainly did not form any branches of those parties in Tarnogrod.

In the last years before World War II there was an association of Tzeriei *Agudath Israel* [youth movement associated with *Agudath Israel*] in Tarnogrod. They had their own *minyan* on Lakhover Street, in the home of Leibl Zaberman, where they prayed on the Sabbath.

There was also a *Beis Yakov* school for girls on Razhenitser Street, in Moshe Feingold's building.

But it was at the library that the liveliest activity took place. The library created a drama section that organized its own theater productions. There was a shortage of female members, so often boys played women's roles. The only girl was Moshe Lemer's sister Freida. They held rehearsals at the home of Itche Ber Adler. He was also the theater prompter. Adler lives today in America.

The First Hebrew School

From the beginning, the library founders were aware of the enormous importance of teaching the children Hebrew. They saw no way to conduct productive Zionist activity without a school that would acquaint the children with the rich past of our people and educate them in its national spirit.

And so a Hebrew school was established. They hired a Hebrew teacher and the Hebrew language proudly began to sound from the mouths of our children. The founding of the Hebrew school led to a big fight with the fanatical Jews. The *melameds* played a certain role, seeing in the school a threat to their livelihood. The rabbi and other religious personnel also sharply opposed it.

When Zionist and Mizrakhi [religious Zionist] speakers came to Tarnogrod they encountered the same vigorous opposition from the rabbi and other religious Jews, who did not permit them to appear in the *besmedresh* or other houses of worship.

The Free Food Program for Children

The library founders also put a lot of energy into creating a food program for children. With the significant help of the Joint Distribution Committee, about 200 Tarnogrod children were fed two meals -breakfast and lunch- a day.

Young volunteers from the Zionist movement carried out the work in and around the kitchen, did the cooking, serving and cleaning and distributed food to the mothers, who came everyday with pots to carry out food for their children.

In the difficult years of the First World War the importance of a food program for children of poor homes was enormous. Later, when food began to become available on the free market, the service gradually ended.

At that time, the tradesmen also founded a cooperative store where they sold their goods at low prices. The longtime chairman of the cooperative was Yekl Schneider (Magram) who now lives in America.

The First Emigrants to Israel

Finally the Polish-Bolshevik war ended and free emigration to other countries, mostly America, began. Later, when America closed its gates, emigration continued to Germany. Gradually, many of the library founders emigrated. Moshe Lemer, along with his entire family – parents, sisters, and brothers – settled in Berlin, where, incidentally, they became very rich. Bazhe Bank, the chairman of the library, also emigrated with his parents and settled in Berlin.

Meir Dinger, the librarian, married a girl from Sieniawa and after the wedding they too went to Germany. When Hitler came to power Dinger left Germany and was able to go to Eretz Yisroel, where he still lives.

Chaim Apteker who was among the most skilled in Hebrew and active in the Zionist movement emigrated to Israel, where he still lives, occupying an important position in Tel Aviv.

Others who made *aliyah* at this time were: Chaim Lipiner and his wife; Avraham-Yitzhak and Golde Kenigstein, who got married there and live today in Tel Aviv; Shmuel Fefer and his family, who live today in Kiryat Motzkin; Shmuel Akst; Zishe Fester and his wife, who came from America to Tarnogrod and soon after left for Israel, taking with them a large crate of books they had brought with them from America; they live today in Haifa; Berish Schorer and his wife, who live in Tel Aviv; Volvish Weiss who several years later brought over his brother Moshe, they live in Tel Aviv.

Jews who lived in the villages around Tarnogrod also had a strong desire to emigrate to Israel. Zalmen Feferman from the village Lukow and Dovid Entner from Rozaniec emigrated, but after living there several years returned to Tarnogrod. Entner was killed several days after Tarnogrod was liberated in World War II. Feferman lives today in America.

A *hakhshore* was established in Tarngorod – a training kibbutz where boys and girls prepared for emigration to Israel by engaging in farm labor and other physical labor. The farming was done at Yekl Sharievker's in the village. The other heavy labor – part time and full time -- was done in town for various employers who considered it their obligation to give work to the Zionist youth dreaming of making *aliyah* and reviving the devastated land.

Tarnogrod also had a *Betar* [Revisionist Zionist] organization, led by Moshe Kenigstein, who several times a week led the group in military drills.

In time Tarnogrod developed closer ties to the larger cities. The words *Eretz Yisroel* resounded deeply in every heart. The new word, "*chalutz*" [pioneer] drew us to our land, to a new life and future. The movement carried us away and interest grew in all the different Zionist organizations. *Hashomer Hatzair* [the Young Guard] was very successful. Young people joined in with their parents' approval, engaged in various athletic exercises and organizational activities, with special insignias and clothing.

Parents supported their children's Zionist activity with the hope that it would help them realize their plans to go to Eretz Yisroel. But only a very small number of Jews from Tarnogrod were able to do so.

The Impoverishment of the Jewish Population

In the period between the two World Wars the town experienced ups and downs. When the [First World] war ended, Jewish life in Tarnogrod, as in the rest of Poland, began to normalize. Although pre-war means of livelihood disappeared, and people could not directly return to their businesses or skilled trades, the Jews gradually overcame the difficulties and slowly began to rebuild their lives.

The Jews demonstrated great initiative in redeveloping the town. People were inspired by social forces. They returned to conducting commerce, and various trades – tailoring, shoemaking, carpentry, et. al. – were revived. There were no large industrial enterprises in Tarnogrod. The Jewish merchants, just like the tradesmen, toiled from very early until late at night.

Waves of anti-Semitism grew stronger, but that also strengthened Jewish feelings of national resistance. Jews participated in political life, actively engaging in elections to the *Sejm* [Polish parliament] and town council, where they had their representatives.

In the early years, Tarnogrod had created a workers' party in which Itsik Farber (Leibl Melamed's son) played a leading role. It had its offices in the house of Avrom Hersh Adler.

One May 1st, the Jews marched through the streets to the Polish town offices, carrying a red flag and singing workers' songs. Itsik Farber stood on a table on the square in front of the town offices and delivered a speech in Polish. He was followed by additional speakers who spoke sympathetically about the Communist regime in Soviet Russia.

Police and town officials, along with other Poles, stood in the square calmly listening to the speeches. No one interfered. But when the group resumed the demonstration and began marching back to their offices, the police attacked, beating them right and left with the butts of their rifles.

A whole slew of worker activists were arrested and put on trial. The Jewish households whose sons had been arrested were in turmoil. They hired lawyers who took from the poor parents their last few pennies. Many of the arrestees were released after a few months pending trial. After trial, many of them received long sentences. Itsik Farber was sentenced to six years in prison. During the Second World War he was sent to a Soviet camp, where he died.

That was the sole public action by the Communist youth organization, which remained illegal the entire time.

Anti-Semitism grew from day to day. The Polish government began to impose heavy taxes on the Jews. In addition to having to buy a special license, a Jewish shopkeeper had to pay all kinds of fees and taxes. The Jews sorely felt the burden of these enormous taxes. In addition, they gradually lost their peasant customers in the nearby villages. The peasants travelled to other towns in Galicia, which were accessible by better roads. They travelled to Lezajsk and Sieniawa, Oleszyce and Lubacow, where they sold their produce and bought whatever merchandise they needed.

The fairs in Tarnogrod grew increasingly smaller. The market days, which were the main source of livelihood for Jews, also had fewer peasant customers. Christians set up stalls in the market and new Christian-owned businesses opened up. They received special financial support from the government, which enabled them to compete with their Jewish neighbors.

The town government officials also aided the Christian merchants by imposing oppressive measures on the Jews, making their lives more difficult. Prominent among these were the town secretary, Witkowski, and the mayor, Rutkin. A Jew had to obtain permission for every little thing, even the renovation of one's home, which was hard to get and took months.

Once the renovation was done, the two officials would visit the home to check on the work, always finding something that didn't conform to the administrative order, for which they punished the Jew with a stiff fine or arrest.

Each year, the tax officials in Bilgoraj held special meetings which lasted several weeks, at which they considered tax calculations for the entire population of the Bilgoraj district. They summoned to these meetings two Jews from every town, who had to give their opinion about the earnings of the Jews in their town. The two such experts selected from Tarnogrod were Khaim Goldman and Yosef Maynes-Royznblat. These two delegates had the difficult task of combating the excessive taxes that the officials wanted to impose on the Jewish merchants and tradesman. But their efforts were in vain. Burdened by heavy taxes, the shopkeepers got ever poorer. They travelled to Warsaw, Lviv and Lublin to get merchandise on loan, signing long-term promissory notes which made the merchandise even more expensive, by 20% and more. When the due date for the promissory notes and for taxes approached, many of them went bankrupt.

For a Tarnogrod Jew, the first bankruptcy was shameful, a slap in the face. He would struggle with all his might in order to remain an honorable man. But he could not see any way out and had to sell his merchandise below cost. Bankruptcy became a common event. Later on, merchants from larger towns would travel to Tarnogrod with the unpaid promissory notes and initiate litigation in the Jewish religious court, where arbitrators conducted negotiations and made adjustments. Afterwards, the shopkeepers continued to do business, employing the same methods and encountering the same problems.

Even if the shopkeeper somehow managed to work things out with the wholesaler, it went much worse with the tax officials, with whom there was no room for negotiation. Every market and fair day, the *sekvestratorn* [confiscaters] from the Bilgoraj tax authority would come to collect taxes from the Jewish storekeepers. They were very brutal, extracting the last penny from their pockets. If they didn't find any money, they took the merchandise.

The taxes were so high, that even after the merchandise was confiscated, the storekeeper still owed money. The *sekvestratorn* would then go to the Jew's house and confiscate any items of value. If these were not sufficient to satisfy the debt and the fees for confiscation, they were sold at auction at half price and the storekeeper remained in debt to the government. Such auctions occurred every week.

Here we should mention the Jewish town magistrates: Khaim-Leib Mantel, Leibtshe Lipiner and Godl Vetsher. They were employed by the town government at a low salary and their job was to accompany the Polish officials and to take care of issues involving the Jews.

The Jewish magistrates felt powerless to help the Jews. But it often happened that a *sekvestrator* would arrive from Bilgoraj and ask the Jewish magistrate to take him to a Jewish shopkeeper to confiscate his merchandise. The magistrate did everything he could to alert the shopkeeper to the arrival of the *sekvestrator*, so he would have time to hide items of value. When the *sekvestrator* got there, he found nothing of value and left empty-handed.

Another source of terrible problems for the Jews was the sanitation commission. Every house in Tarnogrod had a piece of land where night soil was discarded. The peasants would take it away and spread it on their land as fertilizer, paying for it with a few potatoes. The sanitation commission imposed fines for the presence of the waste.

The commission also caused a lot of difficulties for the bakers and food shops. Strict ordinances required the bakers to have seven rooms and a ceramic tiled oven for baking, as well as a separate shop to sell the baked goods. It was strictly forbidden to sell baked goods from a table in the market place. No baker could comply with these regulations and they were constantly at risk of having their business closed, even when it was as clean and sanitary as an apothecary.

In the air hung the feeling of an impending storm. The peasants felt that they could do whatever they liked to the Jews, and just like the Christians who lived in town, felt entitled to goods at half price. The Christian customers increasingly bought on credit and increasingly forgot to pay their debts. When conversing with Jews, the town Christians and the village peasants would, in an ostensibly innocent way, mention the pogrom that had occurred in Przytyk [in 1936], hinting at what might happen [in Tarnogrod].

The economic boycott made itself felt. Christian customers were embarrassed to enter a Jewish shop. In the villages there were violent attacks, robberies, and thefts against Jews.

The criminal acts of the Nazis in Germany and of the anti-Semites in other Polish towns, especially the pogrom in Przytyk reverberated in Tarnogrod and soon had an effect. Encouraged by anti-Semitic harassment by the government, hooligans carried out attacks in Tarnogrod unimpeded.

The air was electrified. There were rumors that a pogrom was being planned. Supposedly, on a certain Tuesday market day, peasants from villages near and far would come to Tarnogrod and attack the Jews.

Jews were worried. A delegation travelled to the *staroste* [head official] in Bilgoraj, requesting protection against the organized attack. The *staroste* promised to send a reinforced police division to the fair. He also asked the Jews to try not to provoke the crowd.

The Bilgoraj *staroste* was known as an anti-Semite and the Jews put little trust in his promises. The young people therefore decided to organize a self-defense. They were relying on the strength of the Jewish butchers, stablemen and other strong young people.

Some people were of the opinion that on the targeted day, the stores should remain closed and that merchandise should not be loaded onto the market stalls. But others feared that the Christians would be angry if the shops were closed and that on the pretext that they wanted to buy, they would break in and loot the goods. The conclusion was that it was better to open the stores and be prepared for an attack.

This was in the summer of 1939, in the Hebrew month of *Tammuz*. Early in the morning, the Jews went out into the street, opened their shops and stacked their stalls with merchandise. In the market place there actually was an enhanced police patrol. Peasants who had never before visited Tarnogrod started to arrive in large crowds from villages near and far, in wagons and on foot, carrying thick sticks in their hands.

At the market place the crush of people kept growing. Christians armed with sticks streamed in masses among the Jewish shops. Despair grew in the hearts of the Jewish shopkeepers, but no one displayed their fear and feigning calm they laid out their wares.

Hooligans armed with sticks stationed themselves at the Jewish shops and businesses and wouldn't allow any Christians to enter. If a peasant approached wanting to enter a Jewish shop, seeking cheaper prices, the hooligans would forcibly drag him away. The Jewish shops were pasted with placards and signs warning in big letters that this was a Jewish store and should not be patronized.

In some stores the hooligans took merchandise without paying, with the intention of instigating a quarrel that would lead to blows. Some hooligans grabbed a piece of goods from a stall and ran away with it. Others waited provokingly for the Jewish owner to try to retrieve the goods. The Jewish shopkeepers submitted to everything and this way avoided even the slightest fight.

In the end, the market day passed without any disturbances, only fear and despair. The Christians dispersed on foot or in wagons not having been able to provoke the planned pogrom.

The Jewish *Kehillah* [Organized Jewish Community]

Until the First World War Tarnogrod did not have an organized Jewish community. Yankl Mentl took care of Jewish issues. He also kept records and prepared birth certificates for Jewish newborns, for which he received a small stipend. Only after Poland became independent did Tarnogrod have a Jewish governing council which consisted of 12 elected representatives and a president. The elections for the council were hotly contested. Placards were mounted on walls and people campaigned in the streets and houses of worship for their candidates.

Yisroel-Noah Pelts neglected his shoemaking workshop and threw himself into the election, as did other tradesmen and shopkeepers.

The *Kehillah* took on the responsibility for paying pensions to the *Kley Kodesh* [religious functionaries], and sustaining other religious necessities. This wasn't easy, taking a lot of effort to figure out how to raise the required funds, and it was necessary to impose a special tax on the entire Jewish population.

The following served as president of the council during the time of its existence: Khaim Goldman, who died in Russia during World War II; Shloyme Mantl, who now lives in Israel; Aron Listrin; Hersh Blutman, who was killed by the Germans.

Gemilut Chesed [Interest Free Loan] Fund

There were Jews in Tarnogrod who appeared to live on nothing but air, who spent entire days looking beseechingly at the sky, wondering where they could borrow money, a few cents to travel to Bilgoraj and earn enough to buy a piece of dry bread.

It must be said that Tarnogrod Jews helped each other out and wouldn't let someone go under. Walking to prayers in the morning, their prayer shawls under their arms, people would ask for the loan of a few *zlotys*. The food shop owners, who themselves were not rich, never refused anyone food on credit. Their account books were filled with unpaid debts.

The tradesmen were in general worse off than the shopkeepers. In some households they were literally starving, not earning enough to feed their children.

Tarnogrod had a *gemilut chesed* fund, run by Yastshes (Royznman). He lives now in Israel. One could obtain an interest-free loan up to 100 *zlotys* that could be repaid in installments. There were instances where people could not pay but no one was sued in court.

Activists who worked on behalf of the *gemilut chesed* included prominent people who were devoted to the work body and soul.

Religious Youth in Tarnogrod

Religious young people in Tarnogrod were organized in *Hapoel HaMizrachi* [religious workers organization] and *Tseirey Agudas Yisroel* [religious youth organization].

There were also young men who were continuing their religious studies, mainly in the Belzer *shtibl* [small, *Hasidic* house of worship] where they sat day and night studying Gemora to the tune of a melancholy *Hasidic* melody. For some of them, Talmudic analysis was the only thing that mattered. They were satisfied with whatever they had, hoped for the coming of the Messiah and focused on the world to come.

When a poor man needed help, he knew to come to the Belzer *shtibl* where he always found young people, as well as older ones, who were ready to come to his aid.

Members of other *Hasidic* sects – Trisker, Sandzer, Kuzminer, and Gerer – also prayed in the Belzer *shtibl*, as did ordinary Jews who were not affiliated with any *Hasidic* rabbi.

During the war the Belzer *shtibl* was turned into a hospital. The biggest Nazi *aktsie* [mass murder or deportation] took place on the square adjacent to the *shtibl*.

Tarnogrod also had girls who belonged to *Bnoys Yankev* [Daughters of Jacob, organization of orthodox religious schools for girls.] These girls from religious homes were modest and quiet, holy in their beliefs and good deeds who studied with their parents and female religious teachers.

First group of girls of the Tarnogrod Bnoys Yankev

Such was the life of our sacred Tarnogrod Jewish community, which was completely wiped out and remains only as a gravestone memorializing a warm, beautiful and vibrant Jewish community.

[Pages 119-120]

II

<u>Personalities, Portraits, and the Way of Life</u>

Shimon Kanc

Translated by Miriam Leberstein

Tarnogrod Jews

The Jews of Tarnogrod led quiet, modest lives. They had no opportunity to funnel their energy into large industrial enterprises, or expansive businesses and so were untouched by the cold calculation and brutality that such enterprises entailed.

They worked at all sorts of trades that served the needs of the Jews in town and the Christians in town and in the villages. They were the tailors and blacksmiths, cobblers and masons, bakers and glaziers, porters and wagon drivers. The shopkeepers worked as hard as the tradesmen. All of them were filled with respect and love for religious scholars, spiritual people, rabbis and yeshiva students, the tales told by the *magid* [itinerant preacher], and the speeches of the Zionists, who brought them the religious learning of past generations as well as visions of a new life. Tarnogrod Jews have maintained this love for people of this kind to the present day, and have eternalized them in this memorial book.

[Pages 121-126]

The Rabbis of Tarnogrod

The Gaon[1] Rabbi Chaim-Elazar Wachs[2], of blessed memory

by Yechiel Muterperl

Translated by Martin Jacobs

We do not claim to be writing the history of the Tarnogrod rabbinate, since the information which has reached us about the rabbinate in our city in general and about each rabbi in particular is meager. It is only because of our desire to immortalize the memory of the community and its martyrs in a book that we began to investigate and research the history of the rabbinate in the Tarnogrod community. And so we have acquired, in part through our own efforts and in part through those of the town's residents, the material for an introduction, which is presented in the present section. To be sure, we have not been able to acknowledge all the rabbis who sat upon the rabbinical throne in Tarnogrod in former days; and likewise we have not been able to get exact information and precise dates for all the rabbis. But every detail has something of interest to those who left the city and those who research its history.

The first rabbi in Tarnogrod about whom we could find information in books was the Gaon Rabbi Chaim-Elazar Wachs of blessed memory. He became famous, however, mainly as the Rabbi of Kalisz. Here is what his grandson writes about him:

My grandfather the Gaon Rabbi Chaim Elazar Wachs of blessed memory was born in the year 5582 [1822] in the city of Tarnogrod. His father was the Gaon Rabbi Avraham Yehuda Leibush and his mother the saintly Chaya Tova of blessed memory. We know very little about his childhood and his youth before he became well known in the Jewish world as one of his generation's great halakhic experts and a spiritual giant whose influence is engraved deeply in every area of Jewish life in his own time and for generations after, and this is not at all surprising, for he was humble and modest without equal. For this reason we do not know much about his origins. From a few slips of the pen, however, we learn that he was of a good and distinguished family. He wrote in one of his responsa (in the possession of his pupil, the head of the rabbinical court in the city of Pietrokov, the Gaon Yakov Aryeh Glazer [may the Lord avenge him!]) – I quote from memory – "And I, a descendent of the Bach". [Bach: The name given to Joel Sirkes (16th – 17th centuries), from the initials of the name of his major work, Bayit Chadash]. From this we may conclude that he was counted among the descendents of the Bach, of blessed memory; indeed as a child I heard all sorts of versions of his genealogy, such as that he was descended from Rashi and Rabbi Yohanan the cobbler, and that his lineage reached as far back as King David, but I was never interested in investigating the sources mentioned, and

I mention these reports merely by way of conjecture. However there is no doubt that his family was numbered among the distinguished families of Israel, and who in this matter can we rely on more than our master, the holy Gaon, the author of "Chidushei HaRim" ("Original interpretations of the Rim") [Rim: Yitzchak Meir Rotenberg-Alter 19th century rabbi. known as the Rim from the initials of "Rabbi Yitzchak Meir"], of blessed memory, who says in one of his writings ("He who illuminates the eyes of the exile", p. 58, section 16), "And he was related ..." (I have quoted from this work below).

We have no definite knowledge who his teachers were, but from his various responsa it seems that his most distinguished teacher in his early childhood was the Gaon Rabbi Sh. Z. Helir, the rabbi of Przemyśl – not to be confused with the Gaon s (of blessed memory), the Rabbi of Safat – whose style of teaching and original Torah interpretations were similar to those of the afore mentioned Gaon.

He mentions his father, the Gaon, many times in his books. In the preface to his great book, "Nefesh Haya" ("A Living Soul"), he brings interpretations in his name (in the study section "Rabutsa"). This is what he says: "I had it in mind to organize these interpretations from the writings of my father and teacher, the Gaon, of blessed memory, and to attach them to this treatise of mine, but many burdens prevented me, and I intend now to mention one thing in his name. It has remained in my memory from having heard it from his sainted lips when I studied before him while still a little child". He also mentions his grandfather (in "Nefesh Haya"): "I well remember the objection which my grandfather had, the astute Gaon, my master Bezalel (may his memory be a blessing) which I saw in a manuscript where he pointed out a difficulty with a saying in the Talmud." But neither his father nor his grandfather served in the rabbinate for reward, whether because they were wealthy or for other reasons.

As we have said, we know very little about his childhood, and the little we do know must be extracted from the opinions and a few lines in the preface to his magnum opus, and also here and there from his responsa in which he lets such phrases slip as "the difficult questions I asked in my childhood" or "how I debated with the Geonim". (In the response to Baumgeld, in the matter of the perjured witnesses, he reveals that even in his early years he corresponded with the "Chidushei HaRim", of blessed memory, and debated with him.) From everything mentioned above we may deduce that even in his earliest years he was well known as learned and sharp of mind, that is, "young yet clever".

In the preface to his book he writes about his life story in a style both joyous and heart-rending, and his words are so fittingly written, with so much feeling and warmth, that we here quote them at length:

"...my saintly mother thought so well of me as to devote me to Torah and the commandments, and while I was still in the womb all the desires of her heart were to bring forth a son for Torah, for she had had a brother, my uncle the Gaon and master Chaim Elazar (his memory for a blessing), after whom I am named, who died young, being only 18 years old. He was very learned in Torah; he knew the "Hoshen HaMishpat" from cover to cover and by heart, and he could speak fluently about many a Talmudic tractate, as though they were engraved upon his lips, and he was a friend of my master the saintly Gaon, master in Israel, my master Chaim (of sainted memory) of Sants, brother of my father-in-law the Gaon (of blessed memory). When my mother conceived, my uncle, her brother, came to her in a vision, and she knew that he was dead, and she asked him to tell her the difference between this world and the world to come. He answered that in this world every one is personally free but there one is like a slave under the hand of his master. When she woke she told these things to my father the Gaon (of blessed memory) and he told her that these things were true, and from that day on she was faithful in her desire to give birth to a son dedicated to the Torah. Afterwards, when she had given birth to me and I was about a year old, a holy man of God, the holy Gaon and head of the rabbinic court of Zakliklw (may the Lord provide a good foundation for it) passed through the city and she carried me in her arms to him so that he might bless me. He spoke of great things for me and said that this boy was ready for greatness, and so all the other Jews in the city of Tarnogod (may Lord provide a good foundation for it) came to know this. Even if the words of the holy man had not been fulfilled in me, not even to a small extent, for everything is foreseen by the Holy Spirit, and despite having wasted my days with the free will granted to us, nevertheless it is not a small matter that the Lord granted me favor to minister among his people Jacob, Israel his inheritance, in holy congregations where the great seats of judgment are in the land. From that day on she placed all the desires of her heart only upon me. When I was about three or four I fell very ill, so ill that the doctors gave up all hope. My mother cried bitterly and prayed to the Lord, and she said, "What I ask I ask as a mother, that all ill decreed for the child be upon me. As a child can do nothing without his mother, so I ask to take on half of his illness." And so it was. I began little by little to get better and she became very ill, so that the doctors gave up hope of finding a cure, but to her too help was sent from the Holy One to raise her up and restore her to life.

After this, when I was eighteen or nineteen, she sought to get me appointed to the rabbinate of the congregation of Tarnogrod (may Lord provide a good foundation for it), which is considered to be among the great towns. There were always great rabbis there, such as the authors of "Tavnit ot Yosef", "Noam megadim", "Yam haTalmud", for whose "Meforshei hayam" they made "a crown of gold for its border" [Exodus 37:12, describing the table in the ancient tabernacle], as well as other Geonim, rabbis, and great people who did not leave writings. I was then but a tender youth, not knowing how to act, or how to lead the rabbinate as it is now led, or how one deals with the personalities of various men , and she fought my battle with a certain man who caused her such distress that she became ill, and she told me that the rabbi who wrote "Tsion lenefesh haya" (author of "Noda bihuda", the Gaon Ezekiel Landau, of blessed memory, rabbi of Prague) made a memorial for the soul of his grandmother who raised him ..."

From the above words of my grandfather, the author (of blessed memory), we see a man's great modesty. But his modesty turned into greatness, for it was not his desire to become famous in the world of Jewish law with innovative Torah interpretations, but only for the sake of his saintly mother could he be urged to publish his works; this was for him a matter of fulfilling the command "honor thy mother". All this we learn from his words above, for from the day he emerged into the world his mission was to serve the leader of the generation, and if indeed he made little of himself because of his modesty, his personality is revealed, in all its scope and glory and its full immense spiritual stature, in several documents which remain from that period.

I will quote from this letter, which is in fact of a detailed nature, and therefore its evaluation is very objective, especially since the letter was drafted by the leader of the generation of Russian-Polish Jewry, the Gaon author of "Chidushei HaRim", sent to his brother's son-in-law Yudel Kaminer (of blessed memory), concerning a marital match. Here is an excerpt:

With God's help, the eve of Sabbath "Vayiqra" 5618

"...; I have investigated the above mentioned rabbi (who is called "Nefesh Haya"); he now studies day and night with great diligence, and if he is not so much esteemed by our followers because he does not go to Kotsk, nevertheless I know him and he is dear to me, and he is a Torah scholar and greatly esteemed for his expertise. There are not many like him, and he is a leader and from a prominent family...."

Anyone who knows the clarity of the style of the Gaon who wrote this knows that he was not accustomed unconditionally to scatter praises of this sort, such as: "Torah scholar greatly esteemed for his expertise", "There are not many like him", "A leader from a prominent family". This letter serves as a sincere expression, faithful to his lineage and the esteem in which he was held, which the author of "Chidushei HaRim" expressed for the Nefesh Haya while he was still a youth.

By the way, the following story shows the esteem in which the Gaon "HaRim" held the Nefesh Haya: They say that the Gaon told his wife of his desire to make a match between his grandson Rabbi Shloymele Alter and the daughter of a Torah scholar. The *rebbetzin* [wife of rabbi] asked him who, in his opinion, was worthy to be called a Torah scholar. The Gaon answered, the Rabbi of Kalisz, Rabbi Lipman of Radomsk, (son-in-law of the "Tiferet Shlomo"), and Rabbi Noah Shahor from Biała (son-in-law of my Master Rabbi Avraham Mordechai of blessed memory, from Góra Kalwaria).

While still very young he married Blima daughter of the Gaon Rabbi Moyshele Halberstam of blessed memory, rabbi of Zborów and elder brother of Chaim, the Gaon of Sanz. It was Chaim who investigated the young Gaon for his brother's daughter and was the "expert" concerning him; consequently it was natural that when the rabbinical office became vacant in Tarnogrod, the city of his birth, in the year 5600 [1840], the Gaon of Sanz would recommend rewarding the young Gaon with this high office.

Many were the stories which were spread among the Jews of Poland about his greatness as a Torah scholar and his generosity in matters between people. We shall limit ourselves to trying to select and bring to the fore the most characteristic of these stories. As is well known, the Nefesh Haya was a very rich man in his youth. In addition to the large dowry which he received from his father-in-law he inherited from his father a rural property in the vicinity of Tarnogrod called Kfar Hammer, with a paper mill attached to it. In his rabbinic office in the course of twenty-two years in his birth city of Tarnogrod not only did he give up his remuneration as rabbi of the city, but he also maintained its great yeshiva from his own private funds, where hundreds of youths studied, a large number of whom served afterwards as well known rabbis, and only after he had lost his fortune and become impoverished, when in Kalisz, did he ask to receive his salary. But even then he set aside most of his income for the needs of the community and especially for his great yeshiva. He protected it as the apple of his eye. The fact that a large number of his students went with him from Tarnogrod on the border of Galicia to Kalisz on the German border serves to show how much he was beloved by his students. He who has ever been privileged to speak with one of his students knows how much affection and admiration they felt for their great rabbi. It is difficult to describe the joy which overwhelmed them when speaking with one of the descendants of their rabbi, and this is not surprising since he truly went out of his way to help them. Not only was he concerned to fulfill their needs while they were within the walls of the yeshiva, but even after they left him he was like a concerned father to them. If a student reached the age for marrying, the rabbi was concerned about making a suitable match for him, and after that a rabbinical position or other appropriate livelihood. If a student became ill the rabbi did not move from his sick bed but supported him and encouraged him. If a youth was having difficulty with his studies the rabbi came to his help until he was doing better. Even school children could say that when the rabbi tested them he never struck fear into them or failed them but, on the contrary, encouraged them with his charming smile.

In secular matters too he was accomplished: he knew several foreign languages and was resourceful and a man of vision. What I heard from my friend Chaim Miller of Haifa is worth noting: *Reb* Chaim, who was a native of Tarngorod, heard from his father, who knew the Nefesh Haya well, that after the great fire (which is mentioned in his book), when the Nefesh Haya was still young but his intelligence and sharp-wittedness were well known, and even the government was charmed by his appearance, which fully did him honor, a chief minister came and the Nefesh Haya stood before him and with moving words asked for his help in rebuilding the "little sanctuary" which is the synagogue. The minister was so impressed with his words and his personality that he did his utmost to get the top government officials to set aside the town's open land as a gift for the town's young rabbi, to do with as he wished. The Nefesh Haya demonstrated his ability in the field of commerce here too. On this open space, the "*rynek*" [marketplace] he constructed rows of houses for dwellings and shops, selling them at a great profit to the townspeople. With the money he made he erected a magnificent synagogue which was the pride of Tarnogrod up to the time of Holocaust. Chaim Miller told me, having heard it from his father, that when the synagogue was being built the Nefesh Haya helped the builders and with his own hands he passed them bricks and other building materials. This was his way from that time forward and he continued to do every good deed with his own hands and his own body.

Translator's notes:

I have not striven for consistency in the transliteration of personal names but rather used the spellings the reader is likely to find elsewhere; thus "Chaim", but "Nefesh Haya", although the "Ch" in the former and the "H" in the latter transliterate the same Hebrew letter.

1.   Title given to someone very learned in Torah.
2.   Also spelled Wax and Waks. In the heading to this essay his name is given as "Chaim-Eliezer", but it is "Chaim-Elazar (Elozor)" in the body of the article, and in all other sources I have seen.

[Pages 127-129]

My Great Father

by Eliezer Teicher

Translated by Martin Jacobs

My father, Rabbi Gaon Mordecha Tsvi Teicher (of blessed memory) was the rabbi of Zamech and later rabbi in Tarnogrod. He was the son of the great Gaon Rabbi Aryeh–Leyb (of blessed memory), the former rabbi of Tarnogrod. My father was the son–in–law of the Gaon Rabbi Asher Zalka, head of the rabbinic court of the congregation of Grodzisk.

Rabbi Mordechai Tsvi and his family. It was said about him that wherever you find greatness in Torah you also find greatness in wisdom and in virtues

My father was born in Lublin in 1880 and died in 1942 in distant Russia (Chardzoi). He was buried in the old Jewish cemetery there. We know very little about his childhood and youth. He was very humble and did great deeds hidden from the eyes of people. He lived in great modesty. When he was 18 years old he received his rabbinical diploma from the famous Gaon, the rabbi of Berezhany. Soon afterwards he replaced the rabbi of Łaszczów, who had just died. My father at the time temporarily carried out all the tasks of a local rabbi, until the town appointed a new rabbi.

As a young man he also had printed the books which he composed from the collected manuscripts of his grandfathers: "Haelef Lekha Shlomo", "Imre Maharan", "Pne Yitshak", along with his own addendum, "Hagahot Mordekhai". Before the outbreak of the World War my father had already prepared the type molds for printing the fourth book, "Imre Man", but the great calamity came and interrupted the publishing of this book.

Aside from his being a great Torah scholar he also distinguished himself with noble virtues. He was a great anonymous philanthropist, and regularly welcomed the poor as guests in his home. He also publically taught the Torah. Evenings in the bes medresh he used to teach youths and elderly a Talmud or Mishna lesson and he used to sit by himself studying late into the night.

When I was a child he used to send me as well as the other children on errands, bringing money and food to the needy who, unknown to anyone in the town, had nothing for the Sabbath. He ordered us to say, "Father has sent you this to fulfill his obligation[1]."

It is impossible to describe all the fine and great qualities which characterized my father. Let me be permitted, however, to record here what I heard in Israel from Mrs. Kruk, daughter of Yona Ber the teacher (of blessed memory). She lives in Israel now, in Ramathaim. She told me that as a youth, when he was still studying in *heder* with her father, her father died, leaving a widow and small children who could have died of hunger. My father, just 12 years old, took over the class and for a time taught the smaller children. Their parents continued to pay the tuition, giving it to the widow and her children. This lasted a long time and left a deep impression on the orphans.

In Tarnogrod earning a living was difficult; my father was far from being one of the wealthy. Yet he exerted great effort to get his oldest daughter Beyltshe a great scholar as a husband[2], Yitskhokl Rayz, a former student of the Chofetz–Chaim and himself very devout and philanthropic. He had room and board[3] in our house up to the outbreak of the Second World War. My father gave him everything he needed to continue his studies.

He and his daughter Rivkele were killed by the German murderers. The Germans also killed his oldest son Joseph–Menashe, his wife Rokhltshe, and two children, Yitskhokl and Osher Zalkele. Surviving were his widow, the *Rebbitzin* Estherl, and two sons, Eliezer and Aaron, and the younger daughter Golda, and a grandson, Moshe–Naftali Rayz. They all live in Israel.

These were the only survivors from the great Teicher family, rabbis of Tarnogrod, who had numbered about a hundred souls. These, the survivors of the great lineage, preserve the memory, the sacred faith, and the striving for noble deeds. With hearts full of honor we hammer out our sparks in the flame of our great father and great grandfathers.

Footnotes:

1. Presumably, the obligation of every Jew to give charity.
2. Literally, "as his son–in–law".
3. It was the custom to provide room and board for one's daughter and son–in–law if the son–in–law was a scholar needing to continue his studies.

Eliezer Teicher (Leyzer the Rabbi's son)

[Pages 130-132]

Our Rabbi

by **Alter** Zitz-Tishbi

Translated by Martin Jacobs

The Tarnogrod rabbi, Aryeh-Leyb Teicher (of blessed memory), was descended from generations of rabbis. He had a stately appearance, with a full face and a handsome grayish rather short beard. He dressed in a beautiful silk long fur-lined coat with a wide silk belt.

Every day, precisely at nine in the morning, he entered the *bes medresh* with his large *talis* and *tefillin* sack under his arm. He looked around with great satisfaction and saw how the youths were sitting bent over their Talmud books studying out loud. He went slowly to his special seat at the eastern wall, near the sacred ark. He sat down, opened a book, and looked into it, waiting for the *minyan* to begin praying.

When the praying had finished he stayed around in the *bes medresh* until twelve o'clock. The town wasn't lacking in things to do, but there were *dayonim* [A rabbinical judge or assistant to a rabbi] to decide questions of Jewish law; these were his son Moyshele, Shiele, and also Sander the teacher. As local rabbi he also had to take care of many town matters. In addition he taught a Talmud lesson every day at four o'clock, for students who came to his house.

Before Passover the rabbi's activity was quite intense. He had to make sure that the wells were not unkosher for Passover and the bakery ovens used for baking matzo were properly prepared. He also had to see to it that everyone should come in time to sell their *hametz* [Leavened bread and anything containing leavening, forbidden on the Passover. The rabbi sells such to Gentiles so it does not remain in the possession of Jews during Passover]; the baking of *shmira-matsos* [Matsot specially watched so as not to come into contact with anything leavened.] was also his concern.

In those days the rabbi was seen every day walking about with his two *shamosim* [Assistants to the rabbi, often called "sextons" in English.]: Nahum and Moshe. The rabbi, carrying his silver-handled stick, walked between them through the town, issuing orders which everyone endeavored most respectfully to carry out.

The rabbi's sermon on *Shabos godol* [The Sabbath preceding Passover] was really something to be experienced. The rabbi also delivered the blessing of Tsar Nikolai on his birthday, when representatives of the police and the authorities came to the *bes medresh*.

The rabbi's wisdom was exceptional. Everyone listened intently to him, and in every dispute the parties relied on his decision.

In addition to taking care of keeping kosher for Passover and all year long, the rabbi also had to make sure that the *eruv* [A cord around the town which designates the town as officially indoors, and so objects may be carried here on the Sabbath; without the *eruv* objects cannot be carried outdoors on the Sabbath.] around the town was in order, so that on the Sabbath Jews could carry their *talis* for praying and women could bring home the *cholent* [A stew prepared on Friday and just kept warm, not cooked, on Saturday, since cooking is prohibited on the Sabbath.] from the baker. It once happened that the *eruv* was torn in two and a dark cloud descended over the town. The men could not leave the town carrying their *talis* and hunger threatened, since without the *eruv* the cholent had to remain at the baker's until the stars came out. The rabbi then allowed employing little children, who are still free from sin.

In those days the congregation gave the Tarnogrod rabbi no problems. They walked in the way of God, kept the Torah; parents sent their sons to *heder* and their daughters to Chaim the teacher, who taught them to write using books of sample letters, so that later on they could write letters to their relatives in America. Chaim also taught them enough Russian to write an address.

I remember the circumcision celebrations, which took place in the synagogue, after prayers. As prayers ended the women arrived dressed in black silk dresses, leading the new mother with the baby. They stopped at the entrance to the synagogue, waiting until the husband took the child from his wife. Then they remained in the corner of the synagogue until the circumcision was over and refreshments were served. All that time they stood with downcast eyes and only caught glimpses of the youths swaying piously in prayer. Later, quietly, with fearful step, they left the synagogue.

Every celebration in Tarnogrod was everyone's celebration; the rabbi participated in it as if it were his own, like a shepherd looking over his sheep.

In addition to the sermons which he delivered on holidays, in private conversations the rabbi taught the townspeople to love truth and justice, to hate falsehood and injustice, because the latter is like one building on sand or trying to glue with spittle. He used to say: "You may think that you are losing money from truth and earning from falsehood, but only in truth is real security, and when the time comes to transmit my heritage to you, I will bequeath to you my honesty, which has been implanted in me through the Torah. There is no greater aristocracy than honesty."

And at times of boundless grief for the Jewish destruction and devastation, take your place, son of man, surviving Tarnogrod Jew, on the bridge of generations, and shed a tear, a hot burning tear, for the shepherd of the Jewish congregation in Tarnogrod, a tear of love, a tear of deep faith, that – **HIS MERITS MAY PROTECT US.**

Sholem Schwartz, grandson of Chanele, the Rabbi's daughter

[Pages 133-134]

**Dedicated to the memory of Arie-Leib Teicher,
Rabbi of the Congregation of Tarnogrod**

The Rabbi's Pipe

Yechiel Muterperl

Translated by Martin Jacobs

Funded by Natalie Lipner in Memory of her father Szmul Josef (Samuel Joseph) Lipner

In my teenage years I became friends with one of the Rabbi's great grandsons, whose name was Shlomke, and I was one of those who had entry to the Rabbi's house. In the front room, in the corner between the walls facing north and west, stood a cupboard with glass doors and sides. Among the items on the shelves several tubes made of white bone made an impression on me. When screwed together they became a pipe of a meter in length.

All year long the pieces of the pipe stayed untouched in the cupboard. But when the eve of *Hoshanah-Rabbah* [the seventh day of Sukkot] came the elderly rabbi would approach the cabinet and take out all the parts and attach them to each other, each one in its proper place, until the pipe was complete and shining in its beauty. Then he would fill it with tobacco and light it.

That night many people were seated in the adjacent *bet hamidrash* [house of study] praying the *Hoshanah Rabbah* evening *tikun* prayers. Some were nodding off between prayers. Then the elderly rabbi appeared and went round the benches on which the worshippers were sleeping, touching each one's shoulder with his pipe. They immediately woke up and saw that the rabbi was collecting donations for the needy. No one withheld his contribution. This was the rabbi's custom from year to year, thus fulfilling two commandments at the same time: to wake Jews to prayer and to engage in charity.

Let us mention that in the second room, in the rabbi's living quarters, was an extensive religious library. Here he received all who came to him with all sorts of questions. Here too he diligently studied the rabbinic writings all his days. Since the walls had not been painted for a long time, his daughter Chanale asked his permission to paint the room with beautiful colors. After many entreaties the elderly rabbi agreed, but only on condition that the black square on one of the walls be left to commemorate the destruction of the temple.

The rabbi was very careful not to give out his *tallit* and *kitel* [long white linen robe, worn by rabbis and other prayer leaders on important occasions] to be laundered. When he was asked the reason, he answered, "My *tallit* and *kitel* have absorbed many tears, and you wish to destroy them with water."

His paths are pleasant paths; [quotation from the book of Proverbs] his life's burden was to dig the deep well of Torah, so that many waters would emerge from it. The Torah is compared to fire, and this fire extinguishes other fires and as there is fire on top of fire, so too is there light on top of light. A touch of gracefulness extended across his countenance.

All this nobility can be understood as well as coming from the suffering of generations which he had absorbed, a suffering forged in fire of a Judaism founded in its own blood and satiating all the fields of the world.

Yosef-Moshe Teicher
Grandson of the old rabbi and son of Rabbi Tzvi

His children, grandchildren, and their descendants walked in his ways, up to the coming chapters of the flames of the Holocaust and the destruction. It is told how the old rabbi's grandson, Yosef-Moshe Teicher, suffered martyrdom at the hands of the murderer.

The Rabbi died two years before the Holocaust, at the age of more than eighty.

May his memory be blessed.

[Pages 135-140]

Rabbis and Hasidim of Tarnogrod

Meir Ringer

Translated by Martin Jacobs

Funded by Natalie Lipner in Memory of her father Szmul Josef (Samuel Joseph) Lipner

Meir Ringer

One of the phenomena which aroused great interest in the Jewish life of Poland was, without a doubt, *Hasidism* [mystical religious movement founded in Poland by the 18th century teacher Israel ben Eliezer, also known as the Baal Shem Tov], which also brought new light and faith to the Jews of Tarnogrod, drove away depression, and filled the hearts of all Jews with joy, from which they derived spiritual exaltation and new strength, love of one's fellow Jew, and good deeds. As in every other town in Poland, Hasidism in Tarnogrod too was a way of life and a culture.

Hasidism in our town was a popular movement. Almost every Jew in the town had great faith in the power of the *tzadikim* [*Hasidic* rabbis], and when the *Hasidic* rabbis visited our town the people brought to them notes on which they set forth their desires and needs and asked their advice about matters of business and also about medicines and treatments for various illnesses.

But, despite the fact that they saw the rabbis as miracle workers, listened with astonishment and wonder to their teaching and to their fervent praying, not everyone thought of himself as belonging to the *Hasidic* movement. Though not everyone was a person of intellect, yet *Hasidism* took over the religious community in Tarnogrod, absorbing within it love of God and of one's fellow man.

Among them were *kabbalists* [students of the Kabbalah or Jewish mystical tradition] who studied and meditated day and night in both the hidden and revealed Torah. Several of them used to get up at midnight for the prayer of lamentation for the exile of the Divine Presence and for the destruction of the Temple.

How great was the sense of community that pervaded the *Hasidim*. They addressed each other in familiar, informal terms. It was considered natural and ordinary to help a *Hasid* on his way down and lacking a livelihood with various means. They celebrated each other's private joyous occasions. They also knew who was in need of help and who was in a position to offer help.

The *shtibl* [literally "little house" or "little room" which served as a house of prayer] served as the best recreation center for both young and old. Here youths sat and learned Talmud with its captivating chant, and here were brought all the questions and requests pertaining to life of the community and town. For everyone, song and melody were tried and tested means of bringing the heart close to the service of the Creator, for not by afflictions and sadness does one reach his state of holiness, but by worshipping the Lord out of joy and by cleaving to Him from inspiration.

Hasidism was always a matter of song and dance.

The *Hasidic* rabbis did not make their home in our city. The *Hasidim* of Tarnogrod used to travel to their rabbis on special occasions and on the High Holy Days and were united with their rabbis through prayer, *tish* [literally "table", a gathering of *Hasidim* around their rabbi, perceived as a moment of great holiness], and gifts to the rabbi. The sign of adherence to the *Hasidic* movement was praying in the *shtibl* in a group, according to the accepted usage in the house of prayer of each "*rebbe*". The *shtibl* was like a world to itself, a kind of extended family. All who belonged to this family remained connected to their rabbi, the *tzadik*; his image always hovered before their eyes. At his holy word they came in and went out, acting in the power of that longing for the rabbi and his *tish*, for his teaching and his illuminating words. They were not pacified until he traveled to be with them, so that they might find shelter with him, look at him, gaze upon the brightness of his face, hear his interpretations of the sublime secrets of the Torah and learn from his deeds and his character.

The material conditions in Tarnogrod did not permit a separate "*shtibl*" for every group, and so the *Hasidim* of Belz, Trisk [Turiysk], and Kuzmir [Kazimierz Dolny] were concentrated in one *kloyz* [a small synagogue], which was called the "Belzer shtibl". In the "Sieniawa shtibl" the *Hasidim* of Sanz [Nowy Sącz] and Gorlice also prayed. The *Hasidim* of Rozvedov [Rozwadów] prayed together with those of Rudnik and Cieszanów, etc.

The *shtibl* gave the *Hasid* confidence that he was not alone in the world. He was assured support in time of need. The *Hasidic shtibl* became both a religious and communal institution. It was sanctified for prayer and for the study of Torah. In the *shtibl* the *Hasidic* atmosphere of Tarnogrod was created.

After a hard day's work the Jew went to *shtibl* and there put away his cares, forgot the burdens of the day and absorbed the joy of a page of Talmud and some small talk. Each one studied at his own level and everyone achieved satisfaction, not merely satisfaction of the soul, but also enjoyment in the literal sense of the word. Jews renew and refresh themselves in these hours, they restore their souls, as the *Hasidim* say: "*M'hot zikh mekhaye geven*" ["We got great enjoyment"].

From time to time the *Hasidic* rabbis came to visit their followers in our town, and people flocked to them from nearby communities to drink in their words with great thirst and to seek advice from them on family matters. The rabbis' *tish* was set with pride on *Shabbos* in the great study house. The rabbi distributed *shirayim* [remainders of the rabbi's meal, eagerly eaten by his followers] and joyfully greeted the Guest with the Radiant Face. The *Hasidim* sang melodies full of longing and devotion.

There were many pearls among these melodies. The sounds were filled with splendor and innocence and dramatic-mysterious tension, and they had the power of softening men's hearts and awakening a man's conscience.

During the rabbi's stay in the city people drew closer together, and not just the Jews of the town, but also of nearby towns. Even though the rabbi did not have the power to join them all together as one, since they were jealous admirers each one of his own rabbi, for only through him was it possible to reach complete wholeness, and they traveled great distances to reach him, and they related to a second rabbi with a negligent attitude, not believing in his power, nevertheless he influences a great part of those who are indifferent to come together under one banner, that of *Hasidism*.

There were not a few among the *Hasidim* who were warmly compassionate Jews, full of pain and love for Jews, and who emphasized simple and perfect faith. Is not love one of the foundations of *Hasidism*? They turn in love to all men and receive them with open arms; therefore they look favorably upon the great congregation that gathers around every *rebbe* who comes to the town.

Thus the essential nature and character of *Hasidism* as a whole come to it from the existence of the *rebbe* rather than from its doctrines, streams, and ways. This is the greatness of *Hasidism*: in him is the secret and explanation of its strength; he is the center of its being. For a man who has a *rebbe* the whole human template is different from one who does not have a *rebbe* in his world. In the image of the *rebbe*, *Hasidism* expresses one of its essential foundations. The faith of the *rebbe* in the *Hasidic* world is such that even for those who have turned away from religion the authority of the *rebbe* has not faded for them.

In those days the movement was strong in the city. Every evening people gathered in the home of the *Hasid* with whom the *rebbe* was staying; they stood crowded together and his admirers told "holy stories". In that hour both young and old forgot the world and its sorrowful existence, and were transported to the spiritual world, to the most fantastic stories in the world, and to every word and sign coming out of mouth of the *rebbe*.

The day the *rebbe* left the city everyone recalled the saying of Rashi: "When a righteous man leaves the city his glory also leaves, his splendor leaves, his majesty leaves". Hundreds accompanied him and did not leave him until they received a parting blessing from him.

The Elderly Rabbi of the Tarnogrod Congregation

Rabbi Arie Leib Teicher, grandson of the rabbi and *tzadik* of Kreshiv [Krzeszów] and a descendant of Yom Tov Lipmann Heller, was a great and sharp-witted scholar, learned in Talmud and commentaries, head of the rabbinate for 72 years, at first for a time in the new city of Zamość, similarly in the community of Czchów near Lublin, but most of the years he officiated in our congregation.

In his capacity as *mara deasra* [local rabbi] and zealot for the religion and sanctifier of the people, he fought strongly against all freethinking. With the awakening of political life in our town he beseeched us to free ourselves from the 49 gates of impurity (may the Merciful One protect us), citing the Biblical verse: "None who go to her come back" (Prov. 2:19). In the study of the Modern Hebrew language he saw only a striving to learn a modern language, and therefore preached that it was better for us to learn Greek. In his naivety he saw Greek science as ruling the modern world.

In the founding of the library and of the first Hebrew school in the town he saw the root of all evil and so he proclaimed, with all the means in his power, that we had an obligation to a holy war against them, even to the point of his pronouncing a ban on them. He did the same with regard to all Zionist activity carried out on behalf of the branch of the Zionist *Histadrut* [Federation of Laborers in the Land of Israel] here.

He had four sons, all of whom became rabbis or religious teachers in Israel, and two daughters. He remained the rabbi of the congregation until his death at the age of 95. He passed away two years before the outbreak of the Second World War.

The Last Rabbi of the Congregation

Rabbi Moshele Teicher, son of Rabbi Arie Leib, was the congregation rabbi until the Holocaust. He supported matters of interest to the town with knowledge and intelligence.

His form and appearance spoke of honor to both Jews and non-Jews alike. He was easily approachable, and he knew how to talk to everyone, according to that person's education and class. With his sharp intellect he was very knowledgeable in all branches of commerce; people came to seek his advice. His wife, the *Rebbetzin* [wife of a rabbi] Malkale, bore him 12 sons and daughters, because of which supporting his household was as difficult for him as splitting the Red Sea.

During the Holocaust his whole family, already numbering several dozen, found a hiding place in a bunker. This became known to a Christian in the city, who informed on them. They were all brutally murdered; not one of his descendents survived.

A Man of Wide Learning

Yehoshule, the third son of the old rabbi, swam in the sea of Talmud and *Poskim* [Rabbinical scholars who settle matters of Jewish law and ritual]. He was a kind of *tsena demale sifra* [Talmudic expression defined in Jastrow's dictionary as "a basket full of books", a man full of learning, but without method].

As a young man he was isolated in his thoughts; he neglected himself and everyone close to him. He withdrew from the life of this world. He imposed fasts and afflictions upon himself and he constantly walked about the streets, until one day he caught cold, took to his bed and departed this life while still young, to the sorrow of his family and the townspeople.

Yakov the Intermediary

Yakov, or Yekil Mantel, the leader of the congregation throughout his life, was the *Shtadlan* [official representative of the Jewish community to the government. Such people were generally chosen because of their knowledge of the official language of the country in addition to their own Yiddish] with the Russian authorities and high officialdom. Knowledge of the Russian language was also the source of his livelihood as a scribe, skilled in worldly affairs and in Russian law. He was dedicated to the needs of the community. At one time I had the privilege of working with him in the children's open-plan kitchen, and I saw his great dedication to the congregation in his community.

In his twilight years he lived in poverty because he was not on good terms with the Polish administration and they put someone else in his place, depriving him of his livelihood.

The old rabbi, Arie Leib, with his sons and a grandson

Rabbi Moshe Naphtali Teicher at the time of his stay at the bathhouse in Szczawnica

There are those who reveal themselves as great persons by revealing a new path in Torah or in wisdom, in leadership or in their qualities. Then there are great people, exceptionally virtuous people, even more so than the first, who outwardly do not bring all new Torah interpretations to our attention; to ordinary eyes they seem like mediocrities in all their talk and activity, but their praise is great in that they do not arouse praise for themselves with their peculiar ways and exceptional deeds. On the contrary, they are gracious in their power of restraint and in the appropriate superiority of modest behavior. They cover themselves in unpretentiousness. They are deliberate in judgment and deliberate also in the use of the virtuous grace that protects them; they are humble and modest, and their ways are quiet. They return as it were to old ideas, but with renewed pleasure; they do not boast of the performance of some method, and so they act not in accordance with their method, but in accordance with their own interpretation. They are careful not to separate from the community.

Such was Rabbi Moshe-Naftali Teicher, wonderful in that he was not eager for wonders, so as not to excite the people in an unlawful manner. *Reb* Moshe took great pains not to abandon the protection of humility, for humility is the source of all virtues.

[Pages 141-146]

How the Enlightenment
and Zionist Movements Arose in Town

by Meir Ringer

Translated by Joseph M. Lipner

The youth of Tarnogrod was divided into three classes: manual workers, merchants, and those who were dedicated to the study hall. Those in the study hall would sit there, day and night, laboring to learn a page of Talmud and its commentators. They were always enclosed in the four cubits of Jewish law and all changes in the life of the outside world were foreign to their spirit. They were considered in town to be the elite among the young men, and every Jew wanted to obtain on behalf of his daughter, when it came time for her to marry, one of these elite young men mentioned above. Mostly, the rich were able to achieve this for their daughters.

In that period, it was accepted among the Jews that any book without religious content was impure, and a book in Hebrew or Yiddish which contained criticism of accepted ideas or the way of life of those times was seen as heresy and apostasy and was forbidden to read.

Until the First World War, life flowed quietly. Old as well as young knew that heaven was God's heaven, and the world was given to humans as a sort of hallway in which to earn the world-to-come. They likewise knew that one does not inquire about what is above. And then came the events of the war, which also influenced accepted ideas. And just as the order of the world below changed because of the war, so too changed these concepts above.

Organization and Collection of Funds

We were at that time several young men of the study hall who began to leave the traditional four cubits of Jewish law and to become interested also in what was happening in the wide world. We also began to read books in Hebrew–and in Yiddish, that were of the class of heretical books. We did this all in complete secrecy. We read them in the attic, in the bathroom, or in some other hiding place, until one day when this secret came to light. Suddenly the matter of our reading these books became known. And it also became known that from time to time we were visiting Moshe Lemmer who was called Moishe Yantshes, who was known as a heretic, because of the books that were found by him and because of his views, which were judged to be heretical.

This news also reached the ears of the elderly rabbi, Rabbi Leibele Teicher, and he warned us about the danger awaiting us in reading these books and in particular Hebrew books, which contained the root of heresy. And to prevent any problems from recurring, he particularly forbade us to be found within four cubits of Moishe Yantshes the heretic.

This warning reached us too late, after we had already peeked and been injured, because in the meantime we had already read the book "Ahavat Zion" (by Mapu), the book "On Beliefs and Opinions" by Dr. S. Bronfeld, and a reference book with all its parts, "Each Generation and Its Seekers" by Dr. A.H. Weiss. These books exerted an enormous pull on all the young men of the yeshiva. Because of this, we received the warning of the rabbi, to prevent any problems from recurring, but we continued reading the books. We also found it necessary because of this, whether voluntarily or not, to approach Moishe Yantshes to exchange books.

When the elderly rabbi learned that all his warnings did not work, and that there was no way to fix us, he then approached us, in person and in his honor, when we were learning in the study hall among the other young men. He announced to us that from that day forward, we no longer had the right to sit in the study hall, on the grounds that he wanted to save the other young men who had not already been exposed to heresy like we had been. All our arguments did not prevail, and we were forced to stop attending the study hall.

This expulsion caused the youth in all its circles to organize to establish a library and reading room in town. But this matter was not at all easy to accomplish, because of the opposition of the pious zealots, at the head of whom stood the town's rabbi on one side, and Tobele Herbstman, who was the driving force of the opposition, on the other side.

We needed money at that time in order to buy books and rent a room for the library and reading room. Our approach resonated with only a portion of the merchant youths, as the project needed strength and resolve, given the incitement and defamation from the side of the zealots, and most of these youths were still dependent on the goodwill of their parents. On the other hand, our approach resonated strongly with the laborer youths. Not only did they donate money with a wide hand and generous spirit, but they also volunteered to take part in everything, from organizing to the collection of the money.

Here it is appropriate to remember one curious occurrence: one day around that time I entered the study hall to pray (the prohibition that applied to us was only not to sit and study together with the other young men who were learning there) and it happened that the old rabbi saw me (as before the rift I was counted among his students and also among those who visited his house; I learned Talmud and halachic authorities together with his grandson Eliezer for several years). The rabbi asked me: "Meir'l, for what foundation are you going around collecting money? And what is the degree of your poverty that you have joined together with tailors and shoemakers?" And when I answered him that the gathering of this money is not for charity, but rather to establish a library, he said to me as follows: "Know that in the town, where I am the leader of the community, there was not and will not be a bibliotheque, and those new friends you have nowadays are a sure sign of the level to which you have already fallen, exactly as it is written: "From the high roof to the deep pit.""

We gathered a nice sum of money and bought books, but struggled with renting a room, for all the Jews in town were afraid of the threats of the zealots. Having no other choice, we agreed to the suggestion of a certain widow, to rent for good money half of her room, which we divided with a cloth curtain.

The Zealot's War

At the opening celebration, which occurred on a Friday night, we experienced several unpleasant events. In the middle of the celebration, parents of boys and girls who were celebrating with us suddenly came in, grabbed their children and took them out by force. And there were those who slapped their children's faces in everyone's presence. Understandably, this caused an awful depression to the rest of those present.

Before many days passed, the zealots reported us to the authorities, claiming that we had founded a communist organization. Immediately the police appeared and demanded a permit from us. When we did not have one, the police sealed up the bookshelf and forbade us from gathering until we produced to them a permit from the authorities.

In that predicament, we turned for help to the cultural committee of the Zionist organization in Warsaw. After a little time, Dr. Emanuel Allsonger informed us that he had designated and listed us as a chapter in the network of Hebrew culture of the

Zionist Histadrut, and that in the coming days they would remove the prohibition from us. And so it was. After a week, the police removed the prohibition, and we started to organize with redoubled strength. And in the language of the zealots: "The power of impurity again became stronger than the power of holiness."

At that point we succeeded in renting an appropriate room whose owner was considered one of the important people in town. His economic situation had become suddenly unstable, and we paid him a high rent. And we decided to establish in that place a Hebrew school also. We brought in a very successful Hebrew teacher, and we opened the school. In the beginning the school had few students, because of the prohibitions and bans which were announced evening and morning in all the synagogues against any of the parents who had the nerve to send their children there. And those who sent their children to the school experienced bad situations in which others did not want to pray together with them and chased them out with force. There were also those who did not allow these parents to be called to the Torah and the like. But this school exerted a great attraction to both children and parents.

A Polish Christian teacher, a member of the faculty of the local government school, also joined our school. This later had a good influence on the school in another way.

The religious zealots again informed on us, and the police again closed the Hebrew school pending receipt of a license that we had already applied for, which depended solely and only on the local cultural council, the majority of whose members were anti-Semites. Among the members of this council was a principal of the government school of Tarnogrod. We bribed him with a designated amount of money. He persuaded the members of the local council that (a) his school no longer has space to absorb additional students; and (b) the Hebrew school stands virtually under his supervision thanks to the fact that one of his faculty members serves there as a teacher. And this influenced most of the members of the council to grant us the license and led to the opening of the closed school.

The Hebrew School

Among the students sitting from the right: M. Ringer, M. N. Mantel, M. Lemmer, the teacher Bloomstein, Chaim Rokeach, S. Adler

From Loneliness to the King's Highway

Then our influence increased greatly in town. Having no other choice, the religious people recognized our existence as an established fact. The school developed nicely and there was a need to expand to another room, which we rented at that time with greater ease.

We took advantage of this comfortable atmosphere to establish a Zionist organization with all its committees. Many members signed up and we left our loneliness for the king's highway, and at that time we were recognized in town as an official public body.

I would be remiss if I skipped over the following details: (a) Together with the decision to establish a Hebrew school, we chose an administration. We required that the members of the administration, from that day forward, should speak among themselves only in Hebrew to the full extent possible. Because of this, instead of calling us "heretics" or "Zionists" as they had earlier, they began to call us "shalom-niks" in town because of the greeting "shalom." (b) After the establishment of the library, and the struggle we had with the pious zealots, we searched for ways to be accepted by the majority of the people who are called "amcha." When we learned about the American Joint Distribution Committee's activities to nourish children, we made great efforts to convince the Joint's local administration to hand over to us the management of feeding the children of Tarnogrod. And we succeeded in convincing them that we were the most appropriate to perform this task because of our dedication. We rented a large room and opened a children's kitchen with a dining hall and there we distributed parcels of food three times a day to more than 400 children. Obviously, all this work was done on a volunteer basis, and without the expenditure of funds, and it was a large operation, which the pious ones always wanted to take away from us, albeit without success.

(c) The celebration in honor of the Balfour Declaration took place in the middle of the summer of the year 1919. Everywhere in the Jewish Zionist world, people celebrated the Balfour Declaration. By us, this occurred after the end of the struggle that we had with the zealots. Our influence on the Jewish street increased, and almost everyone made peace with us. Then we also tried our best to organize demonstrations of support for the Balfour Declaration.

On Lag Ba'Omer in the year 1920 in celebration of the Balfour Declaration

In the middle of the photograph sitting from the right: Y. Wolfish, G. Kenigstein, Ch. Rokeach, M. Ringer, M. Lemmer, Ch. Grubman and P. Lipiner
Among those standing: Ych. Lipiner, H. Strausser, S. Topler, M. Lustrin, Z. Lustrin, Yechezkel Sinaless, S. Lemmer, S. Richter, Ch. Lipiner

The elderly rabbi agreed then to permit us to open the gates of the great synagogue and to hold a large assembly there. This was an enormous national experience that the people of the village had never seen before. At the head of the demonstration marched in exemplary order the teacher and children of the Hebrew school with the blue and white flags and the flags of the country, and after them the youths marched, and after them the elderly and the children flowed across the width of the whole market square to the great synagogue, which was filled from one side to another.

The school's children's choir sang a song in Hebrew. Afterwards speeches were heard about the value of the Balfour Declaration to the land of Israel and the people of Israel. And then a national enthusiasm rose among all the participants, reaching the heights of heaven. And in the end, everyone sang *Hatikvah* and this was the first time and also the only time.

(d) In the end, as we know, all Jews in our town, from the zealots to the laborers were very religious, and any small deviation was a deviation from the straight path of Judaism in their eyes. They saw, in the ideas of Zionism and Socialism–without understanding their substance–something that opposes Judaism. The vast majority of people could not even differentiate one from the other and they lumped them both together under the name "Ziosocialism." What resulted from this was that the rest of the Jews were passive participants in the zealots' opposition to us. Among them were our parents and their situation was the worst, for they were in the predicament of "ice on one side, ice on the other side." On the one hand, they too hurt from the deviation from the straight path by the children who came from their loins. On the other hand, they served as targets for the braided arrows of the zealots, for the bans and decrees that were decreed also against them because of us. (They placed a ban on my father's house and forbid anyone from entering his bakery; only after three days did the rabbi recognize his error, correct it, and nullify the ban.) Apart from this, the parents absorbed shame and embarrassment that cannot be measured. Obviously, our situation at home was extremely unpleasant, and when I recall today the great suffering that our parents underwent at that time, I feel their pain to this day.

So did there arise among us the movement of the enlightenment, and so arose the movement of Zionism and Hebrew speech.

In connection with the struggles of the religious zealots against us, I give testimony today–notwithstanding the great pain and insult that they caused us–that their motive was honest and acceptable, because they suspected every new thing and did not understand the spirit of the youth or the time.

As the years passed there arose in our town different organizations, both secular and religious. There were some in those years who were enthusiastic about looking for solutions to the questions of the diaspora and the questions of class exploitation while working towards a single solution. Who knows which way the wind blows? Out of the distress of the diaspora, constant longings, operations and activities, a strong feeling of changes and upheavals in history, contacts and interactions with the revolutionary movements in Poland, material and ideological motives–the Zionist-Socialist movement spread and became strong in our town too.

There were, however, ups and downs, achievements and failures which were all mixed together, and they made the winds stormy, activated people's thoughts, caused ferment to the forces of the young people and caused rebellion among the complacent. There were some who fought against those lacking faith from the right and left camps, and who placed dams against the malicious surges of anti-Zionism. With this they inserted themselves into the operation of the youth movement, and especially the pioneers, who were the first to make aliya to Israel.

[Pages 147-149]

The Home From Which
the *Haskalah* Movement[1] and Zionism Emerged

by Meir Ringer

Translated by Sara Mages

R' Yakov Lemer, who was called by all, Yantshe Fakhtsher[2] , worked hard all his life to support his family. He previously lived in the village of Plusy near Tarnogrod, in the yard of a Polish landowner as a milk tenant. Every morning he traveled to the city with the milk, and its products, to sell them. During the First World War he moved to the city of Tarnogrod.

R' Yakov was a religious Jew, always liked to prolong the prayer and the recitation of Psalms. Besides that, he used to hum all sorts of traditional melodies to himself, and when the Sabbath, or a holiday, came, there was no end to his singing. Only in one thing he was very different from all the other local Jews, he did not interfere and not disturb his sons in the course of their thoughts and their ways of life, which were also slightly different from the conventional concepts in those days.

In this sense, it is especially noteworthy to praise his wife, Sheindil, who understood the spirit of youth and time alike, and she enjoyed seeing the youth's desire for life in society and in the movement. Her house was always wide open, and was a kind of a meeting place for sages under the guidance and devotion of their eldest son, Moshe, who was a type of a distinctly Russian-Jewish scholar and was called Moshe Yantshe the heretic. For this reason, the ultra-Orthodox zealots kept away the students of the *Beit Midrash* from this house, those who were thirsty for some education and wanted to know what was happening outside the world of *Halacha* [Jewish law]. They snuck into this house secretly and in the darkness of the night, so that they would not be seen, to get a book there or to talk about various matters. Woe to the one that the eye of the zealots has found him there. As a result, a boycott and banishment was imposed on this home, and it was forbidden to a young man from *Bait HaMidrash* to go there.

R'Yakov Lemer and his wife Sheindil

But, it was not long before this home became a symbol for all the residents of the city and the surrounding area: that from there emerged the Haskalah, Zionism and the speaking in the Hebrew language, and it was the reward for R' Yakov Lemer and his wife Sheindil for the humiliation and banishment they had gone through in the past.

Several years later, R' Yakov Lemer won a bigger reward. It was at the time that his son, Moshe, settled in Berlin and informed his father that he was donating all his Vilna Edition of SHAS[3] to *Bait HaMidrash* in the city of Tarnogrod.

In honor of this great event, R' Yakov held a great *mitzvah* meal at his home, and also those, who had previously been careful not to approach this house, came. And then, he got to hear, with his own ears, from the elderly rabbi, R' Leib'le Teicher, that this SHAS is really the Torah of Moshe, in double meaning, of *Moshe Rabbeinu* and also of his son Moshe. Then, there was no limit to R' Yakov's happiness.

Thanks to their sons, who had big businesses in Berlin, R' Yakov Lemer and his wife Sheindil also immigrated there. They lived there for several years of rest and satisfaction, but not for a long time. Following the Nazi revolution in Germany they returned to their hometown in Poland together with other German Jewish refugees. When the Second World War broke out they fled to Lvov where they were victims of the extermination of all the Jews of Lvov.

May their memory be blessed.

The young women in the Zionist Movement
From the right: Malka Silberzweig, Dvora Adler (USA), Ita Teicher daughter of HaRav R' Moshe'le, Chana-Mela First

A group of young people activists in the General Zionists

Among them are - in the first row, from the right: Berkel Weintraub, Rivtz'a Nissenboim, Yisrael Adler, Zelda Kendel (now in Israel), Azriel Bas, Malka Kalikstein, Yosef Weiss, Chana'le Aptiker, David Groisman, Dvora Adler (America), Rivka Zukerman.
They conducted a beautiful job, in which they wrote a great chapter in the history of the town, which was wiped out and disappeared.

Footnotes:

    1.   *Haskalah* Movement – The Jewish Enlightenment – was an ideological and social movement that developed in Eastern Europe in the early 19th century.
    2.   Yantshe Fakhtsher – Yantshe the Tenant.
    3.   SHAS – Hebrew abbreviation of SHishA Sedarim, or, the "six orders" of the *Mishnah*

[Pages 150-159]

Town Figures

Meir Ringer

Translated by Zvika Welgreen

Edited by Ben Knobloch

Reb Gedalia

Rabbi Gedalia Mindles– as he was called, was a man of high moral character, an extremely humble scholar, who lived in poverty and made his living as a *"Schpiditer"* [shipping agent], bringing goods for the town's shopkeepers from Lublin. With horse and wagons which were covered with canvas as shelter from the rain and snow, and with the help of a driver who took care of the horses.

Reb Gedalia sat inside the wagon while traveling and studied the Talmud and Jewish Law. The wagon served *Reb* Gedalia as a traveling Talmudic school, for he was always traveling except Shabbat and holidays. He left on Sunday morning and returned back home before sundown on Friday.

He was honored by all town people, congratulating him when passing in the street, treating him with due respect.

Once he was carried away and took part in the dispute between Shinova Chasidim and the local Rabbi and when angry quoted an insult from the Talmud.

A while later he regretted his deed and the insult caused to the town Rabbi, and he didn't rest until one weekday, when the towns people saw *Reb* Gedalia walking bare foot along the market square to the Rabbis' home, to ask his forgiveness for the insult he caused in a moment of anger.

When he died, while washing his body before burial, he was treated as a holy person for he was worth it, and all the townspeople took part in his funeral.

Tebale Herbstman

Tevl Nachum, his parents and family members called him, the townspeople called him Tebale.

When he was young, he studied in the *Beit Hamidrash* and knew his way in Talmud and medieval commentators.

Was very clever and yet knew very well day-to-day life, selling agriculture machines to farmers.

As a typical Belz Chasid, he was opposed to any non-orthodox movement, and so he opposed the Zionist and the Enlightenment movements, the Hebrew school and all other cultural establishments founded in the town and was a bitter opponent to the Zionist youth, a symbol of fanaticism and extremism.

Never the less we respected him for his integrity and his true belief and saw in him an honorable opponent.

Tebale was a proud and brave Jew, and at the last day of his life he brought it to light.

The day that the Germans gathered part of the town's Jews and claimed they were communist Jews and led them outside the town for slaughter, behind the Christian cemetery, and ordered them to dig their own graves, Tebale was among them.

At a certain moment he stood up and admonished the murderers for their cruelty and predicted their bitter end, then he addressed his fellow brothers and urged them to recite *Vidui* [a special confessional prayer recited on Yom Kippur and at the deathbed, by, or on behalf of, the one who is dying] and to sanctify G-d's name in front of the murderers.

Suddenly a gunshot was heard and a Nazi bullet hit his pure heart, Tebale fell into the open grave, and then a machine gun started shooting, spreading death among our holy brothers.

Tebale, the same way you stood all of your life for your pure belief, you exceeded yourself in standing in front of your grave, and you shall be remembered forever.

In Memory of the Souls of my father's House, May Their Memory be a Blessing

Berish Ringer, some called him Berish Baker, made a decent living out of his bakery until eradication.

He was a man of honor, his generosity came from his heart and he always helped the needy, in small amounts or substantial support, and so he was known in town.

He always welcomed every guest at his home, with a cup of tea, a good cigarette or news from the newspaper to whoever was willing to hear.

Poor passers-by ate at his table, especially on Shabbat. It did not occur even one Shabbat that he go home from synagogue without a guest

My mother Rivkale died of natural causes during the war. Before the Shoa, she secretly helped those who addressed her, and on several occasions she provided her jewelry as collateral in order to borrow money and help someone in need.

My eldest sister, Goldele, who married before the German-Russia war, died tragically on Lochov Street outside the Ghetto, by a Nazi bullet when going to the Balonia district to buy some food. She was buried not far from the place where she died, leaving at my father's home a young baby.

Etla my other sister, who impressed everyone with her beauty and manners, stayed with my father until the eradication period.

Sheindela, my youngest sister, managed to run away from the Germans and stayed during the whole period of the war in Soviet Russia. She fell ill with heart disease in the Siberian forest and then got well. At the end of the war, when she came back to Poland and heard about the misfortune of our family, she fell sick again in Szczecin and died there extremely lonely.

My brother Wolf, his wife Miriam and their five children all died in Lvov by the Nazi murderers.

Teacher, Player and Poet

Avraham Moshe Melamed, was a scholar with a slow and quiet voice, different from others in his qualities and manners which he fulfilled without considering mockery of his acquaintance, who didn't understand his spirit.

He didn't name his sons after deceased close relatives, as was common among Jews, but named them with biblical names such as Dvora, Efraim and Menashe, most likely taken from the weekly torah portion.

Once he decided to honor Shabbat by speaking in Hebrew, which was the holy language instead of Yiddish, which was seen as the every day language. Quite often his behavior was laughed at as people considered it laziness, even though he didn't change his ways till his last day.

He liked art objects and with his own hands built a violin and played it. He wrote lyrics in Hebrew and Yiddish and composed for each song its melody.

Once he invented a machine to count the Omer, a contribution to the *Beit Hamidrash* and they used it every night during the *Omer* period, between Pesach and *Shavuot* and this way he built different articles using only a knife and chisel.

He was also talented in drawing and carving and was always busy in all sorts of delicate art works without learning it from anyone.

On top of everything, he was gifted with fine and rich humor, which he used in the right time and place.

I am sure that by the death of this man a huge talent was gone.

He earned his living by teaching and his wife was selling different items on market day and they lived modestly and he didn't merit to reach an old age.

Gone to Heresy

He was called Israel Kuki, as his surname was unknown. He was a scholar in his youth and was married very young. He studied Kabala. Gone to heresy, he lost his mind and did things that are not done, such as eating pig in public, smoking on Shabbat and other horrible things.

Rabbis allowed his young woman to divorce him so she could be free from him. For a few years Israel Kuki wandered like this until he regained his sanity and became a quiet and normal person, but by that time he was ignorant and forgot his studies completely.

There was a poor girl in town – Tovale, that had recently been married to a poor hunchback and the wedding took place in the cemetery as a supernatural cure for the cholera disease that spread in town. Shortly afterwards her husband died and she was remarried to Israel Kuki.

He chose matchmaking as his profession even though he never succeeded to make one. He received a small amount of each match done in town in some kind of protection so he will not damage the betrothal by saying something wrong, because Jews have a saying that "even a cat can damage".

During the First World War, there were only few matches and weddings among Jewish families and until things improved, Israel Kuki had to find some other work to make his living. Searched and found, each town citizen who had to serve some days in prison for some administrative violation, Israel Kuki would serve time instead and was paid small amount for that.

Once in a while there was no one to serve time for, and deprived of his income, he approached the police complaining about that. The Police understood his distress and decided on the need to go to the Jewish district, find someone who did something wrong, then they would fill the form and Israel Kuki will get his payment.

Out of all those occupations he would make a modest living of bread and water.

Memories of Old Days

Each time I sit listening to the radio hearing music of the Cantors, I remember ideas and memories of old times, I imagine myself wearing a long black coat, boots, the black hat and with long side curls, a complete Jew with only a beard missing. At my youth I already knew everything a Jew is forbidden of, just like a fifty year old Jew. I knew it is forbidden to get off bed without washing hands, forbidden to eat without blessing the food, forbidden to rejoice because of the destruction of the temple and generally forbidden and forbidden again.

During the winter we were in the house due to rain, snow, mud and cold. When springtime came, it was between Pesach and *Shavuot*; the days to count the Omer, and every Jewish boy knew that at that time almost everything was forbidden. New clothing and footwear, bathing in the river and especially joy. We were taught about ten kingdom martyrs, about Rabbi Akiva's followers who died in the plague etc. etc.

And than *Shavuot* finally arrived with its "*Akdumos*" [liturgical poem recited on *Shavuot* consisting of praise for G-d, and Torah] music which we loved so much with the green leaves we brought into each home and the different kind of food, specific to *Shavuot* with their special taste. Like a miracle we felt the winter's burden lying off our shoulders and we became free to reach out to the green fields and enjoy ourselves.

We didn't have enough time to enjoy ourselves because there came the three weeks (before 9 in Av) and everything was forbidden and forbidden again, and again we were studying the destruction of the temple.

Because of Kamtza and Bar Kamtza Jerusalem was destroyed, and we couldn't be happy. Shortly afterwards came "Shabbat Nachamu" and we hoped to enjoy a bit with our life ahead of us and the free world just waiting for us, according to our standards of course, and here comes the month of *Elul* slapping our faces as if calling us, "Hey where are you running, have you forgotten that judgment days will soon arrive?"

"Have you forgotten that during *Elul* the fish in the water shiver?" We stood astonished, we had not taken anything out of all the good things, didn't enjoy yet all the beauty of the summer, the gardens calling us with a wink, "Come guys climb the fence, see all the wonderful fruits and the cool shadows in the hot day." A huge conflict was created in us, the drive calling us to reach the open fields, water and wonders of nature, against the drive for concession and being satisfied with what we had according the spirit of *Elul* and its companionship, Rosh Hashanah and Yom Kippur and the ten days between them. These ten days had important values, and are not named the Holy days for nothing. They determine your fate to bring you back to study and to forget that there is something else in the world.

Finally, when also these days have passed, we were standing before the rain season and the wheel started its new turn again.

Godel Wetscher

In his youth Godel was a *Beit Midrash* student, familiar with Talmud and other holy books, but his behavior distinguished him from other Jews in his education and clothing.

Among all the children in town, he was the only one who studied in the Russian school, a Jewish child was not welcomed and even other Jews didn't like it.

He was perfectly familiar with the Russian language and with Polish Yiddish and the holy language, knew all kinds of official matters and therefore was approached mainly in tax matters. He wrote the request or the appeal to the right authority. At first he made his living as a private teacher of those languages, later on he dealt with different home industries, mainly soap production.

Godel was a scholar who cherished the religious laws, wearing the *daytshmerish* [overly Germanic] clothing and his beard always done carefully with scissors (not shaved), following the French style, in which he was unique in town. Nevertheless he was treated with respect by all town Jews due to his profound knowledge of the gentiles' languages written and oral. He was treated the same way by the gentiles.

When Zionist movement was established in our town he headed it, taking part in all committees.

His wife, Lea, was a clever woman and was his main help in commercial business as well as in social life. She rejoiced every achievement and grieved for every failure encountered in the Zionist activity locally and out of town.

Their home was always open for any public activity especially Zionist. Godel was ready to help any public activity with advice or action at any time, even when this was not in accordance with his political opinion, as he understood the spirit and ambitions of the young generation.

During eradication they were within the last victims of towns people. They hid for a while in the forest, but suffered so much that they left the forest and reported to the Nazi murderers.

Reb Shmuelke Stokman

As the manager of towns "Hevra Kadisha", *Reb* Shmuelke Stokman did his work with no hesitation due to any difficulty or obstacle.

During the cholera plague, in WWI, he buried the dead according to Jewish law, and encouraged others to do the same in spite of the big risk of catching the disease, *Reb* Shmuelke was an energetic man with a great will to perform all the tasks he took upon himself.

At the beginning of WWII, the day the Germans captured the town and shot a young man, no one dared to bury him as the Germans forbid to bury the dead. *Reb* Shmuelke dared to address the head of the German police about this matter. He managed to submit his request in a way that beat Germans' pride and after short negotiation they permitted burial of the man according to Jewish custom. In his youth *Reb* Shmuelke was a grain dealer, and as an adult he opened a bakery at his home and made decent living out of it.

He was murdered in the Holocaust along with other Tarnogrod Jews.

Reb Shmuelke Stokman

Reb Zalke Melamed – The Doctor

He was an important man in our town, nevertheless he lived all his life in poverty and was forced to change his profession from time to time to make his living, and everything was very difficult for him. From watchmaker he turned to be a teacher and here also he faced many difficulties and turned to other occupations as Matzot baker etc.

At the time a doctor was needed, they didn't go directly to the doctor but called the doctor to *Reb* Zalke. *Reb* Zalke, being full of *chesed* [kindness], would accompany the doctor to the patient.

As time passed *Reb* Zalke learned the profession from the doctor and later on even substituted for him, visiting patients and writing prescriptions according to which the local pharmacy prepared the drugs. Doctorate became his main occupation on which he made his living. During the cholera plague in WWI, he was the only medical expert in town and did his work without considering the danger and immense overworking.

As a Chasid he had special mental life, in his youth he was part of Sandez Chasidim and was among those who went to visit the Rabbi Chaim and spent the holidays there. Rabbi Chaim was the *Admor* of Sandez also known as "*Divrei Chaim.*"

When the *Admor* passed away *Reb* Zalke learned truth and integrity from his son Rabbi Baruch Halberstam, the *Admor* of Gorlitz, and was one of his devoted followers.

Reb Zalke was sharp, open minded and vital till old age and till his last day was devoted to the Rabbi and kept visiting him. When Rabbi Baruch died he followed his son Rabbi Tzvi-Hirsh of Rudnik praising him for his Torah knowledge and greatness.

Shneur the "Litvak"

One day, many years before WWI started, on a sunny day a man named Shneur came to Tarnogord, he was 40-50 years old entered *Beit Hamidrash* and stayed there for several years living, eating sleeping and learning there.

He was a weird man in his behavior, clothing and character, and made his living out of the support and charity he received.

His appearance was repulsive, he was short, chubby with a wild beard, hair and side curls. Was shortsighted and very sloppy but was a diligent Torah scholar and knew Scriptures Talmud and Jewish law adjudicators. Day and night he would study Torah.

When speaking Yiddish he had typical Lithuanian accent, and therefore was known as "Shneur the Litvak."

Somewhere he had wife and daughter whom he left. Once his only daughter – Rivkale, came to visit him and he was very happy to see her, she stayed with him for a while in *Beit Hamidrash.*

One day he saw children playing in the street instead of learning and decided to do something. He addressed the children and somehow convinced them to enter *Beit Hamidrash* and taught them Torah and *Gmara* for several months.

Later on, for some unknown reason, the group separated and only few of them continued studying and remained *Beit Hamidrash* students.

This man named Shneur, the same way he appeared out of nowhere to Tarnogrod, so did he disappear without leaving any trace.

Chana the Half Deaf and Dumb

"The Deaf Chana" – that is how people called her, was a big and strong woman with hands of a boxer, worked all her life very hard and lived in poverty.

Her husband was Efraimke the drummer who earned a small amount of money playing during each wedding held in town. He ate to be full only from wedding to wedding.

Chana was the one who provided for their home, her main job was kneading. She was kneading the dough for the town bakers. Day and night, cold or hot, she was running from one baker to the other, from one side of town to the other one and in addition to that she was carrying different stuff out of which she stitched sacks – a side job she performed between one kneading to the other.

During the whole week she didn't sleep in her bed, but took sleeping breaks somewhere on the hard floor.

Only on Saturday she slept in her bed but because of her exhaustion and deafness, she accidentally strangled her baby with her heavy weight.

She kept this way of life till old age and life was not kind to her, until one day she suddenly dropped dead in the middle of the street.

[Pages 160-165]

Trifling Stories About Prominent Men in Our Town

by Moshe Lemmer (London)

Translated by Joseph Lipner

Rabbi Koppel Lukower

One of the prominent Jews who graced our town Tarnogrod was Rabbi Koppel Lukower. He lived all his days in the village of Lukow and was buried in Tarnogrod.

Legend tells us:

One day the priest gathered all the farmers in the surrounding areas and commanded them not to buy the *Hametz*, the bread and other leavened food, from the Jew Koppel before Passover. What did Rabbi Koppel do? On the afternoon of the day before Passover, he opened all the doors of his store and announced: All leavened foods which I have in my possession may they be *Hefker K'afra D'ara*—ownerless and available to everyone like the dust of the earth. Then all the village farmers gathered to take this ownerless food for themselves. In that moment pouring rain fell. The water surrounded the entire area and for the eight days of Passover no one could reach the Rabbi Koppel's store.

And legend also says:

Every Tuesday, market day in Tarnogrod, Rabbi Koppel would come to town. One time it happened that a village woman from Lukow, while bartering about the price with a Jewish storekeeper, fell down and died. The farmers gathered to take revenge from the Jews. The news reached Rabbi Koppel. He hurried to the store of the Jew, kneeled on the floor, bent over the non-Jewish woman and called out with a commanding voice, "Get up, Kashya!" Suddenly, a miracle happened. The woman got up on her feet and looked all around her with confused glances. A roar of admiration rose from the crowd, which quietly dispersed.

That much is legend.

When I was in Berlin, I came across a German book. In it, I read about the Council of the Four Lands that gathered in Lublin to choose an emissary to travel to Rabbi Koppel and ask him to work to have the Pope in Rome influence the Polish government to nullify an evil decree about Poland's Jewish residents. This book relates that Rabbi Koppel traveled to Rome and succeeded in his task.

The Seer of Lublin was Rabbi Koppel's grandson.

The *tzadik* Rabbi Chaimel Sandzer was born in Tarnogrod. His mother passed away and was buried in our town.

Rabbi Jakob Teomim

They tell the following story about Rabbi Jakob Teomim, a rabbi in our town. In one of the meetings of the community members who deliberated about building stores and a synagogue, the members suggested building the synagogue first. Then the rabbi stood up and opposed them: "The people of Israel need to make a living. Therefore, we should build stores and afterwards build the synagogue."

And so it was.

Rabbi Gedalia Mendeles and Rabbi Reb Leibele Teicher

The scene in the study hall remains in my memory: Rabbi Gedalia Mendeles decided to ask forgiveness from Rabbi *Reb* Leibele Teicher for the embarrassment caused by words that had escaped from his mouth.

The study hall was filled with people. Rabbi Gedalia took off his shoes and approached the rabbi wearing his socks. Tears choked his throat as he turned to him. "Rabbi, forgive me for the pain I caused you." The rabbi pulled Rabbi Gedalia Mendeles towards him with by the corner of his clothes and said, "I forgive!"

Rabbi Yonah-Ber Who Makes Do With Little

Who in Tarnogrod did not know Rabbi Yonah-Ber? He was a Torah scholar who lived in awe of Heaven. He wrote many comments on the Talmud and lived all his life in poverty. He lived on meager bread and drank only a little water. When I once came to his house I heard his wife crying out that their neighbor had moved the boundary marker between their properties. Rabbi Yonah-Ber closed his ears and said as follows: "Do not curse, we need to forgive a Jew who sins and ask G-d to forgive him. Nothing will happen if we have a little less land."

The Father of Getsel the Water-Carrier

Aharon-Isaac, who built and fixed roofs, the father of Getsel the water-carrier, was a sort of primitive philosopher. He was not satisfied with dry laws. Instead, he always tried to find in the stories of the Torah an explanation more appealing to human intelligence. He exercised that intelligence when he taught *midrash* or the weekly Torah portion to a group of men each Sabbath.

I remember that one Yom Kippur he dozed off in the study hall in the middle of the prayers. When they woke him and told him that on Yom Kippur one must not sleep he answered them as follows: "Don't worry about me, I know what I'm doing. For in Heaven they first judge the "heads of the fish:" the rabbis, the righteous ones, the synagogue officers and the rich. Today, those people need to ask for forgiveness and atonement. But beggars like me are the last to be judged, and the Master of the Universe also does not waste much time on their fate – beggars they were and beggars they will be. For this reason I will not tarry too long in my prayers."

The Doctor Rabbi Zalk Lipiner

Everyone knew him in the final years of his life as a doctor also. I too saw him primarily in this role, until the following happened and I got to see another side to him:

Early morning, at four o'clock, I got out of bed to go the study hall. Outside it was pitch black, and the cold chilled my bones. I was the only one in the street, other than the moon traveling along the paths of heaven above my head. Suddenly my ears noticed a voice crying, and the voice was coming from inside the study hall walls.

Trembling overtook me. I stood quietly and I could not muster the strength to enter. Only after a few moments had passed did I overcome the dread and fear and I entered. And what did my eyes see? By a table sat Rabbi Zalka and in front of him was an open book. From his eyes tears dripped down, wetting the book's pages.

I waited for a moment that seemed to go on endlessly until he calmed a little and I asked him:

"*Rebbe*, what happened?"
Silence prevailed. He looked at me with his pure gaze and in a paternal voice replied:
"A great disaster has occurred. I received the news during the night that the Rabbi of Gerlitz has passed away from this world."
At that moment I understood the hidden inner life of Rabbi Zalka the doctor.

Rabbi Chaimel the Kosher Butcher Who Loved Israel

I remember one day, about two weeks before Passover, the roads were full of mud from melting snow, and I saw Rabbi Chaimel the kosher butcher dragging his feet and walking slowly. He travelled on foot from the village of Plusy to Tarnogrod. On his face was not the slightest shadow of resentment. He walked along deep in thought. What did Rabbi Chaimel, the lover of Israel, think about? Where to get money to bake matzo? Other expenses for the coming holiday? No one suspected he had thoughts like this. Everyone knew that Rabbi Chaimel did not worry about himself. All of his worries were about how to supply the poor of our town with matzo. Suddenly he heard a voice call, "Rabbi Chaimel!" A carriage drawn by four horses pulled up next to him. Inside, wrapped in his mantle, sat Rabbi Avraham'le Fabricant.

Rabbi Chaimel climbed up and got into the carriage. He greeted Rabbi Avraham'le with, "Shalom Aleichem and Rabbi Avraham'le answered "Aleichem Shalom." Rabbi Avraham'le looked at his clothes and his torn and dirty boots. After several moments Rabbi Chaimel broke his silence and said:

"You know, Avraham'le, I do not envy you. You do not really enjoy the pleasures of this world. You do not experience enjoyment like I do. After the frost outside and in my house all day, I go to the study hall and sit by the fire to warm my bones. You cannot even imagine the pleasure I get."

There was always a light smile playing on Rabbi Chaimel's face. He was never resentful and he never complained. Only one time on Tisha B'ab when we, the young men of the study hall, were talking about the destruction of the Temple, when the hunger was bothering us and we were counting down the hours to the end of the fast, the door opened and Rabbi Chaimel entered. He went to the bookcase and took out a book. Deep in thought as usual, he opened the book, looked into it and tears fell from his eyes.

This was the first time I saw him sad. For a whole hour he sat and cried and afterwards closed the book and left the study hall deep in sad thoughts.

Itche Pirsht – Religion and Enlightenment

Itche Pirsht was known as a man of Torah, and the Enlightment was also not foreign to him. His favorite book was the Torah with the Malbim's commentary, which never left his table.

As though he were still alive he stands before my eyes, like the first time we met. I did not knock on his door, as was the custom among Europeans, but I just opened it and went straight to his room. I held out my hand and greeted him in Russian. And he, a tall man with the face of an intellectual, responded to me in Russian. Our conversation concerned literature, Tolstoy and Dostoyevsky, and when I parted from him he went to his bookcase and took out the book, "The History of Religious Philosophy in Israel," by Dr. Bernstein. He held the book out to me and warned me not to tell anyone that I got it from him.

The Enlightenment did not stop him from remaining a religious man all his life, praying in the *Shinovar Shtibl*. Once a year he travelled to the great rabbi the *Admor* from Sidigora. He made his living writing pleas to Russian courts and sometimes appeared personally to defend a Jewish defendant. The Russians and Poles also honored him.

He died before the First World War. If my memory does not deceive me, he died on Friday afternoon before the Sabbath.

An hour after his death I met in the town square the son-in-law of the rabbi, Yankele, and he turned to me and said as follows:

"I was always afraid of death, but now I'm not afraid any more. Why should I be afraid? If I die, I will be together with Itchele."

His brother, Eli, had an entirely different personality. He was educated in the lap of Russian culture. Before he came to our town he was sympathetic to the movement for assimilation, and in his early days in Tarnogrod too he joined the Russian and Polish intelligentsia. But after a little while he joined the youth of our town in the Zionist movement and dedicated all his energy and initiative to the movement. He became interested in Hebrew and Yiddish literature and helped us in our struggle, internally and externally, against the Polish anti-Semites.

Eli Pirsht was a Jew dedicated to the national problems of the Jews and was proud of his Judaism.

Before I left Tarnogrod to travel to Germany I went to his house to say my farewells. When I asked him not to forget to answer my letters, his eyes closed for a moment and afterwards, he turned his gaze as though he were surveying the table and suddenly his head fell to the table and he broke out in deafening sobs. His wife Merimel approached him to calm him down and tears were in her eyes too.

He wrote me every week. He did not finish his last letter, because he died of a stroke, a sudden death.

That was in 1929.

Godel Wetscher

Godel Wetscher was the only Jew in our town who went to a Russian school and he obtained much knowledge in two languages: Russian and Polish. Hebrew, he had learned from his father, Moshe the *shamash*, who was a grammarian who sent his son to a secular school. The Jewish people in town grumbled and complained, but he paid no attention. He trusted his son not to fail in his faith. And so it was. Godel did not leave the path of his fathers and remained faithful to the Jewish religion. On his days off from school he supported himself with his knowledge of the two languages, teaching Russian and Polish to the daughters of the Jews of Tarnogrod.

He was active in the Zionist movement and regarded it as the only way forward.

From the rumors that came to me after the war I learned that he and his family were among the last Jews of the village who were murdered by the vile Nazis.

Getsel Richter

Getsel Richter did not attend the secular school. Nevertheless he knew Russian and Polish better than those educated in these languages. He also wrote fluent Hebrew. He excelled in history and geography.

After World War I he was elected secretary of a certain Polish committee, which had been founded at that time.

One time he came to me confused and undecided and told me about a speech given two days before by a Polish anti-Semite, who asked the farmers in his audience to drown the Jews. Getsel showed me the protest he wrote to the Polish government in

Warsaw. It was a ten-page essay. I showed it to the principal of the Polish school, who admired his style and said that the person who wrote it deserved to be a Polish author.

I spent a lot of time with him. Few days passed when I did not visit his house or store and enjoyed his conversation. When he was sick, too, I visited him and sat by his bed many hours.

One time, when I opened the door of his house and I saw him lying down with wide open eyes, I wanted to leave, but he felt I was there and he asked me to sit by his side. His breaths could be heard rising and falling heavily and he started talking about the highest mountains in the world. Two hours later his soul left him.

[Pages 166-168]

Town of My Youth

by S. Chaper

Translated by Zvika Welgreen

Tarnogrod, town of my youth, I was not with you during the Holocaust, during your occupation by Hitler's troops, didn't hear the groaning of my brothers and sisters, of my childhood friends and acquaintances, when the human beast preyed mercilessly upon you. We lived remotely and knew too late our towns' disaster. The horrors and terror were beyond comprehension. Since then and forever, the terrible nightmare and its cause pursue us and does not give us piece of mind and we shall never forget you, both your life and your death.

22 *Cheshvan* [November 2, 1942], the day of final elimination of the Jewish life in our town, is the day we commemorate you, to remember and remind for eternity what happened to the people of our town, whose lives were destroyed lawlessly by the murderers of our people.

I shall not forget you, Tarnogrod, the Torah schools and the magnificent synagogue, the streets and alleys, during weekdays and holy days, when you transformed from one shape to another.

From Passover to *Shavuot* the period was half grieving, in spite that everything came alive after the cold winter, we didn't dare to joy, to walk in the green fields, except for one day, *Lag ba-Omer* [minor holiday celebrated on the 33rd day after Passover]. And then from *Shavuot* to 17th of *Tammuz* and again a break till Tisha be-Av, the day when tables and chairs in the school when turned upside down and we sat, youngsters with white bearded men, to mourn the destruction of the Temple and the deportation from our land.

When *Nachamu Shabbat* [Sabbath of Consolation, the Sabbath following Tisha be-Av, the date Jews mourn the destruction of the Temples in Jerusalem] arrived, everything returned to its normal course. Weddings took place; we travelled in the fields and bathed in the towns' river, which "demanded" human life each year.

And then came the month of *Elul* and sound of the *Shofar* [ram's horn blown during the high holy days] was heard from the *Beit Hamidrash* [house of study], the town transformed again, the atmosphere of the ten days wrapped homes and streets and Tarnogrod Jews asked forgiveness from each other, pardoned each other and had a new start.

Sukkot [holiday celebrating the harvest of Israel and commemorating the Israelites' 40 years of wandering in the desert] arrived, the longest and most complicated holiday. Our ancestors embraced the Torah commandment: "be happy during your holy days". During this holy day, the school walls noticed wine drinkers, but not a single Jew lost his mind due to heavy drinking. Yet the wine did its trick -- and Jews sang and danced, each *Hasidic* group to its tunes.

How phenomenal and deep is the fact that the joy embedded in the calendar is connected to what brings to the people of Israel the high tension and the upmost solemnity - the Torah.

The holy days were the partition between year periods. In *Elul*, cold winds began to blow and seriousness found its place in people hearts. Right after *Sukkot* the long winter arrived and with every passing day the frost and livelihood worries intensified.

During long nights we sat at the *beit hamidrash*, as there was no other place to spend the time. We counted the weeks from "Bereshit" [Genesis 1:1-6:8] to "Vayechi" [Genesis 47:28-50:26] the *Gemara* [record of the discussions about the *Mishnah*] was opened in front of us but our minds were elsewhere. Each period had its problems, until we got older and began thinking and then to action in Zionist activities.

Deep in my heart remains the memory of the rabbi's house, which I entered at the age of three until I grew up at the age of seventeen. The rabbi's grandson, Elezar, was the same age as myself, we were born the same day, and together were brought to the *heder* [small Jewish elementary school] for the first time, and at the same time we left one *heder* and entered another one. Friendship and love tied us together during the whole time. I loved Elezar's parents, Moshele and Malkale, as town people called them, and their twelve children: Beila-Sara, Elezar, Chantzi, Yekhezkel, Mottel, Etaleh, Hershl, Roza, Shosha, Tzvia, Saul-Joel and Itzik.

I learned with Elezar from the age of three until thirteen at the same *heders* and then we continued to study together at *beit hamidrash*. I had to wake him up every day at 4 a.m. and in order not to make too much noise we invented a system: when going to bed Elezar tied a string to his arm and left its other end outside of the door, a delicate pull of the string was enough to wake him up.

When I was seventeen I dared to show up at *Beit Hamidrash* wearing a stiff collar, and then, on the second night of *Shavuot*, Moshele, Elezar's father, approached me and took off the collar without me feeling anything. I was offended and decided not to visit their home anymore and since then avoided *Beit Hamidrash* studies as well.

I read a lot of non-religious books and joined the Zionist movement and participated in one of the first groups which prepared itself mentally and practically for the bold step of pushing the end and leaving the Diaspora before the arrival of the Mashiach.

Meanwhile, Elezar moved to Tomashov, far from our town, and during this whole period we didn't have the chance to meet each other. But one day, before I made *aliyah* [act of immigrating to Israel], when everything was already packed and ready for the voyage, the door opened and Elezar showed up.

Youth Group

From the right: Yona Fiter, Aharon Teicher (lives in Israel), Hersh Teicher, Shlomo Fink, Yosef Zucker, Avraham Mahler (in Israel), Shalom Schwartz-Teicher, Moshe Shettfeld (in US), Efraim Kenigsberg (in US), Eliezer Teicher (in Israel).
Truth and vision, innocence and dream, passion of youth, where its prose is poetry, and dream become reality, where its trope* is reality, and reality overcomes trope. Trusting in good, with the hope of fighters, tried by themselves to find their way in life.

He came to say goodbye, was excited and said: "I just wanted to see you once more…" Did he have a feeling that we would not see each other ever again? Only God knows. The fact that he dared to come showed his deep and sincere friendship to me, as most of the town's Jews and especially the Rabbi's family opposed my *aliyah*.

The old Rabbi, who was authorized by the government, refused to sign my birth certificate declaring openly: "I shall do my utmost to stop you from going to Ishmael land…" finally he was forced to sign within the duty of his position but departed angrily from me.

His grandson, Elezar, who was an orthodox Jew and devoted to his family tradition, needed lot of courage to come and say goodbye to me.

*Editor's note: Definition of trope used here is to mean: a figure of speech consisting of a word or phrase in a sense different from its ordinary meaning.

[Pages 169-170]

Cantors and Prayers

by Alter Zitz-Tishbi

Translated by Zvika Welgreen

Tarnogrod Jews highly appreciated their cantor *Reb* Itsik-Shaya as a good cantor. He prayed without notes but his prayer was overwhelming. Especially good were his prayers during the High Holidays such as "Kol Nidrei", "Shema Kolenu", "Unetaneh Tokef" or " HaAvoda". He was helped by the poets Yitzhak Shlomels, Moshele Shohet, Mechl Dudes, Eli-Elishas, and Yoseleh Megides, and others...

The cantor *Reb* Itsik-Shaya was famous in the whole area. On Yom Kippur night for Kol-Nidrei, many intellectual Christians came to the synagogue, to listen to the cantor and the choir. The Jews were proud of that.

Reb Itsik-Shaya was known as a loyal and honest man and all dowries were given to him to watch.

Cantors were a hobby for the Jews of the town. Whenever a Jew who stayed in Warsaw came to the town everyone wanted to hear from him about Sirota: How did he look? How did he sing? How many poets helped him? And so on.

It happened that the town Judge bought a gramophone with different albums.

In his apartment, a two-story building owned by Leib-Shimonhe would take out the gramophone to the second story balcony and played different songs. Once he played some recorded songs by Cantor Sirota.

The whole thing with the gramophone left a tremendous impression in the town, because this was the first time they heard a "playing box," but they were much more surprised hearing Sirota himself with his choir singing.

People didn't move until the singing ended at midnight. The next day everyone in the town was talking about it.

Those days another singer appeared in town, the Yeshiva student *Reb* Yoseleh, son-in-law of the *Gvir* [literally, rich man but can be used as a term of respect], *Reb* Naftali Sobol. He was gifted with a strong and pleasant voice and brought from his town of Zaklików a collection of tunes from different *Hasidic* trends. These were new melodies that were never heard in Tarnogrod. His songs were moving and the Hasidim were very pleased.

The wife of *Reb* Yoseleh was the only child of *Reb* Naftali the *Gvir* and he promised Yoseleh, as was common in those days, full economic "*aybik kest*" [support for the rest of his life]. He didn't have livelihood problems and sat all day in the "*shtibl*" [literally "little house" or "little room" which served as a house of prayer] of Sieniawa Hasidim and practiced the lovely tunes and melodies along with other yeshiva students. Among them were my brother Arele, Chaim Mahler, and others.

Eventually, *Reb* Yoseleh was considered as the best *ba'al-tefillah* [leader of prayers on special occasions] and was leading choir of "poets," musicians and music fans who learned music from him.

Yoseleh's name was famous in the town as a *ba'al-tefillah* who excites and touches his listener's heart with his warm prayer and his charming voice.

There was a difference between the Hasidim *ba'al-tefillah* and a cantor. *Reb* Yoseleh belonged to those *ba'al-tefillah* who were scholars as well as having a sweet voice like silver bell.

We couldn't have enough time counting all the *ba'al-tefillah* and cantors who served the *kehila* [jewish community] throughout time. The *kehila* didn't have special lists of all the cantors, rabbis and scholars. In this aspect, we were not unique.

As in all Polish towns, our town had many versions of cantorial music, ours was mainly free style which intended to stimulate admiration and fulfill a moral-religious role. Cantor's imagination played a crucial role in it by developing new melodies and versions by his inspiration.

Later on came Hasidim that hid the cantorial music along its numerous versions and tunes, claiming that the cantor emphasized his beautiful voice over the meaning of the words. On the other hand, this gave birth to new *Hasidic* liturgical music with popular cantors. Those were the *ba'al-tefillah* and the public liked their melodies and listened to them with great joy and willingness.

[Pages 171-172]

During the First World War

by Alter Zitz-Tishbi

Translated by Zvika Welgreen

It was in 1914.

Right in the first days after war broke, in spite of the Austrian army's victories, Tarnogrod Jews started preparations in case of enemy attack and were terrified.

Indeed Kaiser Frantz-Josef was well known for his sympathy for the Jews, but rumors spread that among his soldiers there were "*Sokals,*" Polish volunteers, and they were enemies of the Jews.

On top of that was the fear of the Russians, especially the Cossacks and the Circassians, known for their hatred of Jews and the sight of their faces and their clothing was enough to terrorize anyone.

Rough time was not far away.

And then one day, on Friday morning, a few lone riders were seen galloping through the town. Their appearance and clothing were strange and copper helmets were on their heads.

Before the people had sufficient time to look at them, they disappeared.

Very quickly a rumor spread quickly among the people: The "*Sokals*" had arrived. The news got to the *Beit Hamidrash* [house of study] and passed from person to person. Worshipers quickly removed their prayer shawls and the students stopped their study. Everyone prepared to run home.

They barely went out on the Lochow side street, when a company of soldiers appeared on horseback with drawn swords in their upraised hands.

There was exchange of fire that hit the enemy patrol and they were forced to retreat leaving behind some dead and wounded on the street.

The Russian soldiers chased them to the edge of town when they saw in the distance, a large army of the enemy preparing to attack, they turned back and took two peasants with their carts, loaded their wounded and killed and fled from the town.

It is difficult to imagine the panic that arose in the town, like a storm that went through them all. The shops were closed and everyone ran home to pack their belongings and run for shelter.

Where to?

Everyone ran to the synagogue, men, women and children from all over town came with their belongings. The great hall was full. Urgent sounds of prayers and reciting of Psalms was heard along with the children's screaming, adding to the loud noise of the crowd, sounding like a storm descending to groans, whispers and moans rising like a huge wave to the ceiling, shuttering all barriers.

And the voice of the Cantor broke into a bitter cry.

The crowed answered, crying in loud voices from the bottom of their hearts, "Please God save us! "

Suddenly from all corners of the town there appeared Austrian soldiers with guns in their hands. They came to the synagogue and ordered all the people to come out.

The women and children were released and ordered to return to their homes and all of the men were taken to the marketplace square. They were kept there surrounded by guards.

Without knowing the reason for their imprisonment, the Jews were full of fear. The men thought they were going to be killed and whispered the confessional prayer, sighing and crying.

The men were held until late afternoon when the army commander arrived to warn them that their detention was due to shooting at his soldiers and if any soldier is injured, the blame would fall on all Jews.

At the same time, he ordered all the shops to reopen and to be kept open on Shabbat for the benefit of the soldiers.

Rabbi *Reb* Arie-Leib Teicher allowed the desecration of Shabbat in this emergency and due to the command of the army.

Shabbat passed by and Tarnogrod Jews were alarmed again upon hearing that a Jew was arrested for hurting a soldier from the "patrol" who ran away from the shooting and was hiding in the yard of a Jew and was captured by the Russians. The Jew was blamed for calling the Russians and telling them that the enemy soldier was hiding in his yard.

This was an old Jew, Shmerleh Mahler, who gave an account of his actions and thought with complete innocence that his civil duty was to help the Russian authorities.

The old man stood before the military tribunal and Polish witnesses testified against him saying that they saw the Jew hurt the soldier. He was sentenced to death by shooting and was publically executed in the presence of the Polish citizens who rejoiced in the event, and for the Jews of Tarnogrod it was a day of grief and mourning.

[Pages 173-177]

The Power of the Cradle of Childhood

by Alter Zitz-Tishbi

Translated by Zvika Welgreen

Tarnogrod Jews condition was similar to the conditions in most of Poland's towns. Most of them lived in poorness and some in poverty. Shopkeepers and craftsmen.

Who can describe poverty!!

Who could find the correct description that will fully draw the profound suffering of Tarnogrod's poor people?! This would need a writers pen to describe, a crying pen as Jeremiah's, to fully describe the profound poverty.

But one thing only, strengthened their hearts and gave them vitality, that was their faith which encouraged them even on surly and wild days.

The faith in the future, in the afterlife, because "anyone of Israel has his place in the afterlife" and the righteous shall live by faith.

Merchants, peddlers and shopkeepers, supermarkets' owners, in which one could get a whole herring – although usually it was sold by its parts- and all other market needs of the town people, their main income was from Tuesday market day in which everyone took part.

The situation of the blue collar workers such as carriers, water carriers, tailors, shoemakers, bakers etc. was no different. With hard work they made their living and thanked God for that.

The shoemaker, the tailor, the wagoneer, the shopkeeper everyone found his place and was satisfied. One by learning a Gemara page, one *Mishnah* chapter, or simple Psalms, saying in private or in public.

Everyone by his class and the group he belonged to, Shas group, Misnayot group etc.

Raising children to be Torah scholars was the desire of every parent. The luxurious life was not the desire of Tarnogrod Jews. Only in one way could a Jew excel himself – by the fruits of learning.

Even the poorest people would take this burden upon themselves. Does anything else count when you consider such life fundamental basic.

The cheder, where children studied, was at the *melamed's* [religious school teacher's] house and served as bedroom, dining room, cooking and baking place as well. All of the furniture was placed along the walls.

At the center stood a large table around which the children sat close to each other.

The *Melamedim*

Most town's Jews share a common desire, that their children would learn and become rabbis, or at least *shochetim* [ritual slaughterers], or *dayanim* [rabbinical judges], any kind of profession related to religion, therefore there were many *melamedim* as well.

As a *melamed* prototype, one can describe *Reb* Leibeleh. A short, light colored haired Jew, known scholar, always occupied with deep thoughts. They said he asked too many questions.

Gemara with interpretation were taught in his *heder* and he tried to explain the lessons thoroughly. He explained the temple construction with its ritual objects. He drew us the Kohen's clothes with its bells, the forehead decoration, and the Menorah with its beautiful decorations.

Students who finished their studies at the *heder* went to continue learning at *Beit Hamidrash* [house of study] or the *shtibl* [literally "little house" or "little room" which served as a house of prayer] where they continued studying until they came to age and got married.

Upon leaving Leibeleh's *heder* I went to Shinovar Hasidim *Shtibl* and felt great responsibility while I was only 12 years old.

Some preferred *Reb* Leibeleh to *Reb* Senderel Melamed, in spite of the fact that he was scholar and questions about Kosher and non Kosher were placed with him, meat and milk problems, but *melamed* Reb Leibeleh topped him with his talent to explain and teach.

Pairs studied at *BeitHhamidrash* and at the *shtibl* and I have found as partner Yekhezkel Teicher, the Rabbi's grandchild. It was a great honor for me and I achieved it due to my knowledge and studiousness.

The contact with Yekhezkel went on for some years, I went to their home and sometimes I participated at morning in tea with milk drinking as it was accustomed for them daily before prayer. This was rabbi's wife Malkale's demand and it caused me sometimes unpleasant situations, meeting some girls who starred at me while I was shy and was afraid to look back. I avoided the situation whenever I could in spite of *Reb* Moshele, the Rabbi's son.

A while later another friend joined us – Yehoshua Schlechterman, a single child serious in his studies, very much spoiled by his parents who lived at the end of the town in a house surrounded by a big garden with many trees. We loved coming to this garden where we studied secular studies such as calculus and Russian language.

After a while I realized that studying at *Beit Hamidrash* was better for me as most of the scholars studied there: Binim-Mendel, Hersh Meir, Shmuel Fefer, Meir Ringer and others, so we went there and I managed to drag my father there as well, but we kept praying at the *shtibl*.

The "Shinovar *Shtibl*," in spite of being small, hosted about thirty prayers, but spread light and life all around and everything was done voluntarily.

The *gabbai* [person responsible for keeping ritual order and collection of dues] was chosen once a year and he was the *shamash* [synagogue caretaker] as well. He had to take care of cleaning the place, collect the *nedarim* [declaration or pledge] money, and prepare wood and oil for warming during winter, etc.

Sometimes money was needed to be sent to the rabbi. To charge everyone, prayers were forced to leave their tallit [prayer shawls] on Saturday and collect it on Sunday, paying according each one's ability.

When it was my father's duty to become the gabbai, he asked me to help collecting *nedarim* and on Friday I helped swiping the *shtibl*. It was an honor for me that my father was the *gabbai* and he was able to call people to read the Torah at his will.

Some known people prayed at the *shtibl*: *Reb* Naftali Wakslicht ("Yukter"), Gershon Apteker, whose son Chaim Rokach was among the first people to commit to Zionism in Tarnogrod and started reading secular books in spite of the strong opposition of his parents; Leib-Shimshon Wientraub, Yosef Mahler and his sons Yekhezkel and Chaim, the wagoneer Moshe Goldbaum (Moshe Punis), Wolf Herbstman and his son Baruch and others.

Yosef Kalkstein wanted to pray in the *shtibl* in honor of his father *Reb* Moshe in spite of the fact that being a wagoneer, he had to go twice a week to Zamo. He suffered as his seat was in the corner and the praying took a long time while he always wanted it to end quickly.

His desire was that his sons continue their studies at the Gemara *Melamedim* or at *Beit Hamidrash* but he didn't succeed and they, Yekhezkel and Libtche , became wagoneers as well.

Rabbi's aura influenced the day to day life at the shtibl, a group of Chasidim was much more than the sum of its individuals, a current like electricity connected the group's members in the bondage of *hevruta* [to study text with a partner].

A Chasid's most important time is when he forgets himself. In the *Chasidic* world, holidays had special effect. *Shavuot* meant the *shtibl* was purified and clean, green branches decorated the walls, the stage and the ark.

There was another kind of purity, inner purity, purification of the soul and cleaning the soul form all impurities it gathered during the whole year in order to enter clean and purified to the New Year.

Those were the *Yamim Noraim* [High Holy Days].

Before Yom Kippur a wagon with straw was brought and spread on the floor to make it easier to walk bare foot.

Purity is everything that surrounds people and cleanness means no insults or hard feelings among people. Chasidim were asking for forgiveness and forgiving each other.

Then *Sukkot* arrived, the longest holiday and the most complicated one and Chasidim took very seriously the specific Torah command – rejoice in your holidays.

The joyous climax was on Simchat Torah, which ended with a great feast in honor of the Torah. At that time *Reb* Chaimel Shohet was invited to pray "*Ata Hereta*" (you were shown). In spite of his sometimes hoarse voice, his prayer was special. His voice came out of his heart and entered sweetly other hearts.

Even towns girls entered the *shtibl* and stayed at the corners, next to the door as they were forbidden from taking part in the hakafot [processions] and were allowed to watch only. Then the boy's voices became stronger and livelier.

Sender the Blind

Sender was a special character, he was known as "Sender the blind" and no one knew how he was making his living, or when was he eating. At the shtibl he would be standing behind the fireplace, moving and praying.

When he lifted his eyebrows, white eyes were seen frightening the children.

Sometimes children were picking on him, he chased them and when he caught someone took his revenge, therefore frightening the rest.

Once a year he had special role, he had a whip with some strips with which he would whip anyone who fell down 39 whips. He was paid small change for his task.

Aharashkeh Papiroshnik

Aharashkeh got this name from his occupation as he made his living by producing cigarettes and selling them at the *beit hamidrash.*

He was holding the cigarettes in his pockets as it was forbidden by law. The boys were taunting him during the service. As *Tisha b'Av* mourning eased somewhat, men threw things in his beard and he struggled pulling them out along with his beard. The mourners stopped their praying and were laughing along with those who did it.

Reb Israel "Koko" - The Match Maker

He was a short Jew with a big beard, long eyebrows that shaded his glittering eyes, and he wore long *kapotah* [black coat] with big pockets in the back.

People said that his pockets were full of boy's and girl's addresses. While walking in the street, girls blushed and boys pretended to be serious so he would find them attractive.

Even *Beit Hamidrash* boys treated his with respect. Everyone hoped that one day he will be the one to find a spouse for them.

The Jewish town of Tarnogrod had many types of people, regular ones, day dreamers and those who were always engaged with day to day troubles, and it had a positive driving force for youngsters. Tarnogrod's youth was vibrant, excited, and hoping to get out of the small town and promote themselves to better life.

The Austrian army invaded and conquered the town. Along with the army, many Galician Jews came, among them liberal Jews with Zionist orientation. Two Galician sisters stood out, they established a restaurant where Zionist ideas were spread. At that time Chaim, Gershon Apteker's son came back from Tomashov where he studied. He fell for the liberal ideas as well. A group, out of *Beit Hamidrash* boys was established among them Shmuel Fefer, Meir Ringer and others.

Out of curiosity they started reading newspapers during the war. As scholars they could read. Youth groups were established. At first for the purpose of mutual help during the cholera plague. The group took an important part in saving people.

Upon Poland's independence many left Poland to Germany and Czech Republic. I did the same leaving to Czech Republic to Reichenberg, where I have worked and kept the idea of returning to Zion.

I had organized a Zionist group in Reichenberg and two years later, I went back to Poland and settled at Rzeszów along with my parents.

In Rzeszów I had opportunity to practice my Zionist ideas, but due to family matters I couldn't fulfill it and made *aliyah* only in the year 1935.

I didn't have the chance to bring all my family with me, my father Itzhak z"l, my brother Aharon z"l and my sisters Miriam Zilberzweig and Rosha Zilberzweig were killed by the Nazis.

The Jewish community in our town was destroyed. It was very difficult for me to accept that this happened and I shall not see my beloved ones and my dear town where I had spent my youth in the years of beautiful dreams and great hopes.

[Pages 178-179]

Celebrations and Children's Games

by Alter Zitz-Tishbi

Translated by Joseph Lipner

Parents did not throw birthday parties for the Jewish children of Tarnogrod. The children certainly did not receive presents and were not used to ready-made toys. Instead, they invented for themselves various games, amusements and toys that they made with their own hands according to their own inventions.

On the holiday of *Shavuot*, you could see in the windows of all houses where there were children multi-colored pictures on biblical subjects, such as: the binding of Isaac, the giving of the Torah, the joy of bringing the first fruits, the exodus from Egypt, David and Goliath, Ruth and Naomi, and similar topics. Some children drew present-day village scenes: the digging of a well in the middle of the marketplace, the customary way farmers ate, galloping horses harnessed to a wagon and many other things.

These were simple things and they were also magical in the same measure. Yekhezkel, the son of Sineleh the tinsmith, especially excelled in creating these pictures. He was a thin and skinny young man like his father, his fingers long and thin. From right after Passover he began to work at drawing and the rest of the children learned from him. Their sole concern was where they would get money to buy a sharp blade and various paints.

The children devoted a lot of attention to preparing for Hanukah, making dreidels from the lead that they took out of the sacks of sugar, in order to melt down the lead and pour it into a wooden mold.

It took the children a long time to manufacture "*kvitlech*" [lit. notes or slips — to be used in a card game] so that they could play cards with them. Onto thick dark paper they glued white paper with the numbers showing in ink.

The children also hand-made the noisemakers and "Haman-klappers" for Purim. They had a wealth of experience with the game of buttons and nuts on Passover and Sukkot.

Young life filled with longing, lost forever, forever?!

To Far Away Places

It was not an easy thing, the worry the Jews of Tarnogrod had about how to raise their children in Torah and the fear of Heaven. That worry became seven times harder when the time came to draft their children into the army.

Although "the law of the land is the law," how is it possible to raise sons who are learned, keepers of the commandments and having reverence for Heaven, and then to send them off to far away places where they could not keep their Judaism: eating kosher, keeping the Sabbath, not shaving their beards, an act that by itself violated five separate prohibitions. There was no way out other than to take every means of obtaining release from the draft. There were various possibilities: physical unfitness, accomplished by means of various discomforts such as lack of sleep or fasting, which caused weight loss; intentional disfigurement, such as pulling out teeth, cutting off a finger, and the like; or defection, by crossing over the nearby border into Galicia. Upon defecting, the son lost his connection with the family, and the government imposed a fine of 300 *rubles* on the parents.

When it came time for my big brother Ahrele to report to the army he chose to defect, and my father was required to pay the fine. But he did not have the ability to pay the sum of 300 *rubles*. The governing authorities chose market day, when the shop was full of merchandise that had been bought on credit especially for that day. Then the collectors came with a policeman and destroyed and emptied the entire store.

This completely impoverished us and because of this my father was forced to travel to America to get his footing and fix the situation. He stayed there until the end of the First World War.

Sitting from right: Rabbi Yitzhak Zitz, his daughter Miriam Silberzweig with her two children, Chanaleh Zitz
Sitting from right: Alter Zitz — lives in Haifa — and his sister Rosa Silberzweig

[Pages 180-191]

Mere Figures

Meir Ringer

Translated by Tina Lunson

Edited by Lorraine Rosengarten and Tom Merolla

There are sources that allow us to determine when Tarnogrod was established as a settlement. It is accepted by the Jews that the town arose in very old times but in general the Jews in our town had their own way of reckoning time: So many years before the great fire, so many years after the great fire. Large catastrophes remained etched in the memory for a long time and served as dates for further chronological events.

Chaim Tsibelkale

Its age was characteristic of the town: Old houses, old ideas, little power of conception and naive enthusiasm for newly discovered beauty.

And such was Chaim Tsibelkale.

He was a small, thin little Jew with a long, hoary gray beard; the teacher of the young children's *heder* [school-house] who lived his whole life in peace and quiet and never traveled outside the town until the day came when he had to travel with his son Eli Meir for conscription in Bilgoraj.

Upon his return he gathered his pupils and with great ardor told them about the wonders that he had seen on the on his six-mile journey to Bilgoraj. The point is, he had only now realized how large the world is. He had never imagined that beyond Tarnogrod the world was so large and so wonderfully beautiful.

This same picture, this same kindergarten teacher's ardor, was still in my mind years later after I had left the town and perceived the wonder of the larger world. The naiveté of those people lives forever in our hearts and just as we use wood to keep a fire burning, so we remember those naïve people with the belief that the world is full of greatness and wonder.

Baruch Bank

Who of us does not remember Bazshe Bank?

Properly speaking he was not a Tarnogroder, not born and not reared in Tarnogrod. He was only a guest there for a while, passing through. Yet he managed during the short time of his stay in Tarnogrod to make such deep ties with the people of the town, especially with the youth, that we felt he was our own, a person from our town.

He came to us at the beginning of the First World War. He came as a refugee from Shinova and was dressed in the clothing of a yeshiva bocher [yeshiva student]. That was his appearance, his dress. He became a pupil in the Oshvyentsimer yeshiva and used to sit with the other study-house youths and study, appearing to be an observant Jew. But even then he possessed secular knowledge, had been infected with the *haskole* [Jewish enlightenment movement] currents of that time. In secret, he continued that study and gained secular knowledge and education.

In secret he also found a language with the Tarnogrod youth, who had felt the thirst for knowledge and had begun to take the first steps toward the goal of developing a cultural society in the town. He helped us a great deal then, cooperating with us in word and deed to revive and to create the cultural atmosphere in our town.

And later, now in Berlin, he still felt connected with us, and with our cultural institutions and often helped us financially as well.

Bazshe Bank died suddenly after the war, of a heart attack in America. We, his comrades and friends, all who saw him at work and felt his bond with our town and with the ideals of our youth, will never forget him and always hold his memory dear.

Getzel Wassertreger

Really, in Tarnogrod, besides Getzel Wassertreger, there was another Getzel who was very much the honorable proprietor, a Jewish scholar, who could write in Yiddish, Hebrew and Polish too. So no one ever called him just Getzel but by his family name too, Richter, or Getzel Faliks. But it was enough to say just Getzel and young and old knew who was meant. Getzel Wassertreger was unique among us. There are not many such Getzels in God's creation.

Getzel was born into the poverty of Aharon Itsik Dakhbashleger, with whom he grew up hungry and going around in rags until someone had mercy on him and gave him something to put on. No one ever paid tuition for him to go to cheder. Nevertheless he learned to pray. What else would a Jew like him need to know?

He also had no time to learn a trade. Already in his early childhood years he had to go out to earn money and so became a water carrier.

He was still almost a child the first time he put a pair of collar-straps with two wooden cans on his narrow shoulders, went to the well, filled the cans with water and carried them off to the wealthier houses. So he began to earn a livelihood and that is how he always stayed.

In Tarnogrod there were other water carriers as well. But it would be a mistake to take Getzel for one of them. Getzel was completely different, even though he carried water the same way. For when he went around with the buckets, full or empty, that was not the only way he spent the time: He sang the psalms for the whole year as he walked and had a good word for every Jew that he met, reminding him of his ancestors, knowing exactly when every *yahrzeit* [anniversary of a death] was. He was literally a living calendar.

Getzel loved people and everyone loved him. He was always happy, always content, even when he had nothing in his pocket and had to fast a little. In summer he generally did not wear any shoes, he went around barefoot. In winter he bound his feet with rags, as he was accustomed to doing from his early childhood.

He had a fine folksy humor and used to find a joke with which he could make little of wealth, not to be overcome by never having known the taste of new clothes. He was happy with his lot.

People in town used to whisper that Getzel was a *lamed-vovnik*, one of the thirty-six righteous people on whose merit the world exists. Jews were very careful not to speak about this openly, so that Getzel would not be redeemed and so would have to, God forbid, depart from this world.

Kuni-Leml - The Tarnogrod Job

He was called Aharon, but very few people knew his real name, had already stopped using his family name, because everyone called him Kuni Leml.

He was the watchman for the poorhouse and busied himself with the poor and sick residents of that place, and had to be ever ready to intercede in the quarrels among the crazy people, the permanent and temporary residents of the poorhouse.

He was also the one who set up the taharah bret [the board on which the dead would be washed and purified] with all the accessories, and watched over the bodies so that they would not be alone before burial.

Besides that he was also a locksmith. He was called to houses to repair a lock or iron, tin and wooden casks, or to fit a key.

Every Friday morning he went from door to door collecting donations. Otherwise he would shame the holy *Shabbos* and, heaven forbid, starve along with his wife and children.

He went around hungry all week, never complaining. He silently bore his deep grief over the horrible death of his two grown sons. With that same stoic calm and quiet he worked around his wife Shifra, who had become blind. No one ever heard a sigh from him, no complaints about his bitter fate.

If *Reb* Levi Yitzhak of Berditchev were alive then and the Ruler of the universe ordered Kuni Leml to a Rabbinic Court and laid out all his errors before him, Kuni Leml would win the case. His sufferings were not smaller than Job's. But Kuni Leml had never made any errors.

Poor yet strong Kuni Leml! You did not heed the warning from Zalke Melamed; the doctor of our health committee while the cholera was raging. He warned every sick person not to drink any water. Kuni Leml, while he was sick, had his wife draw water from the well and he swallowed one bucket after another. But despite all predictions he got well and went on living in want, torment and loneliness, which he bore with such extraordinary heroism.

On the day that Kuni Leml departed this world, the gates of all the seven heavens opened wide and there was a commotion in the world above; angels and saints came out to welcome the great saint who had come from the world below before even the slightest sin, who had with such strength carried all the troubles and not complained. With great honor, the angels led him straight into the bright Garden of Eden.

The World to Come

Lipele The Shoemaker

The Talmud teaches us: "All Israel has a portion in the world to come, for it is written: all your people are righteous."

A relevant story:

Lipele the shoemaker, a small, thin Jew; a plain and simple person who still possessed a great heart and that heart was full of love for God and of the great desire to do something in the world so that, when the time came, he would not go into the next world with empty hands and empty pockets.

One ordinary weekday afternoon, Lipele stood up from his shoemaker's bench, picked up the two empty wooden buckets and went to the well to bring water for the needs of his household.

Near the well stood the house of Itsik the elementary teacher, my *rebbe*, with whom I was then studying in cheder.

Itsik Melamed, already elderly, a very revered Jew, used to go every *Shabbos* and holiday to study the commentaries with other elderly Jews who were artisans.

Those people with whom he studied approached Itsik Melamed with great respect and reverence. Lipele was also among those attendees and, usually, when he went to the well, he would leave the buckets outside and go in to visit Itsik Melamed for a pinch of snuff and to listen while we, the young pupils, sat and studied Torah.

But one such afternoon Lipele stayed with us in *heder* longer than ever, listening attentively to what the *rebbe* was studying with us.

After a while Lipele, with great humility, turned to Itsik Melamed:

"*Rebbe*, please, tell me, how can a soft-hearted Jew like me merit the World to Come? I cannot learn Torah, I don't have the opportunity to pray or recite psalms frequently because of my livelihood, which takes up all my time. I don't have the means to give charity, because I am a common Jew myself. So what can I possibly do to merit a bit of the World to Come?"

He stood twisting around for a while and then added, "*Rebbe*, tell me, is this a good thing that I do? Say I walk on the street and I see two pieces of straw lying on the ground, one on top of the other, like a cross. I cannot pass them by unless I am careful not to disturb them. Am I right?"

After thinking for a while, Itsik Melamed answered with these words:

"What you do with the straws is a very good thing. That you want to do the other good things, but you do not have the possibility of doing them, you should know that, to the Master of the Universe the point is the intention, the good will. For the Eternal such things are considered as *mitsvos* performed."

When the *rebbe* finished speaking the room was so quiet that we could hear the buzzing of the flies. Such sighs of relief tore from the childish hearts. They joined him in the great joy of knowing that he had found his portion in the World to Come.

Lipele straightened himself up and left the *heder* happily.

When later in *heder,* we studied about Jacob our ancestor's beautiful dream about the ladder that stood on the ground and whose top reached the heavens; Lipele's exultation came to mind. When I was older and encountered the dream of "a ladder set up on the earth, and the top of it reached to heaven," I saw even more clearly the comparison to the lovely figure of that simple, salt-of-the-earth Jew who had, in his longing for the World to Come, raised himself up to the level of "his head reaching into the heavens".

Peysakhl the Sacrifice

The goat has always been surrounded with a special feeling among Jews. More than other animals, the goat has brought out a warm attitude. Many stories and songs are interwoven with the motif of the goat.

In our *shtetl* too the goat occupied a special place, became almost a piece of the history of the town. Especially interesting is the history of the goat that had a special name among us:

"Peysakhl the Sacrifice".

Who among us does not remember Yosef Leibeles? He was a kind Jew, a wagon driver, a jokester. He owned two wagons and three or four horses and used to take long trips with them, driving back and forth with merchandise from the Tarnogrod merchants to other, far-off towns.

He watched over his horses like the eyes in his head. And his horses were connected to him, expressed love for him and it even seemed that they understood his language. They never strayed from the path, they went wherever Yosef Leibeles indicated with the reins, and served him faithfully.

Yosel Leibeles also saw to it that a nanny goat was always part of his household. A nanny goat, he said, is like a second mother. She gives milk and from milk one can make many things, to wit, sour cream, buttermilk, cheese, butter and from those all kinds of other good things.

A nanny goat could also do the favor of giving birth from time to time to a little goat, sometimes also a he-goat. This was no small heritage, because if a nanny goat belonged to the category "eat and contribute", the he-goat was simply an "eat and contribute nothing", a sponger and a mischievous fellow as well, who only makes trouble, and who needs him? It happens that when a holiday came around, he was slaughtered and people had a jolly holiday with him.

A he-goat was born at our Yosel Leibeles too and it seemed that he would wait to slaughter him until Pesach. But his tongue stumbled in speaking, and he was caught out with a wrong word. Instead of saying that he would slaughter him on Pesach, he was understood to say that he would be a sacrifice for Pesach.

He did not have to do anything else.

His words were repeated to the *rebbe*, who promptly sent the beadle to bring Yosel Leibeles to him and announced:

First, that from today forward, no one could slaughter the he-goat. He would live as long as the Master of All Worlds gifted him with years.

Second, the he-goat could do whatever his heart desired in the town, and no one could beat him, or lay a hand on him, to say nothing of a stick.

Since that day Yosel Leibeles has not been one to envy. But the whole town became involved as well.

The he-goat knew his way around and knew where to go, sometimes to a roof on which grass grew; sometimes to a window where potted plants were set out. Sometimes it pleased him to go to a basket of apples in the middle of the market, to baskets of cabbage, or potatoes, and the poor market-stall sellers were afraid to chase him away, and with pounding hearts had to watch as the he-goat played them.

No one dared to raise a hand to him.

Quite a bit of time went by and the he-goat never stopped making trouble and creating anguish for the people of the town. Until the day came when thank God may His Name be blessed, finally had mercy on them and they found the he-goat stretched out with his feet in the air. He was truly dead.

People ran to the again and the *rebbe* ruled:

Since the *Peysakh* sacrifice was a holy animal, he must be dressed in shrouds and buried in the cemetery.

Yosel Leibeles and a few other Jews dealt with the holy animal and did exactly what the *rebbe* had said.

Yosel Leibeles and the whole town of Jews with him were united and restored.

Since that time the Tarnogrod Jews know to be careful with the tongue, so that, heaven forbid, they will not stumble and bring unwarranted troubles upon themselves.

A Jew Travels to Eretz Yisrael

Let us return for a while to Itsik Melamed and tell about his journey, together with his wife Rachele to Eretz Yisrael.

Itsik Melamed's material circumstance was really an unusual one. Besides his teaching, which he had done his whole life; he also had a small candy factory. In addition his wife knitted underwear and had several assistants in that industry. But in all their years, may heaven preserve us, they had never had any children and in their elder years they decided to travel to the Holy Land.

Itsik Melamed liquidated everything, packed up the very essential things, and the entire town came to accompany him and say farewell.

Such a distant journey in those days was not taken on lightly. When they arrived in Jaffa they got two Arabic camels to which they were tightly strapped so that they would not heaven forbid fall off on the way to the holy city Jerusalem.

The journey from Jaffa to Jerusalem lasted almost one week. Rachele was greatly weakened by the long journey and the difficulties of the trip, became ill and died a short time later. She found her eternal rest on the Mount of Olives.

Itsik Melamed spent days and years in Jerusalem. He married again at the age of eighty and his wife favored him with a son.

He wrote a letter twice a year from Jerusalem to Tarnogrod. In the letters he recounted all the names of his students, the artisans, he mentioned the holy places such as the Western Wall, the Tomb of Rachel, the Tomb of Rabbi Meir Baal Haness. So from time to time his students in town collected a small sum of money from among themselves, which they sent to him.

With the outbreak of the First World War the connection to Eretz Yisrael was broken and we did not hear anything more about our *rebbe*, Itsik Melamed.

Shomrim [Guardians] Knocking

The sages of the Talmud said:

"There are three partners in the creation of a human being: God, father and mother. When the human dies, heaven forbid, it is said, the Master of the Universe takes back his portion."

Just as in many other small towns, Tarnogrod had for generations observed the custom that every *Shabbos shomrim* went through the streets and alleys early in the morning calling: "To the Shul".

They pronounced those words with a special melody that awoke the sleepers behind their locked doors and shutters.

On ordinary weekdays, the "*shomrim*" knocked on the doors and shutters rather than calling out.

That knocking by the "*shomrim*" represented the call "to the shul" or "Get up for the worship of the Creator".

On hearing that knocking that had its own special rhythm - two knocks one after the other and then a third knock - the Jews in the dark, damp houses woke up from their sleep, washed their hands using the ritual cup , recited the "*Modeh Ani*" [prayer said upon waking, before getting up from bed] with great intent, wiped the sleep from their eyes, quickly got into their clothes and hurried to the study-house.

If someone had died in town, God forbid, the *shomrim* tapped out just the first two knocks. This was the sign that during the night, the Master of the Universe had taken back his portion from some house in the town.

For many years Kuni Leml was the *shomrim-knocker*.

In that dawn when only two knocks were heard, screams of terror were heard from behind the closed shutters and barred doors. Soon doors and windows were open and in the completely dark outdoors voices could be heard calling out and asking with curiosity:

"Who? Who died?"

Kuni Leml felt more important than usual on such a day. Everyone turned to him with questions. Each person looked his in the eyes with curiosity, waiting for his answer.

If the deceased had been an eminent proprietor, a person with property, Kuni Leml did not conceal his satisfaction and would add:

"Today, thank God, there will be some livelihood."

Kuni Leml was also the one who set up the washing board and the accompanying vessels necessary for ritual washing of the corpse.

The two concepts, death and life, flowed together as one for Kuni Leml. He was not shocked by death just as he was not enamored of life, which for him was full of trouble and suffering. In the hovel where he lived he saw life in its lowest state. At the funerals where he always served, he heard the lamentations of mothers over dead children, of wives over young husbands. Thus, death never upset the equilibrium of his ever-silent rigidity.

In his later years the charity house where he lived was in danger of collapse and had to be closed. Kuni Leml - who after the death of his wife Shifra had remained a widower - lost his home and had no place to spend the night. He went to the cemetery, which was located outside the town, and spent the night there in the hut for the guard for the corpses.

Then one dawn no one heard the *shomrim* knocking. When they went to the cemetery they found Kuni Leml there, dead. In that dawn there was no one to announce to the town by knocking only twice, that Kuni Leml was dead.

[Pages 192-204]

Schools and Teachers

Meir Ringer

Translated by Tina Lunson

I was three years old when my mother took me off to *heder* [small Jewish elementary school], to the elementary teacher who they called Fife. His real name was Hersh, but no one knew his family name. Every day my mother gave various candies to the children, and especially to the teacher and his helpers.

The teacher sat me at the table, showed me the alphabet and told me to repeat: This is an *alef* [first letter of the Hebrew alphabet]. For a few days my mother went with me into the *heder* and later took me home again. She had to be in *heder* the whole time because I did not want to be left alone with the teacher and the boys. But that did not go on for long. One day my parents decided that it was time for me to go to *heder* by myself. The point was that they wanted me to get used to staying by myself in *heder* for the whole day.

I put up a fight in my own way and did not want to go to *heder* by myself. Then the teacher's helper came; he had not anticipated my crying and screaming, but he just set me up on his shoulder and went out in the street with me. I fought like a lion, I screamed and scratched his face. The helper accepted everything patiently, but the passers by spoke to me: "Phooey, this is not nice. A boy should go to school." Their words did not calm me and I never stopped crying and screaming the whole way, kicking my feet and scratching his neck and face with my nails, and that is how he carried me wailing into *heder*.

The teacher heard my protestations and saw the helper's scratched face, and thought that I should be punished. The great punishment with which he would finally put an end to my stubbornness was a "*pak*" [burden]. That happens like this: My long coat was turned inside out, and they did the same thing to my hat and put it on my head. The teacher stuck a broom into my inside-out coat, hoisted me up and sat me on the top of the oven. All the boys and the teacher shouted "Hoorah! This is what happens to a boy who doesn't go to *heder*!" This had a powerful effect on me. The following morning I took myself to *heder*. But I could not forget the humiliation of the "*pak*" for a very long time and I still carry it with me to this day.

The *heder* consisted of a single room in which about fifty boys studied. The same room served at the same time as a residence for the teacher and his household, for cooking and sleeping. There were two tables in the *heder*, one before the teacher, the second before the older helper, who also worked with the children.

The helper also went with the children to recite the *Keriat-Shema* [central prayer of Jewish liturgy, which expresses the concept of monotheism and declares faith in God. *Keriat-Shema* includes the recitation of three paragraphs from the Torah] at the home of a woman in confinement after giving birth to a male child. The helper only took the very small children into *heder* and at lunchtime he brought them all food from their homes.

Long benches stood on one side of the table. On the other side stood the bed-benches that by day served as seating for the students and by night as sleeping places for the teacher's household.

The teacher often suffered from toothaches. Still in my memory is the time he took a string and tied one end to an aching tooth and the other end to a doorknob. Then he told a student to go and open the door. The student did so and briskly opened the door, and the tooth sprang out of his mouth.

There were levels in the *heder*. When one level was studying, the other played outdoors. It was harder in the winter, when it was very cold outdoors and we were all packed together in different corners, and also under both tables. One time, one boy poked a button into the eye of another boy. The boy, of course, cried out and there was chaos. The teacher worked long and hard, and sweat ran down his face, before he got the button out of the eye.

There was a bed standing right by the door on which the teacher's sick wife lay, completely covered up, and we could always hear her moans and cries of terrible pain. One time she became suddenly still and the teacher became very agitated, went to her bed, uncovered her face and shouted out, "She is dead! Children, go home!" On the way out each of the boys glanced at the bed, saw the white face of the teacher's wife and, terrified, we left quickly.

In the morning the teacher went around to the parents of his students and collected a little money for the burial expenses.

For three days we, his students, were running around merrily, happy with the freedom and thinking that we would be so free for the whole seven days of the *shivah* [initial seven-day period of mourning that follows burial] but our joy was destroyed on the fourth day when the town *Rav*[rabbi] arranged with the teacher to study with the children.

I studied with the elementary teacher for four terms. Half a year was considered a term. After ending a term one went over to a higher level. In the elementary school I learned the Hebrew alphabet, praying from the prayer book, and Hebrew language. After that I was ready to go to another teacher who taught Torah, *Rashi* [Rabbi Shlomo ben Isaac, regarded as one of Judaism's greatest commentators of Talmud] and Talmud.

Faiwel the Talmud Teacher

When I was five years old I could already pray from a prayer book by myself and my father sent me to study with *Rebbe* Faiwel in his *heder*. There, I began to study the Five Books of Moses. After I short time I learned the *Rashi* script and soon the commentary also. After studying for two terms I began to study Talmud. The teacher was satisfied with me and reckoned me among his good pupils. Therefore I had to pay a dear price, which was going every *Shabbos* [Jewish Sabbath] to be heard. None of the boys liked to have to do this, really like today a category in the *shul* [synagogue], and it also cost me a lot of well being. My father, proud of the *rebbe*'s praise, sent me to his friends every *Shabbos* so that they could observe and praise my knowledge. The *rebbe* sent along another student as well, someone not so adept at study, in order for me to help him out. So, *Shabbos* was for me the hardest day of the week. The people outside who saw me walking with a Talmud volume used to laugh and call out, "The Talmud is bigger than you are!" The distinction I received from my listeners consisted of a pinch on the cheek.

With Faiwel I also learned to write Yiddish. That study went like this: At first he wrote out a whole line of alefs and I had to fill the whole page with the same letter. He repeated this with all the letters. After that I had to write out the alphabet backwards. This was called the *tashrik* [reverse] style. After that we moved on to spelling. The *rebbe* wrote out a line: "I went to Lublin to purchase some merchandise", and I had to fill the whole page with the same line. Finally the *rebbe* had us write a whole letter. Writing such a letter took us entire months, and this was a sign that we had reached the highest level in writing Yiddish.

After some time, when I was already sixteen years old, that same Faiwel would come to me from time to time and ask me if I would write a letter to his children in America. He was embarrassed about it, and would answer, "My letters spoke words and read themselves."

The fact is that I learned my first knowledge in Yiddish from Faiwel *melamed* [teacher]. In comparison with other teachers, who were always going around angry, Faiwel was a calm and quiet person and showed his students a great deal of love and devotion.

At the *rebbe's* there were two kinds of water. From one well, one got salty water, and from the second, sweet water for cooking and drinking. That was harder to bring, and on the day that I brought the *rebbe* new-moon money or money for a holiday like *Lag ba-Omer* [33rd day of the counting of the Omer, celebrated as a minor holiday - the reason for this holiday has not been definitely ascertained], *Tu b'Shevat* [15th day of the month of Shevat, originally the yearly date for reckoning the age of trees for tax purposes and to know when the tree's fruit could be eaten, which would be the fourth year. During the Zionest movement, planting trees became symbolic for Jewish reattachment to the land of Israel], or *Purim* [feast which celebrates the deliverance of the Jews from the plot of Haman to kill them in the days of Queen Esther of Persia] - which not all the students did - then Shoshale, the *rebbe's* old mother would come to me and say, "Meirl, come, I will give you I nice drink of sweet well water."

I studied with Faiwel Melamed for four terms and afterward went over to a great Talmud teacher, Itsik Melamed.

Itsik Melamed

I studied with Itsik Melamed for four terms also, two years. Besides Talmud, we also studied the Five Books of Moses with various commentaries.

At the entrance to his house was a very small room, which served as a kitchen, and was also a workshop for his wife, who knitted underwear and employed a few other knitters as well. In the second room where we studied there was also a little factory for candies, where the *rebbe's* adopted son Hersh worked. It often happened that the *rebbe* helped him in his work and got us to help too. In time, we children became experts and knew the craft of making candies.

After Hersh's marriage, Itsik elamed and his wife, both in their elder years, made *aliyah* [the act of immigrating to Israel] to *Eretz-Yisrael* [land of Israel].

Shmuel Natan

At Shmuel Natan's, I studied Talmud with more exegeses. There too the *heder* was in a single room where the *rebbe* also lived with his family. There too the sick *rebbetzin* [wife of rabbi] lay all day in bed, in the same room where we studied and she often moaned or cried out in pain. Still the *rebbe* was good humored by nature, and we boys loved him very much.

Leibel Melamed

When I became *Bar-Mitzvah* [at 13 years, a Jewish boy becomes responsible for fulfilling Jewish law] I was turned over to Leibel the teacher. I had given a fine *Bar-Mitzvah* speech and my study now took on a serious character, with additional glosses to Talmudic commentaries and the exegesis of *Rav* Shmuel Edels. It was said about Leibele Melamed that he was a bit of a philosopher. That is, he occupied himself with inquiries and philosophy. The truth is that I never noticed this in him. It is possible that this came from the fact that he stemmed from Shebreshin [Szczebrzeszyn], where they said that there were many heretics.

Sender *Melamed*

Sender the teacher was a great scholar, an ordained *rav* and had authority to respond to difficult questions.

Certain householders in town had demanded that the community counsel make Sender a recognized decider of matters of rabbinical law and pay him a monthly stipend permanently. But the *rav* and his sons opposed it and *Rav* Sender stayed with his teaching, living in poverty and want.

His students had the reputation of being good pupils and the study was deepened with a lot of exegeses.

One time on a winter day Sender Melamed called me aside and asked me very earnestly: "Meirl, do you want to study *SHaKH* [Rabbi Shabtai ben Meir Ha-Kohen, eminent 16th Century interpreter of Jewish law]?" Of course I quickly agreed and he told me that I and Leibush Shachnas should come to him three times a week before dawn, at four in the morning. He really had no other time because he was busy the whole day with the other students, who were not yet competent for such difficult study as *SHaKH*.

When I relayed this news at home my parents were very happy. My father woke me at three o'clock from a deep sleep, my mother saw to it that I dressed myself well, and with a lantern in my hand I went over the dark streets in the cold, in the snow, in the rain. The *rebbe* was still asleep, but at my arrival he quickly got up, washed his fingers and promptly sat down to study *SHaKH* with us.

Leibush Shachnas and I, as young as we were then, saw ourselves as grownups, felt as though we were adults. No small thing that we were already studying *SHaKH*. That's what those who dreamed of becoming *rebbes* studied.

One time when we arrived at *heder* completely frozen we could not wait long for the *rebbe* to open the door for us. We had to knock and knock harder and harder. When the *rebbe* finally woke up and let us inside, he told us the reason he was so fast asleep and did not hear how hard we tried to wake him.

The story was so:

In the same room where Sender and his wife and six children lived, there were another two beds. The older children slept in one of the beds. Mirlin or Yonelen were put to bed on the table. The smallest child, Pessale, was laid in a small crib, and the other four children in the beds of the father and mother. That night little Pessale would not stop crying and they had to take her out of the crib and put her in the mother's bed. So they had to move another child over to the father's bed and the *rebbe* had to sleep in the crib. According to what he said, he got so warm and cozy and was so fast asleep that he did not hear our alarms.

It remains a puzzle for me to this very day how the *rebbe* got into the small, narrow crib and then felt so rested afterwards. In later years when I read Avraham Reisen's poem: "A Family of Eight and Only Two Beds", I saw again the home of my *rebbe*, Sender Melamed.

*

During that time my father was studying how to combat *yetzer ha-ra* [inclination toward evil] and achieved a high level in it. In his view it was yetzer ha-ra that persuaded me to sleep and made it hard for me to get myself up at dawn when he woke me and I went back to sleep. My father had to wake me two or three times. So he told me a story:

It happened that a young man who was supported by his father-in-law after his marriage and who studied day and night, was pestered by *yetzer ha-ra* and on a particular morning when he had just wakened himself from sleep, *yetzer ha-ra* argued: "Look, man, you went to sleep very late, now it is still early and you are still tired, it's cold and wet outside, while in bed it's warm and pleasant, why torture yourself, go back to sleep just once." The young man went back to sleep but when he woke the second time the immediately understood that there had been a bit of *yetzer ha-ra* that had bewitched him with its speech. The young man had, however, reached a certain level and already knew how to wage war with *yetzer ha-ra*. He decided that every time *yetzer ha-ra* pestered him at dawn to talk him into sleeping, he would take the finger-water, which stood by his bed, and simply pour it into the bed. Yetzer ha-ra would have no power in a wet bed.

My father ended the story and sighed deeply, adding, "Meirl, you have not yet reached that level and you do not yet know how to overcome *yetzer ha-ra*."

Sender Melamed in Eretz-Yisrael

Some time after I had made *aliyah* to Eretz-Yisrael, my childhood friend Shmuel Khefer (Fefer) came from Haifa to visit me, and among other things he told me that our *rebbe*, Sender Melamed was here in the country with his family, on Allenby Street in Tel Aviv, near the old age home. He was there with his wife selling cigarettes. My friend had met with Sender and learned from him that he was here to get a certificate to be a rav, as *Rav* Kook, of blessed memory, had accomplished through the English authorities and when my friend had asked him if he belonged to the *Mizrakhi* movement [religious Zionist organization], he answered him with a joke: "The *Mizrakhi* took from us observant Jews the word Torah, and from you Zionists the word service and made itself a political party. What do I need them for?"

I was then living in Rishon LeZion, and traveling once to Tel Aviv I decided to visit my *rebbe*, Sender Melamed. Arriving there, I encountered an old woman standing by a little shop. I bought a pack of cigarettes from her and asked if she was Chanale. She said she was and asked if I was from Tarnogrod. When she heard my name she exclaimed, "You were one of our students!" I asked her about the *rebbe* and she pointed upwards with her finger. At first I thought she was indicating the fourth floor, but she soon told me that he had recently not been feeling well, that his strength was going, and that on *Tisha be-Av* [A day of mourning marking the destruction of both ancient Temples in Jerusalem], sitting in *shul* where he studied with a group of Jews, he was suddenly taken ill and breathed his last.

Yossele Wigdors

His father was named Avigdor and he himself had started his teaching career in Tarnogrod. But after a time he moved to *Mlave* [Mława, Poland], where he studied with two sons of a very wealthy man who paid him well and supplied him with everything. Yossele came home to his family only two times a year for holidays. That went on for many years, until his wandering became tiresome and he decided to return home and become a teacher in Tarnogrod.

At that time Yossele was already an old Jew, but still full of courage and with a reputation as a good teacher. He was strict and severe. He was a *Kohen* [A Jew who can trace his ancestry to the priestly tribe descended from Aaron] but because of his anger people said that he must be *Kohen gadol* [high priest] because we, his students, did not eat honey.

Yossele's method was:

Every Sunday he read us the Talmud passage. Monday and Tuesday were for questions. On those days one could ask as many times as one felt necessary. He was friendly; he patiently explained the answers to all the questions. But when Wednesday came, no one dared to turn to him with any question. He asked the questions then and woe to any student who did not know the correct answer. He struck with whatever was close at hand. For Yossele Wigdors the concept "forgot", the word with which we sometimes answered, did not exist.

It did happen, in some good-humored moment when we had correctly answered the questions, he posed a question and one of the students tried to take pride in his knowledge. The *rebbe* then would say with a smile on his lips and in a thoughtful voice, "You are still young and you don't yet know that the end of knowledge is to know that you don't know. When you are older and you attain a degree of knowledge that you still know nothing, it will be the beginning of your knowledge." His words and the tone in which he said them are etched in my consciousness until this day.

Yossele was an honest person, and when it happened that a student was weak and could not take in the study in his *heder*, Yossele would go to the father and ask him to take his son and teach him a trade, because it was a waste of his money that he was throwing away in paying tuition for him.

When his young daughter Chaia-Beile was married and moved to Bilgoraj, he sold his house in Tarnogrod and also moved to Bilgoraj, to live close to his daughter whom he loved more than all other children and used to call her "my precious little daughter."

Only many years later, walking along the street, I spied a Jew with a long white beard and patriarchal appearance, but also very bent over with age. When he got closer I easily recognized my old teacher Yossele Wigdors. To my greeting, he looked at me and asked:

"Who are you, scoundrel, wait, wait, you are Meirl Berishes?"

"Yes, *rebbe*, it is I."

"They say that you became some kind of a Socialist, Zionist, some kind of thing, Meirl? For God's sake, stay a Jew."

In my tone there was certainly a little heat:

"*Rebbe*, I am a Jew like all Jews."

He looked at me, inspecting me, and said:

"Yes? If you say so, if you say so."

He said good-bye, shook my hand and his last words were:

"Meirl, be a Jew. You should know, that I have always loved you."

I did not see him any more.

Lesson Readers and Study Partners

After Yossele Wigdors, I no longer studied in a *heder*. For a year Yossel Avraham Itches (Apteker) and I studied every day before lunch in the Shinovar [Sieniawa] *shtibl* [literally "little house" which served as a house of prayer - see page 135] with Yossele-Shaye-Shayes (Milch). We studied the tractate *Nedarim*[vows]. After lunch we studied separately in the *Beit Midrash* [house of study].

After that, Eliezer Mosheles (the young rav's son) and I studied "*Yoreh Deah*" [volume of The Code of Jewish Law - *Shulchan Arukh* - dealing with charity, torah study and dietary laws] each morning at the *Beit Midrash* with commentaries by Berishl Rotenberg. In the afternoon Wolf Pinie Bentz (Weissman) and I studied independently; Wolf is now in Israel. Our *Rebbe* Bereshl was a great scholar, an expert with a sharp mind, one of the best students of the *rav* of Bilgoraj, *Rav* Silberman, who people used to call the genius of Matsheve.

While studying the "*Yoreh Deah*" about the laws of kosher and *treif* [foods not allowed to be eaten under Jewish dietary laws], Eliezer's father Moshele took us to the slaughter house where he gave us practical examples that helped up to better understand the laws in "*Yoreh Deah*".

Watching how they examined the lungs and liver of the slaughtered cow and how the butcher took the tube of the lung in his mouth and blew it up so that the inspection by the *rav* or the *shochet* [ritual slaughterer] would be thorough, I was disgusted to nausea. *Reb* Moshele, who noticed this, said to me, "Meirl, a *rav* cannot not be a delicate man, must not be disgusted by bad odors and other things. Otherwise one cannot be a *rav*."

At that time the older *rav* was also teaching a lesson on tractate *Hulin* [Talmud tractate containing laws of ritual slaughter and details on kosher and nonkosher foods]. Among the select students who studied with him, I also took part in the lesson, which was at a very high level. We studied on the winter nights, three times a week, with the *rav* in his home.

When the First World War broke out I was already completely independent in study. I studied various tractates with commentaries with Itche Yakiv Galis (Zychler). Itche was a serious youth by nature, very friendly, and our relations were very sincere. But in time we went our separate ways. I began to read apocryphal books, as modern literature was called in those days, and he saw me as someone who had gone badly astray, and he broke off our relationship.

In those times even the others in the *Beit Midrash* began to look at me askance, they were afraid that I would despoil the other boys, and the *reb* forbade me from further study there.

The "Prison"

Since time immemorial it had been the practice in town to throw dirty water out into the street. But if the watchman suddenly passed by and caught you, he had to be slipped something, something put into his hand, and if you did not have anything to give him he would promptly write a report. People referred to a report from the watchman as going to sit in the prison.

Such things also happened when a Jew covered his roof with wooden shingles instead of with tin, or built a house without a building plan, or differently from the way it was in the plan. If it had not previously settled it with the watchman, he would put together a report and take it to the court. The punishment was almost always to go sit in the prison for a few days.

True, one could exchange the sentence for a monetary fine. But what Jew would do such a foolish thing, and instead of going to sit, throw money away in the street?

Krotshek, the watchman for the town council, was also the overseer of the prison. Krotshek's work consisted of coming to the Jews to remind them that it was time to go sit in jail. Then one would put something into Krotshek's hand and put off going to sit until later, that is until a more convenient time, for example after the non-Jewish holidays when trade was dead and it was cold outside. That was the most suitable time for the Jews to go sit in the prison. Then one packed some bed linens, took the *tallis* [prayer shawl] and *tefillin* [small black leather boxes with straps that contain pieces of parchment on which passages from the Torah are inscribed] under their arms and went to the prison, to sleep well and rest up the whole time. Food they brought from home, the very best.

The prison was always open, because Jews still had to go every morning to pray because there may not always be a *minyan* [minimum gathering of 10 people necessary for communal religious service], and then Krotshek looked the other way while the Jews went out to pray with *tallis* and *tefillin*. People also came to visit those who were sitting in jail, to chat about their own matters or about the news that was printed in the gazettes. In winter, when there was a singeing frost outdoors, people used to go to the prison to warm up.

But it happened that a control commission came from another town, and Krotshek had to lock the prison and keep it closed until the commission went away.

One time when such a commission arrived in town unannounced it was a market day and the prison was, of course, completely empty. What Jew would go to sit in jail on a market day? For Krotshek it was a big trap. His whole career was at stake. He ran out to the market and told the first Jews he saw what had happened, that a commission had come; someone had to save him and go sit in jail.

How hard it was for a Jew to give up the market day, but he had to realize that Krotshek was correct and he had to go sit in jail, locked up for several hours, until the commission left. Both Krotshek and the Jews were equally happy that all ended well.

[Pages 205-212]

The Song of My Town

by Yitzhak Karper

Translated by Miriam Leberstein

And no matter how much I sing to you
it's only the sparks that you'll hear.
The flame, the flame remains within me,
silent and enclosed.

--Yehoyesh[1]

1.

In the second half of the last century, the Jewish population of Tarnogrod numbered about four thousand. The Tarnogrod Jews were religiously observant and possessed rabbis of great renown and learning. The rabbinical seat was held by such famous rabbis as the former Kalisher Rabbi,[2] זצ״ל after him, Rabbi *Reb*[respectful term of address] Yakov Toyvim, זצ״ל and later Rabbi *Reb* Aryeh Teicher, זצ״ל, whose lineage reached back as far as the Tofsos Yom Tov [Rabbi Yom Tov Lipman Heller, 1579-1654]. Rabbi *Reb Hatsadik* [holy man] Aryeh Teicher held the post until his death at the great old age of 104.

In addition to his great learning, Rabbi Aryeh Teicher, זצ״ל was also a good cantor. During the entire time he served as rabbi, he led the *Neilah* [final prayer service on Yom Kippur] and *Musaf* [extra prayers during the morning service] prayers during the High Holy Days. He prayed with great fervor and sweetness.

At *Hoshanah Rabbah* [Seventh day of Sukkot] he was the cantor for the *Hallel* [Psalms of praise] and *Hoshanot* prayers [said while holding the lulav and etrog]. His chanting moved the congregation to great excitement and everyone was in tears.

After his death his oldest son *Reb* Moshele became rabbi and held the position until the Holocaust. He was killed, along with the entire Jewish community of Tarnogrod; God will avenge their blood!

2.

Tarnogrod had a beautiful synagogue, a large *besmedresh* [house of study and prayer] where people prayed in various *minyans* [groups of ten or more] from six in the morning until ten at night. Hundreds of worshipers prayed there, summer and winter. In the winter months, the worshippers came more frequently. In the *besmedresh* there were long tables and benches over which hung oil lamps by the light of which people studied. There were young boys, young married men and old men, grey haired scholars who immersed themselves in their studies until late at night. It was warm, heated by a large brick oven with three iron pipes that gave off a pleasant heat.

In the evenings, until eight o'clock, the *besmedresh* was as bustling and noisy as a stock exchange. People talked about everything in the world, discussed political news, and conducted various kinds of business. The *besmedresh* was the only place where Tarnogrod Jews could spend their free time in a social setting. There were no places of entertainment, no boulevards or gardens to stroll. So the *besmedresh* was the center where everyone gathered.

When the merchants and politicians left, there remained the religious scholars who sat for hours over their Gemores [commentaries on the *Mishnah*]. From time to time, when they wanted something to eat to relieve their hunger, they would bake potatoes on the hot oven pipes and would devour them with great pleasure.

The *shames* [sexton] had a little shop in a small room in the besmedresh. There he always had a bit of whiskey, some cookies, and herring. The richer boys would buy a piece of herring to go with their potatoes. After eating they would return to their studying with renewed enthusiasm.

Tarnogrod Jews followed the practices of giving charity and aiding indigent travelers. The town took an interest in every needy person and marshaled every possible means to alleviate the want both of those who lived in the town and those who were passing through, providing the latter with food and lodging. On the Sabbath, every Jew took home a guest. From time to time, a poor Jew from out of town would arrive, who seemed to be a respectable man, someone who had come down in the world. The young men would take up a collection among the worshippers and provide him with a good meal and a place to sleep, so that he didn't have to be ashamed. The young men from the *besmedresh* also followed the practice of giving anonymously. They would collect money for various respectable men from Tarnogrod who, embarrassed by their poverty, continued to pretend that they still had money, when in fact they lived on the secret funds that the young scholars collected.

The town had a big *Hasidic shtibl* [*Hasidic* place of worship] where several hundred Hasidim – from the Sendzer, Belzer, Shiniave and Gorlitzer sects --studied and prayed.

3.

The lifestyle of the Jews of Tarnogrod was far from luxurious or fashionable. People lived thriftily, spending carefully. They wore their traditional Jewish clothing until it was no longer wearable. Clothing for the Sabbath was well-cared for and lasted a lifetime. When a girl got married, she received a Turkish shawl that she wore to synagogue every Sabbath and to weddings and other celebrations for the rest of her life, despite the fading of its colors.

The first Sabbath after her wedding a young wife would come to synagogue sporting a pretty hat on her head. Such a hat would generally be one of two that were lent out to the brides of the town. A wealthy man brought home from Warsaw for his daughter a light colored straw hat which she wore to her wedding. It had a broad rim, and was beautifully decorated in multi-colored silk. Such a hat had to have cost several *rubles*.

Once, a wealthy man married off his son to a girl from Galicia. She arrived in town wearing a hat she had bought for herself. It elicited a lot of interest among the women and it was later loaned out to other brides who couldn't dream of buying themselves such a lovely hat.

These hats were cared for like jewelry. They lent the bride charm and beauty. Wearing such a hat the bride proudly strode across the big market square on her way to synagogue and back. This was the only day in her life that she wore such a beautiful hat. Every such hat served twenty to thirty years, each year adorning the heads of at least twenty brides – that is, a total of five hundred brides enjoyed its beauty.

4.

The villages around Tarnogrod were rich and well supplied with food. Peasants in the thousands would gather at the fairs that were held in Tarnogrod's big marketplace. They sold their grain and bought various kinds of merchandise. They had a good relationship with the Jews, living in mutual trust. Yet there were instances when one party tried to trick the other. So it was that there once occurred a curious event that was long talked about in town.

At one of the fairs, a peasant brought a barrel of honey from his beehives. His Jewish customer bargained with him for a long time and when they finally agreed on a price, the peasant began to fear that he would make a mistake in counting out the measures of honey. The Jew briefly thought about this, then told the peasant that after each measure was poured, he would give the peasant a ten *groschen* coin, and at the end they would count the coins and thereby determine the correct number of measures.

After thinking about it for a while, the peasant agreed. After each measure was poured, he was given a coin by the Jew. But while the Jew was busy pouring the measure into his own container, the peasant would now and then drop the coin into his boot. In his Polish head he thought he was cheating the Jew by stealing the coin. It didn't occur to him that the Jew had noticed and had pretended not to, saving himself the cost of the measure represented by the coin. Both were content with the result.

Zishe Ulrich

In Tarnogrod there were several families named Ulrich, and while none of them was wealthy, they were honest, respectable Jews. One of them, named Zishe, went to Warsaw as a sixteen year old boy, having decided to settle down there. In those days such a thing caused a big stir, just as if someone had set off for a distant land. Zishe arrived in Warsaw without any money, but he possessed a lot of energy, zest for life and a will to work hard. He began selling in the street, whatever goods he happened to come by. He was a success, and whatever he did, he made money and in time became one of the rich men in Warsaw. His store was at #1 Banga Street, in the passage. He maintained a beautiful home, gave his children a good Jewish upbringing and education and was one of the prominent men in the city.

Reb Zishe was an intelligent man. He retained the modesty of his Tarnogrod family and would say, "Wealth is like a ball, a wheel that turns. When it starts to roll, you never know what will happen, where it will finally wind up."

He decided to make a good marriage match for his daughter, to find a son-in-law who was a great scholar. He applied all his energy and initiative to this goal and in this too he was successful. He took as his son-in-law the son of the Krakower Rabbi, who was renowned throughout the Jewish world, the learned and saintly *Reb* Shimen Schreiber, who was the son of the Hatam Sofer [Rabbi Moses Schreiber, 1763-1839]. *Reb* Shimen's son *Reb* Bunim [Schreiber], a well-known scholar, became the son-in-law of the rich Warsaw Jew, *Reb* Zishe of the Tarnogrod Ulrichs.

The father-in-law, the Krakower rabbi, besides being well learned and a saintly man, was a wise man and was highly esteemed not only among the Jews, but also the Christian population. He was elected deputy to the parliament in Vienna and when he appeared in the Austrian parliament, the deputies treated him with great respect and warmly received his proposals on behalf of the Jewish population in Galicia, Austria and Hungary.

Reb Zishe Ulrich brought his esteemed son-in-law to Warsaw and set him up very nicely. *Reb* Bunim spent many years engaged in religious study and prayer and was a prolific writer. The scholars of his time often referred to his Biblical and Talmudic interpretations.

After *Reb* Zishe Ulrich died, the family used the money remaining in his estate to rent the Zamakher farm, one of the properties outside Tarnogrod owned by Graf [Count] Zamoyski. It was in the (18)80's that *Reb* Bunim came to Zamakher farm with his wife and two sons, Zishe and Akive, and three daughters, Toybele, Sorele and Perele.

The eldest, Toybele, stood out for her refined manners and good qualities and was renowned for her beauty. They called her "The Krakower Beauty." At the farm *Reb* Bunim continued his religious studies and turned his house into an inn for scholars.

In the [18]90's *Reb* Bunim had to leave the farm and went to Krakow. His daughter Toybele became the daughter-in-law of a rich man in Krakow, but for various reasons they had to separate after a while. The middle daughter also got married in Galicia, while the youngest married the son of a prominent merchant in Vitebsk, the owner of a large tobacco factory.

Until 1935 I remained in contact with the Schreiber family, frequently exchanging letters. In May of that year, I made *aliyah* [immigration] to Israel and settled in Jerusalem and from then on I lost contact with them. From what I later heard, their factory was completely destroyed by fire during the war.

*

Around Tarnogrod there were rich agricultural estates owned by Zamoyski, which were rented by Jews, often with large areas of forest. Among these renowned Jewish aristocrats were Fabrikant, Wayntraub and others.

These rich Jews would come to Tarnogrod to pray on Rosh Hashanah and Yom Kippur. They contributed a lot to charity. In winter they sent potatoes for the poor and wood to heat the *besmedreshes*.

The Zamekh Estate was held for a time by *Reb* Bunim Shreiber, a grandson of the Hatam Sofer. He would invite me to visit several times a year. I was then a young scholar in the *besmedresh* and very much enjoyed listening to his Torah interpretations and legends, which he liked to relate.

In 1893 the Russian government evicted all foreign Jews and *Reb* Bunim, as a Galitsianer, had to leave the estate and transfer it to a Christian, who quickly ruined the huge property. *Reb* Bunim at that time delayed his departure for several days past the deadline set by the government. The police arrested him and brought him to Tarnogrod, from which he was to be sent to Galicia. His arrest dismayed the Jews of the town, and they interceded to make sure he would be kept in a separate part of the jail and not together with other arrestees.

The next day I went to visit him. I imagined that I would find him in an oppressed mood. How great was my surprise when I found him cheerful and merry, as if nothing had happened. Even in jail he abided by his *Hasidic* custom of not falling into despair. He told me, "See, for the first time in my life I'm drinking *koze* [goat] milk," pointing to the milk I had brought him. This was a pun, for in our town, we called a jail a *koze*.

He then immediately launched into a discussion of Torah topics and sparkled with erudition and keen wit.

After several days they took him to the border and he went to Krakow, where he was received with great honor and named *magid* [preacher] of the city. He held that post until his death. He was buried with great honor in the Krakow cemetery.

* * *

In the (18)90's there was a significant increase in the excise tax on alcohol in Russia, leading to an increase in alcohol smuggling from Austria. The chief of the excise officials was Khalimovski, an evil and cruel man. One winter a merchant from Vienna came to us and angrily related that on the way back from the customs house he had encountered an official on horseback riding behind a Jew who was walking in the mud, his hands bound together with a rope, the ends of which the horseman held in his hands.

When the merchant asked what crime the Jew had committed, Khalmovski explained that he had been found in possession of several liters of smuggled whiskey and that he was taking him to the customs house where an official accusation would be drawn up and he would be brought before the court. At such trials Khalimovski appeared as the accuser and demanded the most severe punishment.

The brutality of this official was widely known outside the town. There were non-Jewish Russians who could not condone his brutality and they appeared at the trials on behalf of the Jewish merchants and thereby mitigated their punishment. Among them was the priest of the Russian Orthodox church, a wealthy man who had good relations with the judge and always obtained lighter sentences for the Jews.

Footnotes:

   1.   Yehoyesh (Yehoash): pen name of Yehoyesh-Shloyme Blumgarten (Solomon Bloomgarten), 1871-1927, poet and translator of the Hebrew bible into Yiddish.
   2.   זצ״ל: Honorific for deceased holy or righteous person: May the Memory of the Righteous be a Blessing.

[Pages 213-225]

Not the Song They Sang in my Town
(From My Memoirs)

by Shmuel Eliyahu Puter

Translated by Helene Roumani

Jews have been living in Tarnogrod for hundreds of years. No one knows exactly when the first Jews came, but the learned say it was during the time of Kazimierz.[1] There was even a house in town with architectural features from that period. Some say, the name Tarnogrod stems from the Tartar Invasion of Poland, when the Tartars were posted there.

Tarnogrod is situated on a hill. Rivers flow on three of its sides in the direction of Bilgoraj, the Czarna Lada and the Potik. There used to be bridges on all sides with gates. The only one that remained was called the *Bramin* for the Polish word *brama*, which means gate.

To get to the nearest train station, you'd have to ride 30 kilometers by horse and buggy. The roads weren't paved. Only in 1937 was the road to Bilgoraj paved. The first bus started running then, but transportation was still mainly via horse and buggy. Cart owners drove great distances to Yaroslav, Zamosc, Lublin, and all the way to Lemberg, carrying merchandise of all kinds and passengers back and forth.

Electrical lighting was introduced in Tarnogrod only in 1938, but not every Jew in town could afford it. The lack of electricity was not felt much as, for generations, people were accustomed to using petroleum and oil lamps for lighting.

Houses were generally low-level, mainly one-story, made of wood. There was a large plaza in the town center called the market. Most of the Jews lived around there, on the side streets, leading from the market, where the houses were clustered densely in no particular order, lacking the most basic sanitary facilities. After a rain, the streets were lined with deep muddy puddles. There were no sidewalks. In busy areas, with lots of pedestrian activity, wide wooden boards were placed on the ground, instead of pavement. We called them laves.

The town's central business district was located in the market. The Jewish shops were there too, in two long buildings with booths, small wooden structures, somewhat like cabins on a yacht, where the Jewish butchers sold meat. Until1936, the sale of horses, livestock and pigs was also conducted in the market. Afterwards, in the final years, a garden was planted at the site. There was also a wooden tower there, where the firemen learned their skills and practiced extinguishing fires. If a fire broke out somewhere, the siren would go off from that tower, alerting the whole town.

All major government institutions were located in the provincial capital. Only minor government institutions operated in Tarnogrod. They managed every day affairs. The Municipal Building was located to the south of the market. It also housed other official functions. The prison was located there. We called it the koze [case]. Minor detention was conducted there, mainly for administrative offenses. Major issues were dealt with in the Court of Appeals, in Bilgoraj or Lublin.

The police played a major role in Tarnogrod. Because of the situation, the police functioned as the main authority.

Until 1938, mail was delivered daily by horse and buggy from Bilgoraj. There was no telegraph service in Tarnograd. Telegrams had to be dispatched by phone to Bilgoraj. Jews in Tarnogrod played close attention to the mail service, anticipating letters and packages from America. Young people waited eagerly for newspapers. They came in from Warsaw and Lublin.

The mailman knew every Jewish house, every single member of the family and their connections with the outside world. He wasn't always a welcome guest. At best, he was seen as a reminder to pay bills. Sometimes he got everyone together in the synagogue claiming he heard people gossiping about him. He even heard that his name - Naritz - was cited. Seems he confused that with the Hebrew word "na'aritzcha," from the daily Kedusha prayer.

On the Sabbath, Naritz would come with his mail bag straight to the synagogue. Everyone gathered around as he called out the names. Those present immediately collected their mail. But those who were not there at the time, didn't fare so well. They had to search him out later, far and wide, to collect their mail which he was obliged to deliver in the first place to each recipient by hand.

Another important institution in town was the Fire Brigade. Since the houses were made of wood and usually covered with straw, fires broke out often. Until 1936, the fire station was located in the municipal building where the firefighting equipment was kept.

In 1936, a fire station was built, which was called the Depot. By then, the Fire Brigade already had a motorized pump to draw water, but no modern transport. If a fire broke out in a nearby village, the fire fighters would get there by horse and buggy. As you could imagine, by the time they arrived, half the town was already up in flames. The alarm could be heard during the whole ordeal, blown by mouth in those times. Only later, was a mechanical siren introduced.

Another institution that played a prominent role in the life of the town was the National Public School, where Christian and Jewish children were in attendance together. Needless to say, anti-Semitic remarks were often heard, from teachers as well as pupils.

The Jewish population was sustained mainly from trade and craftsmanship. Everyone had connections with the peasants in the surrounding villages, the rich and the poor. In general, the soil in the area was good so the peasants lived not badly. Jews who frequented the nearby villages, usually by foot, were merchants who sold the peasants all sorts of city goods and in exchange purchased grain and fresh vegetables from them. They were usually received hospitably, but it was a difficult way to earn a living. The merchants had to be prepared for encounters with shady characters, often hostile and full of hatred to the Jews. There were also craftsmen, tailors, shoemakers, carpenters, etc., who frequented the villages. They would stay with the peasants for the entire duration of the work week.

The way of life, and the rhythm of life, at home and in the street, was clearly Jewish, through and through. One's greatest pleasure was visiting the Beis Ha'medrish, [the study hall], to learn a page of Talmud, a chapter of Mishna, or simply to read a few Psalms, whether in solitude or with others in a quorum, each according to his level and community affiliations. Once, a *maggid* (an orator) came to town and held a sermon. It was a wonderful treat for everyone, both men and women were delighted as they listened to the speaker with great joy.

Jews in Tarnogrod were proud of the distinguished personalities the town produced. The mother of Rabbi Levi Yitzchak of Barditchev came from Tarnogrod. Her name was Shasha Devorah. They told wonderful stories about her great wisdom and generosity. She herself stemmed from a highly prestigious family that included the eminent Ra'sha - Rabbi Shlomo Aaron Wertheimer and the renowned Rabbi Moshe Margalit. The latter served as head of the town's Beis Din (Jewish Court), and descended from a lineage of rabbis that went back 26 generations.

Tarnogrod was also the hometown of the Apter Rav, Rabbi Avraham Yehoshua Heschel of Apt (1748-1825), whose progeny continues till this very day, with a huge dynasty of famous rabbis. He had two sons, Rabbi Yitzchak Meir and Rabbi Yosef Moshe. His father, Rabbi Shimshon was an illustrious scholar, one of those distinguished personalities the town folk loved to boast about, as if they were great celebrities. He was the son of Rabbi Chaim Heschel of Lublin. Rabbi Shimshon's wife, Rachel, was the daughter of the revered sage, Rabbi Feivish. She traced her ancestry all the way back to King David.

Another acclaimed personality born in Tarnogrod was the Sanzer Rabbi. And there were others, but no documentation on them has remained as the town suffered fires several times. Nevertheless, the Jews of Tarnogrod continued to talk about these illustrious individuals, with great fuss and fanfare. They raised their children on the values the great rabbis professed, hoping the young ones would adopt their good traits and continue living according to their teachings.

Farewell event marking Yaakov Puter's departure to Argentina in 1938

A group of young people from different organizations celebrate the departure of their neighbor, who was associated with them in common dreams and beliefs. They professed all sorts of great thoughts and dreams about how humanistic ideals will finally be achieved when the Jewish People establish their own national entity. Only a few members of that group survived. They are now mainly in Israel and in America

Mutual Assistance and Benevolence within the Community

In town, there were Hassidic *shtibls* [small prayer houses], a *beis medrish* [study hall] and a *shul* [synagogue] that everyone took pride in. It was the largest building in town, built by the same engineer who constructed the famous synagogue in the Belzer rabbinic court. The synagogue was built following a fire on the spot where a wooden synagogue had stood before.

When the synagogue construction began, the Rabbi called a meeting with all the influential people in town, from the various different activist groups, and requested they contribute a *kopike* (a coin) for the construction of the synagogue. They did and were then followed by the common Jews who responded in kind.

Laying the foundations entailed great difficulty. They hit water and had to dig deeper which increased the costs.

A path made of wooden boards led to the synagogue. It extended all the way from the beis medrish to the entrance to the synagogue. Another area nearby was covered with a wooden platform. *Chuppas* (wedding canopies) were placed there. On the platform, there were two large gates were that lead to the synagogue's entrance lobby. To the right, there was a small prayer hall that we called the Tailors' Synagogue. The craftsmen prayed there. In winter it was full because the main sanctuary was too cold to sit in.

In the lobby, there was a large flask with water. Half of it was imbedded in the wall. Nearby was a copper cup with two large copper handles, used for washing hands. Opposite stood a large box where the *posul* [invalid, worn out] Torah scrolls were kept. All year long the box was closed. On Simchat Torah, the Torah scrolls were removed and used in the traditional *hakafot* (annual festive dancing with the Torah scrolls).

On the left wall, in the foyer, there was a small door that led to a dark room where mortuary instruments were kept. Wooden steps led from there to the women's prayer hall, which was a low structure attached to the main synagogue.

Immediately upon entering the synagogue, beyond the doorway, there was a set of steps leading to the main sanctuary. There were 12 steps. Inside were wide benches. Four large pillars held the ceiling. They were incredibly thick. The reading table was in the middle of the room, on a *bimah* (podium) surrounded by a metal rail.

Approximately 20 steps led up to the holy ark which was adorned with a work of art, painted on either side, depicting two large lions and the ten commandments. A podium stood to the right of the arch where the *chazen* [cantor] led the services and adjacent to that was the rabbi's seat. He would forfeit sitting there on occasion when a distinguished guest came to town.

Until 1938, the synagogue was illuminated with oil lamps and large hanging candelabras. Electricity, which was introduced in 1938, did not change its appearance.

The beis medrish (study hall) was the center of life in Tarnogrod, year-round. But, during the high-holidays, the focus shifted to the synagogue. There the *kaporas* [traditional absolution rites before Yom Kippur] were conducted when entire families came to pray together. Not only townspeople, but folk from the surrounding countryside came too. Hundreds of candles illuminated the synagogue at such times.

Regularly though, the *beis medrish* was more of a focal point than the synagogue. People of all kinds gathered there, even from different affiliations. In the morning it was used as a study hall, filling up later in the day for afternoon and evening prayers. Lots of social activity went on there. Conversations were conducted about everything - world politics, business affairs, people sat around the fireside for hours, conducting dialogues and meetings of all sorts.

On the Sabbath, after the mid-day meal, children would gather there to play their childhood games, far from the sight of their parents.

The atmosphere was entirely different in the Hassidic *shtibls*. At the Belzer and at Shinever, where the ultra-orthodox prayed, services were much more exciting. Each *shtibl* was a world unto its own. There, they had a sense of unity, equal standing among rich and poor. The *shtibl* was like a second home, and for many, the only home. It was where one escaped from everyday worries and despair, where one found compassion, support and comfort in times of need.

Eli Hon, Eliezer Teicher and Yitzchak Teicher, z"l

Eli and Eliezer, survived. Like many of the Jews in Tarnogrod, they were bible scholars, studied the Talmud and had great aspirations.

Sometimes arguments would break out, often about religious matters, or about hiring a rabbi, a teacher, a s*hochet* [ritual slaughterer], and the like.

It was always lively in the *shtibl*. And there was no lack for a shot of whiskey. Here a *brit* [circumcision event], there a *yahrzeit* [anniversary of someone's death]. On Purim or on Simchat Torah, when everyone went from house to house, sampling all the food and drink on display, together in unison, it was truly a *sason v'simcha* [joy and delight] for the Jewish people. Those were the few happy days in the life of a Jewish town in pre-war Poland.

And that is how I will always remember Tarnogrod, the enchanted world of my youth, an incredible dream. The memory will never dissipate, nor will the sorrow I feel for those very many Jews who perished in the terrible disaster that ensued. Their memories will always remain deeply embedded in my heart.

My Grandfather Reb Mendel Yashes

My grandfather, *Reb* Mendel Yashes, was known to be a great Torah scholar and revered for his integrity. But making a living was difficult. He worked till a ripe old age. At 80 he was still working. He did not want to become a burden to anyone. He would wake up early in the morning, harness his horse, hitch up his buggy, and wait for passengers going to Bilgoraj.

He conjured quite an image: a great Torah scholar, glowing with spirituality, tending to his horse and buggy, unabashed by everyday physical labor, totally in harmony with the biblical dictum, "In the sweat of thy brow shalt thou eat bread."

Well-regarded by everyone in Tarnogrod and highly respected, he was the head of the *Chevre Kadisha* [sacred society for performing rites for the deceased] and a *mohel* [a Jew trained to perform ritual circumcision].

Quite a personality he was, awe-inspiring on the one hand and easy going on the other, while at all times scrupulously religious in his behavior. I remember accompanying him to synagogue on the Sabbath and on holidays, holding his *talit* [prayer shawl] bag and *machzor* [prayer book used on high holidays]. He wouldn't carry anything on the Sabbath, least the *eruv* [ritual enclosure allowing activities which are normally prohibited on the Sabbath such as carrying] be down. He used to pray in the Belzer *shtibl*, even though he wasn't a Belzer *Hasid* himself. He identified with the Belzer's ultra-orthodox lifestyle and had a permanent place in their synagogue, on the western wall, where he stood in prayer, from start of services to finish. On *Yom Kippur* [the Day of Atonement], he would stand all day long, not moving an inch, not uttering a word to anyone around.

On holidays, the Belzer *shtibl* would conduct their evening services late in the day. My grandfather used to utilize the break time between afternoon and evening prayers for a catnap. I was summoned to fetch him and when I returned, announcing that my grandfather was on his way, the cantor immediately began "*v'Hu racham*" ["And he being merciful" the beginning prayer of the evening service].

My grandfather, *Reb* Mendel Yashes, was blessed with enormous strength, he was considered to be a hero, not only by the locals, but also by the residents of the surrounding villages. Many stories of bravery were told about him. I remember once when grandfather was on his way to synagogue for afternoon prayers, two *goyim* [gentiles] started beating him up right in front of Pini Becker's house. It was when the Nazis first came to town. At the time he was more than 80 years old, but he retaliated bravely, returning their blows and leaving them wallowing in the muddy gutters. Afterwards, he came straight to our house, afraid the felons might follow him home and take revenge on him there.

He perished in the morning of the terrible massacre.[2] The murderers shot him while he was still lying in bed.

Grandfather never boasted about his virtues, not about his prowess as a Torah scholar, nor about his acts of kindness, and not about his courage. For him the essence of a person was what was inside. He didn't need to put his spirituality on display, didn't need to shine, or stun or overwhelm others. He did nothing for exhibition. Everything was for the service of the Almighty.

My heart weeps with sorrow when I recall his tragic death. I will forever cherish his memory.

Shlomo Marshelik

He was a small man, with short arms and a thin face. But, his head, that was something else. He was capable of thinking up the most amazing things, weaving words and music into poems that he sang each time there was a wedding in town. That's why we used to call him *Shlomo Marshelik* Shlomo the Marcher - as in a marching band].

He was a jack of all trades, worked as a tinsmith, shoemaker, locksmith and carpenter. If you needed a suit, he would also become an expert tailor. With his nimble hands, he made magic, so they said.

Making a living was the everyday mundane thing in his life. Not at all exciting for him. But, when a wedding was celebrated in town, he transformed into an entirely different being. He would suddenly become jolly, mingling with the hosts as if he were a member of the wedding party, puffing on a cigar he got from the groom's father, enveloped in smoke. At that moment, everyone knew, *Shlomo Marshelik* was thinking about the songs he was going to sing for the newlyweds, and the speeches he was going to give. It was a thrilling moment.

And when the guests crowded the entrance to the groom's room, where he was surrounded by bocherim [young lads, the grooms buddies], a path was cleared for Shlomo to pass through. He promptly took his place at the dais and began reciting whimsical lyrics rhyming with the names of the bride and groom, words of wisdom and festive greetings, praising the newlyweds and their distinguished pedigree.

All along, the guests stood by in awe, enthralled with Shlomo's amusing rhymes and lively melodies that just flowed and flowed. It seemed as though he would never tire. Everyone hoped he wouldn't, that the show would go on forever with his endearing and witty skits.

Shlomo's act didn't end there, not even after the chuppah, when the guests were seated for the festive meal. It was then that Shlomo really showed what he could do. He sang and danced to the delight of the guests, leaving everyone mesmerized and thinking, "He is truly a wonder of wonders!"

He had a way of getting to the hearts and souls of the guests, inspiring them to leave substantial gifts. When the time came for announcing the gifts, he would crack a joke while describing each one. The crowd enveloped him. Young girls, women, pushed themselves forward, bursting out in laughter with each joke.

When it came to dancing, he was particularly outstanding. Rolled up his sleeves, bent his knees, turned his head to the side and broke into a *kamarinskaya*, a *Cossack* or a *mazurka* [traditional Russian and Polish dances]. Then he'd grab one of the mothers-in-law, whirling her into a waltz as the guests cheered them on and the young ladies giggled away.

The next morning, everyone in town was tired and aching, but Shlomo Marshelik went about as if nothing had happened. He was pleased with himself and once again full of humor. Everyone wondered, "Where does he get so much energy?"

One day, there was a funeral in town. Everyone joined the procession, marching solemnly, with downcast eyes. From the front rows, where the mourners gathered, a cry could be heard. The widow and the orphans were sobbing, close relatives sighed. Suddenly, Shlomo Marshelik appeared. Tapping his cane on the ground, he broke out in a lively dance. An uproar ensued. People shouted, "What are you doing, Shlomo? This is a funeral, show respect for the dead!"

Shlomo cried back, "And what about the living? May they be disrespected?"

It seemed the deceased was actually one of Shlomo's rivals, someone who caused him great hardships, ruined an opportunity for him to perform at a wedding and robbed him of other lucrative prospects. He was a strong man and everyone was afraid of him. Once Shlomo felt his hand come down on him and for the rest of his life bore the shame of not being able to face up and get even.

But now, Shlomo was alive and he was dead, a reason to celebrate, so he broke out in a dance and tapping his cane, shouted, "So, where is your strength now? Go ahead, let's see if you can harm me now!"

At that point, no one could suppress a smile. Then suddenly, he turned serious again, dismissing his previous words and actions to a mere jest, and quickly reverting to a somber mode of behavior as would befit a funeral. Marching on quietly, he whispered, "The Angel of Death seizes its victim without being challenged. Life is nothing more than a game."

From top right: Gittale, Yisraelke (perished), Sini (Argentina), Sarah (America),Yona-Chaim (perished), Shmuel-Eli (Israel), Tobche and Yaakov (Argentina), Mendel-Yoshes, Yoskeh and Esther (perished)

Translator's Footnotes:

1. Casimir the Great, 14th century
2. The Jewish community of Tarnogrod was liquidated on Nov. 2, 1942.

[Pages 226-228]

The World of our Yesterdays

Shlomo Mantel

Translated by Martin Jacobs

The Miracle from Heaven

As soon as the first World War had begun the Russians withdrew from our town, which was taken by the Austrians, but several weeks later the Russians, in a great offensive, succeeded in retaking Tarnogrod, driving the Austrians beyond Cracow. Among the most difficult memories of that time is the arrest of the rabbi, Aryeh Teicher, and his son Moyshele. The Russians were looking for scapegoats for their earlier defeat and accused them of secretly working for the Austrians. The Russians led them out into the marketplace and placed them against a wall. Two Cossacks were already there and took aim with their rifles, ready to fire.

At that moment the Russian Orthodox priest appeared on the marketplace. He went over to the officer and began to argue with him for the release of the rabbi and his son. His talk must have had its effect. The officer ordered the Cossacks to free the Jews and let them return home.

In their release the Jews in the town saw a miracle from heaven.

Hakofes[1] with the Talmud

Chaim–Leibush Okst and his son Simkha were builders. They built Israel Fluk's house by themselves, without help from Christian builders. They were simple but honest and pious Jews who had great respect for a Torah scholar, for the learned men of the town.

Such were the Jewish craftsmen in Tarnogrod. They themselves worked hard and had no time to study, but for this reason they showed the greatest respect for those who did.

There were learned men not only in Tarnogrod but also in the surrounding villages. in our times in the village of Likev [probably the nearby village known to the Poles as Łukowa], where the kabbalist Kopl Likever once lived, Hertsl Zilberlicht was living, a great scholar, with rabbinical ordination. In the village of Lachow lived Joshua Milekh, a great scholar and a God fearing man. In old age he settled in Tarnogrod.

It once happened that the *gabbai*[2] did not call him up to the *hakofes* on *Simkhas–Torah*, along with all the other notables. This irritated the old scholar very much; he grabbed a Talmud volume and carried it around as though a *hakofe*, and called out to the gabbai:

"Moshe son of Khana, I don't need you to call me for a *hakofe*. I've learned the entire Talmud and it Is a great honor for me to go on a *hakofe* with a Talmud volume."

Jewish Heroes

At the time of the Tsarist military draft, when Christian boys from the surrounding villages came to present themselves to the military committee in Tarnogrod, they used to attack Jews along their way. One day the wild draftees spread out over the marketplace and started beating Jews. At that moment Lipe Adler the butcher arrived; he tore up a little tree which had been standing in the middle of the market place and began to rain blows on the draftees.

Blood was already running from some of the Gentile boys, but they weren't leaving yet, though the beating was becoming more and more savage. Only when the other butchers arrived, along with the stablemen, and began landing blows left and right, did they run away.

Such happenings were often repeated.

The power of a holy man

Old Jews from Tarnogrod used to tell a story that they heard from their parents and grandparents:

On the left side of the road to the cemetery there was a hill two storeys high. On top of it stood a cross. At one time, many, many years ago there was a church where the hill now is. Every time someone passed away and was being conveyed to the cemetery Gentile boys came out of the church and threw stones at the Jews who were following the funeral procession. And so it happened too at the funeral of the *Tsadik* [holy man] of Kraszew. The Gentile boys started showering the procession with stones. Then the Jews placed the casket to the side and started reciting the verse "*Shakets teshaketsenu*"[3], which is what the *Tsadik* some time before had commanded his followers to do in case the Gentiles should stone his funeral.

When they had finished reciting the verse several times the little church suddenly sank into the earth, and in its place grew this little hill, which is there to this day.

As a remembrance that there was once a church there the Gentiles of the town set up a cross on the hill

Translator's notes:

    1.   Processions around the synagogue with the Torah scrolls on Simhat Torah.

    2.   Manager of the synagogue, who assists in the running of the synagogue services. The word is sometimes translated "sexton" or "beadle".

    3.   "You shall utterly abhor [an abominable thing]" (Deuteronomy 7:26), with a play on words of "sheygets" (a Gentile boy) and "shakets" (to abhor).]

[Pages 229-232]

The Religious Life

Y. Ben–Efraim (Yechiel Hering)

Translated by Chesky Wertman

    Amongst the varied associations in Tarnogrod there was the *Agudah* and *Mizrachi*, referred to as the religious organizations of the youth, they actively and vibrantly participated in the national activities of the *Hapoel–HaMizrahi* and in *Tzeirei Agudas– Yisroel*. They participated in educational work, and in the preparations of religious pioneers for *aliyah* to *Eretz Yisroel*.

Beit Yaakov School

    From moment the "Beit Yaakov" movement was formed there arose amongst the young girls a yearning to engage in spiritual activities and they began to assume an important role in the lifestyle of the shtetl. Contrary to the traditional view of the Rabbis who established boundaries for young girls and forbid them to study torah, these young girls participated in activities that were productive and far reaching and in doing so they acquired for themselves the eternal *mitzvah* of Rabbi Shimon, son of Chalafsa, of developing a proclivity for Torah and an appreciation of the supremacy of Torah in their home, and in worldly pursuits even under difficult conditions.

[Translation of Hebrew. Paragraph is same as above in Yiddish]

Young Girls From ";Hashomer Hadati"

Young women played an enthusiastic role in the organizational activities of *Mizrahi* in Tarnogrod they were imbued with religious spiritual verve and idealistically sought to build a Jewish home in *Eretz Yisroel*.

Hapoel HaMizrachi offered evening courses in the Bible and conversational Hebrew, to help gain knowledge about the land of Israel. The *Mizrahi* members participated in *Keren Kayemet* [Jewish National Fund], *Keren Hayesod* [United Israel Appeal], and in distributing the shekel.

Among the young members of the religious organizations there were a group of young men known as the Villerner, they gathered in the Belzer *Shtiebel* [literally "little house" which served as a house of prayer], where they sat and studied Torah all day and night.

Inside the Belzer *Shtiebel*, were long tables and benches and along the walls were bookshelves filled with the Talmud and other scholarly works. It was there that we prayed, learned and held chassidic gatherings. The holidays were lively.

There was immense energy during the Chassidic gatherings. They danced and sang Chassidic songs that expressed intense spirituality and fusion with G–d; the songs that were sung in the *Shtiebel* were heard throughout the shtetl. At Chassidic *Melaveh Malkahs* [a meal in honor of the departure of the Sabbath], and at other events we spoke about many topics that pertained to the *Shtiebel*. The activists of the community listened, and provided assistance to help the destitute, or to arrange a Chassidic celebration, or to assist in the marriage of a bride, and so on.

Belzer Chasidim were infused with the ideal that every gathering strengthens the love of a fellow Jew, which in turn draws down the Divine Presence.

In the Belzer *Shtiebel* there were renowned eminent scholars:

Henekh Blum, Berish Itzekels, Israel–Chaim (Yechiel's son–in–law), Hersh–Meir Zichler, Avrahmele Shohet and his father R' Yankel, Teyvl Nachum Herbstman, and my father Efraim Yankel.

There were many others, many other G–d fearing scholars. Unfortunately, their names have escaped my memory.

A needy person — a Yid, a *Ben–Torah* [literally, "son of Torah" who leads his life according to the Torah], who would come to the *shtetl*, already knew the path to the Belzer *Shtiebel*. There he would always encounter people young and old, who would help him in an honorable manner.

Belzer Chasidim were not only ones who davened [prayed] and learned in the Belzer *Shtiebel*, there were also the Chasidim of various other Chassidic *Rebbes*. Trisker, Chasidim, Kozmerer, Sanzer and Gerrer, also davened there.

The first Chasidim in the *Shtiebel* were the followers of R' Yossela of Lublin. He was R' Koppel Lukower,'s brother – – a Tarnogrod native.

One of the interesting role models of the *Shtiebel* was R' Chaim Yecheil Shohet, an extremely pious person, who as a rule on Friday nights arranged meals for all the needy people that would go to the *Shtiebel* to daven. R' Chaim would not allow Friday night prayer services to start until all the needy people had a place to eat the *Shabbos* meals.

When he died, my father Efraim Yankel z"l [of blessed memory] took upon himself the responsibility of arranging the meals for the needy.

R' Chaim Yecheil Shohet, also had an inn that provided lodging to the needy who would come to Tarnogrod and were unable to leave quickly. A poor religious Jew who would come to town, already knew the address of R' Chaim Yecheil Shohet, and knew that was the person who would do everything possible to assist him.

Another fine role model was R' Avraham Moshe Melamud, who was a sofer [scribe]. On *Shabbos* he would only speak in the holy language and he wore a *shtreimel* [black, broad–brimmed hat]. On *Tisha B' Av* [the fast day commemorating the destruction of the Temples in Jerusalem and other calamities] he would place a sack on his head and lament the destruction of the Temple.

But, on Purim he would cheer up the entire crowd with amusing rhyming songs and until late at night he would lecture and discuss the holiday, and other Torah topics.

In the Belzer *Shtiebel* there also davened *Misnagdim* [opponents of chasidim] who did not follow any *Rebbe*, but they were pious, punctilious Jews, who were very learned, that is how R' Yossel Wertman and his son were, pious but not connected to any *Rebbe*.

It was unnoticeable that davening and learning, in the *Shtiebel*, were *chassidim* of various *Rebbes,* I never heard of any arguments. The *Shtiebel* imparted unity and friendship.

At the time of war, in this *Shtiebel*, was the Ghetto Hospital. The Nazis, near the *Shtiebel*, in this very place, used it for their murderous acts they perpetrated on the entire town.

[Pages 233-236]

"Yavneh" School

by Y. Ben-Efraim (Yechiel Hering)

Translated by Sara Mages

The Last Graduating Class Before the War

It was not easy to support the school. If we remember the poverty and distress that prevailed in the Jewish community - we will understand the difficulties that the school faced at that time. The school endured thanks to invaluable virtues: extraordinary dedication of a group of activists, loyalty of the teaching staff and national recognition of the parents. And indeed, the school has been very successful thanks to these factors.

The history of the youth in the small towns of Poland has not yet been written, and if this history is ever written the youth of Tarnogrod will also take its place among them. Although the goals between the youth movements were different, the common line in all of them was the revolt on the present and the desire to establish new patterns for the Jewish people.

Many were the roads that led to this goal, but the central road was the road of the Hebrew schools, although this road was more difficult than all other roads.

The road chosen by the activists, teachers and parents was always illuminated by the sacred idea of redeeming Zionism, and they had a great influence on social and public life.

The movement, which imposed on its members to speak Hebrew from early age, carried on its shoulders the Hebrew education and the study of the Hebrew language. Not only the children and the youth, but also the fathers and mothers strived to succeed in it, and in this the school gave its respectable part.

Here, children and teenagers dreamed of a more beautiful future when they will settle in Eretz Israel. An educational environment was created for the belief in the resurrection of the people and pioneering Zionism.

The regular trips out of town helped the social unification. The youth was slowly trained for independence and pioneering roles in his life.

In the Hebrew school we saw the perfect national school. We were joined by members whose souls are thirsty for freedom and human and national renewal, and they saw their future in pioneering fulfillment in Eretz Israel.

The aspiration of Mizrachi[1] for the fulfillment of the prophetic vision -; for out of Zion shall the Torah come forth, and the word of the Lord from Jerusalem" - found an extensive area of operation also in Tarnogrod.

The men of Mizrachi said:

"With all our strong desire to revive our language and make it the language of education and life, the language alone will not give us the light in the Torah and the affection for our ancient literature. The Torah is the first source and the fertile nucleus of Judaism and should not be replaced by different streams."

The men of Mizrahi had talented speakers who lectured and taught, in simple and clear words, about Zionism, religion and work, about the nature and mission of HeHalutz HaMizrachi[2] and Hashomer Hadati[3], and the great work entrusted to them. The general feeling among the religious youth in our town was in terms of "*Na'aseh V'nishma*.[4]

The young and the adults knew how to organize and get along in meetings and debates, in practical work, in activities on behalf of the Jewish National Fund and for the behalf of other institutions.

At the time that Lord Balfour issued his well-known declaration, the Holy Land was drawn all at once into the arena of European-American-style cultural-political life - at the same time the observer of the Torah was placed before the sublime and difficult experience.

The gaze, full of longings of the Jews in the Diaspora in front of the Tabernacle of Testimony[5] of God, united the religious Jews and in the thousands they began to express the yearnings to revive the desolation of Jerusalem, for indeed, the desolation of Jerusalem heralded and declared that the fulfillment of God's will within life on this land, the Holy Land, is a precondition to full national life.

Hashomer Hadati

A Group of Young Women in the Last Years Before the War

A Group of Young Women from Different Streams in Tarnogrod

Roize Teicher, Ite'la Teicher, Rivka Zetzer, Chaya Apper, *Malka Silberzweig, Tile Adler, Tzvia Teicher, Dvora'le Adler (lives in America), Sosha Teicher, Leah* Feifer, *Finkel* Eisenberg- Teicher, *Golde* Alpenbain-Teicher *(lives in Israel), Beiletche Teicher*

The boys and girls of Hashomer Hadati in Tarnogrod believed that the closed gates of the countries of the Diaspora and the open gate of Eretz Israel - are not just the results of the reasons of its history - they are only guidelines and means of education on behalf the Providence to the Jewish people.

However, historical events can be understood in several forms, the order of his history depends on changes and transformations - while God's voice is concealed in his Torah, the same voice speaks to us from the commandment of the settlement of Eretz Israel.

This voice taught us the way we should go, with all our strength and spiritual and physical efforts, without deviating slightly to the right and left, without becoming dependent on the thought processes of others, without seeing in any political change a kind of destruction of our national hopes."

This is how the national religious youth in Tarnogrod thought and acted.

Translator's footnotes:

1.   Mizrachi - a religious Zionist organization founded in 1902 in Vilnius.
2.   HeHalutz HaMizrachi (lit. "The Mizrachi Pioneer") movement was established by Mizrachi.
3.   Hashomer Hadati (lit. "The Religious Guard") is a religious Zionist youth organization.
4.   The Jews standing at Mount Sinai signal their acceptance of the Torah with the words "Na'aseh V'nishma"–"We will do and we will hear/understand."
5.   The term "tent of witness^#147;/"tabernacle of testimony" first appears in the Book of Numbers as a reference to the portable temple structure that the Levites were in charge of dismantling, transporting, re-erecting and camping round about it.

[Pages 237-240]

Bais Ya'akov[1]

Y. Ben-Efraim (Yechiel Hering)

Translated by Miriam Leberstein

The girls who belonged to Bais Ya'akov in Tarnogrod possessed special ethical qualities. In addition to engaging in communal activities, they were devoted to the land of Israel and contributed a great deal to the Zionist movement, bringing it to life in their homes.

Among these ordinary Jewish girls were some who understood the deeper meaning of all the principles and religious laws of the Jewish faith, how one must conduct oneself in all communal situations, the laws about Sabbath observance and other aspects of Judaism.

These girls learned a lot about the meaning and goals of Judaism. They knew that there wasn't just one interpretation but many, that Judaism contains a world of symbols that reflect the great truths of the religion, and which conceal various secrets and meanings the depths of which cannot be fully comprehended.

What did these girls think as they took their final steps to a horrific death? Did they believe that the Jewish people was the one among all the peoples of the world chosen to serve as proof of the greatness and uniqueness of the Jewish god, as they had learned? Why did God look on with such indifference as his army was annihilated? And where was the news of the coming of the Messiah, who is supposed to liberate us?

Perhaps they thought that this was what the beginning of the time of Messiah's coming was supposed to be like. Perhaps they accepted the law, the most terrible law ever promulgated against a people. After all, they had always held high the flag of Judaism, and from their education knew that everything in life is swallowed up in suffering. Their teachers and school administrators died along with them. We note here those who were the most active: Aron David Honikman; Henekh Blum; Berish Vayser; Saul Mordkhe Frukhtman; Yisroel Levinzon; Tuvye Kroyn; and the rabbi's son, Saul Teicher.

The Nazi murderers killed the Jewish children but could not break them. As strong as oaks they fulfilled their tasks under the sword that hung over their heads until the last moments of their lives.

Piety and Beauty

Just like their mothers, the young girls in Tarnogrod practiced the rules of piety in the most refined and quiet manner. On all the lonely roads I travelled, my way was brightened by the virtuous glances of the girls in my former home.

Walking on the noisy streets of big cities I would feel a yearning for the beauty of my poor home, for which I still feel the anxious and lonely love of an orphaned generation.

Throughout my life there has remained in my heart the yearning for that piety and beauty and now I remain so sad and ashamed for these lives cut off so young. I will never relinquish my sadness over the horrific death of these dear and holy Tarnogrod girls who did not abandon their parents in their last days.

Bine and Royze Teicher

Translator's Footnote:

1.   Network of youth movements and schools for Orthodox girls.

[Pages 241-255]

Tarnogrod Between the Two World Wars

S. Chaper (Fefer)

Translated by Tina Lunson with Martin Jacobs

Tarnogrod had an exuberant Jewish life, with every charm, with all the joys and all the suffering and problems that existed in Jewish life in all the other Jewish towns in Poland. Until the year 5685 there was a Jewish community in Tarnogrod, that numbered some 500 families. They lived in the center of the town, in the market square and in the lanes around the market. Around them, on all four sides, the town was occupied by Christians.

Right upon entering the town, even from a distance, one could already tell where the Jewish houses began. The first sign was the end of the trees and fields that surrounded the Christian houses. There began the naked, poor little houses without the least adornment of a tree or a little green.

The Jewish houses cold also be recognized by the shutters on the windows, which were closed from inside with a strip of iron. But the Christian houses did not have closed shutters, not because of poverty, but because they had less to fear an attack than the Jews. The Jews in town had always lived in fear of the Christian attackers. True, in a real crisis the shutters would be of little help, the shutters were an unconditional component of a house and in a certain sense gave an illusion of security, of protecting oneself from the enemy.

The Jewish children always longed for a tree and they were drawn to the forest, to the fields. In free hours one ran outside the town, climbed up in someone's tree and tore off an apple, a pear, a bunch of currents, except that this was tied up with fear, with the terror of the Christian proprietor, for the dog, that could exact a price. We were often caught, but that did not stop us from repeating the same thing a little while later.

Jewish Livelihoods

Our town belonged to Czarist Russia up until 1914. The Austrian border was 7 kilometers from Tarnogrod. The village of Meydan already belonged to Austria. The Russian border post was on our side. We called the border soldiers "*obyeshtchickes*" [freeloaders / scroungers][a] and they bought everything at Jewish stores.

The horse dealers in our town used to buy up horses from the surrounding peasants and in the dark nights at the end of the month, smuggle them across the border into Austria. There were some rich people among those horse dealers, but they lived apart in a certain sense, among themselves and the butchers. They prayed with the butchers in a separate *minyan*.

Their trade was one of the good livelihoods in town, just as was smuggling certain linens, handkerchiefs, shawls, silks and woolens and various other goods from the Austrian side where they were much cheaper.

None of these livelihoods were easily pursued. Besides the dangers at the border there were also inspections in the warehouses, where they looked for any signs of Russian manufacture on the goods. The Jews also informed one another about such activities although that could lead to misfortunes, as in the case of Zelda Opfer who was killed by a border guard.

For each item of merchandise that Jews touched, some special permission from the government was required, and not everyone could obtain it. Yet Jews dealt in flax and linen and other agricultural products used to make clothing.

Trade in grain was well developed in Tarnogrod. There were big merchants who had warehouses in town and farmers brought grain to them. But there were also some who left home early on Sunday for the village, where they spent the whole week living on roasted potatoes and a piece of dry bread because they would not try any of the peasants' food. People called them the village runners. They bought from the peasants the various goods that they had worked on all week and returned to town with them on Friday afternoon, selling the goods to the bigger merchants after *Shabbos*.

The main problem was how to earn enough to make *Shabbos*, to pay the teacher for teaching the children. Because of that Jews labored the whole week, were exhausted and very busy.

The fairs that took place in town each Tuesday were an important source of livelihood. The peasants brought their grain, chickens, eggs and milk and for the money they got for those products, bought fuel, salt, clothes, boots and other household goods in the town.

There were others in town – rabbinic judges, elementary teachers, cantors, ritual slaughterers, match makers and plan poor folks, people who literally lived from the air.

The bakers had an honorable livelihood.

Merchandise was bound up with many difficulties. Besides the border guards there were also Russian officials in the town whom we called *smotshkes* [meaning unknown], who watched that the goods in the shops had Russian seals, showing that they were of Russian manufacture.

True, there was also a way around that. Little machines were made that could copy the original seals and stamp them onto products after they were in the stores.

Once it happened that Zelda Opfer was carrying such "*kashered*" goods from home to her shop, and met up with one of the officials who shot her as she was already on the threshold of the shop and killed her on the spot.

It is not hard to imagine the impression this incident made on the Jews in the town at that time.

Jews also dealt in flax, linen and various other agricultural products, from which all kinds of clothing articles were crafted for the peasants. Also commerce in hair was well developed.

There were also larger merchants who owned warehouses and conducted their business in the town. Others left on Sunday in the morning to go to the villages and returned only on Friday evening. Those Jews lived the whole week on roasted potatoes and a piece of dry bread.

However hungry they may have been, they did not take any other food from the peasants.

Those Jews – whom people called village-runners – bought up goods from the peasants and sold them in the town to the larger dealers.

The chief problem of chasing after livelihood was to earn enough for *Shabbos* and to pay the teacher to teach the children.

One of the bases of Jewish livelihood was the fairs in town, that were held every Tuesday. On that day the peasants brought into town the things that they had grown in their fields, what they had raised in their barns – chickens, cows and horses – and with the money that they earned for all those things, bought clothes, boots, kitchen utensils, tools, fuel oil, salt and other things in the town.

The greatest number of the Jewish merchants lived in poverty. Around them lived the elementary teachers, rabbinical judges, cantors, ritual slaughterers, match-makers and other religious functionaries. The hardest and poorest livelihoods were all kinds of porters and the water-carriers.

The Wealthy

Tarnogrod's rich people did not possess any big houses. Most of the houses there were built of wood. A proprietor of such a little wooden shop among the four rows of shops that stood in the middle of the market square, was considered a rich man.

Naftali Sobol did not even have that. No one knew what his wealth consisted of, but he was reckoned as the first among the town's wealthy.

He was no great Talmud scholar. He had a lovely daughter, Malkale, who was his entire hope since he expected nothing from his two sons.

When Naftali Sobol brought his son-in-law Yossele into town, it resounded through the entire village.

It appeared that this was a match made in heaven, except that the Tarnogrod match-maker had not had any part in it...

When Naftali Sobol went to *shul* on *Shabbos* to pray, we went with his son-in-law Yossele, who wore a velvet cap with a broad visor, a little different from what people wore in Tarnogrod. He wore his velvet-collared black overcoat unbuttoned so that people could see his modern silk coat inside.

Naftali Sobol was then the happiest Jew in town and knew that even the most wealthy were envious of him.

Most of the Tarnogrod Jews were followers of some rebe or another. They generally could not comprehend how one could live without a *rebe*. In the home, in family life, in rearing children, marrying them, especially daughters, in presenting one's self for conscription – for each thing one had to get the advice and the blessing of a *rebe*.

One did not necessarily travel to the *rebe*, whichever one the followers considered theirs, because if was often too far, so one went to the Belzer *Rebe* or to the Rozvadover *Rebe*, and they often visited the town.

On the contrary, the wealthy, like Yosef Munis or Moshe Yoynes, could indeed travel to distant *rebeiyim*. They wanted to be sure that the followers would not fall away from their *rebeiyim* and sought ways for them to visit the town more frequently.

So, the rich men used to bring in the Trisker Maggid's son, a grandson of Rabbi Motele Tshernobiler, and the joy in the town was incalculable. The *rebe* held the *Shabbos* table in the study house, a natural place that belonged equally to all the Jews. The cabinet-makers and carpenters volunteered to put together seating for one thousand. The boards for the benches were borrowed from Moshe Leibushes and Yetshe Fogel. The benches were made like steps and reached up to the ceiling. The table rituals took a full half-day, into the night, and the joy in the town was great.

The Kuzmer Rabbi and the Trisker used to come to town in a carriage drawn by four horses that had been borrowed from the Jewish magnate, Avrahaml Fabrikant.

When the rebe left the town all the splendor, the joy, went with him, and life went back to being gray and gloomy.

There were also some *rebeiyim* who lived on the other side of the border in Austria. But coming over was not difficult. One had only to buy a ticket in the township for 30 *kopikes*, with which one could cross the border freely for 30 days.

The Tarnogrod Rabbi Moshele Teicher with his son Eliezer, his daughter Itele and her husband

These were the points of light in the grey life of the town. They healed sick spirits, bringing happiness and courage and giving content and sense to life.

Hasidim

During a visit from the Trisker Rabbi, or from the Kuzmer Rabbi, who came to visit their followers in the town, they stayed at Yosef Munis or Moshe Yoynes. With the arrival of the Trisker Maggid's sons, and of Rabbi Motele Tshernobiler's grandsons, the joy in the town was immense.

Often such a visit was accompanied with difficult problems. There were no separate *Hasidic* prayer houses. The Hasidim prayed in various study-houses. Where would the *rebe* pray? Where would he host the *Shabbos* table? True, both Kuzmer and Trisker Hasidim prayed in the prayer house in Belz, but in order to maintain neutrality the *rebe* prayed in the study-house and held the *Shabbos* table there as well.

None of the prayers, even those who did not belong to the *rebe's* followers, opposed this. The Tarnogrod carpenters Simcha and Hershl took on the work of building the tables and benches and preparing seating for more than a thousand people.

The table was set up in the very center and the benches were each higher than the one before so that no one would block another. The boards for the benches were borrowed from Moshe Leibushes and Yetshe Fogel. The top row of benches reached the ceiling.

The *rebe's* table rituals lasted late into the night and the joy in the town was great.

Everyone in the town knew that they had Yosef Munis and Moshe Yoynes to thank for the *rebe's* visit, as they had taken care of the expenses and of getting him across the border.

Jewish Aristocrats

Avreml Fabrikant was a landowner and people actually called him the Jewish nobleman of Lukow.

At that time there were other Jewish aristocrats besides Avreml in the area of Tarnogrod. But for the others the property was used only for commerce. He rented it out for a certain time and for that term the property and all its inventory could be rented out by a second aristocrat for whom the property was not merchandise that went from hand to hand. Just like the gentile aristocrats he was well established on his estate in Lukow, retained a Jewish lease-holder all those years, and conducted himself like all the other Christian aristocrats who were so attached to their land.

Getting into the estate of the Lukow prince was just as difficult as getting into any Christian estate, where the dogs threw such a fit and guards kept things in order. Before every *Hoshanah Rabbah* [seventh day of Sukkot] Avreml came into Tarnogrod, bought an *etrog* [citron] from Moshele the *rebe*, prayed in the study-house on holidays, made the circuits with all the respectable Jews, the rabbi at the head. He then was given an *aliyah* to the Torah and donated wood from his forest to heat the study-house through the winter.

When his wife Tirtza died and had to be buried in the Tarnogrod Jewish cemetery, the burial society demanded the highest sum from him, with which they mended the fence around the cemetery and there was enough left over for a celebratory dinner for the members of the burial society.

The Jews of my Town

Jews in Tarnogrod did not plant any trees, but the Jewish children were very drawn to the trees – perhaps not so much the trees as to the fruit that drew them to climb a tree, pull off an apple, a pear, or something else.

Despite the fact that there was fear of the gentile proprietor and of the dog that guarded the orchard, we boys still tested fate and more than once our test ended with heavy blows and bites from the dog.

A longing for trees and vegetables lived in our hearts, and when the Tarnogrod "pioneers" took to the land their first thought was to plant trees and flowers. In that we saw the symbol of our ancestors' rootedness in in the earth.

My Teachers

The Elementary Teacher Reb Chaim Tzibelkale

First, of all it is my debt to mention the elementary teacher with whom I studied. He was called Chaim Tzibelkale. To this day I do not know whether that was his real family name. At the time he was already in his seventies, but it did not bother him to be the teacher of three- to seven-year old children. After age seven they moved on to a Talmud teacher.

The *heder* consisted of one big room in which the oven was also located, and there was also something cooking in that oven. The two big beds were covered with sheets. There were other small things besides that, and there was still space for the approximately forty children who studied with him. They all sat around the big table on which there were always lying various pieces of bread that the children had brought with them from home, smeared with butter, chicken fat or jam. Flies flew around over it all.

The old teacher had a good relationship with the children. He had never traveled outside the town. Once his son Eli Meir, who even then was burdened with a large family, but was registered as being several years younger than he was, and in his later years was called before the conscription board in Bilgoraj. His elderly father went with him. That was the first time that he had traveled from the *shtetl* and made such a long trip of 18 kilometers.

Our elderly teacher was full of surprise from his long journey and sought someone to express his inspiration to. He knew that most of the adults in town had made such a trip more than once and would not understand his enthusiasm, so he turned to us children and began to depict how he had traveled to Bilgoraj and back and for the first time had seen what a large world God possessed, and how much beauty there was. Inspired, he told us: "You may think that over there, behind the pharmacy where the sun sets is the end of the world. I also thought that at one time. But as one travels to Bilgoraj one can see God's great world, one rides and rides, and one goes a little way by foot to show mercy for the horse who must drag a wagon with people so far, one rides for hours and God's world does not end, it becomes ever more wide and beautiful. If you don't see it with your own eyes, you cannot imagine it."

Reb Avraham-Moshe – His Poems and His *Sefira* Box[1]

Translated by Martin Jacobs

Reb Avrom-Moyshe was a *melamed* [teacher], a very poor man. When Purim came he wrote his own Purim story, including poems, to which he also fitted melodies.

On Purim night *Reb* Avraham-Moshe went around the town wearing a *shtrayml* [hat worn by pious Jews on Sabbath and holidays] and disguised as a "Purim Rabbi" [comedian parodying rabbinical ways]. With fiddle in hand he sang the song he himself had created in Hebrew, which began with the words:

> Light for Mordechai darkness for Haman,
> A blessing for Mordechai, shame for Haman,
> In the elevation of the righteous is joy,
> In the destruction of the wicked is joyous shouting,
> Haman's name will be erased
> And Mordechai appointed in his place …[b]

So the song that he had written went on for a long time, according to the alphabet. If his voice held out, he sang other songs too, also of his own composition.

I remember how I went around with him to a lot of houses, when I accompanied him and a lot of other boys on Purim evening to collect money to buy and repair books for the *beit midrash*. His songs drew out a great deal of cheerfulness and seeing this effect, his face beamed with joy.

In the morning, *Shushan Purim* [15 of Adar, when Purim is celebrated in walled cities such as Jerusalem], I also went with him to the square between the Shinovar and Belzer *shtibl*, where both had set up tables and *Reb* Avraham-Moshe, a short man with a long beard and broad fur hat, danced on the tables by himself while playing his fiddle and singing the songs, his own new creations.

The audience that gathered around the tables clapped their hands, children and adults recognized the melodies and tunes to which he sung his songs of praise. It was literally happiness and joy. The joy of those days has remained in my memory all this long time.

Purim and Simchat Torah were to two happiest days for the Jews in Tarnogrod, and just as Avraham-Moshe was for Purim, so were for Simchat Torah the dozen Jews who had taken upon themselves the task of bringing joy to the town by dancing and singing in the streets.

Avraham-Moshe was also famous for his sefira-box. This was his original invention. One just had to turn the specially-constructed handle and out came the date of tomorrow's counting day and the basis for the accompanying special characteristics, according to the receipt for that day. The box was square and nicely carved. On the top is was covered with glass and inside were the counting days in the usual order with their characteristic bases.

In all probability the construction of such a box must have cost – besides money – a lot of craft and months of work.

He later gave it as a gift to the *Beit Midrash* and would not accept any payment for it.

Reb Chaimel Shohet

Among the most distinguished, eminent Jews to take on making people joyful on Simchat Torah was Chaimel Shohet. On the night before Simchat Torah he took all the children from the *Beit Midrash* and with a Torah scroll in his hands led the children through the streets, all the while shouting:

"Jewish people!"
The children answering him in one voice:
"Meeeh, meeeh".
Chaimel went through the streets like that late into the night. On the morrow, Simchat Torah in the morning, he would be drunk and no one knew where he had gotten so much whisky.

After praying the Simchat Torah service late he came over to the Belzer *Beit Midrash* and took Itchele Treger by the arm and went off with him to eat *kreplach* at various homes. Their first visit was to Simchale Lemel's, who lived right across from the *beit midrash*. Everyplace he went, he was followed by laughing children.

I recall how Simchale's wife, Tchepele, pleaded with *Reb* Chaimel that she had only prepared enough for her own family. But Chaimel considered himself a drunkard on that one day, who was always invited. No talking helped. He and Itchele Treger both sat down at the table that was set with the holiday dishes, and Chaimel ordered, "Itche, eat!"

And Itche ate.

And so it went in the other houses where they went, singing jolly tunes and sitting down once again to eat with the appetites of people who had not eaten anything all day.

Itchele Treger made it known to the children in the *Beit Midrash* what the Garden of Eden [heaven] was and what hell was. He described to us children how he, Itchele, would be placed after his death in the Garden of Eden in a huge ritual bath full of small farfel, cut fine, and big navy beans. Good angels would fly around singing songs and talking to him, saying "Itchele, east, eat to your heart's content!" He would sit for three full days in that bath full of farfel and beans and eat without interruption.

We children stood with open mouths and listened to his depiction of this satiated Garden of Eden. When it came to hell he was sad, because he envisioned being put into a similar bath with the same farfel and big beans that came up to his neck, but above him flew black angels with eyes that spit fire and who told him with devilish laughter to eat. He wanted to bend his head and start eating and felt that his neck was stiff, his hands and his whole body were paralyzed yet inside in his stomach and mouth he felt a great hunger, but he could not bend. His eyes would bulge out of their sockets and he felt that he would faint from hunger...

*

Jewish life in Tarnogrod developed and achieved a certain level in all areas. But as each rise was accompanied by a crisis, the life of the youth became one of emigration and decline.

There were times when the economic situation was difficult and there appeared to be no way out. Tarnogrod did not have any factories or big workshops. The craftsmen worked from very early to very late at night. When it seemed as though there were not enough hours, they grabbed another eight hours of work on a winter *Shabbos* evening. In the morning they would run to the first *minyen* in the *beit midrash*, pray quickly and hurry right back to work.

That is how it looked in the times when there was work. Then you could hear through the windows the sound of cantorial singing and various songs.

Then came the days of crisis, when it was dark in the Jewish homes, and no one hurried to pray and there was no singing.

A depression hung over the town.

But even in those days the Jewish youth was busy with cultural activities. With the greatest stubbornness and determination, with the with the limited human and financial strength, work continued in the library which was the home and center for the youth in Tarnogrod.

Almost all the youth were grouped around the library. The Library became more than a place where one got a book. It became an educational institution, where there was concern for the intellectual development of the youth, and with a watchful eye saw to it that each member or reader would read the appropriate book that would enrich and broaden his horizons.

Its ascent also began to be expressed in other cultural forms. The drama circle was created, and everything together became an integral component of the general Jewish life in Tarnogrod.

*

Thus were the scholars and the ordinary Jews. The scholars taught, formed and shaped the Tarnogrod boy, who was not inclined to drunkenness and hooliganism, who walked through life with the fineness and elevation that he learned in *heder*.

The modesty and purity that we learned in *heder* accompanied us all through our lives.

The community ways in the home and on the street were Jewish through and through, and the Jews in Tarnogord, various, but bright, kind, heartful and smart, not only in their minds but also smart in their hearts, with a certain wisdom that comes from vigilant senses.

This was always the particular characteristic of the Tarnogrod Jew, who did not have the opportunity to expend his energy in any big industrial undertaking, in any many-branched businesses, and so was also far from any cold calculating and brutality.

Their strength was their belief, that is deeper than all wells and clearer than the deepest human understanding, and thus the assignment of telling about their life is so huge and so holy.

Translator's footnote:

1.   "*Sefira*" is the ritual counting of the forty-nine days between Passover and *Shavuot*. To aid in the count sometimes decorative boxes are used which contain scrolls which help keep track of the day.

Editor's Notes:

a.   The editor would like to thank the following ViewMate responders for their help in translating "*obyeshtchickes*": Ite Doktorski, Emma Karabelnik and Martin Jacobs.
b.   End of translation by Martin Jacobs.

[Pages 256-259]

Days of Fasting

A. Tishbi

Translated by Irving Lumerman

Edite by Lorraine Rosengarten

Tarnogrod Jews have always kept the fasts such as: Seventeen *Tammuz*, Tisha B'Av, Yom Kippur, Fast of Gedaliah, Fast of Esther, Monday and Thurday, and the Tenth of Tevet, etc. However, when it came to the evening before Passover, and the Fast of the Firstborn, who would fast in memory of the plague in Egypt and would thank G-d because the Jewish firstborn sons were saved, the Jews of Tarnogrod found a way not to fast.

The evening before Passover, every firstborn son came into the *bet hamidrash* where the teachers were waiting for them having prepared a *siyum* [completion of a tractate of the Talmud, followed by a celebratory meal], that they learned all year and left the last page with the "*Hadran alakh*" [prayer recited at the end of each tractate] for the evening before Passover, and would finish together with the firstborn of the town.

The happiness from the *siyum* and finishing the tractate required a small meal and the firstborn did not have to fast. Thus all firstborn had a gift.

On the day before Passover the scholars had true satisfaction from their study. Those who persisted and studied a lot could, on that day, serve a great number of firstborn and so received more money.

I remember when it came to Hanukkah, in the *beit midrash*, the boys studied small tractates such as Masechet Megilla, Ta'anit and Horayot that had only twelve pages. This was done so that on the evening before Passover they would be able to complete more tractates.

It was strange to observe, in those days, when every Jew had so much to do in the house by cleaning and bringing in the Passover dishes and cutlery and various other *erev yom tov* [evening before holiday] duties, the *Beit Midrash* boys all sat at their tables with the Gemorahs and taught the unlearned Jews: Hersh-Meir and Itche "Jokim Galis," Shmuel-Itskik-Hersh, Meir Bershis, Leizer and Yekhezkel Mosheles, Alter Itsiks, Shiala the Biala-Vans (Schlechterman), Hershele-Yossel Retczyks, etc. The money that they received brought them great joy, but this was not the only important thing they gained on this day.

I also remember something else. My grandfather, *Reb* Avraham, may his name be blessed, was a firstborn son, and I remember that he left a page of the *Gemorah* to finish on the evening before Passover.

Removing the Evil-Eye

There was a time when Doctor Libely left Tarnogrod and the town was left without a doctor. However, the Tarnogroder Jews were not afraid. At any rate, people did not go to the doctor immediately with each little thing. First, they tried other things among themselves. First they went to get rid of the evil-eye. Three learned people in the town did this: Shmuel Zeiss, Yentche Melamed and Avraham Moshe Melamed.

From about the age of 7 years I studied at the house of Yentche Melamed. I remember that on the first day of *heder* [small Jewish elementary school], a woman came in with a shawl around her neck, stood by the door and waited until the Rabbi finished his lesson. He already knew why she came to him, went to her and asked the name of the sick person, the name of the sick father. He had all of it written down and when the woman left, the Rabbi washed his hands, put on his *gartl* [cloth belt worn around the waist, either at all times or while praying], took down a small book that was hanging on the wall and turned to the eastern wall and murmured something with his lips. When he was finished, he put the book back in its place. We children were in awe of the book; there were the names of the angles, which the Rabbi used to help against the evil-eye.

First, if it was determined that removing the evil-eye did not help, then they called Yankele the doctor. He received the name doctor from his father, Yossel the doctor. Neither one of them were doctors. They could only make enemas, set leeches, do cupping and other measures.

Yankele the doctor was a tall man, very skinny, with a pointed beard. He dressed in new clothing, including a coat lined with fur and deep galoshes, like a prince. Upon entering, he carried himself as a doctor. He took the temperature with a thermometer, prescribed medicine that had to be bought in the pharmacy, made enemas, and prescribed "cupping," which they did in those days.

In general, these measures were enough for the sick in Tarnogrod. After several days, the sick got better. But, if the condition did not improve, the women of Tarnogrod would move "heaven and earth." They would get together with the neighbors of the sick man and go to the *beit- hamidrash*. As soon as they approached the door, they broke out in powerful lamenting, up until they approached the ark, where they parted the curtain, opened the doors of the arc, told of all the virtues of the sick person and what would happen to his wife and children if he did not recover.

While the women wept and cried, the worshipers stopped their prayers. The learners were left sitting and listening to the women cry.

After the "wailing," the women turned to those in attendance in the *beit-hamidrash* and thought that all should say prayers and study for the sick. After the women begged G-d, the men put together a *minyan* and said prayers for the ill person. Because of this, the Jews of Tarnogrod were able to have long periods without a doctor.

In 1916, in the middle of the war, Tarnogrod had a break out of an epidemic of cholera. The Jews created their own committee with it's own powers and resources to save the people.

There was no doctor in Tarnogrod. Among the measures used against the epidemic was a note, affixed to the door, with the following inscription: "Nobody is here and whoever is here should remain as is."

People said that it helped.

*

The Tarnogrod Jews were sincere and religiously observant. Therefore, their memory has been written down by the remnants of their people.

Today, their whole lives are but a vanished story, but the nostalgia, great beauty and goodness, which they carried and left behind as our surviving inheritance, will never be forgotten.

We are not able to describe everything. However, we do know of some usual events from dates, from ordinary happenings and from words spoken by restrained voices, once concealed and now a living spring.

This is the spring that was left to the Jews of Tarnogrod. We draw from the river, full of nostalgia, the everlasting-benevolent Jewish kindness.

[Pages 260-261]

Sabbath Eve in the Town

Yechiel Muterperl

Translated by Miriam Leberstein

On Fridays, the whole town took on a different appearance. From dawn, the narrow streets were filled with the aromas of fresh baked goods to be eaten on the Sabbath and the rest of the week. Among these were *varenikes* [dumplings] filled with blackberries. The berries grew mostly in the Lakhower woods, and peasants from the surrounding villages brought them to town on Thursdays in large earthenware pots and sold them in the market for a few pennies. Boys and girls from the town also enjoyed going into the woods to pick berries and filled baskets to bring home. The blackberry *varenikes* left their traces on the faces of the children, who by Friday were already wandering around with stained mouths and teeth.

The children ran off to *heder* [religious school for young children] happily, because they knew the school day was a short one on Friday. In summer, right after eating their midday porridge, they would run off to the streams and ponds. They longed for a big river to swim in, but the mothers thought it was a lucky thing that Tarnogrod did not have a large river and that they were therefore spared the possibility of a drowning.

When the sun began to cool off a bit, Jewish men would emerge on their way to the steam baths, little whisks in their hands. The bath was on the left side of the synagogue courtyard and was reached by descending a few steps. At those times a black smoke rose from the bathhouse and through the windows you could hear the voices of the overheated men sweating on the highest benches [where it was the hottest].

But the men did not indulge themselves in this pleasure for a long time. The approaching Sabbath hurried them along. When they had finished with the steam bath they still had to immerse themselves in the *mikve* [ritual bath] three times in honor of the Sabbath. Only then would they put on their clean underwear and with their beards and side locks combed, and panting heavily, slowly set out for home, ready for the Sabbath.

Meanwhile, the women, clad in their greasy aprons, were carrying their Sabbath stews in clay–sealed pots to the baker [to be baked in the ovens overnight]. They rushed to get back home as quickly as possible. It would soon be time to go to the synagogue and there was so much left to do to get ready. They had to wash themselves and the children, and polish the silver candlesticks for the blessing of the candles.

A few Jews were still arriving from travelling, from business, from the villages and fairs. And then *Reb* [respectful form of address] *Kalmele Shamesh* [beadle of the synagogue] appeared, walking with measured steps, knocking on doors and shutters with a special hammer to announce that the Sabbath was arriving.

The sun began to set in the west and the Jews closed their shops. A Jew would run past with a bottle of wine for the *Kiddush* [blessing of the wine.] A wagon driver who was running late would whip his horse to speed their arrival home.

Quickly the house filled with Sabbath and a beautiful feeling of holiness spread over everything. On the table lay two fine challah breads covered with a cloth. Candles sat in the polished silver candlesticks and Mother stood gently bent over them, tender and pale, covering her face with her hands as she blessed the candles.

Her lips quietly murmured the prayer. She prayed on behalf of her husband and children, of every Jew. Her hands, like the wings of the *Shekhinah* [divine presence] hovered over the candles, full of compassion, faith and trust, and from her eyes, made holy by sorrow and suffering, a tear fell upon the white cloth.

The vision of mother's gentle dove–like eyes, so holy in the glow of the blessed candles on a Friday night, still accompanies me wherever I go.

[Pages 262-263]

The Brothers Yakov and Zalke Akerman

Tzvi Rozenson

Translated by Miriam Leberstein

Who in Tarnogrod did not know Yakov and Zalken? Tarnogrod business owners made much use of their services. They would carry out commissions on behalf of the kasha makers, the oil processors, the soda water factories and the hat makers. It was a special treat to hear Zalke tell his stories about Abyssinia, about wars and fires and other catastrophes.

Once Zalke attacked the Polish official Staronievski and beat him badly, because Staronievski had rummaged through the drawer in Ite Moshe–Sheindel's store, looking for the money she owed in taxes. Zalke was arrested and beaten so badly that he was sick for several days.

Yakov worked as a watchman for Aron, the manager of the *hekdesh* [shelter for poor and sick Jews] and people called him [Yakov] Kuni–Lemel [a fictional character typifying an awkward simpleton].

When Aron died, Dr. Kratskevits came to issue a declaration of death, permitting burial. While filling out the declaration he asked Yakov if he knew the name of Aron's mother. Yakov replied [jokingly] that it was "either *Asoro–B'Teves* or *Ester Ta'anit*" [both names of Jewish fast days that can be read as puns on women's names].

About Shlomo Marshelik– A Few Added Words

Others will probably also write about this wonderful character, whom I knew from the time when he and I prayed in the same *minyan* [prayer group], that was called the "*pol–zhidkes*" [Polish; "half–Jews"][1]. May I therefore be permitted to add a few words about him.

He was always bustling about industriously, with the energy of a young man, even when he had grown old. Always happy, cheerful, every Purim he would make the rounds of the households holding a stuffed hen, which he had fashioned by removing the skin with the feathers of real hen, and then skillfully stuffing it, providing much jollity among the people he visited.

He once told us how in his younger years, every Passover, he would, after celebrating the seder, gather several cheerful young people who would hide outside the windows of certain householders and eavesdrop. Listening to how the householders conducted their own seders and recited the haggadahs, they would burst into laughter. Sometimes they would push a goat into the house, just at the moment in the seder when the door is opened and they recite the verse that begins, "Pour out your wrath."

Once, they went to listen in on the seder of a householder who was expecting them, and when Shlomo Marshelikset foot on the step in the darkness, he stepped into a bucket full of whitewash. He didn't lose his wits, however, and directed and all of his companions to take a dip in the whitewash as well. And all of them had a good laugh at themselves.

Footnote:

1. This somewhat derogatory designation seems to reflect a view that the members of the *minyan* were not sufficiently observant. It is possible that it was a designation the *minyan* members ironically gave themselves.

[Pages 264-269]

My Father

Fajwel Kenigsberg

Translated in His Memory by His Great Nephew Yaakov Willner

My father Moishela *shochet* [ritual slaughterer] was born in 1893 in Tarnogrod. He became orphaned at a very young age and was left with a brother and two sisters. His grandfather, *Reb* Levi Yitzchak, who had taken over responsibility for him, taught him *shechita* [kosher butchering] so that he should be able to support his younger brother and sisters.

He was doing this divine work for some time, and when a few years later the town needed a *mohel* [person trained to perform ritual circumcision], he accepted upon himself the additional job of *mohel*, in which he served Tarnogrod and the surrounding neighborhoods as well.

For this job he didn't take any payment. He had done it with great devotion. When it was necessary to do a *bris* in an outlying village, nothing could prevent him from traveling there, even it meant traveling by foot, in the worst weather, in freezing temperatures and in blizzards.

There were times that he had to travel away from his town for a *Shabbos*, or a *Yom Tov* [holiday], or even a Passover Seder, and spend them at the tables of strangers, at strange lodgings. However he never complained, he did it with the full understanding of the tremendous *mitzvah*.

Not only didn't he take money for this *mitzvah*, but also, often, when he knew that he was going to a poor family, he would take along money to give them, and a chicken for the mother's recovery period.

He was loved by the people of the whole town, regardless of occupation, by merchants and tradesmen.

In the last years before the war he was also the *baal tefillah* [prayer leader]. As a child he had helped *Reb* Itsik–Yeshaya, who was from the prominent *baalei tefillah* in the town. Everyone would say that it was the biggest delight to hear my father pray. On Yom Kippur they would forget that they were fasting.

People from the town would often speak of my father's praying. When he used to sing out his "*malchuyot, zichronot and shofarot*, [three unique blessings said during Rosh Hashana] it would melt into our very beings. The words entered the heart and awakened our spiritual uplifting.

His life flowed along this way, peacefully, and quietly, filled with beautiful deeds and elevated character. Every year before the High Holy Days he would study over the prayers and sing with the children the High Holy Day melodies.

I remember the last year 1939, three weeks before Rosh Hashanah like every year, we would get ready by reviewing the prayers, but in the air there was already a feeling of suspense over the coming war.

Late at night we would run to hear the radio, and with trembling hearts we would return with feelings full of fear for the coming war.

It came September 1, 1939, five o'clock in the morning, when the Germans crossed the Polish border, and the same day Jews started escaping. They did not know where to run.

Exactly on Rosh Hashana Hitler's troops came into the town. My brother, Efraim, who now lives in America, was at the time crossing the street called Lachover Street, together with Hyman, son of Avrahamle Shoichet, and Yossel, son of Pinie Itzikel, when the murderers opened fire on them. Pinie Itzikel's son fell dead on the spot.

He was the first victim of Hitler's murderers in Tarnogrod.

The Friday night of *Shabbos* Teshuva is forever etched in my memory.

By us at home it was packed with people, fugitives, who had escaped from Galicia. In the middle of the night, 2 AM, we heard a terrible gunfire of heavy machine artillery. The windowpanes were trembling, and the men who were lying on the floor raised their heads and the fright was showing in their eyes. This lasted until daybreak. We heard yelling "Jews Out!" We heard running footsteps. Soon after we heard people yelling that there was a fire.

When I looked out of the crack, I saw flames that were shooting to the heavens.

The people from our house fled. Myself, my father and my mother went down into the valley. On the fields we already met up with a lot of people but no one knew what was going on, where there was a fire, and what had happened.

Women said that the murderers had, at daybreak, taken away their husbands and children.

It was only after a few hours, that someone came from the group that the Germans had taken away in the morning. He was extremely frightened and due to his tremendous fright he was unable to answer the questions that were pouring at him from all sides.

It went by an hour until he became calm and was able to say that in the marketplace, near the City Hall, he saw Jews that had been shot, men, women and children. Others, the Germans had forced to dig a grave in which to bury the murdered.

Suddenly, there came a command that they should halt the digging and throw the bodies into one of the houses near the City Hall. Afterwards the Germans doused the house in benzine and lit it. The fire then caught on to the neighboring houses.

When we heard this, our fright grew minute by minute. People were afraid to return to the town. People began running to the surrounding villages. We ran to the town called Majdan Sieniawski.

On the way we encountered German battalions. All this time they would stop anyone they saw. They were saying that Jews from Tarnogrod had shot at them.

It was dark already when we were getting closer to the courtyard of the "lame" Leibush. There we saw set up a German military kitchen. There were soldiers on horses wandering about.

We felt terribly afraid. It became bitter on the heart but we had no choice, we could not turn around. Soon, as we feared, the soldiers spotted us and surrounded us. Again, they were yelling that Jews from Tarnogrod shot at them. One of them aimed his revolver at us and the others searched us to see if we were carrying arms.

We felt that these were our last minutes. I saw how my father's lips were murmuring. I understood that he was saying Vidui [prayer recited at the deathbed].

His eyes looked at us with tremendous warmth, in such a way that he wanted to encourage us, and strengthen our hearts. There wasn't a trace of fear on his face.

At that moment Leibush's wife approached the German officer and with a cry of despair and began pleading with him that they should let us go. Her cry was so emotional and with so much beseeching, that it moved the murderer's heart and he told the soldiers that they should let us go.

They allowed us to stay there overnight, and on the second day we returned to Tarnogrod and met everybody with a lot of concern and uncertainty.

The Germans wandered about with their revolvers in their hands and tread with death in every footstep.

That's how we lived in deathly fear until Sukkot.

On the evening beginning Sukkot, people in the town started murmuring that the Soviet army had crossed the Polish border and was marching through Polish territory. They were saying that they would come to Tarnogrod.

On the third day the predictions began to happen. From the side of a street called Kuchever Bram there appeared a Russian tank and behind it were full military services.

The Jews in the town were enveloped in an indescribable joy. We allowed ourselves out of our houses, from our hiding places, and began to stroll in groups through the marketplace. We greeted each other, falling on each other's necks from great joy. It, the fear of death, was evaporated in a moment and we saw ourselves released from their murderous hands.

Several days went by and again rumors began spreading, this time that the Russians were leaving Tarnogrod and the Germans were coming back to the town.

As soon as the rumors reached my father he declared that we were not allowed to wait for the murderers to arrive, but rather we should leave with the Russians.

He went out into the street and called out to every Jew that he met not to stay with the Germans, but rather as soon as possible to leave the town in the direction of the Soviet border.

We went through several difficult years of wandering over the wide expansive Russia. In even the most difficult days my father did not lose his hope. With tremendous self–sacrifice, in the bitterest of circumstances, he watched himself not to pass even the slightest judgment.

Occasionally, his lips would move in a manner of one who would whisper a secret in the ear;

"Master of the Universe, enlighten my eyes how I should act in a hard time such as this…"

His words and his way of living, gave us encouragement and consolation, and breathed into us new powers, to be able to withstand the hard time.

Finally, it came to the end of the war, and we traveled from Russia and settled in Shtetshin.

The information that my father was in Shtetshin also reached Wroclaw, where Weli Shprung was then the president of the kehilla [Jewish community], and he invited him to come to Wroclaw.

The city needed a *shochet* and my father was therefore welcomed with a lot of *kavod* [honor, dignity, respect]. He wasn't only a *shochet* and *mohel* there, but also a *hazzan* [cantor].

Unforgettable is the day when the news reached us that a Jewish country had been set up. Hot tears flowed from my father's eyes, and he began preparing himself to be immigrated to Eretz Yisroel.

Just like by a lot of others, the aliya was accompanied by more than a bit of trouble. But he accepted everything with love and finally in 1950 he arrived in the land.

The Tarnogrod Jews and all those who knew him showed him a lot of heartfelt warmth, and in the first year of his arrival he was already accepted as a *shochet* in Haifa.

Not for a minute did my father forget the old home. That world of Jewish joy and happiness, of tears and longing, the pain of yesterday and the hope for a better tomorrow. Every year he took part in the memorial for the Tarnogroder *kedoshim* [martyrs]. Making the "*Yizkor*" was for him a great and sacred charge.

5 Adar 5722, my father passed away in Haifa.

Blessed is his memory!

[Page 269]

Eliezer Teicher and Fajwel Kenigsberg
at the Tarnogrod synagogue
Both live in Israel

My Father

Translated by Martin Jacobs

All silent heavens reflect your glances,
All winds bear your ash and dust,
All lands become your dispersed graves,
Souls flutter in space like dove's wings.

All   birds   sing   a   mournful *kaddish*.
All woods murmur in lamentation and weeping,
Who can forget you? Who can forget?
Left orphaned, forlorn, like a stone.

[Pages 270-274]

My Holy Father, Mr. Shmuel Schorer

My Parents' House

Yosel Schorer

Translated by Gloria Berkenstat Freund

Tarnogrod for me was my own homey Jewish world. But after the hellish fires of the greatest destroying Satan of all times, not even graves or ruins of that world remain. Yet, in my memory, sparks of that dear and loving world still glow. As I imagine once again my parents' house, the sparks are encouraged to a merry little fire that warms my heart day and night.

I can never forget the sweet faith that my parents' hearts were so full of, although need so often looked in on us. What did one have to worry about? The Master of the Universe is a father, everything would work out…. And my father went off to the *Beit Midrash* [house of study] for the afternoon prayers.

More than once as my father worried about his livelihood, he had headaches and went around in a heavy mood as he watched the children in his house chewing on bread with nothing on it.

Our fathers and mothers are no more. No more the dear souls who used to cuddle and kiss each of our limbs, who trembled with our every step. No more those in whose eyes glimmered tears of joy when we were happy, tears of pain and suffering when we suffered.

No more our brothers and sisters, or all the dear friends with whom we went through our best childhood and youthful years, days in high or in low spirits, dreams and hopes of a better life.

Dear and Holy Figures

They all, our dearest and closest, who we will never forget, perished in the most outrageous death.

I am sitting today in my beautifully arranged apartment, where a television set sits in a corner and on the screen is seen all of the particulars about the flights of the American astronauts in distant space; another room, the kitchen, is full of electrical appliances that save time so my wife need not toil, so that we have time to amuse ourselves, to rest. In this life, where luxury has become a daily phenomenon, the past years in Tarnogrod would seem not to be important to remember, describe and immortalize. However, for me, Tarnogrod, my family and all our closest people remain dear and sacred.

The years of my childhood and youth live in my memory: the *heder* [small Jewish elementary school] where we spent mornings until later at night. We would go home in the dark. Over us was a sky of sparkling stars and we lit the way with lanterns, which we, ourselves, made out of cardboard and colored paper.

When we studied the *Humash* [Five Books of Moses], we lived along with the Biblical figures and with the stories: felt like a part of Eliezer's retinue, wandered with him to Mesopotamia to search for a bride for Yitzhak, crawled into the water up to our neck before Moses split the sea; we welcomed the Torah at Mount Sinai and said, "We will obey and we will listen."

There were also other games, where everyone could show their dexterity and physical power. Today the Passover game with walnuts, the daily game with buttons, because we could win a great deal of buttons, all kinds, sizes, forms and color - a vast sum!

When the heat of the month of *Tammuz* [tenth month in the Jewish calendar, it falls in June or July] arrived, we paddled around near the stream, jumped into the water, paddled, and chased each other with joyful noise. This small river was changed to a large ocean in our imagination and we were creatures who were found in its depths.

Sroltshe Adler, Eli Adler, Eli Mantel, Sheindel Mantel

Common economic, cultural and family cares and joys bound the young people together in Tarnogrod. In the most difficult times, when the Jewish young did not have a place to go and ran wherever their eyes carried them, there were obstinate people who, in the time of scholars and Psalm readers, forged the golden chain for being Jewish, hoped and longed for redemption and did not stop demanding from themselves an account of the day that must give a sense and an explanation to their own lives.

Thus the years passed for the Jewish children in Tarnogrod. I was then already a *Gemara-Yingl* [boy studying the rabbinical commentaries on the Torah] and I also read a chapter of Kings and Prophets. Then I saw the way my teacher shook and rocked with his thin body, with a mournful, sweet melody he sang out the legends of the destruction of Jerusalem and we saw the violent manifestations of the flames of the burning Temple.

Ideal of Building Zion

At that time, a deep respect took root in me for the great scholars who swam the sea of Talmud so expertly. Later came the break; my friends and I began to think about the great and interesting world. We matured and began to be interested in national Jewish events and problems.

There were times when everything appeared without prospect and without hope. There were also times of joy and good fortune. Our young were always active, always searched. Our pious Jews were truly God-fearing; we could truly envy their constant "this, too, is for the best." Our Zionists were devoted heart and soul to the ideal of Zion rebuilt and we, survivors, will never forget them.

There are no words that can express our heavy spirit and grief at their death. We stand mute in regard to remembrance of our dear Tarnogrod Jews, the martyrs, and will remain their mourners.

[Pages 275-281]

Our Former Tarnogrod

Moshe Naftali Mantel

Translated by Gloria Berkenstat Freund

Tarnogrod, the *shtetl* [little town] of my childhood years, lies in a mountain of ash, ruins and devastation.It is hard to imagine that Tarnogrod is now a city without *Shabbosim* [pleural of *Shabbos*: Jewish Sabbath] and without *Yomim-Tovim* [religious holidays on which work is not permitted], that our Jews no longer hurry to prayer, that there are no longer houses full of *Shabbos* and grace and sanctity.

There are no longer tables with two beautiful challahs [braided egg bread eaten on *Shabbos*], covered with a tablecloth; there are no mothers who lit the candles in polished silver candlesticks and quietly and softly murmured a prayer.

What did our mothers desire then, when they stood with hands spread, slightly bent over the *Shabbos* candles?

Their children who were growing up and those who had left for distant places stood before their eyes and they asked God to guard their way, so that they would remain good, dear Jews.

It is difficult to believe that all of this is no longer here; that the lives of our dear ones were so horribly extinguished.

Our former Jewish Tarnogrod is dead and devoured. Only we, the remnant, remain, those who left the *shtetl* long before the destruction of Poland, settled in Israel and in other nations, as well as those who miraculously saved themselves from the Hitler pestilence and are with us in Israel.

We are now writing the history of our *shtetl*, about the scholars and simple Jews during the course of a year, about the merchants and artisans, about the difficult struggle that they carried out for their existence.

This was a difficult existence. Poor and miserable – in the material sense, but with a great deal of spiritual elevation, with a great deal of longing and love, with dreams about a beautiful land, with high moral worth.

The past swims in my memory of when we were very small boys and our father brought us to the teachers of the youngest children and they began to teach us the first little bit of Hebrew.

When we became a little older, grew up, our fathers delivered us to *Reb* Chaim Tsibelkale, with whom we studied *Humash* [Five Books of Moses] and *Rashi* [Rabbi Shlomo ben Isaac, regarded as one of Judaism's greatest commentators of Talmud], *Gemara* [rabbinic legal and ethical commentary] and although his inefficiency was evident in his bearing, he, however, had a very good comprehension of the matter and that which he said was intelligible to us.

The *melamedim* [religious school teachers] had assistants who every day brought the children to *heder* [small Jewish elementary school]. No matter how poor the houses were, each child wanted to stay at home rather than go to the heder. Therefore, the assistant was not much loved by the children, although during the winter days, when it was slippery, he carried them on his shoulders, under his arms, four at a time.

The functions of the assistant also included saying the blessings with the children as they entered the *heder* and 50 to 60 children were already assembled.

The *belfer* [assistant teacher], like the *melamed*, was exalted in Tarnogrod for his entire life, was a very poor man, but like the majority of Jews in the *shtetl*, he was full of hope. If one would suddenly stop such a Jew and ask him: from where and how do you support yourself? At first he would be confused, not knowing what answer to give. Then a little later he would recover and innocently answer:

"What kind of question is this? There is a Lord of the Universe present who does not leave His creations; He sent and He will probably again send income."

There was the type of Jew who, like worms who lie in horseradish, thought that the world ended on the other side of Tarnogrod. There was no sweet, no better life than here.

A small bench stood in the *heder* for the *belfer*, on which he sat and taught the first lesson to the youngest children and later they went to the *Gemara* teacher himself for the second lesson.

He was a user of snuff and the *rebbetzin* [wife of a rabbi] shouted about the tobacco – he was spending all of the money.

The *melamed* had a daughter in Bilgoraj, a nearby *shtetl*, and when, with luck, she gave birth to a son, the *melamed* traveled out of the *shtetl* for the first time.

The distance was eight kilometers, but for him it was a distant trip and he possessed no words to describe and to tell of the wonders that he saw in Bilgoraj.

He saw a train there that was, all told, a small railroad, but he did not stop speaking about the wonder after wonder of its great strength. A blackened man sits at an oven like a chimneysweeper. Smoke comes out of a small chimney and water pours underneath and this pulls 20 railroad cars with people, with goods. All his life he had not met a wagon driver who was so fit with such strength.

We children would be enthusiastic about these wonderful, beautiful stories.

The Kreszówer *Tzadik* [righteous one]

Tarnogrod was proud of the great spiritual credit (it received) because this was where the Sanzer *Rebbe*, the author of *Divrei Chaim* [Words of Life] was born. His parents lived in the village of Borowicz, eight kilometers from Tarnogrod. They had a house in Tarnogrod and the mother came here when Chaim, whose genius later was spread over the world, was ready to be born.

At that time the rabbi in Tarnogrod was *Reb* Yakov Taumim. When he died, *Reb* Chaim Halberstam was already the rabbi in Sanz.

For a short time Tarnogrod was without a local rabbi. When Chaim Halberstam came to visit his father, the prominent residents turned to him, asking that he search for a respected rabbi, a great Torah sage. The Sanzer Rabbi answered them:

"If the Kreszówer *Tzadik* would want to be your rabbi, you would have a magnificent rabbi."

The Kreszówer *Tzadik*, *Reb* Moshe Naftali Katzenelenbogen, who then lived in the small town of Krzeszów, was a great man of moral character and a scholarly luminary in Torah and in wisdom.

The Sanzer Rabbi added:

"I am not confident that his relatives will let him go; they love him very much. But I would happily see him with you. Tarnogrod would have a great rabbi."

Being very receptive to new ideas when one is already capable of influencing people through reasoning is not only a good trait, a sign of humility, but also shows with this strength a great mind. And the Sanzer Rabbi was blessed with this strength. Therefore he spoke with such enthusiasm about the Kreszówer *Tzadik*, said that he corresponded with him often and advised the esteemed city residents [that they should send a delegation of scholars who would travel to Krzeszów and offer him the rabbinical seat in Tarnogrod.

Therefore, he added in passing:

"He will probably write about this; I will urge him to become your rabbi."

And the day came and *Rebbe* Moshe-Naftali Katzenelenbogen with luck became the rabbi in Tarnogrod where he was called the Kreszówer *Tzadik* for all his days.

In addition to his becoming rabbi and a Torah giant, he also was the *rebbe*, took *kwitlekh*, [notes requesting the rabbi's intervention with God for a marriage for a child, a child for a barren woman, etc.] worked hard over them and there were tales in Tarnogrod about him and the great things, miracles, how he became great in the doctrine of what is manifest, as well as in esoteric doctrine.

It was said about him, that while still in Krzeszów, a Jew came to him with a kwitl and cried greatly that he ran a mill that belonged to the landowner, near Krzeszów and now the landowner did not want to renew the contract with him because he intended to transfer the mill to a Christian and throw out him and his six children into the street.

The Kreszówer *Tzadik* told his *shammes* [synagogue caretaker] to hang the Jew's *kwitl* on a nail and he led home the distressed Jew and assured him that the landowner's wife would again rent the mill to him.

When the Jew came home, he heard that the landowner had hung himself and it did happen that the landowner's wife rented the mill to the Jew for the coming years.

It cannot be concealed: Hasidism is drenched in miracles and magical signs and it was also true of the Kreszówer Tzadik, who demonstrated things beyond the usual.

Reb Pinkhesl, the Konsker Rabbi, as he was called, was the son-in-law of the Kreszówer. *Reb* Hershele Taumim, the *Vlodawar* [Włodawa] Rabbi, one of the greatest rabbis at that time, was also his in-law.

Several rabbis, who wished to receive rabbinical ordination, would always be studying with him. Each of them was sure with this of his standing in life because rabbinical ordination from him was so widely respected in the rabbinical world.

The Kreszówer *Tzadik* was the rabbi in Tarnogrod for 20 years and died in 5627 (1867).

At his death, there was a consultation of three doctors at his bed and, when they said that his hours were numbered, the *Tzadik* called over his two sons: my grandfather, *Reb* Saul-Joel, and his second son, Avrahamle. He asked the doctors to leave and he blessed his sons.

He asked the *shammes* to bring water for washing, his *tallis* [prayer shawl] and *kitel* [long white linen robe, worn by rabbis and other prayer leaders on important occasions which also serves as a burial garment]. He put it on and got off the bed and stood to *daven* [pray] *Mincha* [afternoon prayer service].

He recited the *Shemoneh-Esrei* [Literally, "eighteen." A silent prayer said while standing that had eighteen benedictions until an additional one was added. Also known as the Amidah] for Yom Kippur with all of the *Al Het* [Yom Kippur prayer of repentance] and the doctors could not get over their great amazement; they said that the strength that the rabbi had with which to stand was incomprehensible.

After finishing his praying, the rabbi returned to his bed, recited the *Shema Yisroel* [central prayer of Jewish liturgy, which expresses the concept of monotheism and declares faith in God] and breathed out his soul when saying *echad* [one, the last word of the Shema].

His son, *Reb* Saul-Joel my grandfather, was a homebody; he was the son-in-law of *Reb* Hershele Taumim, the *Vlodawar* Rabbi, and studied his entire life.

The other son, *Reb* Avraham Katzenelenbogen, was a merchant in Danzig, and exported wood abroad.

A grandchild was chosen as rabbi of the city, a son of his daughter, *Reb* Arie-Leib Teicher.

His grandson was more skillful in worldly affairs but perhaps *Reb* Saul-Joel was a scholar. Therefore, the *kehila* [Jewish community] pledged itself to provide *Reb* Saul-Joel with income and he actually lived every day with Torah and worship until the end of his life.

I was already 17 years old at the outbreak of the First World War. I then left the *beit-hamidrash* [house of study] and began to do business.

A great deal will certainly be written about those violent years, about the particular troubles that the Jews in the village went through. But there were also quiet days and young people began to become interested in what was happening in the wider world. We began to subscribe to Jewish newspapers, bought books and discussed important problems.

We, the youth, organized a group in the village, "Supporters of the Poor." Everyone gave a certain amount. A *minyan* [minimum gathering of 10 men necessary for a communal religious service] came to pray every *Shabbos* and we also attracted several older men.

The communal energy was used not only for social purpose, but also to bring basic information, education and knowledge to the population.

Conflicts also took place, particularly at the sale of Passover flour. We did not want the poor to pay the same expensive prices that were demanded from the rich men. I then appeared in the *beit-hamidrash* with a speech in which I called on the group to take to heart the situation of the poor Jews.

Tewel Nachum immediately appeared after me and began to thunder against me, that I need to be thrown out of the beit-*hamidrash* because this is not a group of "Supporters of the Poor," but a band of heretics.

This was our first great victory. Our activity won the sympathy of the population and we were approached to create a Hebrew school.

We brought a Hebrew teacher from Bialystok, a Vilna Jew, and despite the fact that the rabbi in the *shtetl* issued a call that children should not be sent to Hebrew school because children were being led there to conversion, we were successful in acquiring a certain number of students who received a nationalist education in the school.

I was then chosen as a member of the trustees of the school and with everyone we gave all of our energy to it. A longing for a Jewish national home lived in our hearts. Our aspirations for Zion became more earnest and stronger.

[Pages 282-283]

The Woodbinders of Kneshpol[1]

by P. Lumerman

Translated by Irving Lumerman and Chesky Wertman
and
Translated and Edited by Martin Jacobs

What didn't we have in our town? From grain, flax, and lumber merchants to cobblers and tailors, saddlers and blacksmiths, carpenters and glaziers, traveling merchants, who for entire weeks wandered about among the farmers, buying and selling, rushed and overworked, until, with the coming of Friday evening, they returned to the town, to their *Shabbos* home.

On the Tanew River, between Tarngorod and Bilgoraj, a rafting river, the Jews used to send the lumber cut from the nearby forests, which used to go as far as Danzig [present day Gdańsk] and from there on to Germany, England, and other countries.

On the river stood the village of Kneshpol. There, there was great activity in the summer time: Jews were there sorting and binding the logs to send them out on the river. In that village, among several Jewish families, lived our family, the Lumermans, tall, slender, handsome people. The men, Chaim's three sons, were like oak trees, and they worked extremely hard[2]. The girls, six sisters, blossomed with all the Jewish charms. The village resounded with their clear ringing laughter and their sweet singing. The eldest of the sisters, Gnendl, married a Tarnogrod lad, Shmuel Shorer, who was called Black Shmuel, although he had sky-blue eyes, from which shone kindness.

Shmuel was not tall, but his beard was that of a giant. He was taught how to bind the timber as part of his dowry. This is what is called being a "kusher", a wood binder. It was hard work. It started in early spring, just as the ice on the river was starting to break up, and lasted until autumn. With their trousers rolled up and in high boots, they bound logs into rafts from the grey of dawn to late evening.

When it became light they put on *tefillin* right where they worked, wrapped themselves in their prayer shawls, and said their prayers. At that point the Gentiles began to speak more quietly, showed themselves to be above the noisy commotion, and looked upon the praying Jews with great respect.

All week long they lived on a bit of dry bread dipped in water. They saved their pennies to pay tuition for the children's studies. Their passionate desire was that their children might study and grow up to be honest Jews and good people.

Mother at home was filled with worry. With tears in her eyes and a song on her lips she entreated the Master of the Universe for a little kindness: "You have prepared so many beautiful things and provided the world with everything good, bless us too that we may never be punished. As the fruits bloom on the trees, as grass is luxuriant on the earth, as [the stars are many in heaven, so may it be with my sons and daughters."]

Translator's notes:

1. Known in Polish as Księżpol, a village in Bilgoraj county.
2. Reading "gebrent" for "gebrengt".

[Pages 284-292]

Our Teacher and Friend
Traits and personality of Moshe Lemer, of blessed memory

by Meir Ringer

Translated by Miriam Leberstein

Meir Ringer with Moshe Lemer z"l shortly before his death

Born in the village of Plis near Tarngorod, where his father, *Reb* Yakov, held the lease for milk production for the Polish estate owner, Moshe spoke Polish from childhood. When he got older, his father brought him to Tarnogrod to study in *heder*, [religious school for young children] where he distinguished himself with his abilities, fluency and comprehension.

After completing *heder* he continued his studies in the *besmedresh*, [house of study also used for worship] immersed day and night in the Talmud and Talmudic interpretations. He was one of the ablest scholars, possessing a sharp intellect, while enjoying the love and friendship of the other students.

He was all of 17 years old when his mother came to see him one day, summoned him outside and announced that he had become engaged to marry. That's how they did things in those days. The parents of both parties agreed to a match and to the conditions of the engagement and then later informed the children that they were engaged.

A year passed and Moshe Lemer, 18 years old, immersed in scholarship, married a village girl. He lived with his father in law, who provided room and board to the couple so that Moshe could continue his religious studies.

As part of the dowry, his father in law had promised to support Moshe as long as he wished so that he could continue to study without having to concern himself with earning a living.

His father in law made his living by running a small shop in the village, which was patronized by the peasants and landowners. It was also patronized by teachers from the village school, and they were struck by the young man who sat there poring over books all day, every day. He aroused their curiosity and they began to engage with him.

He impressed the Russian teachers as an outstanding scholar and they were therefore surprised to find out after several conversations with him that this young man was entirely cut off from the life around him and that all his thoughts were focused on the problems of Jewish religion.

This was at a time when the Russian and Polish intelligentsia was dominated by liberal ideology and the teachers, seeing that they had before them a young man of exceptional intelligence, proposed to teach him Russian and to introduce him to Russian and European literature.

The young Moshe Lemer nervously accepted their offer. The teachers brought him newspapers and books, and somewhere obtained literary and journalistic publications on Jewish topics in the Russian language.

Lemer's eyes were opened and he began to see the world and himself completely differently. His thirst for books grew stronger every day and he began to buy his own books with money from his dowry. These publications in Yiddish and Hebrew captured his burning imagination and caused an upheaval in his mind. He could no longer conceal his thoughts.

He was on fire and he had to share his ideas with others, and he earned notoriety as an *apikoros* [heretic]. The news reached his father in law, who was extremely upset, and withdrew his offer to support him. "What sense does it make," he said, "to support a heretic who will bring non-kosher books into my house?"

Lemer left the village for Tarnogrod, where he opened a kiosk selling drinks and sweets. He didn't earn much. The town Jews learned of his heresy and many of them avoided patronizing his business, despite the fact that he was very friendly.

Actually, Lemer had every prospect of being among the most promising young people in town. He was a very good student and was considered an expert in Talmudic law. In addition, he was able to write well in Russian and Polish and people were often obliged to turn to him for help [in writing letters and documents]. But he wasn't a very practical person and didn't try to enhance his status. He was completely absorbed with helping young people acquaint themselves with Zionism, with knowledge and education, and he helped to create a new era in the life of the town. He paid a heavy price for this, obliged to lead a life of poverty and suffering.

There came a time when his ideals began to bear fruit, with the establishment of the first Zionist association, a Hebrew school, a library, and so forth. The Hasidim viewed him as the source of everything bad and excommunicated him. Not until several years later did their fury abate and religious people began to have social contact with him. He was even elected to the administration of the *kehillah* [organized Jewish community] but his material circumstances did not improve and he continued to live in poverty.

It became clear to Lemer that there was nothing for him to do in Tarnogrod, and having nothing to lose, he went to Berlin. A friend of his advised him to deal in furs, and this went well for him. He brought over his parents and his brothers and their families and they established a substantial fur business.

In 1935 the Nazis forced him to return to Poland where he again had to begin anew. His business did well. In 1939 he travelled to America on business and when the war broke out he could not return to Poland and rejoin his family -- his wife, children and grandchildren from his married daughter. They were all killed in Tarnogrod. He went to London where his brother lived with his family.

The first years in London were difficult and painful, but he did not succumb to despair. He participated in the civilian resistance, served various tours of duty, stood guard all night over the rooftops and carried out his duties diligently.

Sometimes Lemer would find himself conversing with English professors and despite the fact that he hadn't yet mastered the English language, they sensed his exceptional intelligence. During a conversation on Biblical themes he was asked where and in which university he had studied. Lemer, with his sharp sense of humor answered that his professors were Khaim Tsibelkele and Avrom Melamed, etc. [humorous *shtetl* nicknames denoting humble people] but they took him seriously. They were certain that these were renowned scholars from Eastern Europe and that Lemer was one of their best students.

This reputation spread among the other English professionals and when they later met Lemer they treated him with great respect, taking what he said as the authoritative interpretation of a recognized scholar.

His expansive knowledge and brilliance helped to elevate the reputation of the *shtetl* scholars Khaim Tsiblekele and Avrom Melamed.

Lemer struggled his whole life over the problems of Zionism. He burned with love for Israel and its problems occupied the most prominent place in his conversations and thoughts that he conveyed in his letters to friends and his personal writings, always deeply thoughtful and often enthusiastic.

Lemer was suffused with love for Tarnogrod and its Jews, for all that was so horribly destroyed.

His letters to me were always interwoven with memories of the Jewish life of the past. He warmly remembered the various personalities, both ordinary and prominent. In one of his letters, he wrote about Getsl Vaserman's father, Aron Itstik, who used to repair roofs in town. He was a pious Jew who had the habit of seeking a simple explanation for the fantastic feats described in weekly Torah portion, which he taught to a small study group.

Aron Itsik held certain primitive philosophical beliefs. He did not care for dry laws and said the miracles were supernatural things which are possible if God wills them, that anyone should be able to understand them as such.

Once on Yom Kippur he fell asleep in the middle of praying. Someone woke him up and asked, "Don't you know you're not supposed to sleep on Yom Kippur?" "Don't worry," he answered. "In Heaven the first to be judged are the big shots—the rabbis, the prominent men, *gabaiim* [religious administrators], Hasidim, rich men. Only at the end, late at night, do they consider the little people, the paupers. God doesn't take great formalities with them; they are paupers and will remain paupers. Let the rich and prominent people rush to complete their prayers. They mustn't fall asleep even for a minute, but we paupers can take our time."

Godl Vetsher's Letter to Moshe Lemer in London

Here are portions from Godl Vetsher's letter to Lemer which provides a picture of the living conditions in Tarnogrod:[1].

I can't turn to *Reb* Moshele for help in answering these questions. I know in advance that he will rule that everything is in violation of religious law. The matter of the beard is the result of people like him.

Believe me, Moshe, when I heard the news about the beard, I was struck with terror because it affects me too, because my beard would not pass muster [as religiously correct].

I began to inquire discretely because it wouldn't have been wise to let on that I was strongly interested in the matter. What should I do? How could I go to vote? What if I myself were to be elected?

I couldn't rest day or night. Suddenly, I got the idea to sneak into the anteroom of the Belzer *shtibl* late at night. That's where the young people from the *Aguda* [ultra Orthodox organization] gather. Maybe I could get some information from them.

Listen to what I learned from them. For them, this was a great joy, the day they were waiting for. They had figured out, provisionally, who would be allowed to vote and who wouldn't, and I have to tell you under the seal of secrecy, that my name was specifically mentioned.

There were even some people who gave me the seal of approval, but others declared me non-kosher. They had not come to any definitive decision.

Godl and Leah Vetsher

Then someone sprang up and said that the matter could only be decided by reference to [religious] law and authority; only then would it be correct. Someone brought in the relevant book of religious authority and after paging through it they found the applicable portion. Based on the first citation they read, it appeared I was kosher. That was a relief. But wait, they then found a citation according to which I was not kosher. But that wasn't the end of it.

Up sprang a strict interpreter – or simply an ass – who invoked the example of the red heifer in the Bible, which according to a Talmudic ruling is rendered non-kosher by the presence of two black hairs. From that he concluded that anyone who shaves off two hairs from his beard is disqualified to vote, let alone to be elected. As for those who remove their beard for reasons of health, they must provide an attestation from the local rabbinical court to prove it is a matter of necessity.

The strict constructionist went on to consider the case of someone who is physically unable to grow a beard. He reasoned from the example of the bastard, who is not at fault for his status as a bastard, since it was God who made him so, but who is nevertheless deemed non-kosher.

So, too, the man who cannot grow a beard is not kosher even though it is not his fault.

The strict constructionist was also a bit of a doctor; he knew about illnesses and he declared that anyone who lacks a beard has an illness of the sex glands and can, God forbid, eventually turn into a female and a female is after all ineligible to vote in the elections.

They continued to debate at length the Talmudic requirements for the length and other physical features of a beard to qualify it as kosher.

I sat in the anteroom of the Belzer *shtibl* and listened to the debate and was terrified. I barely dragged myself home. I hope to God that the decree about beards will be annulled, that a miracle will occur, like the deliverance of the Jews from Egypt.

The Vetsher brothers. Godl Vetsher's son selling soap at the market place in Tarnogrod

The Jewish community is now located in the house of *Reb* Alter Zilberman (Leib Gerson's son). Previously, the "*pol zhidkes*" ["half Jews" i.e., not fully observant Jews] prayed there. After them came the Zhitomir Hasidim; who knows who else will pray there in the future.

Regarding your questions, I could only ask them of a selected few individuals because your father asked me not to raise them in public. It really isn't appropriate for the son of the *gabai* of the *besmedresh* to pose such questions.

Yours, Godl Vetsher

*

When I met up with Lemer in London a year before his death he was filled with enthusiasm over our yizkor book, the eternalization of the life and death of the martyrs of Tarnogrod.

In the midst of a discussion about various subjects, he suddenly returned to the theme of the Holocaust, and said "How sad that the world caused almost 8 million murders in Europe in order to wipe out an insignificant people, resulting in the most horrific crime in history. After all that, the world turns around and proceeds to preach about democracy; and there are even some who help the Arabs, make deals with them, send them weapons."

Lemer wanted the pain and horror of the Holocaust to serve as a source of moral strength. He wanted to find light, consolation and hope in the future for the continued existence of the Jewish people. From that came his unbounded love for Israeli children; no enemy on earth was capable of destroying them.

He was a proud Jew and an honorable man, one of those people who carry their stubbornness across generations and who ignite the fire of a high moral truth and simple human love.

For that reason, he is among those in whom the survivors of Tarnogrod take pride and all of his friends stand at his freshly dug grave with heads bowed in sorrow,

"It is a pity for those who are gone!"[2]

Translator's Footnotes:

1.   In this excerpt, the letter writer is poking fun at the strictly observant Jews in Tarnogrod who are considering a rule that would ban any man without a beard that conforms to religious requirements from holding office in the organized Jewish community or even voting in the elections for office. The writer clearly expects Moshe Lemer, the recipient, to concur in his opinion of the absurdity of their position.
2.   This is a quotation in Aramaic from the Tractate Sanhedrin that is traditionally used in a Jewish eulogy; the expression laments the great loss of the deceased person who is irreplaceable.

[Pages 293-294]

His Great Love
About Moshe Lemer z"l, who passed away in London

by A. Dror

Translated by Sara Mages

In the last years he used to sit in the big fur shop on London's glorious commercial street.At the back of the sales hall, in a small room, he could be seen bent over, reading a Hebrew book. Occasionally he looked up, surveyed the shoppers who entered the shop, and immediately returned to read Agnon, Haza, or one of the young writers.

A person must have a lot of imagination to believe that the owner of a large fur shop, on London's main street, reads the best of Hebrew literature every day. It is highly doubtful that in the whole of the Britain there are many traders who read modern Hebrew in their store and thereby neglect their trade.

Whoever knew Moshe Lemer in the days of his adolescence and adulthood, knew that he had always loved the Hebrew word, the Hebrew culture and the special folklore of the people, that he so wanted, in his own way, to belong to it. Those who knew him were not surprised that he read and wrote Hebrew so well, even though he had never been to Israel for more than a few weeks. It was enough to watch him when he met an Israeli child in London. The elderly man, with short stature and noble facial expression, looked at the child behind glasses in a gilded frame, and endlessly enjoyed his Hebrew speech and the very fact that he was an Israeli child. He found in every Israeli child only virtues, and any attempt to find a flaw in him, he would encounter quite convincing explanations and interpretations of Moshe Lemer.

A Victim and a Symbol

After he passed away at the age of 76, dozens of articles were also found in his estate, all of them written in Hebrew, and in them book reviews, reactions and thoughts about the Jewish people, its fate and struggles.

Moshe Lemer himself is, at one and the same time, a victim and a symbol of the Jew's suffering. He was born in 1890 in Tarnogrod. From an early age he observed the life of the Jews in his environment, saw their suffering, understood the lack of future in the meager trading life and sought a solution. Even though he never received a regular education, he believed that the Jewish child must, first of all, learn to know his culture and past.

In the photograph, which remained from those days, he is seen together with the first students in Tarnogrod, on the day he founded the first Hebrew School. In the town everyone saw him as a scholar, sometimes called him a "rabbi," but he himself was a "heretic," and believed that in the reality of the Diaspora, as it was then understood, the religion stood as an obstacle in the way of the Zionist movement that several of its members later immigrated to Israel.

In 1928, Moshe Lemer left his hometown and moved to Germany. There, he began to organize, for the first time, the family businesses which flourished until 1935 when, as a Jew, he was forced to leave Germany and return to Poland. Here he had to start from the beginning, the businesses prospered but, once again, fell victim in the hands of the Nazis.

In 1939, while on a business tour of the United States, the Second World War broke out. Moshe joined his brother, son and nephew in London, while his family members, including his wife, a married daughter, two sons and grandchildren, perished in the Holocaust.

Modest Life

From then on, Moshe did not forget for a moment his private disaster, and the national lesson. Often, he would remember and mention the Holocaust. And when he remembered his loved ones - the tears choked him. For nine years he could not free himself from the disaster, and in the ninth year he married a woman again. He saw her son as his son, was anxious for his successes and failures, and later identified him with his beloved son, Amnon, who was murdered with the other children of Tarnogrod and his corpse was on display, with the other children of the city, in the main square.

In his last years, Moshe Lemer lived, despite his excellent financial situation, a modest and routine life. People who knew him and passed by his store, enjoyed entering to his small room at the back of the store, to have a short conversation with him in good Hebrew, to see him smile nobly, and especially, whenever he mentioned his unforgettable visit to Eretz Israel.

In the last months, when he lay on his deathbed, terminally ill, childhood memories suddenly came to him, and always recited proverbs and verses from the Bible and the Talmud, the Gemara and the *Mishnah*, and did not stop reciting them to his last day.

[Page 295]

III

<u>Death and Destruction</u>

[Pages 296-318]

Cry Out, My Murdered Folk

by Yitzhak Katsenelson

Translated by Miriam Leberstein

Cry out from every stone, each grain of sand
from the dust, flames and smoke
formed from your flesh and blood, the marrow of your bones,
your hearts and souls – cry out loudly.
Cry out from the woods, from the fish, the rivers
that swallowed you up; cry out from the ovens, cry out, all of you.
I want to hear your weeping, your pleas for help, your voices.
Cry out, you murdered Jewish souls, cry out.
Show yourselves to me; stretch out your hands
from the graves, miles long and deeply dug,
layers upon layers, steeped in lime and burnt.
Arise, arise! Rise up from the deepest depths.
Come out from Treblinka, from Sobibor, from Auschwitz,
from Belzec, from Paneriai,[1] and more, more, more!
With eyes wide-open, staring – a cry, a plea for help, a voice.
Rise up from swamps, from mire, from rotted moss.
Come out, desiccated and ground to dust
and form a circle, a big circle, around me, one giant hoop --
grandfathers, grandmothers, mothers with babies in their laps.
Come, Jewish bones turned to powder, to pieces of soap.
Show yourselves, appear before me, come, all of you.
I want to see you, I want to look upon my murdered folk,
look at you, silently, struck dumb.
And then I will sing – yes, give me my harp,
I will play!

Footnote:

1.   Treblinka, Sobibor, Auschwitz, Belzec were concentration camps. Paneriai was the site of mass executions of Jews and others by Germans and Lithuanian collaborators near Vilna.

[Pages 319-329]

The Invasion by the German Hordes

by Nuchim Krymerkopf

Translated by Miriam Leberstein

If only one person survives the conflagration he will describe the catastrophe for future generations

Autumn, 1939.

The Nazi troops poured into the big and little *shtetls* of Poland.

Within a few days, the Polish government had mobilized the population. In Tarnogrod boys were called to the battlefront. In Jewish homes, there was worry and fear. This lasted only a few days; the Polish army soon disintegrated. From the first days of the invasion, Jewish refugees passed through Tarnogrod, packs on their backs, barefoot, their feet wrapped in rags. Some stayed in Tarnogrod for a day or two or more.

The Jews of Tarnogrod received the refugees with true Jewish warmth, gave them food and clothing and put them up for the night.

In many houses the women had warm water constantly ready so the fleeing Jews could wash, and soak their tired feet.

Just as had occurred during the First World War, civilians with white armbands – a civil defense force – appeared in the streets, the first sign that the enemy, the new occupiers, were about to arrive. Soon the ruthless fist of the enemy reached the town. The Germans marched through the streets and the sound of their booted footfalls resounded in the houses, where the Jews hid with their doors and shutters nailed shut -- residents and refugees, young and old, children who had lost their parents, parents searching for their children.

The town was instantly transformed, unrecognizable. It was the first night of Rosh Hashanah. People went to pray in synagogue using the back streets, slinking along the walls. The praying was different than in other years, sadder, more fearful, reflecting terror and worry about the days to come. Leibush Chaim Tshipes (Wertman), the cantor who led the night prayer, sped up his praying.

People returned home from praying with pounding hearts. Each one took home several refugees to share in the holiday feast. In some families, no one left the house at all, even to pray. The neighbors got together to pray at one of their homes. Not even the slightest ray of light could be seen from the pitch dark streets; all of the windows were covered and shut tight.

There were houses where no one slept that night. People went to bed in their clothes and stayed on the alert, listening for every sound on the street.

The next morning, the first day of Rosh Hashanah, the town seemed to be completely dead. Cautiously taking back streets, afraid of their own shadows, Jews went to pray in synagogue with their prayer books under their arms. The entire service was one long lament pervaded by fear for the future.

Again, each Tarnogrod resident took home several refugees, among whom were wealthy people. Everyone felt equal, brothers in sorrow.

At 2:00 p.m. a German patrol drove their motorcycles through the blonie [commons] on Lakhower Street, making a horrible noise.

The First Victims

Two Jewish boys, Avrahamle Shohet's son and Pinye Itzekel's son Yechiel, were at the time sitting on the porch of Leizer Silberzweig's house. When the German patrol approached they were terrified and confused and didn't know what to do. Yechiel began to run away. He had only managed to take a few steps when he was struck in the shoulder by a bullet shot by the patrol. He continued to run until he came to the wall where the poorhouse had once stood. There he collapsed and died on the spot.

Avrahamle Shohet's son, also confused, made a movement to run away but at that moment, he heard one of the murderers yell at him to halt. He stood there, frozen in fear, unable to move. When the patrol approached him, he was still in shock, unable to answer their questions. The Germans searched him and found nothing, so they delivered a few blows, told him to go home and warned him not to go outside anymore.

Yechiel, Pinye Itzekel's son, was the first Jewish victim in Tarnogrod.

Right after the motorcycle patrol, the Nazi's regular divisions, infantry and artillery, marched in. Their first stop was at the Polish town government. Several German officers went inside and immediately took over the offices.

The news of Yechiel's death spread quickly. No one, not even the most daring tough guys, would go out onto the street or even stick their heads out. Pinyele, Yechiel's father, came alone to recover his son's body from behind the poorhouse.

On the second night of Rosh Hashanah no one went to pray in synagogue. They prayed at home, with broken hearts. The night passed peacefully. Not a sound was heard on the street. In the morning German soldiers were seen passing by but they took no special action. German officials and military were installed in the town hall. Jews began gradually to slip out to go to synagogue. They felt as if they were risking death, but they didn't want to stay home. After all, it was the second day of Rosh Hashanah and they wanted to hear the blowing of the *shofar* [ram's horn].

No one went to the *besmedresh* [house of study and prayer] to pray because it was in a highly visible location in front of the market and the danger was a lot greater. As a result, the *shtiblekh* [sing. *shtibl*, small usually *Hasidic* prayer houses], which were in the back streets, were packed. The synagogue, located behind the *besmedresh* and less visible to the German soldiers, was also full.

They recited the morning prayers quickly so as not to be interrupted. They waited a bit to blow the *shofar*, until there was no one in the market place; they didn't want it to be heard on the street, where a German patrol could happen to pass by. The Germans were already strolling around town.

The Jews remembered their experience during World War I, when the German occupiers interpreted the blowing of the shofar to be a secret signal to the Poles. They didn't want the Germans to think they were sending a signal to the disbanded Polish army. They waited to blow the shofar at noon when they knew the Germans would be busy having lunch. They stationed two men at the gate to the synagogue anteroom to watch to see if anyone was coming. The *shofar* blowing took place without a problem.

During the time the Jews had been at prayer, a Gestapo division had arrived in town. They took over the house of Yosl Shprung, where the post office was located, on Lakhower Street across from Berish Ringer.

The second day of Rosh Hashanah was a Friday. Despite their tears, people prepared for the Sabbath. But they didn't go to synagogue on Saturday; they prayed at home.

On Friday night the houses were poorly illuminated and doors and shutters were tightly shut. People didn't go to sleep but sat up in their clothes; even children slept in their clothes. Everyone had a fearful premonition about approaching danger.

The Fire and the First Mass Murder

The worst thing imaginable unexpectedly occurred.

In the middle of the night a gunshot was heard, quickly followed by another. The shooting was right near the commons; they said that a bomb had exploded. But this was before the Nazis had entered the town. No one was hurt in the explosion. The bomb fell on the ground and tore out a huge hole.

The shooting from rifles and machine guns intensified. Soon there was the sound of cannons. Hearts pounding, people peered through cracks and keyholes through which they could see the fiery flashing of exploding shrapnel. The shooting grew stronger from minute to minute. People extinguished the lights in their houses. They didn't know what to do with themselves, with the children, where to run in the darkness of night, where to hide from the shooting.

The sounds of shooting and cannon fire ended shortly before dawn. But the streets resounded with the noise made by the Germans. Some daring souls stuck out their heads and saw thick black smoke rising to the sky. All the Jewish houses in the market place near the Bilgoraj Gate were in flames. Instantly, despite the danger, the entire Jewish population took flight, leaving behind their meager possessions, taking their little children by the hand, mothers holding their nursing babies to their breasts, young and old ran to get as far away as possible from the burning town.

They ran to the villages, Bukowina, Yastrubichi, Luchow, Rozaniec, Korchow. They hid in the woods, in valleys, fields and meadows. They ran to the commons, to Christians whom they knew, where they thought the Germans would not yet know to look for them.

There were Christians who didn't allow their Jewish friends and acquaintances to enter their houses, who didn't remember the favors the Jews had done them only a few days before. There were also those who gladly received the fleeing Jews and made a place for them in their homes or barns.

The Jews could see from the distance how the smoke and flames of the burning houses grew and engulfed the entire town. There were no firefighters; no one would have dared to extinguish the fire that the Germans had set.

The fire did not burn out until late afternoon. The houses were already destroyed by then. After the fire the Germans drove around on motorcycles outside the town and ordered the Jews to go home. The Jews who had been allowed to stay with Christians were in no hurry to return. Those who with their families, some with children, were sleeping outdoors in meadows where the autumn cold seeped into their bones, returned to the town.

The Explosion

A terrible picture unfolded before them. Fourteen Jews had been dragged from their homes and shot by the Germans on that Saturday before dawn, and had been thrown into the fire half-alive. Twelve of them were Tarnogrod Jews; the other two were from Lodz.

Among the twelve form Tarnogrod were: Yisrael Zuker and his daughter; Mendele Silberzweig; Aron Kleiner; Shmuel Ritzer's wife and all of his children. Shmuel Ritzer himself survived and after the fire went around carrying a child in his arms; the child's arm had been shot off.

The houses on both sides of the street – the side where Yankl Magram lived and the side where Zalman Lustrin lived -- from the Bilgoraj Gate up to the Korchow Gate, were totally destroyed. Not even the ashes of the victims who had been thrown into the fire could be retrieved from the houses.

People tried in various ways to figure out the reason for this catastrophe. There were rumors that Polish soldiers had hidden that night between Jewish houses and from their hiding places had shot at the Germans.

For the Germans, that was a pretext; the Jews were shooting at them and so they had to burn their houses and shoot the Jews. The entire time no airplanes flew overhead and no bombs fell.

Edicts and Persecution

The Gestapo visited Jewish homes seeking men to work at cleaning out the sites of the burnt houses. They forced the Jews to sweep the street with their bare hands, without brooms, on the street where the Gestapo had its headquarters. The Jews who were captured were forced to polish and clean the German motorcycles, using their prayer shawls instead of rags.

The Kreshever rabbi, who had gotten stuck in Tarnogrod after fleeing his home, was captured by the Gestapo. They cut off his beard and forced him to clean the toilet with his bare hands and to carry the night soil in his hat to the wall where the poorhouse was located. After a full day's work they forced him to put on his soiled hat. With guns in their hands, they pulled the hat down over his eyes and mockingly danced around him. The game went on for a long time, until they finally ordered him to go home.

The Gestapo issued an order that Jews could not walk on the sidewalks, but had to walk in the middle of the road. Decrees followed one after the other. The situation grew worse from day to day and became intolerable.

The Jewish refugees hiding out in Tarnogrod began to return to their homes. There were others who calculated that it wasn't worth trying to go back because death threatened on the roads, and they stayed in Tarnogrod.

The German military units, which had marched from Tarnogrod toward Jozefow, encountered resistance from the Polish army in the Jozefow forest. The battle lasted an entire night, the following day and continued into a second day. The Germans were forced to retreat to the village Dosakhes on the river Tanif.

The battle in the Jozefow forest was fierce and many German soldiers died. They brought the wounded to the Zayentsifker Hospital in Tarnogrod, which was close to the battlefield. The Gestapo ordered the Jews to bring to the hospital white blankets, underwear, handkerchiefs, sheets and various other items. Yankl Walfish, Godl Wetsher and Saul Teicher were selected to call on Jewish homes and gather all the items demanded by the Germans. Not one Jew refused; each gave what he could.

On Sunday, the day after the fire, when the Christian residents of the area came to pray at the church, which stood near the burnt houses, the S.S. squads tore off the doors of the Jewish shops, took the best goods for themselves, and threw the rest out onto the street for the assembled Christians. An indescribable commotion ensured. Christians came running from all directions and pushed and shoved each other in a wild effort to grab the Jewish merchandise. The S.S. officers looked on laughing, then formed a line and began distributing the looted goods to the Christians. From their hiding places the Jews looked on with heavy hearts at the despoilment of their property, the fruits of years of toil. No one dared to protest, to appeal to those in power to stop the looting.

Jews were not allowed outside after 6 P.M. Poles were permitted two more hours.

Every day the Germans requisitioned Jews for various jobs. Often these jobs were pointless, with no real objective. They did it just to entertain themselves with Jewish suffering. Behind the booths in the market place stood a derelict Polish army tank, already half-sunken into the ground. The Germans nabbed two homeless Jews and ordered them to drag out the tank, an impossible task. A German officer happened to be passing by and observed the German soldiers beating the two unfortunates who were futilely trying to drag out the tank. With a gesture, the officer instructed the soldiers to release them.

Fear and Terror

Yoel Hochman who was a prayer-leader in the Belzer shtibl, owner of a hardware store and a prominent person in town, was forced by the Germans to shave the beard of another Jew whom they had apprehended in the Tarnogrod ghetto. This happened in the first days of terror and lasted until the final liquidation of the Jews in Tarnogrod.

Jews avoided going into the street. Houses of worship stood empty. When the Germans saw a bearded Jew on the street they would taunt and bully him. So the women took the place of men in carrying out all tasks that required going outside.

Yom Kippur arrived. No one went to synagogue. Neighbors gathered at home and behind closed shutters and locked doors, like the Marranos in cellars [during Spanish Inquisition], they sang Kol Nidre quietly, by the light of a small candle, with stifled weeping.

The next morning several Jews crept through back streets to the Belzer *shtibl*, which was near the wall and not very obvious. They prayed there the whole day, quietly pouring out their hearts. *Sukkot* was approaching, but no one put up a *sukkah* or opened the roof. They feared that any little thing could be misinterpreted by the Germans and evoke false accusations of wrongdoing.

There was a feeling that something new was drawing near. The Germans began to remove the wounded soldiers from the hospital. Army transports began to move in the direction of Sieniawa. There were rumors that the Germans were retreating and that the Russians were arriving. On the eve of *Sukkot* it was clear that the Germans were retreating. By evening, there wasn't a single German soldier left in Tarnogrod.

Arrival of the Soviet Army

Thursday, the first day of Sukkot, at 1 P.M., the Russian army marched in through the Korchow Gate. There was great rejoicing among the Jews. The young people were especially enthusiastic. Everyone hoped that under Soviet occupation Jews would be freed of all their troubles and they welcomed the soviets warmly.

The day they arrived was rainy but all the young people stood waiting in the street for hours, chatting with the Red Army soldiers marching in. Among the Red Army were Jews, who elicited great interest among the young people.

The Red Army received an entirely different welcome from the Polish population, who hated them. The Poles looked askance at the Jews who welcomed the Soviets so heartily. The Jews were happy to be rid of the German beasts. Everyone had been deeply affected by the persecution and suffering they had inflicted. They remembered well the fire on the Sabbath of Rosh Hashanah and the shooting of 14 Jews. With the entry of the Red Army they breathed more freely.

Jews began to go into the street without fear. People walked more confidently and freely. They greeted the soldiers openly and shook their hands.

The rain stopped as evening arrived and it became known that the army would show a Russian film at the market place. All the Jews stood and watched the film and engaged in a lively discussion afterwards. Then they returned home and slept without fear. For the first time after two nightmarish weeks they undressed before going to sleep.

The next day, the second day of Sukkot, the Jews went to pray in the houses of worship just as they had always done. Red flags flew over some houses and the Jews regarded them gratefully.

That very day, a Communist committee was established, which included longtime Communists, among them two Jews – Leibush Fester and Yankl Walfish. The town was surprised; no one had known that the quiet and self-effacing Leibush, who was self-employed and even had two apprentices in his boot-top making workshop, was quite an ardent Communist. He was elected Vice Chairman of the committee.

A civilian militia was established and young Jews joined it. They walked around town, proud of the rifles they carried on their shoulders, and kept order. There were instances when the tough guys in the militia began to bully the Polish officials who had recently openly demonstrated their ant-Semitism. Thus, the former mayor was slapped and arrested even though there were no formal accusations against him. The same occurred with other Polish officials who were known to be enemies of the Jews.

The day after the Soviet entry into town, the student Frimtche Zilberlicht, Yekele Getzl's daughter, gave a fiery speech in Polish in the market place. Instead of a podium, they set up a wide table on which she stood and addressed a large crowd of Poles. She talked about the restoration and liberation which the Red Army had brought with it. The Poles gnashed their teeth and balled their fists with hate and anger, but they didn't express these openly; they were afraid of the Jewish militiamen who were keeping the peace.

These militiamen were of a lower social status and did not enjoy the sympathy of the Jewish population. The Tarnogrod Jews did not agree with the way they behaved toward the Polish population, aware of the hatred that their behavior evoked in the Poles. There were instances when they warned the militia that they should behave more leniently and humanely. But the militia responded with arrogance and certainty that the Russians would never leave, citing the Russian slogan, "Wherever Russians set foot, there they stay."

This conviction soon proved false. As early as the fourth day of the intermediate days of *Sukkot* there were rumors that the Soviets would leave Tarnogrod and that pursuant to a new agreement [between Germany and Russia] the town would again be occupied by the Germans. The Jews didn't want to entertain this possibility, which meant so much new suffering and death.

But it soon became a certainty that the Red Army was leaving. You could see that the army was getting ready to retreat toward Lubaczow. A panic broke out among the Jews. People were desperate; they didn't know what to do. Among the pro-Soviets, people were urging that they leave along with the Red Army. They even ordered trucks for several families with children. But the majority could not decide to abandon their homes. Many tried to assure themselves that the Germans would now be less brutal and life would normalize.

That was what the town rabbi thought. He had a big family with many branches—sons, daughters, grandchildren – over 100 members. To leave town, abandon their homes and wander aimlessly seemed impossible and they saw no other option but to remain. They were deceived by their faith that God is everywhere and would not abandon them in times of trouble. Many Jews still remembered World War I when they fled to Russia as rich Jews and returned after the war as poor beggars. They didn't want to think about that possibility.

Turmoil

The town was in turmoil. Neighbors ran back and forth consulting with each other, asking each other what they had decided to do and what they thought one should do – stay in place or go with the Russians. They refreshed their memories of what the Germans had done during the two weeks that they ruled the town. People changed their minds from hour to hour. They would decide to throw everything away and go with the Russians. Then they immediately thought about the little children, how they would have no place to put them to sleep, no place to obtain food for them. They imagined all the pain they would suffer in their wandering. They felt their attachment to the place where they were born and raised, to their own poverty, and again began to convince themselves that the German murderers would forget about the Jews of the small town of Tarnogrod.

The Soviets tried until the last day to persuade the Jews to leave town and come with them. They even arranged for two trucks to carry the small children. But only a very small percentage decided to go with the Russians. There were also some who left, intending to come back soon, leaving their wives and children behind in Tarnogrod. They left on foot, with packs on their backs, their prayer shawls and *tfillin* [phylacteries] under their arms. They intended to stay somewhere in a village until things calmed down and then return to town. But in every village they found that there were no longer any Jews left. The village Jews had left with the Soviets.

The Germans Return

The next day, Saturday morning, the Germans re-entered Tarnogrod.

A few days later, the Germans levied a heavy *kontributsie* [tax; demand for payment] of money and jewelry. They gave the Jews 24 hours to turn over the *kontributsie*.

On Sunday, when the Christians went to church, the Gestapo forced half of the Jews in town to the market place and made them crawl on all fours around the square. It was raining hard and the square was full of mud and puddles. The Germans forced the Jews to dance in the mud on all fours and the Poles stood around, clapping their hands and laughing heartily.

After several months of German occupation life for the Jews began to normalize. People began to go out into the street looking for a way to earn some money. It was the wives and daughters who were the breadwinners; it was still too dangerous for the men to appear in public. Jews were not allowed outside after 7 P.M. Some Jewish women travelled to Warsaw, Lublin and Zamosc to do business with Poles.

There were no German soldiers stationed in Tarnogrod at that time. There was just a commandant and several police officers. After they collected the *kontributsie*, the Germans appeared to become more lenient and turned a blind eye to unlawful business dealings by Jews. Not all Jews risked engaging in forbidden business dealings. They stayed home and went hungry rather than risk their lives.

There were Jews who managed to obtain special permission to buy merchandise for the German Wehrmacht, and other Jews made a living working for these Jews.

The town seemed to achieve a certain stability. The Germans established normal prices for goods which the Poles dealt in. Anyone who charged more was severely punished. As a result, people, including some daring Jews, began to engage in smuggling, sneaking goods over the border to Sieniawa and Lubaczow on the Russian side. Saccharine was very cheap on the German side, so they smuggled it to the Russian side, where there was a shortage of sugar. Although some smugglers were apprehended by the Russians, and were sent to prison and camps, that didn't deter others.

There were some Jews who had fled to work in the coal mines and other places in Russia, who were now starving and wanted to return to their homes in German-occupied Poland. They gave their last remaining bit of money to the smugglers to sneak them back across the border. It was a miracle that the winter was so severe with freezing temperatures and heavy snows and that the border was protected for hundreds of kilometers with barbed wire. Otherwise, far more Jews would have crossed the border to return to the homes they had abandoned. They were desperate, regretting that they were stranded in a foreign country where they experienced indescribable deprivation, hunger and pain.

In Lemberg there suddenly appeared a German commission which registered Poles who wanted to return to their homes on the other side of the border. There were many Jews who wanted to register but the Germans would not accept them. All of those who registered were later sent to Soviet work camps and forests in the depths of Russian.

Along with several other Jews from Tarnogrod, I was staying in the East Galician town of Lubaczow, where we refugees set up our own way of life. We met daily and poured out our hearts, talking about the past, how we lived in our former homes.

Once, as I was sitting on a bench in a garden with several other homeless Jews, an elderly Jew with a short gray beard approached. He was emaciated, with sunken cheeks, and looked to be over 60. He sat down next to me and told me how he had made his way to Lubaczow form his home in Rozwadow, a Galician town near Rudnik. All he took with him when he left was some underwear and his prayer shawl and *tfillin*. He walked through villages and towns including Tarnogrod, until he reached Lubaczow, which was then already under Russian occupation.

When he learned I was from Tarnogrod he was filled with enthusiasm. He said he would never forget the Jews of Tarnogrod who so warmly treated the refugees who passed through. He had been immediately taken in at a home where they gave him food and drink, attended to him, washed his tired, swollen feet with warm water and gave him a clean bed to sleep in. This elderly man was one of many in Lubaczow who related their impressions of Tarnogrod. They had passed through many places, but nowhere had they encountered such good heartedness as in Tarnogrod.

Deported to Siberia

The Jewish families from Tarnogrod who fled to the Soviet side mostly settled in towns near the new borders. They wanted to be closer to Tarnogrod so they would be able to get news of their relatives who had stayed. In those towns they would frequently encounter smugglers [who could pass on news from the German side].

Some Tarnogroders took advantage of the opportunity to cross the border and return to their former homes. They let themselves believe that the Germans had calmed down and had stopped committing atrocities. Those who returned home were: Arish Fischbaindegen and his family; Leizer Sore Feigelis (Silberzweig); Sore Magram; Azriel Bas; Patil Akst; Wolwish Han; Zisman Fink; Chaim Futer; Avraham David Lakher; a daughter of Matyas Herbstman; and Zelda Opfer.

In summer, 1940, the Soviet government exiled all the refugees to the taiga in Siberia. The deportees remained in the labor camps and so-called free settlements under strict supervision by the NKVD (the Interior Ministry of the Soviet Union) until 1941, when the German-Soviet war broke out.

Thanks to the intervention of the Polish government in exile in London a general amnesty was issued for Polish exiles in the Soviet camps and the Tarnogrod refuges were freed. They settled in Central Asia, where they remained until the end of the war.

At this time, in Russia, there was formed the new Polish army of volunteers who wanted to fight the Nazis. This army was dominated by anti-Semitism, and had a tendency not to accept Jews. Nevertheless, young Jews did get in, including some from Tarnogrod.

This Polish army left the Soviet Union after a while and travelled through Persia to *Eretz Yisroel*, where it was stationed as a military unit serving the Middle East. In *Eretz Yisroel* the army held to its anti-Semitic ways, engaging in harassment of its Jewish soldiers. Many Jewish soldiers left the Polish army and settled in the land, where they live to this day. Among them were these Jews from Tarnogrod: Yechiel Hering; Moyshe Shprung; Moyshe Dag; Moyshe Rosenfeld and the two Wetsher brothers, Moyshe and Yeshaye.

During the difficult war years in Russia many Jewish refugees died, succumbing to hunger and diseases such as malaria and typhus. Among the Jews from Tarnogrod who died in epidemics were: Chaim Volf Silberzweig and his wife Sheyntshe and two children, Eliyohu and Yoyne; Chaim Goldman and his son and two daughters; his wife Reli went blind in Russia and died after the war in Szczecin; Yeheskl Silberzweig; Moyshe Kenigstein; Eliyohu Adler; Rabbi Tsvi Teicher; Avrom Shveder; Lipe Fefer; Zalmen Weintraub; Brayntse Herbstman; Sheyndl Weintraub; Motl Struzer; Mikhl Model; Volf Leyb Kesler; Aron Shilim; Elboym; Yeheskl Weintraub; Frimtche Weinman; Rekhame Mantl; Elimelekh Tryb; Chaim Blutman; Yoysef-Hersh Wachnachter; Sheyndl Riger.

The refugees from Tarnogrod who survived the times of hunger and illness, lived the entire time with the hope that the war would end and they would return to their homes. When they did return, they found ruins and devastation, a town without Jews.

The Bloody Monday

(according to two Tarnogrod Christian witnesses. Melekh and Share)

Until the end of 1941, when Germany attacked Soviet Russia, the Jews in Tarnogrod lived somewhat more freely and better than in other Polish towns. It seemed as if the Germans weren't paying any special attention to the town. It was not near the main roads that the German army used. There were only a few German police, and they were susceptible to bribery and willing to cast a blind eye on the smuggling carried out by the Jews. The Polish neighbors were not especially hostile and did business with the Jews. There was not yet a ghetto in Tarnogrod and it was possible to visit a nearby village and return with goods.

The situation changed after the German-Soviet war broke out. Things got worse from day to day. The Germans forced Jews to perform the worst work. They ordered the Jews to establish a Judenrat, which was charged with sending Jews to forced labor and carrying out all the decrees issued by the Germans.

More and more decrees were issued against the Jews. The Judenrat was forced to provide lists of names of Jews to be sent to work. The Judenrat was also in charge of collecting money for the *kontributsie* levied by the Germans. Jews were forbidden to have contact with the Christian population, to engage in commerce with them, or to obtain any aid from them.

Hunger grew worse from day to day. It happened that a Jew would secretly meet up with a Christian he knew, who would give or sell him something to eat, and be caught by a German policeman. This was considered a serious crime, punishable by shooting.

Golda Ringer went out of the ghetto to find something to eat, encountered a policeman on Lakhower Street and was shot dead; she was buried not far away. Her child, who was several weeks old, remained with her parents; later all of them died together.

The Jews looked to the Judenrat for protection from German savagery.

Of course, that was an illusion which quickly disappeared. The first chairman of the Judenrat was Hersh Blutman, who was killed by the Germans even before they began their extermination action. The second and last chairman was Sini Graer. He survived the war in hiding with a Christian in Kamionka, the local dog beater. He now lives in America. His work in the Judenrat is spoken of with great bitterness.

[Pages 319 - 329]

The Ghetto

by Nuchim Krymerkopf

Translated by Miriam Leberstein

In the summer of 1942 conditions worsened for the Jews of Tarnogrod. As they did everywhere, the Germans confined the Jews to a ghetto. They ordered the Jews to move, taking with them the belongings they still retained, into the specially designated Razhenitser Street. The Jewish population of Lakhower Street, the market place and all the surrounding streets, all had to move there. All the Jews who still remained in the villages around Tarnogrod were also crammed into Razhenitser Street.

The crowding was unfathomable. Several families lived in one room or in a vestibule. Every attic, every cranny, was occupied. Illnesses broke out and it was forbidden to bury the dead in the Tarnogrod cemetery; they had to be taken to Bilgoraj or behind Badiak's hill.

Just like the men, dozens of Jewish girls in the Tarnogrod ghetto were sent to work for the Germans every day. Hungry, worried, with burning hatred in their hearts, they would put on a smile, throw their shovels over their shoulders and with youthful strides go off to their exhausting labor, so that neither the Germans nor the hostile Poles would see their despair and bitterness.

For the entire time the Tarnogrod Jews were cut off from Jews in other places. It was rare for anyone to sneak out of the ghetto and make contact with other towns and villages. The psychological conditions were terrible and when someone was able to bring news of the murders that were happening elsewhere, no one wanted to believe it. They didn't want to accept the concept that what was happening was a well-planned annihilation of the entire Jewish people. The Germans operated their death machine shrewdly and methodically. In Tarnogrod as in other towns they prepared for the extermination with a detailed plan.

A few days before the liquidation the Germans informed the Judenrat that they required young men for a work assignment. The Judenrat produced the required transport of Jewish youth precisely on time. None of them ever returned. No one ever found out where they were shot, where their young blood sank into the earth.

This was also the fate of the town's Polish intelligentsia. It appears that the Germans feared that the Jewish youth and the Polish intellectuals would share common understanding and join in a common effort. Conditions in Tarnogrod favored such a common effort. The young Jews were exceptionally bold and had an amicable relationship with the Polish intelligentsia. With the necessary leadership, they could have formed a unified organization able to mount a resistance to the German occupation. The Germans understood this and even before they began the liquidation action they eliminated both the Jewish youth and the Polish intellectuals.

The hellish conditions in the ghetto worsened with each day. People were shot for the most trivial reason. Yankev Akerman, Zalke's brother, pulled up an onion growing in a small garden in the market place. They caught him in the act and shot him. Wolf Stockman went to the Korchow gate with a small sack of potatoes, which he had begged from a Christian acquaintance. He encountered a German police officer that shot him on the spot.

On the road from the Lakhover forest, the Germans caught Meyer Share's two grown sons, Azriel and Antsh, who were transporting a small wagonload of wood. Both were shot on the spot.

After the Judenrat had carried out a collection of money and valuables ordered by the Germans, the Germans found a skunk fur in the home of Yoysef Moyshe Teicher, the rabbi's grandson. He himself was in hiding, but the Gestapo officer who found the fur announced that if he didn't turn himself in, ten other Jews would be shot.

The town was in turmoil. After much deliberation it was decided that to save ten lives, Yoysef Moyshe would have to be turned in. He presented himself to the Gestapo and was shot.

As happened everywhere, the Germans found people from among the Christian population who were ready to serve them. Christian youth tormented the Jews as sadistically as the German rulers. The following is an example: On the commons there stood a stack of hay for the German horses. The Germans stationed Jews there day and night to guard the hay. One night some Polish boys snuck in and set fire to the haystack. The Jews were blamed for this and in retaliation the Germans took 30 Jews to the Christian cemetery and shot them.

The Suffering of Jewish Children

The experience of Jewish children forms an entirely separate chapter of the German occupation. Jewish children became shepherds for the Christians, took their cows, pigs, and geese to pasture, and did all kinds of work, for which they were paid with a piece of bread.

A group of Jewish women and girls from Tarnogrod being taken in a convoy under guard by a German soldier to heavy forced labor, for which they weren't paid. In the photo are Blime Rozenfeld and Fishele Beynushke's daughter (third and fourth from the left). The other faces, changed by their atrocious conditions under which they lived, are familiar. There will certainly be people who will recognize them and will denote them by name, each in his book of remembrances. To their eternal memory!

Jewish mothers went to work for peasants digging potatoes, and would receive a few potatoes for a full day's work, which they didn't eat themselves but brought home for their hungry children.

The Jewish women went to work for their former Christian washerwomen, fed their pigs and stole a bit of the pigs' food to bring home. A bit of cooked potato peels was considered a luxury. Children were swollen with hunger and covered with sores and rashes caused by living in such dirty and crowded conditions.

On Sunday night the Jews saw several autos coming from the Bilgoraj gate, carrying S.S. personnel in black uniforms. Everyone got very depressed. They knew what the black uniforms had done in Jozefow and other towns that had already been cleared of Jews.

The news of the arrival of the evil host quickly spread to all Jewish homes and the Jews, in fear and despair, didn't know what to do or where to go. Death loomed in every direction. There were some people who had prepared hiding places but no one held the illusion that this would help them. They knew that the S.S. searched with bloodhounds and uncovered all the hiding places.

No one slept that night in Jewish homes. Mothers sat cuddling their children, stifling their tears so as not to sadden them. Young mothers tried to sing a lullaby, hoping to dispel their children's hunger.

The next day, Monday morning, the 22nd day of Cheshven, 1942, the watchman at the Polish town hall beat on his drum and announced that all Jews, old and young, men, women and children, must assemble at market place. Anyone who remained at home would be shot immediately. In the Christian streets the watchman announced to the residents that anyone who hid a Jew would be shot along with his entire family and their house be burned. Placards were posted all over town with the same announcement.

At the same time the market was surrounded by S.S. troops who were armed from head to toe. S.S. men armed with machine guns were also stationed along the roads and in the fields. As soon as the Jews arrived at the market place they were attacked by the black-uniformed S.S. men, who began driving them toward a large pit that had been dug near the wall beyond Dovid-Yoel's garden. At the edge of the pit the S.S. ordered the Jews to strip naked and began shooting them with machine guns. Row by row the naked Jews fell into the pit.

Shmuel-Elye, son of Alter Melamed, at the time he was being led to his death, as the German murderers laughed and mocked him. We will never forget his hoarse cry, the cry of a deaf-mute, that continues to resonate in our hearts. It is the cry that rises from the mass graves, a harsh sound that welled up and soaked the earth, along with the innocent blood of children and the old. And forever, all over the world, may there be

heard the cry of the tortured victims buried in the mass graves, may it call out in lamentation and with threat,
with that holy vow – never forget!

The huge pit remained open for a long time, until the Poles in the course of the day, collected the bodies that lay in the streets, houses, and hiding places where the German police had shot them. The Poles put them in wagons like heaps of garbage and took them to the pit. Not until midnight did the Poles finally fill in the enormous mass grave.

Melekh, the Pole who lived on the commons, who later told me about these events, was one of the men who collected the bodies and took them to the grave, and transported sand to cover bloodstains in the street. He said that as he was leaving after filling in the grave, he saw the earth heaving and blood seeping out.

In the course of that Monday, horrifying scenes played out in Tarnogrod. It is impossible to describe all the heart-rending events. It is, however, also impossible to forget them. There could be heard the cries and laments of children clinging to their dead mothers, of mothers searching for the children that had been torn from them. The murderers ran wildly from house to house shooting anyone they found – children in their cradles, the sick in their beds. Entire families lay in heaps.

The Pole Melekh told me in a strangled voice of the horrific sights he witnessed: how two S.S. men tore apart the two month-old child of Dine Akerman and then shot the mother; how a two year-old child embraced his dying mother, pleading with her not to leave him alone. The German police shot the child in the head.

After it was announced that anyone who turned a Jew over to the Gestapo would receive one kilo of sugar and a piece of soap, young Christian boys ran to all the hiding places to search out Jews. They brought in Jews from the remote villages and forests. Little Shrizhele found Moyshe Krietner hiding in a chimney on Razhenister Street and dragged him to the Gestapo. Fanetshke's boys, from the commons, caught Zalmen Wetsher in the forest, put a rope around his neck and pulled him by the rope to the Gestapo. The many Jews who were captured in this way were locked up and held in Khaim Goldman's dark warehouse behind an iron door until they were shot. There were also instances of organized resistance. It is known that several young Jews from Tarnogrod mounted a vigorous resistance to German police, defending themselves until the last one fell.

Yosl Weiss, Mordkhe Beile-Rechls, went up into the attic with his sharp axe. Two S.S. men came looking for Jews and began climbing the ladder to the attic. They stood at the entrance and shouted, "Jew, get out! Weiss hit one of them over the head with the axe with all his strength and the German fell off the ladder covered in blood. The second German ran to get help. The S.S. surrounded the housed and managed to drag Weiss out of the attic and beat him to death with iron bars.

Several years after the war, a Polish doctor from Szczebrzeszyn wrote in the American [Yiddish] newspaper, the Forverts [Forward], about what he witnessed in Tarnogord during the liquidation. He described the battle between two young men and the S.S. in the middle of the Tarnogrod market place. He said that there were no words to describe the bravery of the young men at a time when the entire town was surrounded and besieged by the black uniformed Germans and their helpers.

The forest was the only place to escape but the enemy was a threat there as well. There were instances where the Jews, after several weeks of wandering in the forest lost the will to live and turned themselves in to the Germans. That's what happened to Shmuel (Kits), Yoel Hochman and Godl Wetsher and his wife. They had to pay 20 marks each, to boot – that was the high price that the Germans put on the bullet with which they shot a Jew. Those who couldn't afford the 20 marks for a bullet were beaten to death with sticks and bars.

Several young people from Tarnogrod and the surrounding towns were able to tolerate the suffering and hunger in the forest and survived until liberation. When partisan divisions began to form things got easier in the forest and the conditions for Jews in hiding improved somewhat. The Poles who hunted down Jews began to fear going to the forest. The German soldiers who often tried to surround and penetrate the forest encountered a vigorous resistance and had to retreat.

But the entire time until liberation, the Tarnogrod Poles and villagers who aided the S.S., who before the war had been friends with Jews and obtained favors from them, did not cease to search and spy, robbing and killing any Jews they found.

Rabbi Reb Moyshele Teicher and his family. Reb Moyshele, the last rabbi of Tarnogrod, and his family, were all killed as holy martyrs.

In a Sea of Suffering and Pain

David Elbaum's son, left. The Jews in the Tarnogrod ghetto went hungry and worked with unsparing effort in the sole hope of surviving the worst enemy of the Jewish people, the Nazis.

Reb Moyshele, the last rabbi, hid with his family in a bunker not far from the synagogue. It was airless, and a little boy left the bunker for a few minutes to catch his breath. A Polish acquaintance observed this and reported it to the Gestapo, which surrounded the bunker and forced out over 100 people. They were taken at gunpoint to a site behind the Christian cemetery, where they were forced to strip naked and were shot.

Among the Poles who pointed out Jews in hiding places and who themselves murdered Jews were Serkis, Gush, and the Valashins, who lived near the Jewish cemetery, and Deker's young sons and Panetshik's sons who lived at the commons. Some of them suffered revenge at the hands of young Jews who fought with the partisans and entered Tarnogrod at night with weapons and attacked Gush's house, killing the entire family. Other partisans did the same thing to Valashin's sons, who had turned over two Jewish girls to the Gestapo: Dvoyre Lipiner, who was in hiding with Karpik and Brayndl Honik who was in hiding with Maslovski. The same thing would have happened to others, but feeling threatened by the Jewish avengers, they left Tarnogrod.

Groups of Tarnogrod Jews at forced labor. A common sight wherever the Germans set foot, wherever their brown axe fell. Under that axe, in a desperate sea of suffering and blood, the Jews stood, hoping until the last minute for a miracle.

Among those in the photos: Shmuelke Stockman, Isser Aks, Zalman Brandwein (seated)

[Page 330]

God, Take Revenge

by Nuchim Krymerkopf

Translated by Miriam Leberstein

There was a forest
richly green.
Then a wild storm
destroyed the blooms.

Beautiful trees grew there,
glorious, majestic.
Yours and mine among them
now all in ruins.

Oh, forest, our forest,
you were so dear to us.
How quickly they destroyed you
burnt you in their ovens.

They showed no mercy
for the cherished trees.
They burnt them in the ovens
leaving nothing but bones.

Everyone heard the groans,
the groans of the trees,
as they were covered with earth,
"Shema Yisroel"[1] on their lips.

Our hearts are gripped
by anger and sorrow.
The forest burned
and no one could put out the fire.

For no reason at all
they tore
the innocent saplings
from their mother's breasts.

The fire burned
for many years.
Six million Jews wiped out
and the fields soiled with ash.

Old and young
drowned in a sea of blood,

the glorious forest
burned in the flames.

Through fire and flame
through hunger and need
the child and his mother
died a horrible death.

We stand here
heads bowed
and we mourn our loved ones
who are no longer here.

We will always remember
their faces
and we will say *kaddish*[2]
for the trees from our forest.

God, almighty God
take revenge
for the innocent souls
of Tarnogrod.

1.   "Hear oh Israel," prayer recited morning and night, and, as here, before dying.
2.   Prayer for the dead..

[Pages 331 - 332]

Shabbat Teshuvah 1939

by Tsvi ben Efraim (Yehiel Hering)

Translated by Miriam Leberstein

The first day of Rosh Hashanah the Germans entered Tarnogrod, and the first victim, Yoel Kamer, a 16 year-old boy – fell. Terrified at his first glimpse of the Germans, he began to run and didn't hear their order to halt and was immediately shot. The next day the town was eerily quiet. We went to pray in the Belzer *shtibl*, but the prayers went more quickly than usual. The fear was great; people walked home by back streets so to avoid an encounter with a German soldier.

There were already a lot of refugees in town. There were also several Jewish soldiers from the Polish army, which had been driven out. A Jewish soldier, a boy from Krakow, stayed in our house.

At night, all the doors and shutters were nailed shut. It was already 8 o'clock when we heard a commotion. We were sure that it was Germans, but when we fearfully went to the door, I heard people speaking Polish. We soon heard the sound of bayonets clashing in the street. The voices got closer to our door and demanded we open up. Not receiving an answer, they began storming the door. Our teeth were chattering but we didn't open.

Minutes of terror elapsed. Soon we heard them placing a machine gun in our courtyard, and they began to shoot in the direction of town, where German soldiers were stationed. The fight lasted more than two hours. There were dead and wounded on both sides. Several Polish soldiers were brought into the house of our Christian neighbor.

It was late at night when the Polish soldiers retreated from our courtyard and dug in closer to the market place, in Yisroel Khaim Yoyne's attic, from which they shot ceaselessly into the market place.

Not until it began to grow light did it quiet down. The Polish soldiers went somewhere and the Germans began to look for the places from which the shooting had come. They looked in our courtyard, but didn't find anything suspicious so they kept looking until they found the machine gun in Yisroel Khaim Yoyne's house where the Poles had left it. They made everybody leave the house and they shot and then set fire to them. They threw Yisroel Khaim's daughter Tobe, who was still breathing, into the fire alive.

Among those who were shot were Mendele Silberzweig and Shmuel Ritzer and his entire family, three sons and two daughters. They also shot nearby neighbors, Aron Kleiner (Arish) and his son Shloymen and two daughters. Then they began to set fire to the entire neighborhood, including our house.

The terror spread to other parts of the town where they arrested the residents and brought the to the small church on Lakhover Street.

Seeing what was happening, we fled outside the town, where not far from the church was a deep ravine where many Jewish families hid.

On Saturday at noon some Poles came to us and told us that the Germans were approaching and we had to flee. Chaos erupted. Families got separated, including ours; everyone ran in a different direction. I and my father and mother stayed together.

We arrived at Potek and went to Yisroel Shprung's house, where we were warmly received and we stayed there until the next morning, when we found out that things had quieted down and we returned to Tarnogrod.

[Pages 333-334]

In the Time of Kiddush Ha–Shem

by Tzvi Hering

Translated by Zvika Welgreen

If not for you, great forefathers,
where would we be standing?
Nothing will diminish your glory.

The second from the right, in the first row, is my father Efraim–Yakov Hering.
Next to him: Ben–Zion Weinrib, Mordechai Kroin, Moshe Feingold, Yakov Adler
and Joel Hochman.

Dedication to Their Memory

In the memory of the holy persons who were murdered by the Nazis, may their names be forgotten, and died while saying Shema Israel. They had this combination of heroism and glory, and I allow myself to say what the *bat kol* [the echo or heavenly voice] said for Rabbi Akiva while he was executed by the evil kingdom: "Blessed are you, whose soul departed with echad." [One, referring to the Shema].

My Holy Father!

In memory of my father, Efraim–Yakov son of Chaia–Lea, who is in this photo of Tarnogrod holy persons. I want to commemorate him, in few words.

Seeing you here in your last moments, you are in my mind as a noble and great God believer as I remember you. Proving in your existence during your life and death that the moral basis of the righteous Jewish home is a stable and unshaken virtue which shapes one's character even in the most difficult moments in front of cruel and terrible death.

You had, my dear father, the moral strength, which gives me the belief in life and ideals.

I remember you, my good father, sitting every day after *Shacharit* [morning prayers], wrapped in tallit studying *Mishnayot*, parts of Ein Yaakov's clauses in "Mans' Life."

I remember you, my good father, praying in front of the ark on Saturdays and holidays. Shabbat had long conversation with the hidden Holy Spirit, Holy conversation which cannot be interpreted, you sang "Bless him who created us in his honor" and other songs.

My holy father, I shall not forget you till my last day and my heart bleeds whenever I remember you.

There may be no one who can write anything about the other forefathers, but I shall remember them today, shall bow my head and whisper:

Honor to their memory!

[Pages 335-349]

Through Inhuman Suffering and Pain

by Shlomo-Yitzhak Shprung

Translated by Miriam Leberstein

Everyone in Tarnogrod was familiar with the village of Potok Gorny, where I was born. Twelve Jewish families lived comfortably there, making a living and sending their children to school. When the young people reached marriageable age, they moved to the town. Our family was preparing to move to Tarnogrod, but the outbreak of World War II put an end to those plans. People began to run around in a panic, things became wildly chaotic.

I and my brother Moshe fled to Tarnogrod, where our sister Rivkale was living with her husband, Shlomo Zaltsman, from Maden. We arrived on the day that the Germans had shot several Jews and burnt down their houses.

The next day, we fled back to Potok Gorny, taking with us our sister and brother-in-law and Yeheskl Zilberzweig's son. Later, we were joined by Yeheskl Zilberzweig and many more Tarnogrod Jews. They all stayed with us for several days. When things calmed down a bit, they returned to town.

After several days, the Russian army marched in, but they soon withdrew, and the aimless running around and wandering resumed. We bought a wagon and two horses and prepared to leave but we started to receive news that many Jews had remained in Tarnogrod and my parents decided to stay where we were.

I and Moshe rode our bicycles to Tarnogrod, to which my sister and her husband had already returned. We found them with their belongings packed, ready to leave. We decided to join them in going to Sieniawa because the Russian army was there.

Every week Moshe would sneak across the border and go home to check on our parents. He did this several times without mishap, until one day he was caught by Russian soldiers and arrested. My brother in law, Shlomo Zilberzweig, went to the military post to intercede. A military man even promised that Moshe would be released but he was soon shipped to Przemysl, where he was jailed. I immediately went to Przemysl, where I found ways to smuggle him packets of food, and began to look for ways to free him. But soon they sent him to a military prison in Lviv. Again I tried to get him released. But my efforts were in vain and I returned to Sieniawa alone.

Across the Border

One dark night I snuck across the border to Tarnogrod, where I slept at the home of my aunt Breintche Shprung. In the morning I went home to Potok Gorny.

I found my parents in a very bad state. The Germans had looted everything in their house, loading furnishings, clothing, and furs into wagons, and had distributed much of it among the peasants who watched with joy as the Jews were robbed.

I pleaded with my parents to leave the village and go with me to Sieniawa. My uncle Shmuel Peretz who lived with his family not far from us, came over and they all decided not to leave. Their decision was influenced by their memories of World War I, when everyone who abandoned their homes endured terrible suffering; many died away from home. Those who had chosen to stay in their homes fared much better.

In addition, the winter weather was already quite harsh. The very idea of having to travel in freezing weather to other cities, without the means to make a living, horrified them and kept them from taking to the road.

I began to do business. Working with Christian smugglers, I obtained cloth from Tarnogrod and exchanged it with the peasants for various kinds of food – flour, kasha, millet -- which we then smuggled into Tarnogrod. This lasted until war broke out between Russia and Germany, and persecution grew greater from day to day.

The horrifying aktsies began, shootings and deportations to Belzec. One night the Gestapo came to our house in Potok Gorny. Luckily, I was sleeping in a dark corner and the Germans didn't notice me. They seized 10 people from Potok Gorny, but after several weeks they were freed and returned to the village. They looked like skeletons, tortured and exhausted. Shortly after that, it was decreed that any Jew who left his home without special permission would be shot.

In Fearful Anticipation

The decree ruined the Jews who lived in the town and in the villages around Tarnogrod. Defying it, I risked sneaking into Tarnogrod, where the suffering grew greater daily. People died from hunger. There were terrible shortages and Jews could not buy anything to eat. Children would go out into the street to beg for a couple of potatoes. They would also come to us in Potok Gorny and my mother would first cook up a big pot of soup for them, and later fill sacks with potatoes, which the mailman would leave with my uncle Yosl Shprung, for the children to pick up and carry home.

With every day there were new decrees. They began to deport many families from Tarnogrod, ostensibly to work on the estates, among them our uncle Yosl and his entire family. His loss also affected the children, who now were left to carry the heavy load of potatoes by themselves. These six- and eight-year-old boys were the support of their parents and bore the burden of responsibility for their entire households.

Before the High Holy days in 1942 an order was issued that all Jews had to leave the villages and move to the town. This badly affected the Jews in Potok Gorny, Kilne, Lipin, and Shishkov. One day we were transported to Krzeszow, where we were packed in, two families in one room. We didn't know what the Germans had planned for us. And we lived in fearful waiting for the day of judgment, which came on the 23rd day of *Cheshvan* 1942.

On that date they surrounded the town and sent all the Jews to the market place. Anyone who tried to flee was shot. I and my parents sat in our house for an hour and waited for the murderers to enter and drive us out. My mother's last words were: "My dear child, try to escape. Maybe God will help. Try to save yourself." I jumped over a two meter high fence into an orchard near the town hall of Krzeszow. I began to look for a place to hide and saw a barn where a cow was stabled. There I found a boy from Kilne, Yankl Basvitz, Itshe's son. There was a little straw in the barn which had been prepared for the cow to lie on. We lay down on it to rest. But soon the maid came in to milk the cow. When she saw us, she wanted to leave at once, to inform her employer.

Addressing her by name, I appealed to her not to do that. She recognized me and promised not to tell anyone. She brought us more straw, concealing the corner where we were hiding. We lay in the barn for two days until things grew quiet. We found out that all the Jews who had been driven out had been shot on the road.

A Huge Mass Grave

At night, I and Yankl silently left the barn and crept along the empty streets to get out of town. In the dark of night we arrived at the place where the horrific *aktsie* had been carried out, where our families had been killed. We stood there as if frozen, both of us weeping. I don't know how long we stood there sobbing. We remembered where we were, we knew our crying would not help us, that we had to find a place to hide and stay alive.

Finally, we arrived in Potok Gorny. It was already past midnight and we considered whose door to knock on. Suddenly a Christian approached us; I recognized our former neighbor. He also recognized me and told us about the decree to capture the Jews. That day, he said, many Jews had been captured. Among them were my brother Shimon Aaron Bruk; Feyge Knokhen and her daughter; Chaim-Zalman Brandwein's wife, Perele, and her two children; and many other Jews from Tarnogrod who had fled the town and had been caught in Potok-Gorny and shot.

The Poles stripped them of their clothes and buried their naked bodies in a huge mass grave. We later learned that the grave held 54 Jews. Having heard what the Pole said, my friend Yankl was terrified and began running in the direction of Kilne, paying no attention to me. He appeared crazed with fear.

Brokenhearted I silently slipped into a nearby stable belonging to Larva Yaziye. It was full of grain and I stayed there until morning.

It turned out that the owner had heard someone entering in the middle of the night and as soon as morning came, he entered and jumping on the bales shouted, "Who's there?" I crept out from behind the bales and he appeared astonished, telling me that the day before they had been looking for me at his place. The police had gone around with pitchforks, sticking them in the straw, looking for anyone hiding there. Because of that he was afraid to let me stay.

I sat there unmoving for a time and he again recounted how the day before they had captured many Jews, bound them with rope and brought them to the town hall, where two Germans shot them all. Finally, I gathered my courage and said to him, "It's already light out. As soon as I leave here, they'll catch me and shoot me. You had better just tie me with a rope and take me to the Germans."

These words made an impression on him. Perhaps at that moment he recalled the favors that I had once done for him. He replied, "No, I won't do that." I got the impression that he wouldn't do anything to hurt me. I asked him to cover me up with several bundles of straw, and told him I would stay hidden until nightfall, when I would go into the forest.

He did as I asked, without saying anything and I lay there all day, which felt like a year. I listened to the rain which fell unceasingly outside.

As soon as darkness fell, the peasant entered and asked, "Are you still alive?" He started to remove the bundles of straw and handed me some bread with a bit of butter.

As I left the barn, I was enveloped in a thick wet darkness. I walked for six kilometers. The road was muddy from the constant rain. Finally I could see the forest in the dark. With my last bit of strength I dragged myself to the first line of trees and lay there all night and the next morning. Not until it began to grow dark did I start to walk in the direction of Leshnitshvuke, where a Christian woman I knew lived; I expected to be able to hide out there.

Polish Bandits

When I got there it was fully dark. When I knocked on the Christian woman's' door, she recognized me immediately. She told me that only minutes earlier she had been visited by Shemaia and his son Yosl from Gust and Lipinski. They had been in Tarnogrod and fled together with Eliash's son and daughter. They begged her for something to eat but she was afraid that if they were later caught, they would say where they had gotten food. She was sure that they were still near her house.

She led me to their hiding place and I saw a horrifying scene before me. People were sitting, prostrated by hunger and fear. It had been several days since they had eaten anything. I immediately gave them my bread and butter, and asked the Christian woman to make potato soup for them. She hesitated for a while, but then agreed to do so for my sake.

I gave her some money and she immediately brought out bread and butter and we went deeper into the woods. There we immediately set about digging out a bunker in the ground, in which we all hid. On the fourth day we were discovered by Polish bandits who shot at us. We all ran away. On the way I encountered the Christian Mikhl Koziel from Potok Gorny, who had gone into the forest to get wood. I told him the misfortunes that had befallen us. He consoled me and, in the evening, I returned to Potok Gorny, but he didn't allow me to enter his house.

I decided to knock on the doors of Christian acquaintances and ask them for a bit of bread. But as soon as they opened the door, they told me to run away and threatened to turn me over to the Germans.

Again I began wandering around the barns, spending days and nights wherever I could. On November 13th I went into the loft of a stable but immediately heard that someone was already there. I heard quiet breathing and assumed it was the owner, asleep. I asked in Polish who was there and heard someone say in Yiddish:

"Is that you, Shlomo?"
I immediately recognized the voice of Vele Shprung, who told me he had been hiding there since the first days [of the war]. We rejoiced and I stayed there with him.

The peasant brought us food, but with every day, we felt the increasing cold of the approaching winter. Neither of us had anything with which to cover ourselves, but we didn't see any way out. We were not supposed to leave the barn, and we constantly heard stories about the capture of Jews, each more frightening than the last.

On January 12, 1942, we heard terrible screams. I went to the slit in the wall through which we could see outside. It was still light and I saw Christian boys driving Moshe Knokhn's two children toward Krzeszow, where the Gestapo was stationed. I later learned that they were shot there.

The Letter

Fear grew in our hearts, and we were tortured by a sense of hopelessness, seeing no way we could avoid the dangers that confronted us from all sides and survive this terrible time. We heard news of German victories on the battlefront. The German army was moving deeper into Russia.

Several days passed and the peasant told us that Zalman Brandwein had been found dead in a trench, among dead horses. It seemed that the peasant with whom he had been hiding for several months had murdered him and thrown him into the trench, along with the horses. Zalman Brandwein was Yisroel Zilberzweig's son in law and came from Tarnogrod. This news strongly affected us. We foresaw the same fate for ourselves and decided to go out into the forest and join up with the partisans.

It was Purim. We snuck out of the barn having earlier said our farewells with the Christian. I left a letter with him, to be passed on to my brother Moshe, about whom I knew only that he was somewhere in Soviet Russia. I asked the peasant to give my brother the letter when he returned from the war.

The letter reads as follows:

Dear Brother Moshe:

I am now going into the forest and it is possible we will never see each other again. But deep in my heart, I pray that God will help and we will be together again, mourning the death of our dear parents and sisters. But it is all in God's hands. If I am not able to take revenge for the death of our family, I ask you to find out who was the Christian who captured our dear brother Shimon in Lipne and handed him over to the Gestapo, and to avenge his death.

Now, dear brother, I have left a number of things with the peasants. Make sure that they hand over every bit of it; don't give away a single thread. I am leaving a list of which peasants are holding my things.

Dear Moshe, please do your best to support and take care of the peasant who will give you this letter.

Vele Shprung is with me; he is our uncle Shmuel Peretz's son in law. We are going into the forest together. May God help and end our troubles very soon, and liberate us from the danger of death.

Amen!

From me, your brother, who expects to see your face and rejoice together soon in the battle for the people of Israel. Amen saleh! Your brother, Shlomo Shprung.

Potok-Gorny, March 28, 1943

Moshe Shprung and his brother Shlomo-Yitzhak,
the writer of the letter and of this account

The peasant gave us bread and the cooked meat of half a lamb and warmly bid us farewell.

We walked all night. We wanted to reach the Yashtshembitser forest, because we had heard there were Jewish and Polish partisans there. Arriving at the edge of the forest, we lay down and considered what to do next. Suddenly, a peasant and his wife drove up, en route to gather wood. When they drew near, I recognized them as people I knew. I approached and asked them if they knew where the partisans were. The peasant Franek told me that the people in the forest were not partisans but a band of robbers, who had already robbed and killed many Jews. They were located about a half kilometer away. He warned me not to go there, because they would surely kill us.

Our last hope was dashed. The rain did not cease pouring and we were soaked. Hidden among the small bushes we waited until evening and when it got dark returned to our barn.

The peasants were very glad to see us. They told us they had greatly feared for our lives and were truly happy when they saw us return.

Again we hid day and night in the attic, where the peasant brought us food. We didn't move for an entire week, except for Saturday night, after the Sabbath, when we tiptoed down to the peasant's house to wash.

On one such Saturday, when we were in the peasant's house, someone suddenly knocked on the door. We were scared to death. The owner went outside and returned a few minutes later. He told us that Yisroel Korngold and another young man had come seeking a place to hide. I begged the peasant to let them in.

The man who came with Yisroel was Nachman's son. They were both in terrible shape, having not changed their clothes for months. They remained with us. After several days Nachman's son left to go to Bukovina, where his brother was. But he was captured there.

After a short time, the peasants began to talk about how our peasant was hiding Jews, and we had to find another place.

Three kilometers away lived a peasant, whose barn seemed to be a suitable place to hide. I led Vele and Yisroel there, and told them to climb up to the loft in the barn. I then knocked on the door of the owner's hut, summoned him outside and said:

"Stefan, listen to me. I am a member of the partisans. I and my two comrades have been given an important mission, but on the way my two companions fell ill. Give them something to eat and I'll come back in a few days and retrieve them."

My words and the confident tone in which I said them had an effect and the peasant agreed without protest to hide the two "partisans," but just for several days.

I myself went back to our previous place with the loft, but instead of climbing up to the loft, I fashioned a hiding place under the house, which seemed safer. I stayed there for two weeks, too frightened to leave. The entire time I kept thinking about my two "partisans." I knew what they were going through, but I had no choice. Not until a dark night two weeks later did I go to visit them. When the peasant saw me, he began to weep, begging me to take them away. He was trembling in fear.

I put on a hopeful face and assured him that nothing would happen to him, because the partisans were watching out for him. I told him to call the two partisans down from the loft. They were completely frozen and trembled with cold. The peasant wrapped them in fur pelts, and gave them ample food and drink. I promised the peasant a rich reward and he didn't dare to say anything about taking them away.

At that time, the peasant's wife's brother told me that Simchale, Yankl Patiker's son, was roaming around Dombrovke without a place to hide. I asked her to let him know that I would meet up with him and set a place to do this.

At dawn, we met in the Polish cemetery and from there went to Kruk's on the Dombrovke, where we left Simchale. I told Kruk that pursuant to an order issued by the partisans, he was obliged to hide him. This had the desired effect and from then on the peasants treated him well. And so he survived the most difficult time until liberation. He lives now in America.

Believing in Liberation

With the coming of 1944, we heard news about the defeats suffered by the Germans, and of their retreat. We began to fear that while retreating the Germans would set fire to the villages and so we went into the forest.

There were now four of us: I, Shlomo and Vele Shprung and Yisroel Korngold. Quickly, with all our strength, we began to build a bunker among the trees, deep into the ground. We concealed the top and lay there for several weeks. At night we went to the nearest village and tried in various ways to find out what was happening, until one night we saw that the Germans had run away in great chaos. Right after them the Russian Red Army entered.

Several days passed and we didn't see each other because Yisroel Korngold and Vele were still afraid to leave the forest. They were afraid to come into the light of day and didn't believe in liberation. Not until several days had passed, when they heard that several Jews who had been hiding in the forest had arrived in Tarnogrod, did they decide to leave the bunker.

Among the Tarnogroders who left the forest were Efraim and Avrom Haler and their children; Lipe Adler came back from Bukovina. There was also Chaim Adler, Sini Groyer and several people from Rozaniec.

Several Jews from Bilgoraj and Jozefow also settled in Tarnogrod. People thought it would be possible to resettle there, and earn enough to live on, but we immediately felt the Nazi poison which remained among the Polish population.

One night Polish murderers shot Dovid from Rozaniec. The murderers also hunted me, wanting to shoot me, but I managed to hide. They caught my wife and tore out her hair. They tortured and beat her all night, demanding that she reveal where the *Yid* was hiding. My wife saved me, risking her life by remaining silent, not willing to betray my whereabouts.

The murderers left her unconscious and bleeding, having robbed and broken everything in the house, and left.

When it began to grow light, I left my hiding place and escaped to Lublin. After a short while I went to Lodz, where I lived with Sender from Krzeszow. In 1945 left for Wroclaw and soon began thinking of making *aliyah* to Israel.

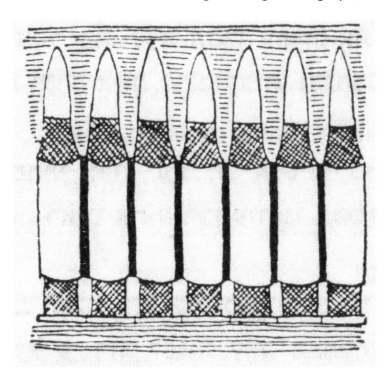

[Pages 350-352]

The Beginning of the End

by Simcha Statfeld (Pardes Chana, Israel)

Translated by David Goldman

It was a small town that exists no more.

Tarnogrod, our little town began to disappear on the first day of Rosh Hashana in 1939 at 12 noon. I was a witness on that day to the arrival of the first Germans into the wide marketplace. However, even before they arrived at the marketplace they had already planted the seeds of death among the Jewish population. The first victim was a teenage boy of 16 years old, the grandson of Itsikel Kaklus, whom the Germans shot on Lochow Street. I heard his mother's restrained but bitter weeping and sensed the end of the Jewish community in our small and poor town.

The destruction of our town began on the second day of Rosh Hashana, Friday night at midnight. A number of Polish soldiers hiding among the Jewish houses in the area between Mendele Bishtcher and Yankel Mantel, attacked the German soldiers who were stationed in the marketplace across from these two houses. As a result of this military confrontation the Germans took the Jews out of their homes and shot them on the spot. The result was that thirteen people were killed, and their bodies were immediately burned together with the houses . The fires quickly spread and nothing could stop it. Jews did not dare go out on the street, they fled to the fields around town and to the nearby villages. The armed Germans patrolled the streets and captured Jews, especially men, and rounded them up in various locations. They made use of a trumped up charge that the Jews attacked them at night, and that if it happened again they would kill all the Jews. But who could be certain that some provocation might not occur again, which would result in the Germans keeping their threat?

My family, several other dozen people and myself from Roznitz Street fled out to the fields at those streets, and we could see how our town was destroyed so quickly. The whole situation was one of tremendous disorder.

This is what happened over several days and nights, where every morning some wished it were already night, and at night others wished it were morning. In general, the town started to empty out in the evening hours. Some went to the nearby villages while others ran out to the fields. This included men, women and children. There was great fear of remaining in town, and the gentile villages refused to allow them to enter their homes and yards.

Anti-Jewish propaganda spread among the villages, and in town the result on Friday night was 13 dead before our very eyes. However, this situation was unavoidable. The world was big, but there was nowhere to run. In the meantime the Germans were satisfied with looting and theft of Jewish property, while engaging in beatings and various forms of humiliation. They captured Jews for all types of work, and in the worksites they abused them in various ways. I was among 10 people caught on Saturday evening to supposedly put out the fire burning since the morning. We were brought to Yankel Magram [sic] and Rivka Mantel's building, and started tearing down the half-burned buildings using tools they gave us, yet even while working they were hitting and kicking us. Finally, at around 11 pm they sent us warning us that anyone who did not disappear from the marketplace within 5 minutes would get a bullet in the head.

This situation of fear and threats continued this way day and night until the holiday of Sukkot, when after a tense period of waiting the Soviet army arrived, which was greeted with flags and flowers. The whole town was overjoyed; finally we were able to breathe a sigh of relief.

This did not last long however, and all the joy ended after just a single week. According to the agreement made, the Russians left Tarnogrod and retreated almost to *Shinova* [Sieniawa]. Then the Germans returned to our town, and the abuses returned with great energy. However, many Jews left Tarnogrod with the Russians, especially the youth. This depressing picture was the view of what was happening in our town. It was on a Friday morning, the last day of the pullout of the Russians from town. I glanced over in the direction of Fishel Foxman and could see teenage boys and girls of various ages carrying full bundles on their backs, making their way quickly to the gates of Korchow. They were accompanied to the gate by parents. When saying their quick goodbyes the parents, and especially the mothers had eyes filled with tears. The question they were asking themselves was whether they would ever see their children again, and in fact, in most cases they never saw their children and relatives again.

That very same evening the Germans entered town. The dance of the devils with the local Jewish population began: abuse, beatings, and various types of mistreatment in full view of the Christian population in the marketplace. This was the fate of the Jews of Tarnogrod.

In view of this dangerous situation Jews in town began their departure from town and to cross the Russian border. However, this could only be done with various dangers and difficulties. When the people of Tarnogrod reached the conclusion that they had to leave everything behind and save their lives, it was too late. But in spite of this, slow movement began in the direction of Shinova, some by vehicle and others by foot. Four other people and I - I remember that two of them were Reuven Richter and Mechl Rinskiss – made our way through the fields and side roads in the direction of the border. We planned to arrive in Shinova to see what the situation was like there, to return and then move there with our families. We arrived at the village next to the border, a place where Mendil Yoshes Futer's son lived. Upon arrival the Germans removed our watches, and in the evening we crossed the border, where we were captured by the Russian border guards. The next day they brought us in peace together with several hundred other Jews.

Two days later we returned to Tarnogrod with the decision to cross back again to *Shinova* with the whole family. On the way back to Tarnogrod we ran into such Jews from Tarnogrod who walked or traveled in the direction of the border. Some left Tarnogrod and returned several times, while others traveled for business purposes, and yet others to bring back something from home. Thus, there was constant wandering and confusion.

News from *Shinova* and from *Yalovtchov* [Naleczow] was not encouraging because of the flow of refugees. There was nowhere to live and not enough food. This situation led to most Jews in Tarnogrod adapting to the new situation in our own town. We had a motto among the people of Tarnogrod that being able to sleep on one's own bed was something of great value, but a few hours later one would change his mind and start packing his bags. The various events occurring through a single day or night affected this instability. For instance, in the village of Rekowka, there lived a Jew named Iser Lumerman. One night they came in and killed his wife. He and the other family members moved to Tarnogrod. Already by 1939 the lives of Jews were easy targets. Only a nearsighted person thought that things would calm down.

I left Tarnogrod on November 15, 1939 in the early afternoon, and great fear spread throughout town. Families and relatives separated, children left their parents, and husbands left their wives. Even I left my parents, and brothers and sisters, both on my side and on my wife's side of the family. Only 5 people left Tarnogrod. My young brother-in-law, 14 years old, accompanied us to the end of Lochow Street, crying bitterly all the way from the house of Zelig the Shoemaker to where I lived, as if he assumed that he would never see us again. So when I returned to Tarnogrod in 1944, two weeks before Rosh Hashanah, I found no one alive except my young brother-in-law.

I left behind 5 members of my family in Tarnogrod, and two of us returned. I found the town burned and destroyed. The population of our town was buried in several mass graves. Most near the Christian cemetery on Roznitz Street and in the yard of David Yoel the shoemaker. May their eternal rest be bound among the living and their memories never forgotten.

[Pages 353-356]

The Testament of Shmuel Peretz Shprung

by Shmuel Peretz Shprung

Translated by Miriam Leberstein

Shmuel Peretz Shprung

With the help of G-d, the week of the Torah portion Shoftim, end of the month of Av, year 1942, here in Potok, near the San River, province of Bilgoraj.

To all those in the diaspora:

It has been almost a year since the issuance of the decree to exterminate the Jews. They began to carry out the slaughter in the month of Cheshvan.

In Tarnogrod, they pulled Jews from their homes, their beds, wherever they found them. Until now, more than 200 have been killed in Jozefow, near Tomaszow; in Zamosc, 1,700 women and children in the course of one day.

In the town of Rzeszow, 17,000 last month, young and old.

In Kilna, near Sahan, 70 people; in Zamosc up to 1,000; in Lublin, more than 20,000; in Warsaw, several thousand slaughtered; plus many more in the villages and other towns.

When the lowlifes wanted to throw a party, they would round up a bunch of people and shoot them. They threw children of all ages alive into the graves where their murdered parents lay.

On the Sabbath of the 47th Torah portion, Parashat Re'eh, they deported 2,000 people from Tarnogrod; we don't know where they were taken. At the same time, they took about the same number of people from Bilgoraj.

It is impossible to describe all the horrors committed by the killers. We must not forgive or forget that the local residents, Poles and Ukrainians, assisted at almost every slaughter. They wanted to get rich on our misfortunes, to get rid of us as soon as possible. They made false denunciations and accusations to spark the powder keg.

The man who is the bearer of this letter is not like them. He does not bear us any ill will. If this letter reaches someone, this man should be rewarded.

We were also expelled from our village, we do not know why nor do we know where to go. We have been set loose to roam. One thing is certain, as soon as one falls into their hands, he is doomed.

From what we have heard of many occurrences, we know that the local inhabitants persecute us as much as the foreign devils. They have already inherited almost all of our property while we still live. And they have taken everything from those who were killed.

According to the news, more than a million Jews have been killed, just in the recent period. That is in addition to what they did at the beginning of the war, through their inquisition-like persecutions. Petlura [Ukrainian nationalist leader and perpetrator of pogroms against Jews in the post-World War I period], in his time, was less horrific than this bloodthirsty tyrant [Hitler].

Hundreds of thousands have died of starvation. In some places there were instances where, just for fun, they ordered all Jews to report and then carried out a selective extermination – the old and weak, women and children were immediately shot. They left alive the somewhat stronger men, assigning them to all kinds of labor on a ration of 70 *dekograms* [about 2 ½ ounces] of bread a day, treating them barbarically. Anyone who was unable to carry out an order to run or lift heavy weights was shot.

The Jews resemble strange animals with large eyes deeply sunken into their cheeks. With no soap to wash with, their faces appear blackened, yellow, dirty and rough. They go about half-naked, many barefoot. Tarnogrod Jews have had to pay more than 200,000 *zlotys* in special tax levies.

They issued an order that strictly forbade a Jew to visit a non-Jewish neighbor; nor could a non-Jew visit a Jew. Both would be sentenced to death.

I, Shmuel Peretz Shprung, am 62 years old, with a family consisting of a wife, a mother, a daughter and a son-in-law with two small children. My brother, Chaim, 54 years old, lives in America, in the Bronx, at 1494 Crotona Park.

We have just received word that the several thousand Jews who were deported were killed. My son, Avram, born in 1906, was taken by the Russians from Sieniawa, near the Sana River, to Omsk in Siberia, along with my wife, our daughter-in-law, Gitl, from Ulanov near Sana, and their son Yosef-Leib.

I want this letter to find its way to someone, and whoever believes in God should take revenge for what has been done, in an even more horrific manner. As I write this, we have received news of slaughters in many places, wherever there are Jews. Polish witnesses have told about what they saw. Someone who worked in the prison in Bilgoraj told how the devils grabbed children by their hair and threw them against the wall and then took them off to be buried alive.

The Germans appointed many local people to official positions to help them accomplish their military goals and these officials assisted in our extermination. They were also charged with beating and pursuing Jews who tied to escape, and turned them over to the Germans to be killed immediately.

What I have described is only a small part of what has happened. I want to finish up this letter because this is a fateful moment. We are waiting, but we don't know for what. One thing is certain, and that is death. They hover over our property. We turn over everything, and many of them are happy with their riches.

May they and their descendants be cursed. Whoever has the means to wreak revenge but does not do so...[1] The blood of the innocents will not be silent until all of the tyrants are destroyed as we Jews were, and meet horrible deaths by sword, hunger and grief.

Notwithstanding their hatred of Jews, many of them raped Jewish women and girls. We now number about 60 individuals or 10 families. If God helps and we survive and all is revealed, people will not believe how the living managed to survive.

The law prohibiting possession of fur was very strictly enforced. If they found one centimeter of fur or even animal skin without fur in a Jew's house, he was immediately shot.

An agency was established to harvest trees in the forest for lumber. The head of the agency is a Pole by the name of Stanislaw Pozdan, from Sanz. He beats Jews mercilessly and takes their money; Jews have also turned over clothing and shoes to him.

I have hidden my good fur coat with a neighbor Jan Zacharer. I have entrusted my son's bicycle with my neighbor Krok. With my neighbor Jan Ugram from Vovzhenietz I have left a lot of bed linens and clothing belonging to my daughter and son-in-law. Everything of mine that he has should be sold and the money used to take revenge on Geresh, the *soltis* [town official] of Kilen, who instigated the slaughter there. His neighbor, Kazhimierzh, the vice-mayor and an officer, told the Jews that they had to be exterminated because if they remained alive they would take revenge if the Germans lost the war.

We appeal to the world, to anyone who has a humane sensibility, not to ignore this appeal, but to take revenge on the bloodthirsty killers.

Translator's Footnote:

1. Phrase unfinished in text.

[Pages 357-364]

Documents

Translated by Miriam Leberstein

These are a few documents that remain from the time of the Tarnogrod ghetto. The originals, in Polish, are now located in the Jewish Historical Institute in Warsaw, to which we express our gratitude for sending us copies of these materials.

*

Translator's note:

These documents all relate to the work of the Jewish Social Self-Help organization (in Polish *Zydowska Sampomoc Spoleczna* [ZSS], in German: *Juedicsche Sozial Selbshilfe),* which was established in Krakow in 1940, with branches throughout the German-occupied territory. The branch in Tarnogrod was run by the town's *Judenrat* [Jewish council established to implement Nazi policies]. The ZSS worked with other Jewish welfare organizations, as well as welfare organizations outside of Poland, mainly the American Joint Distribution Committee, referred to here as "The Joint." Many of these documents appear to be in the format of questionnaires or forms sent by the central office to the local branch to be filled out by them. In many cases, there is a blank space or a line following a question or word, indicating that there was no response by the branch, or in the case of a quantity, an answer of none. Any such blanks or omissions in the translation are in the original. Please see the Addendum for a copy of the original in Polish of the first letter.

From: P. Goldhar
Judenrat of Tarnogrod
Jewish Self-Help

Tarnogrod, December 23, 1940

To: The American Joint Committee in Warsaw:

We respectfully request that you answer the following question: May we sell certain items that you sent to us as gifts? The question arises in the following matter. The branch [of The Joint Committee] in Lublin recently informed us that they had received certain donations, among them nine pairs of shoes. We are in need of a minimum of a hundred pairs of shoes. We have among us many refugees from Lodz, Bilgoraj, Janow, Tomaszow, et al. Hundreds of people have been going barefoot because their shoes were destroyed by working in various labor camps.

This presents the question of how to allocate nine pairs of shoes among 100 people. We were recently sent several sacks of flour. That, too, was not sufficient to satisfy our actual needs, but we could give each person at least a little bit, so that everyone could be treated equally. But there is no way to distribute nine pairs of shoes among 100 people. If one person receives a pair and another does not, we will be in danger for our lives.

The only solution is to sell the shoes and distribute the proceeds, a little bit to each person, so that everyone is satisfied and there is no envy or resentment.

We therefore request your quick response.

Respectfully,
(_____) signature illegible

PS: We are not writing to your department in Lublin because we do not have their correct address.

There is a notation in pencil in response to this appeal, which reads: The clothing was donated by the ZSS and your appeal should be addressed to them. We must inform you that it is strictly forbidden to sell items that were sent as gifts.

*

Community Kitchen

Total for the period January to June

Lunch distributed to adults
Food served to children
Number of adults served
Number of children served

*

Hygiene And Medical Services

Total for January-June

1. Doctor visits
2. Medications
3. Clinic treatments
4. Inoculations
5. Baths
6. Haircuts
7. Soap
8. Laundry

Average number of recipients of health services: _____ persons

Other services _____

Housing assistance -- Number of recipients: --- persons

Financial assistance -- Number of recipients: 850 persons

Dry food products -- Number of recipients: 478 persons

Clothing

Distributed 2925 kilograms of dry products

Distributed 6 clothing and underwear [sic]

Tarnogrod, November 2, 1941

Signed:

Chairman:
Treasurer:
Members: Y. Brezel
Bookkeeper: Y. Kahan

*

AMERICAN JOINT COMMITTEE IN KRAKOW

Krakow, January 1941
Number 291 A
400/ ?4

To: Jewish Aid Committee
of the *Judenrat* in Tarnogrod

We received your letter regarding the distribution of clothing and wish to clarify that the distribution was carried out by the Jewish Community Self-Help in Krakow with the assistance of the Lublin Committee.

Pursuant to regulations, we emphasize that any sale of items which you received as gifts is strictly forbidden.

Respectfully,
American Joint Committee
(Signature not legible)

***

Report of the Social Assistance Program
For the period from March 20 to June 30, 1941

Place: Tarnogrod County: Bilgoraj District: Lublin
Closest postal office -- Tarnogrod
Name of Institution: Jewish Social Self-Help, Tarnogrod Branch
Total number of Jewish residents: 2730
Total recipients of assistance: 450

1. Report of the Treasury
   Semi-Annual Treasury Activity

INCOME			EXPENSES		
Amount in treasury as of January 1, 1941	--	zlotys	1. Aid in form of dry food products		
1. Municipal contributions			a) Community Kitchen	--	zlotys
a) *Judenrat*	600	zlotys	b) Food products distributed	1356.3	
b) Contributions	769.5		c) Child nutrition	1356.3	
c) Payments for lunch			2. Monetary aid	2574.8	
d) Payments for health services			3. Distribution of heating supplies		
e) Disbursement of aid	50		4. Distribution of purchased clothing		
f) ------------			5. Housing aid	--	
g) ------------	1419.5		6. Hygiene and Medical aid	249.75	
2. Internal Subsidies:			7. Institutions for children and orphans		
a) The Joint and other overseas organizations	--	zlotys	8. Homes for the aged	--	
b) TOZ [Society for Protection of the Health of the Jewish Population]	--		9. Investments and repair	150.45	
c) CENTOS [Federation of Associations for the Care of Jewish Orphans in Poland]	--		10. Adminstrative costs	870	
d) Jewish Self-Help	2750		11. Refugees from Bilgoraj	260	
e) Sale of Herring 13	679.3429	13	12. Transport	165	
3. Additional amounts			13. ------------		
a) Repayment of loans	--		14. Additional amounts:	--	
			Repayment of loans		
	4848	zlotys		476.5	
	June 30, 1941			83.5	

*

Jewish Social Self-Help Branch in Tarnogrod

Tarnogrod, November 2, 1941

To: American Joint Committee
Krakow

Along with this letter we are sending two completed reports about our social aid activity for the period from March 20 (i.e., since the inception of our branch) to June 30, 1941.

We ask you to excuse our delay in sending the reports. We had to wait to receive the necessary details from the secretariat of the *Judenrat* for the last quarter, which was not sent until now. The reason for the delay was that the Germans had levied a *kontributsie* [tax] upon our residents in the amount of 40,000 *zlotys* and the secretary of the Judenrat and several members were held as hostages pending the payment of that sum.

Respectfully, For the secretary (---), Ch. Teicher

Bilgoraj station, Tarnogrod Post Office, Addressee Chaskiel Teicher

Town of Tarngorod, Bilgoraj *paviot*, Lublin region,
Submitted July 3, 1941
No. 6174A

*

REPORT

For the Period from December 1, 1939 to June 30, 1941

1.

	Before the War	Now
Number of Jews	2515	2730
Merchants and shopkeepers	220	---
Tradesmen	150	90
Laborers	100	600
Free professions	2	---
Unemployed	50	300

2.   Number requesting support: _____ Receiving support: _____

3.   What institution takes care of social needs?

The branch of Jewish Social Self-Help organization in Tarnogrod

4.   Who provided the funding and in what amount?

The presidium of the Jewish Social Self-Help organization. 500 -- 11.4; 500 -- 20.3;

750 -17.6; 500 - 13.5; 500 -- 13.4; The *Judenrat* in Tarnogrod - 600.

What gifts received, from whom and how much?

From Self-Help organization - 20 kilos oil, a barrel of herring, 25 kilos of marmalade, 20 kilos pork fat, 6 pairs shoes and medicine.

5.   In what form was the aid distributed?

In the form of money, dried goods and clothing.

6.   Is there a hospital? An ambulance service? Who is in charge? Number of patients treated?

_____

7.   Who is responsible for child protection? For emigrants? For invalids?

_____

8.   Number of Jews working in labor camps?

350. Outside the town? 350 in 1940.

9.   How much was spent for this purpose?

_____

10.   How many tradesmen run their own workshops?

60.

Which trades predominate?

Shoemakers and tailors

11.   How many Jewish owned enterprises are there?

_____

12.   Received by Self-Help: 4943 *zlotys*; Disbursed:4765.

What was the source of the monies disbursed?

Voluntary contributions

Do there exist exceptional expenses for Self-Help and what are they?

_____

13.   What food resources were reduced and by how much?

Only bread (50%) and sugar (50%.).

Which foods were not received at all?

Marmalade, flour, honey butter etc.

Jewish Self-Help in Tarnogrod
Ch. Teicher

	JAN	FEB	MAR	APR	MAY	JUN	TOTAL
1 From the Town				600			600
a) Judenrat				667.5		102	769.59
b) Donations							
c) Payments for lunches							
d) Payments for social assistance							
e) Payments for monetary aid					50		50
f) -------------							
g) -------------							
2 External Sources of Aid							
a) Joint Committee and others							
b) TOZ							
c) CENTOS							
d) Jewish Self-Help	50	500	1000	500	750		2750
e) Sale of herring					679		679
TOTALS	50	500	1000	1229	852		4848.5

	JAN	FEB	MAR	APR	MAY	JUN	TOTAL
Food & Kitchen					1272.3	84	1356.3
Supplies							
Child nutrition							
Monetary aid			1362.6	524.65		657.55	2574.8
Clothing							
Transport							165
Sanitation					157.5		249.75
Children's & Orphans Inst							
Investments and Repairs			102.7		57.75		150.45
Refugees from Goraj					260		260
Old Age Homes							
Administrative Expenses					8.7		8.7
TOTALS					2445.9	853.8	4765

Statistics of Social Assistance

(Average number of people monthly)

	JAN	FEB	MAR	APR	MAY	JUN	AVERAGE MONTHY TOTAL
Applied for Aid				1120	600	600	675
Received Aid				850	599	450	600

***

The *Besmedroshim* of Tarnogrod

Translator's note: The *besmedroshim* [houses of study] served both as a place of study and a place of worship. The poem addresses the destruction not only of the *besmedroshim* but also other houses of worship such as shtibls [small simple places of worship for *Hasidic* groups] and the *shul* [synagogue] of Tarnogrod, although the synagogue is distinguished for its partial survival.

*

Addendum

Copy of original letter, written in Polish, From P. Goldhar to The American Joint Committee in Warsaw (translation on page 357). Courtesy of The Joint Distribution Committee Archives.

[Pages 364]

The Study Houses[1] of Tarnogrod

by Eliezer Teicher

Translated by Miriam Leberstein

Written during my last visit to Tarnogrod, in 1949

Where have you gone,
study houses and *shtiblekh*[2] of Tarnogrod?
I've come over hilltops and ditches
to search for you here.

You will search in vain.
The murderers destroyed us all.
Not a trace of us remains
On this cursed ground.

My holy *shul* –
it's a wonder you're still standing.
I've now gathered together
small stones that lay near you.

Listen, you who prayed here,
and I'll tell why I'm still standing.
No one can know this
but the Creator himself.

The Nazi gang did their best
to knock me down, to burn me
But my four thick pillars
prevented my destruction.

They robbed me of the candlesticks and Torah crowns
and the curtains of the Torah ark.
And they took my greatest treasure –
dozens of Torah scrolls.

I stand here like a gravestone, a monument.
No one hears my weeping, my lament.
Within my walls there's only silence
No one's left to say *Kaddish*.[3]

Home to Zion

Lift up your eyes,
Steady your hand.
Enough of bowing down to others
in the stranger's land.

Here you still live in exile.
Enough of slaving for others.
Go east, where the flags wave blue and white
on the shores and harbors.

That is where our home is,
there is holy ground.
There we'll build with clay and brick.
There we'll live unharmed.

There we'll plow and sow
and cut and bind,
wrapping straw around
the sheaves of grain.

Translator's Footnotes:

    1.   The Yiddish word translated as study houses is *bote-midrashim*, plural of *besmedresh*, literally "house of study." The *besmedresh* in the *shtetl* served not only as a place for study of the Torah, but also as a house of worship, as an alternative to the synagogue.

    2.   *Shtiblekh* is plural for *shtibl*, a small (often one-room), modest house of worship, especially for Hasidim.

    3.   Prayer for the dead.

[Page 365]

IV

<u>Heroism</u>

[Pages 367-371]

Author Unknown

Translated by Martin Jacobs

Perhaps the most beautiful songs arise from the echo of the indescribable heroism of the Jewish fighters who came from the Jewish towns and swore that German blood would flow unceasingly. They proved that Jewish blood does not cease seething with revenge and can elevate terrible calamity to the level of heroic deeds. These boys and girls from Tarnogrod and Bilgoraj, just like those from Warsaw and Bialystok, like the descendants of the exiles from Spain, would not be Marranos, would not live in subjugation, but with persistent hatred set themselves against their bloodiest enemy. They would no longer listen to the insults of the Nazis, but with the roar of "Pour out thy wrath" [quoted from the Passover Haggada: "Pour out thy wrath upon the nations that know thee not"], hunted down the Germans, and so the history of their last days is not a Book of Lamentations [a book in the Bible describing the destruction of Jerusalem] but a Song of Songs [a happy love song in the Bible], a song which is elevated above all heights, tears through all the heavens, and will not be stilled until the end of all generations.

Heroes

The Jewish youths of Tarnogrod could have had much to tell about the battles that they waged in the ranks of the various partisan units, in the regular Soviet army, and in the Polish army. Unfortunately almost all fell on the battlefield. These heroic fighters continued our people's tradition of heroism. Physical resistance has always been a part of our lives, which have at all times been beset by a sea of hatred, wickedness, and murder.

A group of Jewish youths from Tarnogrod in the partisan division under the leadership of "Błyskawica" – in the woods near Tomaszow

When the simple village Jew of Likew [probably the village of Łukowa is intended. It is near Tarnogrod] was tortured to get him to betray the *shochet* [ritual slaughterer], as he knew what awaited the shochet, he willingly accepted the torture himself and the death of his whole family. Conquering his fear of death with great heroism, he kept quiet and allowed the German murderers to kill him.

Moshe-Naftali Wasserman *and his family*

They lived in the village of Likev. When the Germans arrived they found a slaughtered chicken in his house during a household search. They tortured him to make him betray the shochet, but this simple village Jew bore the tortures and remained silent. For that the Germans shot him and his entire family.

The Adlers possessed amazing heroism. They fought the Germans with an ax and put fear in their hearts, until they were felled by bullets from German machine guns.

The simple Tarnogrod Jews, who bore the taunts and mockery of their neighbors, showed great moral courage, and, despite all reminders did not lose their sense of inner worth. Deep in their hearts they made light of the carousing, powerful, but spiritually impoverished landowners, and the easily incited peasants, who for generations lived with prejudices against their Jewish neighbors. But even in that situation their wild and unruly neighbors knew that the Jew would not turn the other cheek. Not just once did they feel the blows of the Jewish youths when the hooligans attacked defenseless Jews with mass barbarity.

Such were the Jewish youths in Tarnogrod. The Jewish young men were brought up in this spirit. In those terrible days they breathed the air of glorious moral heroism. Looking at the mountain of Jewish dead, they shifted their look to a higher mountain still, that on which shines the sun of a proud Jewish nation, the equal of all.

Chana Tintfisch

**Heroic Jewish girl from Tarnogrod who fell fighting in the ranks of
partisans against the Nazi enemy**

Honor and glory to you, Jewish heroes of the era of slaughter. Your heroic struggles possessed the great superhuman magnificence of the Maccabees, of the martyrs of all generations. This is the power which Jewish revolutionaries, Zionists, socialists, dreamers and fighters for a better world have shown in all times. Your heroism, partisans and fighters at the front, is the Eternal Light in the history of the life and death of the Jews in Tarnogrod. You, heroic warriors of burnt homes, proud conquerors of death, for centuries we will keep your memory alive and make mention of you and repeat like the holiest of oaths the words of our partisan poet:

"Wherever a drop of our blood has fallen our heroism and our courage will spring up."

[Pages 370]

Acts of Heroism

When historians come to look for material on the terrible Holocaust which descended upon the Jewish people, among which was the dreadful and horrific destruction of the Jews of Tarnogrod and its environs, they will certainly be amazed and astonished at the brilliant pages of supreme Jewish heroism, the heroism of the Jews of Tarnogrod and its environs, heroism without any hope of victory; battles lost from the beginning, daring battles of Jewish heroes in the face of the murder machine of Nazi Germany -- a war for the honor of the Jewish people.

The Jewish youth in Tarnogrod, who felt the destruction and the annihilation even before these happened in the ghetto, did not in any manner or fashion wish to make peace with murder. Immediately upon the entry of the Germans many sought opportunities to escape and fight the Nazi invader. Some set their steps towards the woods, in order to join the partisans; others joined the Russian army.

David Ritzer – Fell in the Polish military in battle with the Germans, and Chaim Wetsher (left) killed in Tarnogrod

All of them sacrificed their lives and did not live to celebrate the great victory over the Nazi enemy. The few of us who remain alive have the duty to immortalize their heroism during the war and the Holocaust.

How many are the hidden treasures of heroism in the struggle of these forest dwellers, who arrived there through their own resourcefulness. But information has reached us only about a few. These we immortalize, lest we forget the destruction of the people and the battle with the cruel enemy.

Let us remember the heroes who fell while fighting.

Let us also not forget those who have remained unknown. Individually they crossed boundaries and overcame dangers. In this way they thought to avoid the enemy, but it was not to be, they determined that they could not run away, they had to fight, they enlisted in the Soviet or Polish army, they fought and fell and no trace was left of them, there were no monuments on their graves.

Let us light an eternal lamp in their memory, in memory of the pure martyrs, in memory of the heroism, the sacrifice, and the dedication.

A Monument for Eternal Remembrance!

Yakov Tenenbaum

(H) Escaped from Tarnogrod after the Nazi invasion, enlisted in the army in Russia, fought and fell by a German bullet in the battles for Stalingrad.
(Y) Fell in Russia where he was fighting as a soldier in the Soviet army. A German bullet hit him during the relentless battles in Stalingrad.

[Pages 372]

Song of the Partisans

Never Say

Never say there is only death for you.
Though leadened skies may be concealing days of blue–
Because the hour we have hungered for is near;
Beneath our tread the earth shall tremble: We are here!

From land of palm-tree to the far-off land of snow,
We shall be coming with our torment and our woe.
And everywhere our blood has sunk into the earth.
Shall our bravery, our vigor blossom forth!

We'll have the morning sun to set our day aglow,
And all our yesterdays shall vanish with the foe,
And if the time is long before the sun appears,
Then let this song go like a signal through the years.

This song was written with our blood and not with lead;
It's not a song that birds sing overhead,
It was a people, among toppling barricades,
That sang this song of ours with pistols and grenades.

So never say that there is only death for you.
Leaden skies may be concealing days of blue–
Yet the hour we have hungered for is near;
Beneath our tread the earth shall tremble: We are here!

http://www.ushmm.org/education/foreducators/resource/pdf/resistance.pdf

Back cover Never say: Hersh Glick, "Jewish Partisan Song," trans. Aaron Kramer in Folks- Shtimme (Poland). Reprinted in Anthology of Holocaust Literature, ed. Glatstein, Knox, and Margoshes, 349.

[Pages 373-380]

The heroic struggle of the two heroes, the Adler brothers

K. Shimoni

Translated by Martin Jacobs

In a bunker where Chava Fefer, two Jewish families from Bilgoraj, and others too, nearly thirty Jews from Tarnogrod, lay hidden, Mrs. Simi Groisman's child began to cry loudly. The Jews hidden there were seized with fear. Not far from the bunker the Germans were running around searching. The German soldier's footsteps were clearly audible above the ceiling. There were also other little children there. It was feared that the crying would become contagious and their hiding place would certainly be uncovered.

The mother of the crying child clasped it to herself and tried in various ways to calm it, but to no avail. The child wouldn't stop crying and, with every passing minute the voices became more and more penetrating and louder. Everywhere people began to murmur and wring their hands with despair: "The child will get us all killed." Someone screamed at the mother: "Take the child outside, unless you want to have thirty human lives on your conscience."

With every minute the mother grew more and more desperate. Suddenly the child was quiet. There was a fearful silence in the bunker. Everyone guessed what had happened: With her own hands the mother had strangled the child.

The bunker was horribly crowded. In the course of the three days they were there they had shared the last bits of food. The cries of the Jews whom the Germans had found in nearby hiding places were reaching them. On the third day the Germans picked up the trail of the bunker, which was approached by a tangle of corridors. Breaking through the first entrance, the Germans stopped, not daring to go further. Standing in front of the bunker, they called on the Jews to come out.

No one answered. The intention was to create among the German the impression that everyone was dead. The Germans were still possessed by a strange fear and they stood for more than an hour calling to the Jews with friendly voices to come out; nothing would happen to them. In the bunker voices were beginning to be heard in favor of giving up and coming out voluntarily. The majority however maintained that it was senseless to come out, as that would mean death.

With Cleaver And Revolver

Finally the Jews in the bunker became aware that the number of Germans lying in wait at their hiding place was small and the two Adler brothers decided to go out and make a sudden attack on the Germans. They opened a hidden door and the younger brother, who had a loaded revolver, lurched in the direction of the Germans. The older brother was holding a sharpened meat cleaver, which struck more fear into the Germans than the revolver; they began to withdraw.

He hit the first German, who had placed himself in his way, with the cleaver, and killed him on the spot. Immediately after this the second German started shooting his revolver at them. Then the second brother had to defend himself and fired. The second German fell and the two brothers fled across the street with the intention of breaking through the surrounding German lines and escaping from the town.

This was in broad daylight. The Germans went berserk; they ransacked the cellars and attics of Jewish homes. They succeeded in finding many Jewish families, used deception to get them to come out, and drove them into the marketplace in the direction of the huge mass grave. The appearance of the two armed Jews, one with a revolver, the other with a bloodstained cleaver, greatly terrorized the Germans. Even the Jews, depressed as they were, began to shout: "Revenge, revenge on the murderers!"

Something out of the ordinary was happening among the Germans. At first fear possessed them and they began to retreat. It really seemed that the two Jews would succeed in fighting their way out of the town. But soon the Germans were seen to come to recover their senses; they took up positions with the aim of capturing the Jews alive. Not one shot was fired, but from time to time one of the Germans attempted to approach the two brothers, but when he saw the threatening cleaver he stopped.

Superhuman Heroism

The circle with which the Germans surrounded the two Jews drew tighter and tighter with every minute. A German officer called to them to give up, but the two brothers advanced silently, and when it finally became clear to the Germans that their victims would not be taken alive, they opened fire.

The older Adler began with great force to clear a way with his cleaver and the younger one covered him with revolver fire. After several minutes of unequal and relentless fighting, the older brother fell, still holding the cleaver. A German policeman immediately ran up to him to tear the cleaver from his hand. He was sure that the Jew was already dead, but just at the moment when the prostrate Jew felt the German over him he suddenly pulled himself up and with extraordinary heroism brought the cleaver down on the head of the German, who fell in a pool of blood. Adler gave his last gasp, as if a gasp of relief, and fell dead, just like a post sawed from the bottom.

Much of the German police unit was focusing its entire attention on this scene and this made the younger brother's battle with the Germans easier. The Germans turned a machine gun on him. He ran a zigzag, never leaving out of his sight any of the Germans, who tried to get nearer to him. He succeeded in killing several Germans before entering a side street. At first the Germans did not dare enter the street. Young Adler made use of this fact and with his last strength reached the road leading to the forest. Here he hid for a while, wandering about hungry and in tatters, until he succeeded in reaching a partisan group belonging to General Kovpak's army [Sidor Kovpak was an important leader of the Ukrainian partisans].

This incident made an extraordinary impression on everyone who was in the street at the time. For a long time the Poles in the town spoke of it and told of the superhuman bravery of the two Jews.

The Last Minutes

The Germans were embarrassed and powerless, and did not dare to pursue him into the woods. They let out all their anger on the Jews they had dragged out of this and other bunkers. The Jews were forced to strip naked and run through a lane of whips, which rained down upon their heads and naked bodies. One after another the Jews fell to the ground from the blows and beatings. The Germans did not stop beating and kicking them, but when they saw that the beaten Jews no longer had the strength to get up they shot them and the young Polish gentiles, who the whole time had been helping the Germans in their murderous work, threw the corpses into the waiting wagons and took them away to the open mass grave.

Long after this the brazen Polish boys, with whom the two Ukrainian bandits Serkis and Kotek very zealously worked continued to murder Jews they found. These bandits lived their whole lives in Tarnogrod and became friendly with the Jewish residents, borrowed money from them, and got various favors from them. Now they dragged these same Jewish acquaintances from their hiding places. The bandits answered all their weeping and pleas not to be delivered to their deaths with cynical laughter: "Shout, cry to your God to forgive you your sins, these are your last minutes, you are about to join your brothers in hell."

When not one living soul was left in the Jewish houses the hyenas went out to loot them of the last bit of Jewish possessions.

Wild scenes that would make you think of the jungle were then played out. At the beginning the Poles and Ukrainians stuck together and helped each other load up their sacks to the top. Later quarrels and fights began to break out among the bandits themselves.

Alone With Her Brother

Little by little everything grew quiet again. After the terrible wailing an empty stillness prevailed, as in a cemetery. Chava Fefer was alone in her house, hiding under a bed. The Germans suspected that someone was still in the house and shot into all the dark shadowy corners and into the bedclothes. It was a great miracle that none of the bullets hit her. The house filled with feathers and the Germans were convinced that there was no longer a living soul there and in resignation left the house.

Frightened and pale as death, Chava Fefer decided to creep out of her hiding place. She became aware that she was alone, the only survivor in the emptied ghetto. She barely took a step, shaking at every rustle. Suddenly she was startled. In a corner of the yard, near the gate, she noticed a figure, which stood as if pressed into the wall. She started to run away, but just at that moment she heard her name quietly whispered. The figure was her brother.

They embraced each other's arms in silence. They would have cried, but their eyes were all dried out. Their words stuck in their throats. They took each other by the hand and moved carefully, like people lost in a dark wood. She remembered the name of a Pole, a close acquaintance of theirs, whom she believed would save them. But at that very moment heavy soldier's boots echoed through the empty street. They stood for a moment frozen with fear. Her brother panicked and without a word began to run back. In despair she wanted to call to him to go on with her, but he had disappeared from her sight and she ran on in a different direction, to the house of the Poles, in whom she placed so much hope.

She finally succeeded in reaching this house. The people there, frightened by her appearance, stood in the open doorway, not knowing what to do. But they let her in and for three weeks hid her in their house.

Her first request was that they find out what happened to her brother. Carefully the Polish people began to creep around every house in the ghetto, looking for a trace of the brother who had disappeared. After long searches they succeeded in finding out that on that same day, immediately after running back to the house, he poisoned himself. The Germans found him dead.

Meeting A Man

Chava Fefer realized the danger in which the Polish people hiding her found themselves. These were good and honest people and she did not want to put their lives at risk. After about three weeks she fled into the woods.

It was on a cold evening at the end of autumn, when, finding herself on the road to Czeplic, she suddenly spied a young man, a Pole, eighteen years old. Fear seized her. In those days young Gentiles stopped fleeing Jews and turned them over to the Germans. Frightened, she looked around for an escape route. As she stood confused the young man approached her. He must have noticed that she was afraid. He began to calm her.

His voice, his polite speech inspired trust. He introduced himself and told her his name was Frantiszek Czapek. As long as he had lived, he said, he had never yet done anyone any harm, and she could be absolutely sure that nothing would happen to her.

They walked along together and he told her the he belonged to the underground and so was forced to hide out at his sister's house. She lived not far from the woods and he believed that she too could hide there. The young Pole did indeed bring her to his sisters'. There she was hidden for several days in the barn.

Every evening the young man brought her bread and water. He was somewhat embarrassed at this and assured her that he too ate the same thing, because he was busy day and night working for the Polish underground. He smuggled weapons for the Polish partisans who were in the near-by woods. In all probability he took no money for this and therefore fed himself very poorly. He really did share his last morsel with the Jewish woman.

After several days the young man announced that he had to go away. He was leaving for Central Poland, which at that time was separated off by a border and was called "General Government". Chava Fefer saw no other way than to accompany him, since no one was left who could get her anything to eat.

They set out together on the road and passed the border, and went on until they arrived at the village from which the young man came. For a short time she hid in his parents' house. When it became dangerous, he reached an understanding with the parish priest, who agreed to hide Chava Fefer in the church. She stayed there until the Liberation, when the Soviet army took the village.

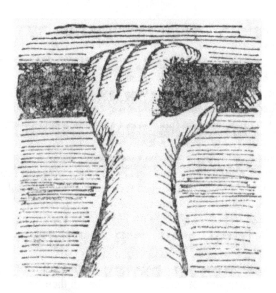

[Page 381]

Through Rivers of Tears and Seas of Blood

Avraham Haler – From My Diary

Translated by Martin Jacobs

On September 1, 1939 a black cloud of fear and anxiety descended on our town. Before our eyes the Polish armies were crushed and the cruel fist of Hitler's gangs began to hang over our heads. The German military entered Likev on the second day of Rosh Hashanah on Friday afternoon. They fired off a few rounds from their machine guns, blindly, but no one was hurt. Immediately the next morning, the Sabbath of Repentance, several German soldiers came into my haberdashery shop and began throwing the merchandise onto the street, where the Christian townspeople immediately gathered and looted it. Whatever it didn't pay for them to take they trampled on and destroyed.

There was a cellar under my shop where I had hidden various goods as well as cigarettes and tobacco. One of my Christian neighbors informed on me about this to the Germans, who broke into my shop and began to beat me furiously. I had to open the cellar and the Germans threw me in and ordered me to hand out the hidden goods. All the time I was handing out the goods, accumulated with years of exhausting labor, the Germans did not stop cursing and threatening me.

Avraham Haler

[Pages 382-463]

Through Rivers of Tears and Seas of Blood

by Avraham Haler – From My Diary

Continued translation by Miriam Leberstein

Having assured themselves that they had robbed everything, they left, and I left the cellar, scared to death and beaten down. It was clear to me that I could expect nothing good and I wanted to go to a Christian I knew and ask him to hide me. When I came out onto the street I saw a group of Jews and Christians surrounded by German soldiers. Someone yelled to me, "Come here, Jew," and soon I was standing in the group, all of us stricken with fear, not knowing where they were taking us. Someone murmured that they were going to shoot us. Another tried to assure himself that they would just torment us a bit and then let us go. All around you could hear crying and sighing. We stood there an hour before they took us to the church. When we arrived, there were already 500 men there, Jews and Christians.

We spent the entire Saturday sitting in the church, some weeping aloud, others silently. Everyone was immersed in dark thoughts, looking into each other's eyes to try to discern what the outcome would be.

At nightfall, the women brought us food, but few people touched it. They began to talk about what had occurred. On Friday night a high level German officer was shot outside the town as he drove by. The Germans suspected the civilian population and for that reason, they had seized us as hostages. If they didn't find the murderer, they would shoot all of us.

The arrestees became increasingly panicky; the air was filled with weeping. People banged their heads against the wall. The guards came and ejected the women and children who had come with the food. After the gates were locked, a funereal silence fell. Tired, broken men lay down on the ground. But no one could sleep. From every corner came moans and sighs.

Nightmares

The night seemed impossibly long. At 8 A.M. they unlocked the gates of the church and people began to go outside. The first to go out quickly returned with fearsome news; the entire church was surrounded by machine guns and it looked like the Germans were ready for a bloody slaughter.

Again, we were brought food, as well as pieces of news. Someone said they were going to send us to a concentration camp. Another had heard from a high German official that they would shoot us all in the courtyard of the church. Another knew for sure that they would line us up in rows and shoot every tenth person. The fear and despair continued to grow. In the afternoon came an order that we should all say *Vidui* [confession before death] because they were going to shoot us.

There were Christian priests in the church to whom the Christian arrestees made their confession. For the first time in my life I saw how Christians prayed. They repeatedly fell to the ground, lay still several minutes, got up and said their confession, cried and lamented. The Jewish arrestees said *Vidui*, made their farewells, and waited for death. This lasted the entire day.

When night fell and darkness enveloped us, they locked us up again and it became quiet. Again people lay down on the hard stone floor. After two days of terror and not eating, the exhausted men gradually dozed off. But the loud moans of others awakened them. The night seemed even longer and more terrifying than before.

In the morning when they unlocked the gates, many people were so scared their teeth were chattering; they thought the executions would soon begin. In the meantime, they brought in food, which nobody touched. People were asking questions but no one had any answers.

At about 10 A.M. a Polish priest came in and said that he had spoken with a German officer, who said that they had investigated the murder of the German officer and it turned out that he had been shot by remnants of the Polish army who were staying in nearby villages. It was therefore possible that we would be freed that day. Everyone was indescribably happy. We were released at 2 P.M.

It is impossible to describe the joy of my wife and child when I returned to our home. Our home had been looted and destroyed, but nobody thought about the looted possessions. All our hearts were filled with thanks and praise for the Almighty for giving us life.

Fire and Death

In Tarnogrod, which was 15 kilometers from Lukow, a Polish officer hid behind the town offices and shot at the Germans. That was sufficient for the Germans to take revenge on the Jews who lived near the town offices. They took away 18 Jews and shot them, set fire to the houses and threw the corpses into the fire.

That was just the beginning. The soldiers said that it wasn't their job to deal with the Jews, but that the S.S. would soon come to attend to their job of tormenting them.

Soon rumors were heard that the Germans were retreating and our area would belong to the Russians. That did in fact happen. The Russians arrived on the first day of Sukkot. The Jews were very happy but their joy did not last long. Within a week we heard that the Russians would leave and give our area back to the Germans.

Thousands of Jews from Western Galicia streamed through our little towns. They were fleeing to towns that were occupied by Soviet Russia. This was a sad sight: women with small children, men laden with heavy packs, dragged themselves along not knowing where. The weather was already wintry and people were already feeling the hunger of wartime. Neighbors came to me in despair asking me what I was going to do; would I leave with the Soviets? I told them I had no place to go with three little children and my elderly in-laws. Later I was tortured by the thought that because of my answer, other people refrained from leaving and remained under the Germans. But who could have then imagined, that innocent people would be slaughtered in such a manner.

The Russians began to retreat on Simchat Torah. They arranged for autos to transport civilians who wanted to leave town with them, but we stayed.

The Germans returned and the Jews were again afraid and bitter. In Lukow, it remained quiet for a while, but in Tarnogrod the S.S. had already arrived and were carrying out their sadistic methods. They assembled the most prominent men of the town and made them drag a wagon of stones along the street. The Poles stood by and laughed. Then they ordered the Jews to wash themselves in mud and smear their faces and clothes, then led them for several hours around town.

At the end of December 1939 the Germans ordered that a Judenrat be established and a chairman selected. On January 1, 1940, they decreed that Jewish men and women, aged 12 and up, had to wear a white patch with a Star of David on their arms. A Jew couldn't walk on the sidewalk. Any German who encountered a Jew could order him to report for work and no one in his home would know where he was. At the various work sites Jews were beaten and tormented.

Despite the difficult winter, Jews began to sneak across the border to Russia. My brother Meyer Haler went over to the Russian side and stayed there for four months. He was able to settle in and even started to learn a trade, but he was homesick for his mother and sisters and in the middle of winter he returned. He was 24.

Labor Camps

After Passover, people began to talk about labor camps and several weeks later Jews were already being seized and sent to these camps. In our town (Lukowa), however, it was still peaceful. Then at dawn on the day after Tisha b'Av, while we were still asleep, there was loud banging on our doors. When I opened the door, several S.S. men rushed in and ordered me to get dressed quickly. At first, I thought that some Pole had made up an accusation against me. The S.S. men goaded me and wouldn't let me dress properly. There was no thought of getting something to eat to take with me. My wife and children began to cry. Terrified and in despair, they accompanied me as I was brought to the town government offices.

There were already about 30 Jews assembled there. I was somewhat relieved. I thought that if the accusation wasn't directed solely at me, the danger was not so great. Our wives and children wanted to say goodbye to us, but the S.S. men wouldn't let them approach. The air was filled with crying and shouting.

We stood there until 10 A.M. when we were ordered to line up and march in rows of three. We looked back and saw our families waving to us, but the S.S. guards angrily yelled at us that it was not permitted to look around. Our Christian neighbors stood on both sides of the street, watching us being marched away, some with laughter in their eyes, some silently indifferent, some loudly proclaiming that it was good that the end was coming for the Jews.

After marching about five kilometers we arrived in the village Khmelki, where the S.S. guards ordered us to stop and rest near a small river. Another S.S. man approached and ordered us to sing a song and told us that if he didn't like our singing, we would have to go into the river in our clothes. He gave us five minutes to begin singing.

We looked at each other in fear, asking ourselves what we should do. Among us was a Jew who had been driven out of Lodz three months earlier, and he was already familiar with Nazi methods. He announced that he would sing first and immediately began singing, "My Little Town Belz." He sang really well and luckily his singing pleased the murderous S.S. man. He let us rest a half hour. Then we marched another five kilometers, when an order came to stop. Again, we sat down on the ground for 15 minutes, and then continued marching until we reached Tarnogrod.

At the Tarnogrod market place, 600 Jews were already assembled under guard by armed Ukrainians. We joined them and the S.S. guard that had brought us there left.

Soon after our arrival in Tarnogrod, women and children from Lukowa came running, among them my wife. I tried to get away from the group, but I immediately saw that we were closely guarded, and I resumed my place, resigned and in despair.

In the meantime, my wife went around town to see if something could be done to gain my release and to find out if anyone knew what the Germans intended to do with us. But everywhere she went she encountered the same despair and no one knew what to tell her.

In the evening all the Jews assembled at the market place were driven into dark barracks, where, exhausted and broken, they fell onto the bare floor and instantly fell asleep. In the middle of the night people started to awaken and from all sides there came stifled sounds, with people moving around, sighing, groaning and awaiting the arrival of day.

In the morning, the gate opened and an S.S. man ordered everyone to go outside to the market place, where they began to register us, writing down our names and addresses and other personal details. This lasted until 10 A.M., when there suddenly appeared about 100 wagons driven by peasants. About 20 S.S. guards ordered us to get into the wagons.

I was able to say goodbye to my wife, both of us unable to hold back our tears as stifled sobs came from our throats.

An S.S. man sat in every second wagon. We rode on the highway to Bilgoraj. The horses walked slowly and it took three hours until we arrived at the small-gauge train station. We were met by members of the Bilgoraj Judenrat, who brought us bread. Among us who had been seized were many Bilgoraj Jews. We were ordered to take seats in the open cars of the train.

In Cattle Cars

At 6:00 P.M. on the 11th day of *Av* [August], 1940, we arrived in Zwierzyniec. As we got off the train, the S.S. men held up a wire at the height of a meter, and we had to jump over it. Anyone who could not do so was hit in the head with a stick. We waited two hours on the square in front of the train station for the train to Lviv. We were crammed like sardines inside train cars used to transport cattle. There was no air. No one knew where we were going.

After travelling for four hours, our wagons were unhitched and left standing. The heat was stifling and there was no water. The wagons were locked and no one responded to our pleas. We remained there all night, pressed together, half-fainting. Not until dawn did the S.S. unlock the doors and tell us to get out.

As I got off, I noticed that the station sign said Belzec. I knew that this was near Tomaszow Lubelski not far from Rava-Ruska. We were led into a large garden surrounded by barbed wire. Inside it was a large building that served as barracks. At the gate stood an armed S.S. man. Inside I saw hundreds of Jews milling around, holding their shoes in their hands. They formed lines that stretched to a kitchen, where they received a bowl of coffee. At that point, I was looking forward to being allowed to go inside where we would get some warm water.

The gate opened and we were admitted into the garden where the (civilian) commandant of the camp took over. He was a Jewish doctor-dentist from Lublin, who showed us where to get a bowl for coffee and we lined up for a bit of blackish water. It took a half hour before it was my turn.

After two days of thirst the coffee smelled good and we were permitted to sit and rest. Not far from us, lined up military style in rows of three or four, were people who had been in the camp several months and who were being taken to work. The commandant told us that we would rest that day and that not until the next day would be taken to work.

We sat there until noon. Through the barbed wire we could see that armed S.S. men were stationed in all corners of the camps. It was clear that we were under strict guard and that there was no possibility of escape.

At lunchtime, we were lined up and walked a half kilometer through town to the kitchen, which was located in the courtyard of a former Jewish-owned mill. S.S. guards now lived in the apartment of the former mill owners, who had managed to flee to Russia. As we passed by, they yelled to us to take off our hats. Anyone who delayed in doing so was hit on the head with a stick.

Jews and Gypsies

At the courtyard of the mill we again saw thousands of Jews and Gypsies with their wives and children. There was loud screaming and the noise was deafening. We were brought to the kitchen, where a Gypsy doled out the food. When it was my turn, he poured into my bowl a half ladle of strange-smelling soup and two pieces of raw potato.

After eating, we were taken back to the garden. Around 3:00 P.M. the people who had long been at work arrived and only now were they given lunch. They didn't return until evening. We were instructed to go sleep in the barracks. Inside the air was heavy and there was a very bad smell. About two thousand people were sleeping on three-tiered bunks. There were people there from Warsaw and Lublin, from Tarnogrod and Piotrkow and several other towns. They had already been there three months and had not had a change of clothes in all that time.

I found the dirt and stuffiness intolerable and along with several other Jews decided to sleep outside on the street. It was not yet cold and it was much more pleasant to sleep outside than in the barracks.

At dawn came a shout: "Get up!" We washed up a bit and again lined up for coffee served from a kettle. At that time, I was still a greenhorn and waited patiently for my turn. But when I reached the kettle, there was no more coffee left. It seemed that some people had taken two turns. If an S.S. man wasn't supervising the coffee, people took the opportunity to fill their bowls more than once, and I got nothing and had to make do with water.

At 7:30 we were again lined up and a supervisor was assigned to each group of a hundred Jews. At 8:00 we went to work for the first time. When we went out of the gate, the S.S. men and Ukrainians took over and led us to a place where each person took a shovel or a pickaxe and we were marched off at a military pace.

Soon we were ordered to sing and we began singing various Yiddish songs and pieces of cantorial music. The S.S. men would place sticks under our feet as we marched and anyone who tripped and fell was hit with sticks over their heads, backs and legs. They would get up and continue to march and sing.

We approached the Russian border, where we dug ditches seven meters wide and three meters deep. The excavated dirt formed a high wall. The S.S. man in charge of us, called Shafirer, continuously goaded and rushed us. Those who didn't adapt quickly to the work methods were badly beaten. I myself saw how an S.S. man ordered a Jew called Leyzer to lay down on the ground and proceeded to stomp on his back, throat and head. The Jew lay there, completely blackened, not showing any signs of life. No one thought he would be able to get up or even survive, but he did stand up, although barely able to move, and was able to pretend that he was still able to work.

Almost no one among the new people was used to working with a shovel, and we quickly developed blisters on our hands. When Shafirer stepped away for a few minutes, people hoped to be able to rest a bit, but at that moment a rider rode up on a white horse. The people who had already been at work several months told us that this was the real Angel of Death, the head of the S.S. named Dolf. He rode through the entire length of the worksite. Apparently, he found everything to be in order and there was no trouble.

The entire day went the same way. After ending work, we were lined up in military formation with shovels and picks over our shoulders and returned to camp singing. As we passed a well, one of the men went over to get some water. The S.S. man saw and shot him on the spot. The S.S. man ordered four people to carry the body of the shooting victim back to camp. When we got there, they laid the body down. Silently and with grim faces everyone opened their packs and took out something to eat. But every bite stuck in their throats. The shooting victim lay in plain sight and everyone thought that tomorrow the same thing could happen to him.

The second night was a lot colder and a lot of people went inside to sleep. I was shivering but I still couldn't resolve to sleep in the dirty and stifling barracks.

The next morning, I heard that several people had escaped from the camp and some of them had been caught. They were shot on the spot and their corpses were brought to camp and laid next to the body of the man killed the day before, to make clear what would happen to anyone who dared to try to escape.

The second day of work was similar to the day before. We met people who looked like skeletons, no longer able to work or even stand up. We learned that every day three or four people were found dead in the barracks. This terrified us and some people decided to escape no matter the risk. They thought they could apply what they had learned from working as smugglers to cross the border to the Russian side. The same day several people did cross the border. I decided to follow their example but then I remembered that my wife and small children would not know where I was and I gave up the idea.

There were days when I felt that I no longer had the strength to withstand the pain and suffering, and was on the brink of suicide. But again, I thought of my wife and children and told myself that I must be stronger than iron and withstand the suffering in order to survive to be a father to my children. Somewhere within me there still glowed a spark of hope that I would emerge from the camp and live to see my home and family. This gave me courage and I worked with all my strength so as not to fall victim to the S.S.

When we returned from work the second day we were ordered to bury the dead.

The First Sabbath in Camp

The first Sabbath in camp arrived. Everyone still felt the holiness of the day within themselves; tears fell from their eyes, but no one said a word. They didn't talk about how the Sabbath was observed in their old homes. I took two small pieces of dry bread and made the *Kiddush* [blessing] over them. Choking on tears, I could barely get out the words.

I was still sleeping on the street and couldn't resolve to enter the barracks. On Saturday morning we got up and like every other morning went to work, sighed and sang, because if we didn't we would be beaten. When we returned from work, everyone had his skinny piece of bread and some water and in this way, we greeted the second week of our stay in camp.

Once an S.S. man came to our group, called out someone's name, and ordered him to run. As he ran, the officer drew his gun and shot and killed him. The S.S. man instructed us to carry his body, screaming that he had shot him because he was trying to escape. We all remained silent. I thought that if I had a weapon I wouldn't have hesitated to shoot the murderer.

We all decided that if the S.S. man should ever again call out someone and order him to run, we would remain standing still and refuse to obey the order. With embittered hearts, we returned from work carrying the body to the barracks, where we set it down. It remained there all night and the next day.

The nights grew cold. Although I wanted to continue sleeping outdoors, my younger brother had been brought to the same camp and was now with me, and I was afraid he would not be able to withstand the cold and would fall sick. So we got together with several people we knew and found a place in the barracks where we could sleep together, so as to somewhat alleviate the suffering there.

That night several of our group had to go outside (to relieve themselves). When a long time passed and they hadn't returned, I went out and woke up the Jew from Lublin who was in charge and together we began searching. It turned out that an S.S. man had seen them leave the barracks and had forced them to lift up the dead body and dance with it for 20 minutes. When he tired of this, he forced them to perform various gymnastic exercises. He then ordered them to go over to the barbed wire fence and dig there with their hands. The hole was fairly deep by the time the Jewish commandant arrived and pleaded with the S.S. man to let them go. The officer's intention was clear: after the hole was dug he would have ordered them to crawl through to the other side, as if they were trying to escape, and he would have shot them.

After this we were even more terrified. We were afraid to leave the barracks at night and the stuffiness was even greater than before.

Once, after returning to camp after work, I received a package which came from the Judenrat. I opened it with trembling hands and found a letter from my wife and children. I was overjoyed and could not restrain my tears. Outside, the people who had brought the package waited on the other side of the barbed wire fence. I quickly wrote a response and gave it to them. In it, I tried to hide my suffering from my wife.

My wife, however, sensed that I hadn't written the truth and the third week of my stay in the camp she herself came to the camp, getting a lift with the people who were bringing packages for the workers. When she saw me, she began weeping, which did not help me to feel calm. She couldn't stop crying and the commandant allowed me to speak with her for 15 minutes at the gate. When we said our farewells, I wondered when I would ever see her again. I already doubted that I would be able to withstand the suffering in the camp.

That night I did not open the package my wife had brought me. I fell onto the hard bunk and buried my head in an old coat and cried for a long time.

The fourth week in camp they took away the Gypsies, who had mostly worked in the kitchen. Everyone knew that they had been liquidated. But there were still people who didn't want to believe that they would take entire families with small children and murder them.

Jews took the place of Gypsies in the kitchen, and saw to it that the conditions were a bit cleaner and that the drinking water tasted better. But every day things worsened and illness afflicted the camp. When we went to sleep we never knew if we would awaken. Every day, one of us was found dead in their bunk.

Trenches Along the Border

One evening we were suddenly ordered to leave the barracks as quickly as possible. There was only one door and the S.S. men thought the exit was taking too long, so they began shooting into the barracks. People panicked and lay down on the floor, afraid to go out.

The S.S. entered and began hitting people with whips. Some people hid under the bunks and the S.S. dragged them out and beat them severely.

Outside on the square, they began counting people. The S.S. commander warned that if anyone was missing, every tenth person in his group would be taken and shot.

The next morning we again went to work. We could see Russian patrols moving around across the border. The Russians waved at us, motioning us to come across the border, but the Germans kept us under close guard. We ourselves watched to make sure no one crossed the border, each of us fearing that he would be the tenth man in each group to be shot in retaliation.

During the fifth week in camp, while we were at work, about 20 S.S. men suddenly appeared and ordered us to stop work and line up. They selected 500 of us and took them away, leaving the rest of us terrified, imagining their fate.

The next day at work we heard a sudden burst of shooting that lasted several minutes. When it grew quiet, we saw that the Germans were leading several people with them. These were Ukrainians who had fled the Russian side, and it had been the Russians who were shooting at them. Two had been shot dead, but five had managed to cross the border to the German side.

A few days later, we learned that the 500 Jews who had been taken away were now in Cieszanow, 20 kilometers from Belzec, where a new labor camp had been established to dig trenches along the border.

Each day in camp brought more assaults, beatings and shootings. The High Holy Days were approaching and I wrote a letter to my wife and children. As I wrote, I could not hold back my tears, which fell on the paper. The day of Rosh Hashanah eve we went to work as usual. Suddenly the S.S. commandant Adolf rode up on his horse. He stopped near me, shouted:

"Damn Jew" at me, dismounted, grabbed the pickaxe I was holding and demonstrated how it should be used. The people who were standing nearby thought that I would soon be killed, but he got back on his horse and rode off. This was the first time he had approached anyone and cursed them, but had not shot them. When I calmed down I remembered my dream from the night before, in which my father was walking with me through the streets of Tarnogrod speaking to me with consoling words.

Temporary Liberation

When I returned to camp I heard that they were freeing the Jews who came from Tarnogrod. I ran to the gate and saw that they were lining up the Tarnogrod Jews on the square. A German sergeant had driven up with two trucks with a permit to remove 62 people from the Belzec camp. I noticed that there were no more than 45 Jews from Tarnogrod because two weeks earlier they had taken many Tarnogrod Jews to Cieszanow. When I approached the S.S. guard, he asked if I had documents proving I was from Tarnogrod and when I couldn't produce them, he hit me with his leather whip, yelling at me to get away.

Moving off to the side, I noticed that people who were not from Tarnogrod were coming forward and people in the lineup were shouting that they were from Tarnogrod and should be allowed in the group. Suddenly I heard the sergeant count out 61 people, saying he needed one more. I ran up, told him I was from Tarnogrod, but that my papers had been taken from me. The civilian commandant, the Jewish dentist from Lublin, took me by the arm and led me from the gate to join the group of people who were going home.

My brother saw all this from a distance. He ran back into the barracks, brought out my pack and we parted. He was happy for me, but he was sad because now he was alone.

Riding in the trucks we remembered it was Rosh Hashanah eve and we started to recite the evening prayers. It grew dark and Rosh Hashanah night fell.

We drove through Tomaszow Lubelski and Zamosc. We began to worry about where we were being taken. Someone announced that it was time to say the night prayer. After the prayer, someone said that in his pack he had two challahs that had been sent by his family. He took them out and we made the Rosh Hashanah *kiddush* [blessing], parceled out the challahs and travelling in unfamiliar parts we observed the Rosh Hashanah meal with broken hearts.

When we rode through Szczebrzeszyn our worry eased a bit. Soon we saw Bilgoraj and then we were in Tarnogrod. But the trucks didn't stop until we were at the barracks outside the town. We sat in the trucks with trembling hearts for another quarter of an hour, when a lieutenant arrived. He gave a speech in which he said he had taken us out of Belzec and we belonged to his military division. If we behaved in a disciplined manner and worked diligently, no harm would come to us. We would work all day building the highway and in the evening would be able to return home. Anyone who failed to report to work in the morning would be arrested and sent back to Belzec.

Joyfully, we returned to our homes. I would have had to walk 14 kilometers to my house in Lukowa, and the road was dangerous at night, so I went to the house of my uncle, Arye Yoysef Tintnfish, who lived in Tarnogrod. There I again recalled my dream in which my father walked with me through the streets of Tarnogrod. Maybe it wasn't just a dream. There I was, actually sitting near my uncle in Tarnogrod and not behind barbed wire in Belzec.

I couldn't wait for night to end. The alarm clock sounded 4:00 A.M. and I got dressed, left the house and flew like a bird to Lukowa. I didn't notice a Christian who drove by and recognized me. He arrived in Lukowa before me and told the first Jew he met the news that I was free and on my way home. My wife got dressed and along with several other people came to meet me. We met on the road and fell into each other's arms.

When I entered my house I saw on the table the letter I had written from camp, hoping for things I didn't even believe I could have.

Later we learned that the Tarnogrod Judenrat had bribed the German commandant to get us out of the camp in Belzec.

Right after Rosh Hashanah came the Sabbath of Repentence. I woke up at 4:00 A.M. so as to comply with the order to be in Tarnogrod at 7:30. I had to walk 14 kilometers. At 7:00 I was already at the market place in Tarnogrod, where the Jews from the Belzec camp along with other Jews assigned to work had started to assemble. German soldiers soon arrived and divided the Jews into groups and took them out of town.

Destruction of the Gravestones

At the cemetery, I saw gravestones lying on the road. Soon, we were ordered to tear up more gravestones from the cemetery[1]. It turned out that I had to tear out the very gravestone that I had placed on my father's grave two years earlier. We felt as if blood ran from the shattered stones. Every piece of stone was wet with Jewish tears.

In the evening I returned home to Lukowa. The next day was Sunday and we didn't have to work. When I told people at home what we had to do at work, they burst into tears.

Monday at dawn I got up, packed food for the entire week and left for Tarnogrod. During the week I stayed overnight with my mother's sister.

We worked on the highway the whole winter. A lot of Jewish families who had been expelled from Poznan and Krakow worked with us. They were not provided with separate housing but were crammed 8 to 10 to a room in the homes of local Jewish families. Things got worse by the day. Jews were allotted only 100 grams of bread per person. The work paid very little. Hunger and need reigned in every Jewish home.

Around Passover, 1941 many German army divisions began to arrive in the towns in our area. Our town was filled with soldiers who engaged in military maneuvers day and night. The ordinary soldiers didn't bother the Jews. Once, in conversation with a German soldier, I mentioned that we were 15 kilometers from the Russian border. I noticed that he became frightened and said that now he understood why they were engaging in so many maneuvers. He didn't want to say more.

New soldiers arrived daily. On June 21, 1941 we noticed that the military had begun to advance. At night all the German soldiers went to the Russian border. The next day, you could hear the noise of airplanes and the news came that the German army had crossed the border. Soon you could see masses of captured Russians being marched along the roads.

At the same time, the German soldiers began oppressing the Polish peasants, imposing heavy taxes on them and confiscating their grain. The soldiers went house to house, searching the rooms. I had stored some grain in my house because there was no bread to be had. The Germans took it all. When my wife pleaded with them, saying that she would have nothing to give her children to eat and to sustain life, the German answered that Jews should not remain alive.

In Tarnogrod, Bilgoraj and Jozefow the Germans imposed a *kontributsie* [demand for money and property] to be paid within a deadline of several hours. In 1941 it was decreed that a Jew was forbidden to go from one town to another. A Jew who was found away from home would be shot. If someone fell ill during that time of hunger, it was forbidden to call a doctor without obtaining special permission.

People risked their lives to go to another town or to the countryside in search of food. A girl who had been forced to leave Poznan and go to Tarnogrod came to Lukowa where she thought she would get something to eat. As she walked in the street, a Christian recognized her as a non-resident of Lukowa and turned her over to the police. The S.S. took her to a trench and shot her there so that her body fell into the trench.

My mother and siblings lived near the town offices. The police commander wanted to take away their house and demanded that they move in with me. Our appeals were in vain and the 15 people who had been living in two rooms had to move out and live with me.

Bad News

I had a neighbor, a Polish professor, with whom I was friendly. His wife came from Krakow. Once, after she returned from a visit to Krakow, she told me that in the train compartment she had overheard two German high officers conversing, saying that by the end of 1942, not a single Jew would be left in Poland. When I relayed this to other Jews, few took it seriously. But I knew she was telling the truth. Every day it became clearer that the Germans were capable of achieving this horrifying annihilation. The Christian neighbors said that on the Lublin-Lemberg (Lviv) train line large transports of Tarnogrod Jews were travelling in closed wagons, but no one knew where they were being taken.

We decided to send a trustworthy Christian to find out where the transports of Jews were going. He travelled to Belzec and observed them unhitching the train cars. Two hours later, the S.S. arrived, unlocked the doors and ordered the Jews to get out. Hitting them over the head, they forced them into the camp where they were led into a building from which they never came out. Several hours, the dead bodies were removed, taken to the crematorium and burned.

The Christian had found all this out by investigating and questioning the local peasants who told him that cremation of Jews had been going on for about four months.

There were still Jews who didn't believe this but I and several others Jews who were convinced that the Christian was telling the truth, began to think about fleeing to save our lives. At the beginning, we wanted to go to the forest, but knowing that other Jews would be punished for what we did, we changed our minds.

Soon there came reports from Bilgoraj and Tarnogrod about mass shootings. During one such shooting a boy, Yoel Hochman, managed to escape. He had been slightly injured, but the murderers thought he was dead. When they left, he crawled out of the ditch and slowly made his way to Tarnogrod where he told everyone about the shooting of the 48 Jews.

On May 5, 1942, which fell on [the Jewish holiday] Lag B'omer, Polish police surrounded my house, burst inside and led away my 24-year old brother Meyer. Despite our pleas, they took him to the police station. An hour later I went there and saw six additional Jews, among them my brother-in-law, Meyer Wartman and his 23 year-old son Moyshe. Also, Yehoshua Fliesswasser and Elimelekh Weissman from Babice. I spoke again to the police chief but it didn't help. The next day the men, their hands bound, were taken to Bilgoraj in peasant wagons. They were then led along Zamosc Street to the Rafis forest, where they were all shot.

Russian Partisans

We were assigned to work in the forest. Once, two armed men approached us and said in Russian, "What's the point of working for the Germans? Come with us deeper into the forest." They were Russian soldiers who had escaped from German captivity, fashioned weapons, and began to organize a partisan army.

We discussed this among ourselves. Should we accept the Russians' proposal or should we stay where we were and wait. We were afraid that the Jews who remained behind would suffer for our actions. So we continued to go to work in the forest.

On May 11, 1942, a Monday, when Jozefow held its market day, several S.S. arrived at the market, rounded up 150 elderly people and took them to the forest to shoot them. Among them were Avrom-Iser Shukhfeld and Yakov Feinbaum

Several weeks later a Christian from Jozefow told the S.S. that the Jews working in the forest were bringing food to the partisans. He gave them the name of a girl, Rivke Honigsfeld. The S.S. took her away and shot her.

On a market day, the 20th of [the Hebrew month] *Tammuz*, 5702 [1942] the Germans surrounded Jozefow and assembled all the Jews, children and adults. They loaded a truck with women and children, took them to the forest, where they were ordered to undress and to lay down on the ground, and shot them. The same truck went back to town, loaded up with another group of women and children, and repeated the action. This continued all day. Only a few people managed to escape and hide. The men were taken to Majdanek. The Jozefow rabbi, a young man, was taken to Lublin. His wife was killed in the forest.

Two Jews from Lukowa who were working in the forest had gone to Jozefow that day to collect their wages. As soon as they entered the town the S.S.put them on the truck which was taking elderly people to the forest to be shot. When he got off the truck, one of them, Yisroel Honigsfeld, a boy of 20, began to run through the trees. The Germans shot at him, and he was hit by 11 bullets, but he kept running until, covered in blood, he reached my house. He looked a fright. He was riddled with bullet wounds, two of them in his cheek.

With the help of a neighbor, I led him through a side street to his house and we went to summon a doctor, who was afraid to come because he didn't have permission to treat Jews, not to mention one who had escaped from a German *aktsie* [Nazi operation or raid aimed at deportation or extermination of Jews].

We returned home and took off his clothes, which were sticking to his wounds, a terribly painful process. We found bandages somewhere and bound his wounds. Not until the next day did we find a doctor, whom we paid well and he determined that the wounds were superficial and that the boy would recover. It took six weeks for him to heal. Not until then did he tell us what he had seen that murderous day in Jozefow, in the forest.

Many of those who managed to hide on the day of the *aktsie* returned home only to find that they were the only survivors, and committed suicide.

Several families that still worked in the sawmills of Gorajec and had documents granting them the right to remain survived the *aktsie*. They too walked around half-dead, deeply depressed. The town felt like a cemetery, the houses empty, with doors and windows left open.

At the same time the S.S. drove around the villages where Jewish families lived, took them from their houses and shot them. In some villages the Jews were ordered to go to Jozefow and the local Volksdeutsche [ethnic Germans living outside Germany] looted their homes. Several Jewish families from Babice hid illegally in Lukowa. In Aleksandrow, a large village seven kilometers from Jozefow, the 40 Jewish families who lived there were shot on the spot.

In Tarnogrod, the Judenrat was forced to turn over 800 people, ostensibly to be sent to work in Wolyn. When the transport arrived in Zwierzyniec, they took everyone's baggage, beat them harshly, and sent them to Belzec, where they were gassed and cremated.

Dispersing to Different Locations

On the 14th day of *Elul*, 5702, Lukowa was attacked by 30 S.S. men who stationed themselves at the municipal offices. I tried to find out from the police what their purpose was, but no one could give me an answer. Around 6:00 P.M. the village magistrate came to see me and told me that the next day, at 4:00 A.M., all the magistrates of the surrounding villages were required to report to the municipal office. We grew suspicious and decided to sleep over at the home of a Christian acquaintance. At 10 P.M. when the streets had grown quiet, we gradually began to disperse in different directions. I and my older son Yehuda went to a barn without the owner's knowledge. My wife and two children and a girl cousin from Warsaw went to stay in the attic owned by another peasant, who also had no knowledge of their arrival.

I and my son burrowed into the hay but we couldn't sleep. When day came my 9 year-old son left the barn and from a hiding place saw that the Germans had surrounded our house. He quickly ran back to tell me. Apparently a Christian saw him running back to the barnyard and began yelling loudly that I was hiding in the barn. When the peasant owner heard that he got very scared and began to look for us. He threw all the straw into the courtyard, entered the barn and began calling me by my name, Avrom. I didn't answer, but lay pressed against the wall and remained quiet. He took the iron pitchforks from the manure pile and began tossing the hay about. At that point, I whispered to him to have pity on me, but he begged me to leave the barn because the neighbor had seen my son running inside and had shouted the news to the entire street.

I had no choice. I had to take my son and leave. But when I got to the gate, I saw an armed S.S. standing in the field behind the houses. I went back to the courtyard and looked through the fence into the neighboring yard, where at the moment there was not a living soul. I didn't stop to think, I jumped over the fence, my Yehuda followed me, and we crept into their barn, which was very small; we barely had room to move.

After an hour, we heard the proprietor and his wife moving about in the courtyard, discussing how the Jews were being wiped out. They said that Ziser tried to run away and was shot; one of Leyzer's sons was shot jumping over a fence and he was left hanging there.

Soon we heard a grenade exploding. The Christians said among themselves that Khane Shmuels was being led away and her leg was hurting so they took her to a Jewish home where Leyzer Mendels was lying in bed gravely ill. They threw a grenade into the house, killing the woman and the sick man.

I heard people saying that they had gone to my house and found no one there.

The captured Jews were taken to the Lukowa courtyard. Avrom Weltz hid out somewhere, but having learned that his wife and two small children had been taken to the assembly point, he gave himself up to the Germans.

Around 2:00 P.M. they ordered the assembled Jews to dig ditches and then shot them all.

This all happened 300 meters from where I was hiding. On that day, the 15ᵗʰ day of *Elul*, 62 Jews died. The rest were able to hide.

When it grew dark, I left the barn. Outside, I found out that the Germans had spared the life of Shmuel the tailor, but when I went to his house, he told me he had been ordered not to let anyone in. Quietly, I slipped into the cellar of a Christian intending to spend the night, but the Christian heard me, came down to the cellar and begged me to leave, because any minute the Germans could conduct a search for Jews and they would shoot him too.

Along with my son Yehuda, I went to another barn and slept until dawn. It had rained heavily all night and a damp cold rose from the ground but I was afraid to go outside. When I saw a Christian acquaintance walk by I came out and asked whether the Germans had left yet but he didn't know. I walked through the field. I remembered a Christian I knew who had done some work for me and asked him if the Germans had left Lukowa. He went to the town offices to find out what they intended to do with Jews who remained.

The Role of Poles in the *Aktsie*

I waited for him to return. My head was afire with all these sad thoughts and I was about to go for a walk in the field when I saw my wife and two children and the cousin from Warsaw approaching. Our joy knew no bounds.

The Christian returned from the town offices and said that the Jews who remained after the *aktsie* could return to their homes.

On the way my wife told me what had happened to her. A Christian woman who lived near the attic where they were hiding knew that they were there. She went upstairs and told them they should come down because the Germans were searching. My wife took the children into the fields. She soon saw an armed S.S. man in the distance, so she flung herself into the grain growing near the houses. After she had hidden there with the children for two hours, a Christian woman passing by noticed her, called her by her name and expressed regret over her situation. But she left quickly and my wife realized that she could report her to the Germans, who would come looking for them. She left the grain field and went further into the fields with the children. They walked about an hour and entered a potato field, where they lay until it got dark.

It began to rain, there was thunder and lightning and they were soaked to the skin, trembling with cold and fear. She snuggled the children, praying to God that they would emerge unharmed. In the morning they began walking back toward the houses. In the field they met a peasant, a neighbor of ours, who was at work plowing. My wife approached him and asked what was happening. The peasant expressed his pity for her and told her what had occurred the previous day.

Frightened, she continued on her way and approached the houses. She went to a neighbor to find out what had happened to me and Yehuda. The neighbors told her that they had heard that I had hidden out. They didn't know exactly what had happened to Yehuda. As she left them, we encountered each other. We returned to our house to find that it had been looted. We were told that the people from the municipal offices had taken the best things, thinking we were no longer alive. We went there and immediately got back our bedding and some other household items. Some of our windowpanes had been knocked out and a feeling of fear pervaded the place. We were afraid to sleep there and went to sleep somewhere else.

There were Poles who took part in the *aktsie* by attacking Jews. In one incident a Pole beat Avraham Yakov, the 18-year-old son of Itsik Leyb Weltz, so badly that the boy could not get up and was blinded. He struggled with death and the Christian doctor took pity on him and gave him medicine that hastened his death.

It was quiet for about two weeks until Thursday, the day before Rosh Hashanah, when an order came that within three days we had to leave Lukowa and go to Jozefow. At the end of Rosh Hashanah Jewish police came from Bilgoraj and supervised our packing and departure from Lukowa.

In Jozefow we moved into the homes of Jews who had just recently been taken to be killed. Our hearts were frozen and we could no longer weep. We had known many of the residents who preceded us and we knew that they were no longer alive.

On Yom Kippur we prayed in a private home. As we were reciting the *Musaf* prayer, we saw through the window how some Poles were chasing a Jew, a refugee from Babice. When they caught him they gave him a terrible beating. He defended himself with his last bit of strength but, his head battered, he fell dead.

Fear of New Developments

My heart told me that new developments were about to occur. I took off my prayer shawl and *kitl* [white robe worn on Yom Kippur] and went home. My wife was very frightened and pleaded with me to hide in the attic, the approach to which was concealed by a tin plate. I hid there among broken crates and soon I heard people downstairs open the door and ask my wife where I was. My wife and children were crying as they answered that I had already been captured.

From my hiding place I heard what was going on in the street. A 12 year-old girl was running, probably to warn her father to hide. An S.S. officer stopped her and asked where she was running. Less than a minute later I heard a shot; the girl screamed and fell dead.

Shmuel Elbaum, the tailor, a neighbor of mine, was the only Jew to have received permission to remain in Lukowa but his wife and two children had to go to Jozefow. On Yom Kippur he joined them there. He was sure that since he had the permit issued by the Bilgoraj town council, no one would bother him. But the Polish police did not take it into account and seized him. He was among 40 Jews who were seized and taken to the firehouse. From the firehouse they were taken to the forest and shot. One managed to escape. They pursued him and shot him in the leg, but he kept running.

After removing the Jews from the firehouse, they came back to my house and took my sister and other women to wash the firehouse floor, which was covered in blood.

It grew dark and I still lay in the attic, stuck there by the fear that any minute they would return. My wife was also afraid to summon me downstairs. I lay there without food or water. In the morning my wife went outside and learned that the Germans had left and things had quieted down. Only then did I come down from the attic.

But we still lived in fear. I went to the train station in Gorajec, where there was a sawmill where Jews from Jozefow, former wood merchants, worked. They lived there with their families in barracks. No one bothered them. With great effort I managed to get myself hired. I received a permit and after working several days in the sawmill asked the director to allow me to bring my wife and children. The director wanted to help but there was no room. I spent the holiday of *Sukkot* in sorrow, suppressing my tears.

Several weeks later, my wife, coming back from Jozefow, told me that she had been in a Christian-owned shop, where they did not recognize her as Jewish, and that she had heard a Polish police officer telling the proprietor that soon they would be rid of the last few Jews. The *aktsie* would not occur at night because the Jews were sleeping in the forest.

I went to see Efraim Lumerman, a Lukowa resident who was in Jozefow with his wife and children, and discussed with him what we should do. We decided that we should go to the forest with our families. I returned to the sawmill and agreed with people there that if they heard any news they would let me know immediately and we would go together to the forest.

Several days later, they conducted an *aktsie* in Szczebrzeszyn and sent the Jews to Belzec. On the way, at Dlugi-Kat, some Jews jumped from the moving train. Many of them were killed; some, wounded, made their way to Jozefow and told about the *aktsie*. My wife immediately sent my 10 year-old Yehuda to Gorajec, to tell me to come home.

I told the sawmill director that my mother had fallen ill, and he released me from working. But I told my co-workers the truth, that the Germans had conducted the final *aktsie* in Szczebrzeszyn and I had decided to go to the forest. A Jew from Jozefow, Yeshaye Kalekhman, said that the chief director had assured him the Jews working in the sawmill would not be harmed. I didn't allow him to convince me of that, and returned to Jozefow. There were a lot of new people – the wounded who had jumped from the train --roaming around there. Everyone was filled with fear.

We had decided that the next day, in the evening, we would go to the forest, but at twilight it began to rain heavily. We couldn't bring ourselves to set off with the small children and we decided to wait until the Sabbath.

On Friday evening we suddenly heard the firehouse sirens go off. We were sure the *aktsie* had begun. We grabbed our packs and the children and ran to the forest. When we got to the hill outside town we stopped and saw that there was a fire in the town. One of us returned to town and came back with the news that there was no *aktsie*, but an actual fire.

Parshat [Torah Portion] *Lech Lecha*

Once again, we returned home. On Saturday morning we went to pray. The Torah portion for the week was *Lech Lecha*. [Genesis 12.1-17.27: God said to Abraham, "Go forth from your homeland to the land that I shall show you...."] I took that as a sign from heaven that we should abandon our possessions and leave.

On Saturday night several of us came together and decided once again that the next night we would go to the forest. I was overcome with worry over my mother, who couldn't walk because her legs were swollen. My heart ached at the thought of leaving her at home. But my mother pleaded with me not to take her into account but to save myself. The entire household was in tears, but she comforted us, saying that she did not have long to live and she didn't want to have our young lives on her conscience.

My sisters Blume, Ratse and Rachel went to stay with our oldest sister, Feige, who lived with her husband Yehoshua in Tarnogrod, where it was still peaceful.

When night fell we took leave of our mother with heavy hearts and slipped out of the house. Outside town we met up with other families with small children and we set off slowly for the forest.

The moon shone brightly; it was 15 days after the new moon of the month of *Cheshvan*, 5703 [October 26, 1942]. When we entered the forest we rested a bit and then continued walking. We had decided to hide in a location that was 9 kilometers away. Because of the children we had to walk slowly and it took us three hours to get there. We laid the children down to sleep and we sat down and pondered our situation. The air was already a bit frosty and we were shivering.

In the morning, when the sun began to shine, we warmed up a bit and began to explore our surroundings. There was a river nearby called the Sopot. The thought that we were near water cheered us. One of us went off to obtain food. On his way back, two Russian partisans spotted him and silently followed him back to where we were. Seeing so many people, they summoned two more partisans and they all attacked us and took everything we had. They even took my prayer shawl.

We sat there, dejected. Hunger began to torment us and we decided that my wife, who knew Polish well and who did not look Jewish, should go to get food, along with another person who had a permit to travel from town to town. Barefoot, like peasants, they went to town, entered the house where my mother was still living, got food, and returned to the forest in the evening.

Our fourth day in the forest, the same partisans came and told us that we weren't in a good location because it was close to the road. They demanded whiskey in return for taking us to a safer location in a young forest. The next day my wife and a few others went into town and went to the house to get food, but as they were there, a woman who had come with her rapped on the window and shouted, "Perl, run back to the forest."

Terrified, my wife barely managed to grab the food and began to run toward the forest. Bullets flew over her head, but she kept running. She lost her way and wandered in the forest for a long while, until she finally encountered a Jewish girl from another group, who accompanied her.

It was Friday evening and I was sitting with our three small children, trembling with cold and with troubled thoughts about why they weren't back yet. It got dark. Two women who had left with my wife were already back but she was still missing. They told us that back in town a deaf woman passing through had been ordered by the Germans to stop, but she ran and they shot at her and killed her. Hearing the shooting, everyone began to run, including my wife, and she must have reached the forest, but gotten lost. I didn't believe them, thinking they just wanted to console me. I didn't close my eyes all night. Not until dawn did my wife arrive with a person from another Jewish group hiding in the same forest.

As soon as morning came my wife set off again to town, along with other people, taking our older son. They encountered no problems and returned at dusk with food.

Several days later they again set off to get food. They had walked several kilometers and were not far from town when they suddenly saw a little girl who told them that the Germans had surrounded the town and had captured the few remaining Jews. They could actually hear shooting in the distance and turned back to the forest with the news.

This was 23 *Cheshvan* 5703 [November 3, 1942].

Yosef Likhtfeld, from Jozefow, was among those in the transport to Belzec and he managed to jump from the moving train. He made his way to us in the forest and told us that those who had been unable to walk had been shot on the spot. That is what happened to my mother, who had been walking with him, leaning on him for support, when the murderers shot her, their bullets passing near his arm.

At night, the partisans who had robbed us came back. We gave them the whiskey we had promised and they led us to another place in the forest that bore the number 176. The forest was divided into separate tracts, each measuring 800 square meters, each designated by a different number.

After the taking of the 600 Jews from Tarnogrod, it was quiet for a while, but it was a terrible kind of quiet. The wife of the German police commandant could not sit down to breakfast until she had first witnessed the murder of a Jew. A victim fell almost every day. People had gotten used to this and never thought that tomorrow the same thing could happen to them.

On 22 *Cheshvan* [November 2, 1942], a Monday, the Germans surrounded the town and began carrying out the final aktsie. Sick people were shot on the spot and the rest were forced into the market place, where the shouts and crying of the small children reached to the heavens. The market place was filled with corpses. All the small children were torn away from their parents and loaded onto peasant wagons. Some of them suffocated in the wagons. Their parents were driven like cattle to slaughter. They were marched to Bilogoraj and those who couldn't walk were shot on the way.

In Bilgoraj they were loaded on to the small gauge train to Zwierzyniec and from there the train took them to Belzec.

Jews in Hiding

There still remained Jews hiding out in various places in Tarnogrod. For days the police searched house to house and dragged them out from hiding. My sisters hid in a bunker, but when it grew dark they went out into the fields. On the way they got lost. Feige was left alone with her 2 year-old child. She encountered some Christians who wanted to send her back to the Germans. She gave them her gold ring and they left her alone. She made her way through the fields in the dark and arrived in Lukowa. She went to the home of a Christian she knew, and found her three sisters already there. The Christian hid them all.

A few days later the Christian heard that people were talking about him, saying that he was hiding Jews. He pleaded with my sisters to find another hiding place. One of the sisters went to the house of a poor peasant woman who lived alone with her daughter. She managed to dig out a bunker in her barn, obscuring it with manure. They all hid there. A few days later, German and Polish police surrounded the entire farmyard and searched for several hours.

After sitting in the forest for a long time Efraim Lumerman and I decided to go to Lukowa and find some food. On the way, a Christian from Lukowa saw us and let it be known in town that we were on the way. He was one of the German colonists, who were under orders from the German police to turn over any Jew found in town.

The local Christians who knew us wanted to protect us, but were afraid to come and meet us. So they staged a fake fight with loud cries and shouting, so that we would understand not to come into town. When we crossed the Tanew River and heard all the shouting, we stopped, not knowing what to do. At that moment, a Christian from Murashkow appeared and warned us not to enter Lukowa.

This man also told me that my brother-in-law Moshe Tintenfisch and another boy had come to Lukowa the day before, had gathered food and were on the way back, having already crossed the river, when they were detained near the village of Osuchy and handed over to the Germans. Today they had been shot.

We became very depressed. How would we return to our wives and children without food?

The Christian told us to wait until it was dark and then to come to his house, that he would give us food. He led us into his grain barn and shut us in, saying he was afraid to let us into his house. Every minute in the barn felt like an hour. We were overtaken by fear and cold. We began to think that the Christian had deliberately tricked us. We would have forced our way out and run away but the barn was locked from the outside.

Finally, he came in with a bowl of hot milk and a big loaf of Polish bread. We ate half the loaf right there, and took the rest with us, along with a 40 kilo sack of potatoes. We left him money and asked him to prepare flour and bread for us for the next night, and went back to the forest, the bags of potatoes on our backs.

It was dark and we couldn't see each other or where we were going, couldn't tell if we were walking in the right direction. Soon it started to rain and we sat down under a tree. We sat there in the cold and dark the entire night. When it grew light, we took up our sacks on our backs and resumed walking, along backroads, until we arrived, lay down exhausted and fell asleep.

The next day we returned to the Christian to collect the flour and bread he had promised us. We silently snuck up to his window to see if we could go in. He saw us and immediately came out with 8 big breads and a kilo of flour. When we left, he asked us not to come back, because he was afraid of his neighbors. When we entered the forest we were enveloped in darkness and couldn't walk further. We didn't arrive at our hiding place until Saturday morning.

Several days later we again began to worry about running out of food and we decided to go to Lukowa via a different route. After a lot of difficulty, we again visited the same Christian acquaintance. He brought us to the barn and returned with a pot of cooked potatoes and sour milk. He took our sacks and filled each one with 40 kilos of potatoes and gave us two breads.

The trip back was difficult and when we got to the forest we sat down to rest, made a fire, and roasted some potatoes. In the morning we reached our location.

Our location was filled with tall, sparse trees and we were exposed to the eyes of every passerby. After a while we moved to another location where the trees were thicker. This was #193. Later we learned that another group of 20 Jews from Jozefow had settled in our original location, from which the partisans had led us away. A few days later they were attacked by Poles, who shot them. Among the few survivors were a wood merchant named Frenkl and a young woman who had gone off to fetch water from the river. She had heard the shooting and sat down under a tree until it grew quiet. When she returned, she found her husband and two small children among the dead.

This woman found the strength to leave the forest and go to a village where she obtained Aryan papers. Later she went to Germany, where she survived the war. I met her in Lublin. Her name is Sarah; she was a granddaughter of Lipe Tarnevaler from the Jozefow Silbersteins. She married a man from Jozefow who had lost his wife and two children. She now lives in Canada.

An old woman from the other group also survived. She had gone to a village to get food. When she returned she found her son, his wife, and their two children dead. She went through the forest and found our group, among whom were her daughter and son-in-law and their child.

Weapons

The next time we set out to get food, we heard on the road peasants shouting on the road. They were chasing a Jewish woman, an increasingly frequent occurrence. Danger was increasing daily, but we had no choice, so we sought out new routes that were rough and isolated.

Once, we arrived at the house of a peasant who had promised to provide us with weapons. He told us he had a gun and 20 bullets that he would sell for 300 *zlotys*. He brought us a pot of cooked potatoes, along with the gun and bullets.

We got back safely.

Several days later, the gun proved useful. We had gone into the fields where we had dug up some potatoes, but when our sacks were already full, we heard the owner of the field shouting at us. We shot into the air and the peasant went away.

On the way to Lukowa several days later, we heard shooting and grenades exploding. We quickly turned back and the next day a boy from Jozefow, Avrahamtche Feingold, told us that a group of Russian partisans, including three Jews, had come to Lukowa the night before. Their assignment was to confiscate grain from the cooperative, but first they wanted to disarm the police station. They surrounded the building – my mother's former house – that held the commandant and five police officers from Bilgoraj. They shot the commandant and his wife on the spot. Two police officers were wounded. The peasants were saying that this was because of me, that it was an act of vengeance against the commandant for having evicted my mother from her house.

Hanukkah arrived. It got colder by the day and we began to build a bunker. We had just barely dug to a depth of two meters when the Russians who were in the same forest as us arrived. They talked us out of building a bunker, because when you are in a bunker you can't hear what's happening outside. The enemy can approach unexpectedly and we wouldn't be able to get away. So we stopped digging.

I didn't want the children to forget the ceremony of lighting the Hanukkah candles, so I carved out pieces of kindling that I inserted into holes I made in a tree and every evening we lit the same number of pieces of kindling as we would have done with candles.

Hanukkah passed. We had no calendar but I kept track of the dates, both of the Jewish and Christian calendars.

The days got even colder. No outsiders came near us, but we still worried that the peasants from surrounding the neighborhood had sniffed out our hideout, and we knew we had to look for a new location.

We looked for a suitable place for several days until we settled on forest parcel #209. We moved there right away, set up a large shelter that could accommodate everyone and began to dig a well so that we wouldn't have to go out for water. The piece of land we selected was on a little hill and all around the hill the land was swampy. It was dangerous to approach and this eased our worries.

Another group of about 20 Jews was located not far from us, at a place called Balitshovka. My sister Chaia and her five children were there. One day, the peasants led several armed Germans there. The Jews heard them coming and fled, but my sister's three youngest children couldn't run away and the Germans killed them. Satisfied with their three victims, the Germans didn't pursue the Jews who had fled, who moved on to another place.

Compassionate People

Again we had several quiet days. Our food started to run out and we again got ready to go to Lukowa to find food. Our money was also running out. In Lukowa I had an acquaintance, a miller who owed me money and also 20 meters of grain. I was certain I would get it from him and persuaded my friend to go with me to the mill to get money, flour and bread.

The mill owner was an honest man and I was sure I could go see him. But the way there led past the police station and the town offices. Going through the field we encountered the peasant who owned it. He was happy to see us and greeted us in a very friendly manner. We were reassured and coming to the mill, we stealthily looked through the window, listening for sounds of strangers talking, and then lightly tapped on the door.

The miller heard us and came out. It was already dark and he didn't recognize us. When I told him who I was he was a little scared but he soon rejoiced, happy to see me alive, and he began to ask questions about what was happening with us.

I gave him a short account of everything we had gone through and how we were living now. You could see how sorry he felt for us in our suffering. He consoled us and said we should hold on because the Germans had sustained a heavy blow at Stalingrad. This was good news and we felt somewhat relieved. We ate the bread the miller gave us with hearty appetite. He asked what else we needed. I told him honestly that we needed bread and flour but it would be hard for him to get it to us and so it would be better if he gave us money so that we could buy food closer to the forest. He gave me 500 *zlotys* and threw in six breads and 25 kilos of wheat flour.

We said our farewells in a friendly way. It was already past midnight and we took our packs on our backs and walked through the fields past Lukowa. We thought about stopping in at the postal official who was an acquaintance, but going through town I met a Christian man who recognized me. He was standing by the courtyard where the postal official lived and he stopped me and asked what was new. After a brief exchange we said goodbye and he went off.

We walked a few steps in the direction of the postal official's house but I soon stopped and told my friend that it would be better if we didn't go inside, because the Christian appeared suspicious; it was possible he had gone directly from us to the police to report our presence.

We went directly into the field, crossed the bridge and entered the forest. When we later went to Lukowa another time and stopped by to see the postal official, he told us we had avoided a certain death. It turned out that the Christian had in fact gone to the police and told them that we were at the postal official's house. The police, along with some firemen, had surrounded the entire courtyard and searched every corner.

The postal official advised us never again to use the same route because it was possible we were being watched. We didn't hesitate, accepted some potatoes and buckwheat groats from him, and went right back into the forest.

About a half-kilometer away from our forest location were several Jews from Josefow, who in need of food, went to a small village near Josefow and stole a cow, brought it to the forest and slaughtered it for meat. The peasants of the village were extremely angry and the next day they followed the tracks in the snow and armed with weapons found the hiding place, attacked and killed all the Jews.

Burning wounds

After living in the forest for three months, the only shirt I owned had fallen to pieces. We slept in our clothing and in our boots. My boots were very tight and I knew that if I took them off, I would never be able to put them back on. My feet were covered with wounds and I couldn't walk any more. Then I tried to pull them off but I couldn't. I asked my friend to pull them off and he couldn't either. It was as if the boots were glued to my feet. There was no option but to cut off the boot legs. I almost fainted when I took off the boots and saw my wounded feet. I could no longer put the boots back on and sat there with my feet wrapped in rags. There was no possible way I could walk 12 kilometers to the village to get food.

My friend Efraim Lumerman, while cutting wood, had cut his foot with the axe and was also unable to walk. We sat there together; looking at our feet, shaking our heads over our wounds, but what hurt most was our sorrow for our hungry children. Without much thought, we each put on one boot, tied the other foot in rags, and set off for Lukowa.

We could no longer take our former route that now appeared to be dangerous. It was raining, the snow had started to melt. Our feet, in rags, were completely soaked. The cold wetness caused us even more pain. We wanted to sit down and rest, but that would have been dangerous, so we continued on, splashing through water and limping along.

We entered the farmyard of a peasant we knew, Makhnie. He came out right away, took us to the barn and let us stay until midnight. Only then did he take us to his house. He gave us something to eat and put together packs of bread and potatoes to take back to the forest. We were so exhausted form the trip and our pain that as soon as we sat down we fell asleep. When we awoke, it was already 3 A.M.

We immediately loaded the packs on our backs and set off, through snow and water, for our place in the forest.

The next time we went to the same peasant, he told us that the night we had last been there, a Jew from Lukowa, Avraham Yakov Gutharts, a shoemaker, had been hiding in his attic. He had been hiding with various peasants the entire time of the German occupation. The peasant hadn't wanted to tell us, because he was afraid that in our amazement we would start talking among ourselves and the news would spread to his neighbors.

His neighbors did in fact find out the shoemaker was staying there and suggested that they take him to us in the forest. The shoemaker believed them and went with them, but instead of taking him to the forest, they led him to the field, took everything he had and shot him.

Our Enemies are Singing

On February 11, 1943, in the middle of the day, we heard a lot of noise in the forest. People were talking loudly and singing. We thought it was drunken Russian partisans. But within 15 minutes, a girl from Jozefow came running, barefoot. This was Rachel Fischel, *Reb* Yakov's 15 year-old granddaughter. Panting, she told us we should flee because Germans and Ukrainians were conducting a raid in the forest. They had attacked her group and killed all the Jews, including her mother and brothers. She was the only one who survived. She lives in Poland to this day.

The singing got closer. We had no time to think. We grabbed the children and some food and ran until we reached a dividing line between two plots of land. When we tried to cross the road to get to the next plot the Germans saw us and began shooting. My wife and two children managed to cross the road along with several others. I ran with another child in the opposite direction, where the Sopot River flowed. We stood there wondering what to do next. Some people thought we should cross the river but I thought we should walk through the bushes that covered the high riverbanks, in the direction of our former location. We did this and after walking several kilometers we thought that the Germans had gone. It was quiet and we let ourselves take a rest. A bit later we learned we had been very lucky not to have tried to cross the river. Those who did so were shot and killed by the Germans, who had stationed themselves along the river on the other side.

At twilight we were approaching the place from which we had fled several hours earlier. Despite the quiet that surrounded us, we were afraid that the Germans had left behind watchmen and we sent someone ahead to see if there was really no one there. He quickly returned to say that all was clear.

We found our belongings untouched where we had left them, but our hearts were grieving. My wife and two children weren't there, nor my friend's wife and child and the other people who had crossed to the other plot. Who knew what had happened to them.

An hour passed. We sighed and wept. Suddenly we heard rustling in the trees and tentative footsteps. Our hearts trembled and suddenly we saw our wives and children. We were very happy. We felt that everyone was here and we had lost no one. But then we looked around and realized that my cousin Blume Fefer was missing. In 1941 she had escaped from the Warsaw ghetto and managed to make her way to us. She had been with us the entire time in the forest. At first I wanted to look for her immediately but this was a crazy idea because it was night and the forest was very dark.

We consoled ourselves with the thought that she had gotten lost and was waiting for daybreak to go on. As soon as it got light we set out to search. This was very hard because we were afraid we would encounter the police or a spy. Convincing ourselves that no one was around, we started to call her name quietly. After a long search we found her lying dead under a tree not far from our hiding place. Near her was a basket that held the *tfillin* that my parents had given me for my *bar mitzvah*. She knew how dear they were to me and had guarded them closely until her last breath.

We stood speechless over her body. The well of our tears had dried up and no words could express our grief. On a nearby hill we dug a grave and thought to ourselves that tomorrow we too could die and there would be no one to bury us. We would lie there like animals until wild beasts devoured us.

A Bunker Becomes a Grave

About three kilometers from us in the forest was a group of about 15 people that included my sister Chaia and her 16 year-old son, and my brother-in-law Pinches Fersht and his two children, a boy and a girl. When the Germans tracked them down and attacked them, four people managed to escape; three were wounded, including my brother-in-law's son. He ran away barefoot in freezing weather and his feet swelled up. He developed a fever and in despair returned the next day to their hiding place. He heard the Germans approach but didn't have the strength to run away and was shot.

The other three managed to join another group. Two – the brother and sister Kielich —asked us to take them into our group and they remained with us the entire time. The brother lives today in Bat Yam (Israel) and the sister -- in America.

A wounded girl joined a group that had dug a bunker in the ground. My wife's sister Sara and her three small children were among those in the bunker. There were also several other women, a couple with a child, and two children, aged seven and eight, without parents. Whenever we went by their place we left them a bit of food. The fate of those children, like that of so many others, broke our hearts. Their father had been captured when he left the forest in search of food. The peasants turned him over to the Germans, who shot him. The same thing happened to their mother when she went to get food a few days later; the same peasants caught her and turned her over. The sight of the two weeping children broke our hearts, but how could we help them when we ourselves faced such enormous perils?

One freezing day, the 20th of Shevat, 5703 [January 26, 1943], when we walked by their location, we were frightened by the silence. All of the people who had been in the bunker had been killed. Their bunker was now a grave and their murderers had filled it in with earth. The peasants from the village Balitshovka, which was just two kilometers away, told us how the Germans had found out about the hideout, stole up to the bunker and threw in several grenades. None of the 13 people there survived.

Not far from us in the forest was a group of 8 young men and one woman. They had four guns and were determined to fight to their last bullet. But one day, after the raid when the Germans attacked us, Russian partisans approached them, demanding that they hand over their guns. We were surprised, because the partisans had always known that some Jews had guns and had not objected. Their confiscation of the guns made us deeply suspicious.

The Guardian Angel who Rescued Us

On February 20, 1943, in the early morning, while the children were still asleep, a Russian partisan, a Georgian named Vashke, came running. Soaked with sweat and panting, he told us that we had to leave immediately because a raid was coming. When we asked where we should go, he told us to follow him. We snatched up a bit of food and the children. My youngest son was five years old and we picked him up, wearing just a shirt, and began running after Vashke.

Burdened by the children in our arms, we couldn't keep up with Vashke and lost sight of him. Confused, we stopped and didn't know what to do next. We entered a thick young forest and stood among the trees. With bated breath we listened to muffled sounds around us. After 20 minutes, it grew quiet and we considered leaving to find out what was happening. But just then we heard shooting nearby. After a few minutes it again grew quiet. We were afraid to say a word and the children stifled their crying.

We stood in the knee-deep snow all day. At dusk we decided that one of us should return to our former location to see what was happening there. He came back in an hour with the news that our shelter had been burned. It was clear that they were searching for us and we must not go back there. We went back to plot #210, where we found an old shelter where we spent the night. The cold was intolerable. But by now we had several times convinced ourselves that a human being is stronger than iron. The hardest thing was seeing our children trembling with cold.

The first thing the next morning, we began to scope out the area. We entered a thickly grown part of the forest, sat down on tree stumps, very quiet, afraid to say a word, stifling the coughs that came from our inflamed lungs. Satisfied that no one was nearby, we went to the location where the 8 young men and the woman had been staying. Our blood froze when we saw all 9 bodies lying there, half-burned.

We later learned that the Russian partisans had worked out a plan together with the members of the A.K. [Armia Krajowa, the Polish Home Army, an underground resistance organization] to kill all the Jews in the forest. The leader of the Polish partisans, Mashke from Josefow, conferred with Mishke Tatar, the leader of the Russian partisans, and they decided to carry out their attack on February 20. Among the Russian partisans were four Jews from Josefow, one of whom was Avrahamtche Feingold. The Russians took their weapons from the four Jews and told them to come on Saturday to collect them, but when they came, they were shot. Only one survived; he told us all of this.

The Poles did not know the exact location of the Jews and had to rely on the Russians to lead them there. That's how Vashke and his friend Lashkali found out about the attack on the Jews. The two of them decided to save us. Lashkali was the guide for the Poles and he led them on a longer path so that Vashke would have time to warn us to leave. If not for Vashke the Georgian we would have all been killed by the Poles, who that day shot 50 Jews.

The Poles later boasted about how they had approached the various Jewish groups, with whom many of them had been acquainted, and engaged them in friendly chats. They then suddenly surrounded the Jews and shot them, then set fire to their shelters, as well as their corpses.

Vashke remained in our memories as a good angel, who saved our lives.

Trembling at the Slightest Sound

The days continued to drag on in cold and hunger. Sometimes we would fall asleep under a tree and wake up covered in snow. Like animals we would shake off the snow and continue our search for food or for a new hiding place.

Our last bit of food ran out and we had to go find more. There was a crackling frost and when we left the forest, instead of going over the bridge, we walked on the ice covering the frozen river. When we were half way across, the ice shattered. By a miracle, I was able to pull back and remained lying on the ice. Had I taken one more step forward, I would certainly have fallen into the water. We re-gathered ourselves and crossed over the bridge. Right after the bridge was a small forest called Soshnine. Several Christians lived there. When I knocked on the door of a Christian I knew, his wife came out and, terrified, told us that 15 minutes earlier a sleigh full of Germans had driven by. She was afraid they would come back soon. She pleaded with us to leave and didn't want to speak with us further.

It was no longer possible to go to Lukowa. We were afraid to go back over the same bridge and we had to go an extra three kilometers in deep snow to get to another bridge and return to the forest empty-handed. We went to two peasants who lived in the forest and after lengthy pleading they sold us some potatoes.

The situation in the forest grew more dangerous day to day. We had lost contact with the other Jewish groups that lived there. We longed to hear something about other Jews but we didn't dare leave our spot. Everyone sat silent, hidden, unwilling to come out, trembling at the slightest sound.

After London's Order to the Polish Underground

It was the week of Purim. A boy from Josefow, Yoske Kalechman, suddenly appeared. He knew the forest well and liked to prowl around, looking and poking into things. We were very happy to see him. He told us that we no longer had to be afraid of the Poles. An acquaintance of his from Leshnits had told him that the Polish underground had received an order from (the Polish government in exile in) London not to harm the Jews who had remained in the forest. This meant we could around freely in the forest, no longer under threat from the Polish partisans.

We were very happy to hear this news. Yoske told us where the other Jewish groups were located and on a Sabbath afternoon before Purim, I, Efraim Lumerman and Yitzhak Onfasung from Josefow went to visit another group four kilometers away, near Biedna-Vioska. They were very happy to see us.

Efraim had to say *yahrzeit* [prayer in memory of a deceased person] that day and wanted to do it with a *minyan* [quorum required for communal prayer]. They built a fire and someone recited the *Megillah* [Book of Esther] by heart. Then our hosts served us a Purim meal consisting of cutlets made from horsemeat, from a horse a Russian had brought them and which the Jews had slaughtered. Someone had brought whiskey and people joined in singing a *nigun* [religious melody]. The oddly joyful sound of singing resounded through the forest, allowing us to forget our troubles for a while.

We stayed there overnight and in the morning we prayed communally, read the *Megillah*, ate a meal and warmly said our farewells, taking with us pieces of horsemeat the others had given us. Then we returned to our place in the forest, where our wives and children awaited us.

The days grew warmer. The snow had started to melt and we began to think about making matzah for Passover. We had no flour and decided to go to Lukowa to get some.

It was a Tuesday, the first day of the month of *Nisan* [7th month in the Jewish calendar, March or April], when three of us – I, Efraim Lumerman and Itshe Onfasung – set off for Lukowa. When we were near Balitshovka, Itshe said his leg hurt and that he didn't feel he could make it to Lukowa. He would go to the house of the two peasants who lived nearby and buy something from them. We decided on a place to meet on our way back from Lukowa. It was in the woods, where there was a pile of dry twigs. We would make a fire there and roast a few potatoes.

Efraim and I went to Lukowa; to a peasant we knew who gave us some potatoes and some whole-wheat flour.

My Encounter With My Four Sisters

Our packs on our backs, we left town. Near the Soshnine forest we noticed someone spying on us. We quickly crossed the bridge over the Tanew and entered the forest. After a short rest, we set off for the place where we were supposed to meet up with Itshe Onfasung. As we got near, we saw a fire burning, but hearing voices we drew back. Creeping forward slowly, we heard that the voices were speaking Yiddish. How astonished I was when I saw my four sisters sitting at the fire warming themselves. I was speechless with joy. We kissed and wept without saying a word.

After resting a bit, we continued on our way. My youngest sister Rachel was not able to walk. My sisters had spent the last five months hiding in a pit under a cow barn, and she didn't have the strength to move her legs. I carried her on my back to our meeting place.

My sisters told us how they had paid the peasant woman who owned the barn well to let them hide under there, but she gave them little to eat. The filth from the barn fell onto their heads. Every time there was word that the Germans were coming from Lukowa the peasant began to tremble and made them leave. When it quieted down, they came back.

My sister Feige had a two year-old child who got sick in the pit and died. They weren't allowed to go out and bury the child. The peasant took the child from them and buried him somewhere.

As Passover was approaching, the peasant didn't want to keep them anymore and they had to leave. They went into the forest at night and walked around for 24 hours. They encountered peasants from the village Osuchy who wanted to turn them over to the Germans. The peasants were not moved by their tears, but the gold ring one of my sisters offered them softened their hearts, and they let them go.

They continued to wander until they came to Bolitshovke and met the Christians who knew us, who gave them something to eat. These Christians knew I was nearby, but didn't know exactly where and they told my sisters to wait in the forest until I arrived.

They had been wandering in the forest for seven days, hungry, despairing, frozen and exhausted. The Christians let my sisters know when Itshe Onfasung entered Balitshovke and he led them to the designated meeting place, built a fire for them, and waited for our arrival.

Rachel, the youngest sister, slowly revived and was able to move her legs. The other sisters also felt better in the forest, freed from the darkness and fear of their hiding place. They all stayed with us in the forest and survived the war. Rachel lives in Haifa, on Mount Carmel. Her husband Tstetshik is a major in the Israeli army. The other sisters live in Australia and Bolivia.

Before Passover, a boy, Baruch Shlicher, the son of Hershele Shlicher from Josefow, came to us in the forest and said that he had sifted flour, which he would give us in exchange for our whole-wheat flour and we would be able to make matzo from the finer flour. He also told us, secretly, that Jews from the ghetto would be coming to the forest.

We cut up a large block of wood and spread it with a dishtowel, and we fashioned a fork and rolling pin from a freshly cut sapling. We made a big fire and baked matzo on the hot ashes. My family received 24 matzos that Passover.

The Sabbath before Passover we went to the Jews living near Biedna-Vioska, who directed us to a Christian they knew in the small village Glakhes, who gave us potatoes. We stayed overnight with the Jews in Biedna-Vioska. In the morning Baruch Shlicher told us that the Jews from the ghetto would be arriving soon. And in fact there soon appeared 15 men and a girl from the ghetto in the town of Yavoriv in Galicia. We greeted them joyfully. They had brought with them a machine gun and several rifles and revolvers.

The newly arrived Jews looked at us, surprised by our appearance after living in the forest for half a year -- tattered, barely clothed, heavily bearded, our faces blackened by the smoke of the fires where we warmed ourselves. They still looked like respectable people and were well dressed. Among them was a lawyer named Forst, from Sudova Vyshnya, near Lviv.

They told us how they had gotten here. In the Yavoriv ghetto there was a Jew from Zamch, a village not far from our forest. His name was Dovid Diamant. A Christian from Zamch would bring him food. The Christian told him that Jews had been hiding in the forest all winter. Dovid Diamant conferred with a group of 15 other Jews and they asked the Christian to lead them to the forest. When they got there, the Christian connected them to a peasant from whom we used to get food.

The First Seder – with Matzo and the Four Cups

We parted warmly and returned to our wives and children. The next day, Monday evening, we celebrated the first Seder. We lit a fire and spread a white cloth on the wooden board we had made. For the ceremony of drinking the four cups (of wine), we cooked red beets with sugar and filtered the liquid through a piece of white linen. We did not sing when we recited the *Hallel* [prayer of praise and thanks to God]. Unable to hold back our tears, we wept.

After the Seder, when we were getting ready to go to sleep we heard a strange cry in the woods. Not far away people were travelling on foot and in wagons and we heard the sounds of their wheels and of human voices. We extinguished the fire and concealed ourselves. In the morning we gathered our belongings and moved to a new place in the forest, plot #212.

After settling into our new location, we went to pray with the Jews who had come from the ghetto. After praying we sat with them a while and listened to their account of life in the ghetto, about how the Germans kept bringing in Polish Jews from other towns, and murdered people every day.

In the midst of our conversation there appeared, as if arising out of the earth, several Russian partisans with their commander Mishke Tatar. They had learned of the arrival of new Jews from the ghetto and had heard that they had brought weapons with them. Mishke already knew that they had a machine gun and he directed them to display it. He regarded it with satisfaction and immediately proposed to exchange two rifles for the machine gun. Everyone had an opinion about this ploy. But we had to remain silent. Mishke was the ruler of the forest.

At that moment, we heard the sound of German airplanes flying over the forest. We all looked up at the sky. Mishke Tatar, who was bending over the machine gun, raised his head and cursed in Russian, "Why are you flying over our territory?" and at the same time, he shot and hit an airplane, which continued to fly for a few minutes, and then fell.

We were struck by fear that the Germans would take revenge and attack the forest, but several days passed and nothing happened. So we went again to get potatoes from the peasant in Glakhes.

When we returned at dawn the next day, we heard shooting. The Germans and the partisans were fighting. Three of the newly arrived Jews from the ghetto were killed. After a short battle, the Germans left the forest and we got back safely to our place.

The Forest is Burning

The third day of *hal hamoed* [intermediate, non-sacred days of Passover] we noticed the forest was burning. Peasants came running from the villages, accompanied by police, and immediately began to put out the fire. We found ourselves between two perils. On one side, the fire threatened our place. On the other side, we feared that the police would spot us. We went deeper into the heart of the forest and lay down among the trees. It took two days to extinguish the fire, which had burned a thousand hectares of forest.

Passover was over and the days got warmer. We began to think about making weapons that would make it easier for us to go out to buy food. Again I went to visit the miller in Lukowa who was now my Liberating Angel. I got 1500 *zlotys* from him. Then we went to a Christian we knew who promised to make us three guns and told us to return the next week to pick them up.

When we came the next week he led us into a field and from a hiding place there he retrieved three rifles and some ammunition, and told us we had to pay 350 *zlotys* for each rifle.

When I lifted the rifle to my shoulder for the first time I felt the fear that had dominated our lives had lifted. I didn't yet know how to shoot; I had never been in the military. Still, I felt safer and freer. My friend was more skilled at handling a rifle and he felt as if he had received the most valuable gift. We felt new strength coursing through our blood. Until now we had been afraid of even the puniest Christian, who could terrorize us and take us to the Germans. The mere thought that we had weapons eliminated that fear. We no longer felt threatened by civilians.

Now, when we went to get food, we would set out with the newly arrived Jews from the ghetto, who also had guns. When we entered a village, we would station a lookout and fearlessly go to visit the peasants, whom we told to provide us with a horse and wagon, with which we used to transport food to the forest. We didn't take anything from poor peasants who themselves had little to eat. Pretending to be partisans, we spoke Russian. We always returned the horse and wagon to their owner, telling him in advance where to wait for them.

These sorties were very dangerous and we tried as much as possible to use single people instead of people who had families to care for.

New Partisans

In May of 1943, we again heard new voices in the forest. We understood that a larger group of partisans had arrived and at dawn we silently slipped up to the place from which the noise was coming. We heard people speaking Russian and Polish and when it got lighter we came over and spoke with them. Among them were two Jewish boys and a Jewish woman with her two children. The leader of the group, who was named Gzhegozh, had a small beard. He was very friendly and warm to us. The partisans had plenty of food and gave us some.

Several days later they moved to another plot in the forest and would come visit us occasionally. After the war we learned that Gzhegozh was a Jew who had to pretend to be a Pole when he was with the partisans.

Once, when I came to Bolishovke, a Christian I knew gave me a letter written in Yiddish from Moshe-Wolf from Babitsh, which had been passed on by my friend Kolye the miller. In the letter he asked me to let Kolye know when we would next visit him and Moshe-Wolf would meet me there to discuss how he could get to the forest. I went directly to Lukowa and agreed with the miller to come on Sunday night of the next week.

I got there exactly on time and waited until after midnight for the mill workers to leave. When I entered the mill I saw Moshe-Wolf chatting with the miller. He embraced and kissed me. It took a long time before he was able to speak. Moshe-Wolf hadn't seen a single Jew for seven months. He had hidden in a stable with his 9 year-old son and could no longer stand to live in the dark and in constant fear. By chance he had learned that I was in the forest and asked the miller to get in touch with me about taking him to the forest.

Moshe-Wolf's sister-in-law Sara was living near Hrubieszow under an assumed Aryan identity. She had obtained false Aryan identity papers. She didn't look Jewish and spoke Ukrainian extremely well. She had brought him the news from Hrubieszow that his wife had been in hiding with a Christian but when she went into the street one day someone recognized her and turned her over to the Germans, who shot her.

We agreed that I would wait for him on Wednesday night at the meadow outside Lukowa. He would be with his son and his sister-in-law who preferred hiding in the forest to relying on her Aryan papers and living in constant fear that her Jewish identity would be discovered.

I arrived on time at the designated spot and sat down to wait. A long time passed and afraid to be seen on the open meadow, I went into the tall grain field to wait. The hours dragged on and I had begun to fear for them. I had already thought of giving up when I saw three figures in the distance, moving carefully toward the designated meeting place. These were in fact Moshe-Wolf and his son and sister-in-law. They excused themselves, explaining that the peasants had been moving about in the village and it had been dangerous to go out.

Moshe-Wolf and his son felt good in the forest. In contrast, his sister-in-law decided after several days to return to her job and suggested that the boy come with her; she would find work for him as a shepherd. After long deliberation Moshe-Wolf agreed. The two of them did in fact survive the war. Sara lives in Detroit and Moshe-Wolf's son lives in Israel in Kibbutz Gan Shmuel, where I attended his wedding.

Moshe-Wolf remained with us in the forest. But several weeks after Shevuot we heard the Germans were getting ready to attack the Jews in the forest. We became very depressed. It was hard to flee with children and we didn't know where to flee. Moshe-Wolf asked me to lead him out of the woods so he could return to Babitsh to the Christian who had hid him earlier. My pleas that he stay with us were in vain. We said our farewells and he left the forest along with three Jews from the Yavoriv ghetto. They didn't get far before they encountered Germans, who shot them. This also happened to Volvish Fefer, Simkhe's son from Lukowa, who fled to the Zamach forest with his wife and two children. On the way, German bullets killed them all

We stayed in the forest, moving to another spot called Sukhi Tshop, named after a tree found there that had a dry top. The threatened attack did not take place. Rather, the Germans seized Poles from Lukowa and surrounding villages and sent them to work in Germany. Many Poles harnessed their horses, loaded their wagons with food, took along their cows, and went into the forests.

One Friday, when we emerged from the dense bushes, we saw the Poles, our neighbors, settled into the forest. We had our rifles on our shoulders, eliciting respect from the Poles, who were, incidentally, happy to see us. They told us about the suffering inflicted on them by the Germans.

The Poles found living in the forest too difficult and they envied us for having already gotten used to it. Our situation at that time was very difficult. The surrounding villages were full of Germans and we couldn't leave the forest to get food. The Polish peasants decided to go back to their villages and turn themselves in to the Germans. They left us some potatoes. They did in fact return to Lukowa and were sent to Germany. Ukrainians settled in their houses. Among the few Poles who remained was my friend the miller, Kolye.

Things worsened by the day, and our hunger became more terrible. Once, we tried to leave the forest but when we came to the river Studzienica, we saw Germans bathing there, and then go into the forest to rest. We retreated into the thick shrubbery. There wasn't anything to cook and we were also afraid to light a fire.

One Sabbath day we heard that the Germans were planning an attack in the forest. We had no other choice but to go deeper into the forest. We gathered our belongings and went three kilometers deeper and hid our things among the white birches and thick shrubbery and sat listening for every sound.

We were exhausted by hunger and one of us went out in the afternoon to the meadow, where he caught a young cow that he brought into the forest. We slaughtered it and at night made a fire, cooked it and had something to eat. But in the morning a woman named Erni came to me and said she had heard shouting not far from the forest. I woke up Efraim Lemerman and told him that the shouting was suspicious and it seemed to be an attack. He wanted to keep sleeping and he said that it was probably shepherds who pastured their cows in the forest who were making the noise.

I tried to calm myself but the voices were growing louder and closer. Impelled by the threat of danger we went deeper into the shrubbery, screened further by freshly harvested saplings. This was Sunday, 2 *Tammuz* 5703 [July 5, 1943]. Lying hidden in the bushes I saw an armed German standing two meters away. I was clutching a rifle in my hands, ready to shoot but I realized that my shot would alarm other Germans who were certainly nearby and that would be the end.

Suddenly I heard someone shout, "Is there a fire?" and someone responded, "No," and the Germans left. Then I realized the meaning of that exchange. A fire was for them a sign that people were living there and it was necessary to search for them. It was a miracle that I had managed to conceal the place where we had made a fire the night before.

It was already late in the afternoon. We were very hungry and Efraim crept out of his hiding place and said that the Germans had left and we could now prepare food. My wife agreed with him. I felt an odd unease thinking the Germans could return and I strongly insisted that we should all remain where we were. Within 10 minutes we heard the footfalls of Germans passing by. We heard an officer order the men to go another kilometer and then to march out of the forest.

The Newborn Child

We left our hiding place at sunset and ate the meat left over from the night before.

The next day, the people who had run away during the raid and had dispersed in various directions began to return. Two people did not return – Miriam-Rachel Wolf from Lukowa and a woman named Sara from Borvitsh.

It was almost impossible to go to the villages to get a bit of food. Ukrainians had settled into the homes of the Poles who had been driven out, and they were ready to turn over to the Germans any Jew they encountered or to kill them themselves. So we had to go out at night into the fields, where new potatoes were already ready, and that sustained us.

Efraim Lumerman's pregnant wife began to go into labor. The news spread quickly among the Jews in the forest and everyone was deeply apprehensive. What would happen? Where could they find a midwife?

Then there appeared one of the newly arrived Jews who had come to the forest after the German raid and he reassured us, revealing his secret, that he was a doctor specializing in childbirth. He went to the woman, who was writhing in labor, and delivered the child, a daughter. A new person had come into the world, fated to endure a life of suffering in the forest. And yet people rejoiced and were filled with gratitude for the doctor, who had arrived as if sent from heaven.

Several weeks went by. The days were summery and the forest was quiet. Blackberries and mushrooms appeared, which helped to make life easier, as we didn't have to leave the forest as frequently. The newborn child was thriving.

Gradually we got used to life in the forest, and it began to seem normal. We forgot about our former lives and the comforts that once seemed indispensable to living a normal life.

About 150 new partisans appeared, who called themselves "*Chapayovtses*," [probably in honor of Vasil Ivanovich Chapayev, a celebrated Red Army commander during the Russian Civil War] and they merged with Gzshogozh's group. They also took in the few Jewish groups that didn't include women and children.

The forest got livelier every day. The partisans went out on diversionary missions, cut down telephone poles all along the rail line, and halted the German troop transports. On the eve of *Tisha b'Av* the partisans left the forest with the goal of attacking the ammunition factory in Stalove-Vole. When they left the forest, they ran into a Polish partisan group from the A.K. Their leader was the officer Penkherski, who had led the *aktsie* in Lukowa a year earlier, in which 62 Jews were killed. The Russian and Jewish partisans now shot him.

When we heard the news we rejoiced. But at the same time, we were overcome by fear that the A.K. would take revenge. We were now alone in the forest so we had to move to a new hiding place.

The partisans marched through the fields on the way to the ammunition factory, engaging on the way in battles with the Germans, attacking a truck and shooting 18 German soldiers and officers inside. They never carried out the attack on the ammunition factory, but in the course of the march, which lasted an entire month, they killed about 200 Germans. Five of the partisans were killed.

When they returned to us in the forest, the Jewish partisans shared their experiences in battle with us. The doctor from Krakow had participated in the march, and on the way he discarded a valise full of medications, which was too heavy for him to carry. When the commander of the partisans heard about this, he threatened to shoot the doctor. Through strenuous pleading we were barely able to get commander to spare his life.

The doctor, along with Avigdor, the boy from Josefow, left the partisan group in the forest without permission and came to us. I tried to convince the doctor that this was the wrong thing to do, but he got angry and continued to hide in the forest.

The partisans began to establish order in the forest and all the Jews had to request permission to remain in their places. The doctor and Avigdor got sick of constantly hiding and they decided to present themselves to the partisan commander. They were accompanied by Baruch Shlicher and Beker, a Jew from the Poznan region who knew the commander and wanted to plead with him on behalf of the doctor and Avigdor. But as soon as they arrived at the partisans, all four of them were shot.

High Holy Day Prayers

The partisans divided into two groups. One went to the Bug River; the other stayed in the forest.

On the first day of Rosh Hashanah the Jews gathered at our place, laid out their weapons, set up a lookout and prayed. There were about 40 people and only one prayer shawl and one Rosh Hashanah prayer book. We prayed with bitterness in our hearts and wished each other a good year. We so deeply hoped that we would survive all our troubles and be completely free in the coming year.

Yom Kippur was approaching. We didn't have a Yom Kippur prayer book but I knew *Kol Nidre* by heart and wrote it out on a piece of paper. We made candles and set them up on a little pile of sand which we dug up from the well; around them we set out our weapons. When we began to pray, it looked as if the young forest with its small trees was weeping with us and we believed that our prayers would in the end be heard in heaven.

The next day we also prayed all day. The mood at the *Neilah* prayers [closing prayers] was one of dread. It was completely dark in the forest when we scattered to our different places, made fires and ate the previously prepared food. We felt a lightness in our hearts. Someone brought some whiskey and for a while we forgot we were in the forest, joined in singing a *nigun*, and the woods echoed with faith and belief.

We continued to live in constant fear that our hiding place would become too widely known among outsiders and right after Yom Kippur we decided to move to another place. It was four kilometers further on, near the river that was called Studzienica. Near the river bank, we built shelters from twigs, making sure that the rain could not penetrate. The winds were already heralding the coming winter.

The next day we received a visit from some Jews from Tarnogrod and Rozaniec, who had been hiding in the Rozaniec forest 20 kilometers from us. Having heard that Jews were living here, they came to meet us. Among them was my cousin Dovid Entner. His wife and four children had been killed and he was alone. Also among them were Hersh Welts, Eliezer Wertman, Temi Trinker, Chaim Lipiner, Chaim Adler, Malka Herbstman and Eliezer Lumerman. They settled in near us and things became a bit friendlier, a bit more relaxed. We had already heard the news about the German defeat at Stalingrad. ?*Sukkot* arrived. We went to pray with a group of Jews who were hiding in the forest outside Sosiets. They were in a hopeful mood. On Simchat Torah we even let loose, had some whiskey and sang *Hasidic* melodies.

We started to get ready for winter. We brought in potatoes and hid them in a pit so that they wouldn't freeze. There was the prospect that we wouldn't need to leave the forest in search of food.

Our second Hanukkah was easier. We lit candles in holders made of potatoes with holes carved in them and wicks made of cotton. Right after Hanukkah, Russian soldiers drove up with two large barrels of whiskey. The Russians began drinking and also shared some whiskey with us. Among the partisans was a Frenchman who liked to visit us. When he got hold of the whiskey, he drank so much he died. The Poles put out a false accusation that we had poisoned him. By a miracle, the Russians testified that on the day of his death he had not been with us, but had been with them the entire time.

The false accusation again convinced us that the Poles' hostility to us was great. For several days we were on high alert for an attack. Luckily, the incident ended peaceably and we stayed in the same place about three months. But we couldn't stay there longer than that and moved to plot #20.

Russian Partisans Bring Jews to Us

When we had already settled in, the Russian partisans brought to us a woman who had been hiding the entire time with peasants. But when she found out that there were Jews in the forest, she came out of hiding and went to the forest, where she encountered the Russian partisans and they brought her to us. This woman, Ratse, was from Kaminke, near Lviv. She had been certain that there were no Jews left in all of Poland and she was very happy to find us. Several days later the Russians brought another Jew, Berger, who had also been hiding with Christians and having learned that Jews were living in the forest, came to find us. Berger lives now in Nahalat Ganim [Israel].

Several days later some Poles brought us a girl with a gunshot wound in her leg. This girl had jumped from a train taking Jews to Belzec, and the Germans had shot and wounded her. They thought she was dead and left her lying in a field, where the Poles found her and recognized her as a Jew. She pleaded with them to shoot her. She had no strength left. But she had happened upon Poles with kind hearts who brought her to a hospital, under the pretense that she was Christian. She stayed in the hospital a long time until they became suspicious and began to investigate where she was from and who she was. The Poles who had brought her there had continued to follow her fate and learning of the investigation, quickly snuck her out of the hospital and hid her in their home. Later they took her to the forest.

A short time later the Russians dropped off troops in the forest and at the same time took wounded partisans away in an airplane to Russia; they also took the wounded girl with them. After the war, having recovered from her wound, she returned to Poland. She lives now in Bat Yam in Israel with her husband and two children.

At the beginning of 1944 the partisans began a period of intensive activity. On February 15, 1944, Kolpakchi's army, [a Soviet field army led by Vadimir Yakovlevich Kolpakchi], numbering 5000 men, arrived. They were armed with cannons and various other kinds of weapons. They settled in the villages around our forest and the Germans in the nearby towns began fleeing in great panic.

Friendly Visits

The partisans would often pay us friendly visits. Among them were two Jews from Lutsk who sometimes brought us whiskey, joined us in a drink and encouraged and consoled us, assuring us that we would survive the war.

Those days we felt free and cheerful. We felt as if we were already rid of the Germans, until one Friday at 8 A.M., the partisan army suddenly withdrew, taking with them some of the partisans who had been in the forest before their arrival. At 10 A.M. German airplanes began bombing the villages, destroying and burning the peasant huts, but the partisans were no longer there.

Panic broke out among the partisans who remained in the forest. They said that the Germans would soon attack. The Jews who did not have families fled the forest, but those of with small children could not go. The snow was too deep. We had to rely on a miracle. We wiped away our tracks on the paths and roads and increased our watch patrol day and night.

Our fear continued for ten days. Once, when I and my cousin Dovid Entner were keeping watch, we heard a sleigh passing by, as well as human voices. Frightened, we hid behind a tree, took up our rifles and got ready to defend ourselves. But when the sleigh drove past, we recognized the occupants – a Jewish girl who was sitting next to a Pole whom we knew from the forest. They were very glad to see us, and told us that the partisans were returning to the forest. We were very relieved.

Purim arrived. The Jews in the surrounding hiding places gathered at our group's place and someone recited the Megillah by heart. By this time we felt like long established residents of the forest. For one and a half years we had been wandering from one place to another, enduring snow and freezing cold. Oddly, this entire time, there had not been a single case of a child catching a cold.

The news from the front was cheering. The cold let up. They resumed dropping off Russian troops. Once, we were frightened by an airplane circling overhead. We could clearly see that it was German and we ran and hid in the bushes, but luckily they hadn't seen us.

At night we went back to our places but the next day we moved to another location, plot #213, where we had once already stayed.

Before Passover we left the forest to get flour and began baking matzo. We prepared apple wine for the four cups, and we celebrated this Passover in a much better mood than the year before. About 30 people attended the Seder.

On the second day of Passover two commanders of the Russian partisans rode up on horseback and spent several hours with us, comforting us and giving us hope that the war would soon be over. But an hour and half after they left we heard heavy shooting nearby. We grabbed our children and ran deeper into the forest.

The shooting lasted two hours. When it grew quiet, we learned that several hundred Germans had invaded the forest and attacked the Russian partisans. There was a bloody battle and the Germans withdrew, leaving behind several dead.

The partisan army grew stronger by the day, numbering several thousand, and that made us feel safer and more free.

The week of *Shavuot* we ordered bread from a peasant in Lukowa and when we went to pick it up, a Christian came running, shouting that we should run away immediately because a large group of Germans was approaching. Running through the fields we heard the loud noise made by the German army. The next day we found out that the forest was surrounded by German soldiers. A few days later heavy fighting broke out. German airplanes bombed the forest for two weeks, until the Germans withdrew and the partisans regained control.

The [Russian] troops who were parachuted in made things lively. Their parachutes were made of good silk fabric that we could use to make clothes. The Russians asked for whiskey in exchange. We went around the villages buying up whiskey and traded it for the parachute fabric.

The Peasants Begin to Treat Us with Respect

On June 15 we heard that another group of Germans was coming to attack the forest. The people in the bunker where Efraim Lumerman was living with his 11-month-old child were very fearful because the child kept crying. So, they wrapped her in shawls and cloths until she stopped crying and when they unwrapped her, they found that she had suffocated to death.

A relentless battle raged overhead. There was constant roar and thunder of various weapons. When night fell it grew quiet. But we could hear the Germans speaking quite near to us in the forest. The next day it again thundered. Suddenly the branch that obscured the entrance to our bunker lifted and there entered a man who looked frightened to death, murmuring a prayer to the Virgin Mary. This was a Pole, a member of the A.K. who had fled the fighting. He had wanted to hide in the tree that concealed our bunker, but when he lifted up the branch, he fell into the bunker.

We told him we were partisans. He was starving and begged for a bit of bread. Although we had very little, we gave him some.

Finally, the Germans left the forest. When we emerged into the sunshine the Pole recognized us as Jews and was grateful to us for saving his life. He said his farewells and we went further into the forest, seeking more detailed information. We met other Jews who like us had left their bunkers. Nothing had happened to the Jews in hiding. But many Poles who hadn't wanted to join with the Russian partisans were killed. Their corpses were everywhere. As many as a thousand had been murdered.

The Germans had in fact left the entire area and we resumed our trips to Lukowa to get something to eat. The peasants regarded us with respect. They realized that the Germans were suffering defeats and they change the way they treated us, providing us with food and drink.

The Russian partisans who in the recent battles had withdrawn to other forests started to return and each day brought fresh news. The partisans had radio equipment and we heard news from Moscow about how the Soviet army was seizing one town after another. But one day we heard loud cannon fire. We again prepared a new bunker and concealed it well. The shooting lasted three days and then suddenly stopped.

On a Friday evening when we were already asleep, airplanes began to fly over the forest in the hundreds and thousands all night. It didn't get quiet until the morning, when we learned that Lubaczow, just 25 kilometers away, was already in Soviet hands. We went to pray in a joyful mood at forest plot #26 where all the Jews gathered.

Suddenly a peasant from the village Boroviets came running and told us that the Russians were already here and we were free. Our joy was boundless. People embraced, kissed and wept. But in the midst of this great joy we felt our loneliness. We could leave the forest, but where and to whom could we go? All of our family and friends were dead.

Until now we had lived in such a frenzied effort to escape death that we hadn't felt pain and sorrow for those who had been killed. Now our wounds opened and began to bleed. On the way back to our place I fainted. When I came to, I felt a terrible weakness. I could not move and lay there about two hours. When I felt a bit better, the Russian army was already marching through the forest. I stood up and greeted them. They were very friendly and advised us to leave the forest as soon as possible, because it was possible that the German divisions that had not managed to withdraw were hiding in the forest and could attack us.

Back to Lukowa

It was Saturday, the second day of the month of Av, 5704 [July 22,1944]. We were still sleeping in the forest and the next morning I, along with another Jew, went to my house in Lukowa. A Christian was living there and I demanded that he leave immediately. We rented a wagon and drove back to the forest, loaded the several packs and pots that we had, settled the women and children in the wagon and drove out of the forest.

The entire time that we were driving through the forest we still had the old feeling that we were being pursued, a feeling that had permeated our blood from our long stay there. We constantly looked around as frightened as wild animals, despite the fact that we were armed.

At the beginning of our stay in the forest, we had numbered 300 Jews. When we left, there were no more than 75. All the others had been killed.

Our Christian neighbors visited us, looking at us as if we had risen from our graves. They expressed pity for us, but we knew that many of them would have been glad if we hadn't returned.

For the first time in two years we slept in a house under a roof. We didn't have beds so we slept on the floor and oddly it felt cramped and stuffy inside. We opened the windows to get some air but the stuffiness continued to oppress us and the night was difficult.

The next day Christians from the nearby villages began to come to visit. They wanted to see how we looked – tattered, shoeless, half-naked. But when they saw our weapons hanging on the wall, they showed their respect and fear.

I went to see my friendly miller Kolye, who owed me money and who had supported me all this time. He received me warmly, gave me a little money and 100 kilos of rye flour. I and Efraim Lumerman started to make whiskey and sell it to the peasants, making a living this way.

Rescuing Parchment Sheets to Make a Torah Scroll

The month of *Elul* was approaching and we began to seek out a shofar and a Torah scroll for the High Holy Days. Passing through the village of Mashtshiniets I met a Jewish woman with two children who had hidden with Christians and she told me that there were a shofar and Torah scroll in the attic of her house. We went straight there and found them, but the scroll was missing the first two of its parchment sheets.

I drove to Tarnogrod where several Jewish survivors were living. We searched the vacant houses of the murdered Jews and found several parchment sheets. I took them to Lukowa where we sewed the sheets together and produced a complete Torah scroll.

In the house of a Lukowa peasant I found the Torah ark from our *besmedresh* [house of study also used for worship]. He immediately handed it over and we began to prepare for the Holy Days.

On the day before Rosh Hashanah we went to the mass grave and wept copiously. We resolved to transport all the corpses to the cemetery in Tarnogrod. This entailed various formalities. We had to obtain certification from a doctor and a permit from the local authorities.

On Rosh Hashanah, the Jews of Tarnogrod and Bilgoraj, lacking enough Jews in their respective towns to constitute a *minyan*, gathered together in Lukowa. We prayed together in my house for the High Holy Days and for *Sukkot* as well. We celebrated *Simchat Torah* with singing and dancing but we remembered everything we had gone through and all of our near ones who had not lived to see this holiday.

A short time later soldiers of the A.K. Polish underground army surrounded my house and searched it. I wasn't home at the time. It turned out they were looking for Efraim Lumerman, whom they suspected had informed on a pharmacist who was connected to the Polish underground. The pharmacist's son, a member of the A.K., had instigated this action against Lumerman.

Luckily, Efraim Lumerman was not in the house. When we came back together from the villages, we shuddered to hear what had happened. Efraim immediately fled and hid. The next day he and his family went to Tarnogrod, where the number of Jews had grown.

Gradually, other Jews from Lukowa also went to Tarnogrod and I remained alone. It was hard for me to abandon my own house. But I had no choice. I didn't want to be the only Jew in town and I decided to go to Tarnogrod. The Christian who had lived in my house while I was in hiding came back.

In Tarnogrod I moved into a house that had once belonged to Manish Shtatfeld. It was near the house of the Tarnogrod rabbi and the *besmedresh*. I collected all the religious books that were left behind in the attics of vacant Jewish houses, loaded them in a large truck and brought them to my home.

Like many other Jews I set up a shop and began doing business. I made a living but I was very sad. When Sabbath came we thought of the hundreds of thousands of Jews who used to stream into the synagogues and *besmedreshim*. Now, everything had withered away.

The way to the *besmedresh* was overgrown with grass. The windows had been knocked out and the doors broken and it seemed as if the dead were hovering in the air. There I was, singing at the Sabbath afternoon meal the same songs with the same melodies that used to come from the rabbi's window. But all around it was dark, dead. Terror seeped into my bones and the melody ceased. I couldn't contain the tears that tore through me.

During the week, I was increasingly absorbed in work. The winter passed and Passover arrived. Again the joy of observing the Seder as free people was mixed with grief over the murdered Jews.

A Jew from the town of Lezajsk, 20 kilometers away, arrived and told us that at night Poles had surrounded a house in which several Jewish families lived. They tried to break in but all the doors were hammered shut, so they threw in explosives, destroyed the house and killed several people. Panic broke out among the Jews in town and they all went to Lublin.

The panic spread to Tarnogrod, where 30 Jewish families were living, and many of them decided to also go to Lublin. Those remaining became increasingly anxious. There was a feeling that something was about to happen. On May 3, 1945, after midnight, we heard a bang on the window and the panes shattered. Several armed bandits broke in and began looting. Pointing their guns at me they demanded money and took my last 2000 *zlotys*. One of them hit me over the head with an axe and I was knocked unconscious. The bandits revived me and again demanded money. I appealed to their consciences, telling them everything I went through hiding in the forest. The children cried, my wife appealed to them, but instead of answering her, they began to beat her. One of them hit her near her eye and she fell down, covered in blood.

Finally, they took everything from the house and fired a shot in my direction. The bullet flew past my ear and as he left the leader told me I should warn the other Jews that we should all leave Tarnogrod or they would kill us all. They also warned us not to move from our places or leave the house until morning.

Morning came and fear still hovered in our emptied-out house. The bandits had taken all our household goods and clothing. I was wearing only underwear and had nothing to put on to go outside. Then I remembered that I had hidden a sack with some items in the attic and I soon found some pants there.

I got dressed and went out into the street. I told the first Jews I encountered what had happened that night and we started to think about leaving Tarnogrod. Many were opposed because we knew that Polish partisans from the underground were in the forest outside Bilgoraj and they attacked Jews who drove by. We were in despair. To leave would be to risk death from the Polish partisans. To stay where we were would expose us to attack in our houses in the middle of the night.

The day passed in desperate indecision. When night fell we were afraid to stay in our homes and went to sleep elsewhere. Quietly we locked up our houses and went to the abandoned ruined building near the bathhouse and slept on the ground. At dawn we returned to our houses, slinking along the walls so no one would notice we hadn't spent the night there. We did this for several nights. Then we were afraid someone had seen us in the abandoned house and we switched to Naftali Wakslicht's half-ruined vacant house and slept in the attic there.

My cousin Dovid Entner was also living in Tarnogrod. Before the war he had lived in Rozaniec and then with me in the forest. Now he was all alone; his wife and children had been killed. One day he went back to Rozaniec to see what had happened to his property. When he got there some Poles attacked him. He escaped them briefly but the bandits pursued him, caught him and shot him.

That Tuesday, the third day of Sivan 5705 [May 15, 1945], several Christians came to my house and told me that Dovid Entner's body was lying outside of town. I got together with several other Jews and we went to the location and took the corpse to the Tarnogrod cemetery.

Newly Dug Graves

The murder produced a sense of urgency among the Jews. After emerging alive from five years of Nazi persecutions and murders we were once again in peril of being killed by our own neighbors. The desire to flee the town grew constantly stronger.

After *Shavuot*, a truck from Lublin came to Tarnogrod to sell eggs and we took the opportunity to get a ride to Lublin. There we rented an apartment at #21 Lubartowska Street and began to look into how to make a living. With the help of friends and acquaintances I began to deal in clothing. I travelled to Katowice and Wroclaw where there were a lot of Germans and they sold what they had stolen during the war.

Our material circumstances were satisfactory but we were still oppressed by fear. Every day there was news about the murder of Jews on the road. A Jew was thrown out of the window of the train to Prashnik. A Jew who had gone to Belzec to sell his belongings was shot. Outside of Lublin a Jewish soldier was shot.

Many freshly dug graves appeared in the Lublin cemetery. They were all for people who had survived the war in bunkers and forests who faced death the entire time and emerged alive. Now they were being killed by Poles in whom they had trusted, thinking that they too rejoiced in having rid themselves of a shared enemy, the Germans.

One night, when we were all asleep, there came a knock on the door. When I asked who it was, there was no answer, but the knocking grew louder. I opened the window and shouted into the street to summon the police. I refused to open the door and the people at the door threatened to shoot into the house. They then broke open the door; it was the police.

One police officer began to question me as to why I had been shouting. Meanwhile the other officer went into the next room and opened the window and got ready to throw my merchandise out the window. When I saw that, I began shouting and the police demanded that I show them a receipt for the merchandise. Of course, I had no such accounts. But I categorically opposed their demands. They placed a seal on the door to the room with the merchandise and left.

The next morning I went to the commissariat and demanded they unseal the door. The duty officer denied responsibility saying it wasn't he who had issued the order. I waited and when it became clear that no one else was coming, I myself tore off the seal, removed the merchandise and went to sell it in the market place.

Some time later a libelous rumor circulated in Lublin, that Jews had killed a Christian child. The child was supposed to have lived at #18 Lubartowska Street and there were Christians who said that they had seen traces of the child's blood there. Groups of frenzied Christians began to gather, getting ready for a pogrom. The threat of murder was again in the air. Jews were afraid to go outside and locked themselves in.

At the time, there were Jews who held high-level positions in the army as well as in the secret police. When they were alerted to the danger confronting the Jews in town they quickly organized the military forces, which energetically began to repel the inflamed mobs. Some of the agitators were arrested and this quieted the angry mood of the Christians.

But this incident forced the survivors to consider their future fate. It became clear that there was no longer a place for Jews on Polish soil, soaked with Jewish blood.

Note from the editors [in the original]:

Avrom Haler lives in Israel and is an active member in the Council of the Tarnogrod Landsmanshaft [organization of townspeople].

Translator's footnote:

1. The implication is that the gravestones were being removed for construction of the road.

[Pages 464-465]

Annihilation and the Struggle for Life

Sender Spiegler

Translated by Tina Lunson

Each word that is written about the dreadful destruction that befell our people, I swallow with great sorrow, and I think that every surviving Jew must from time to time read through a book that tells about the life in the ghetto. We are forbidden to forget the great destruction that has no comparison in the history of human kind.

One must learn about the destruction not only of one's own *shtetl* [small village], but also of all the towns and villages in Poland. The memorial books and everything in which the murderous Jewish annihilation is spoken of are our *keyver oves* [graves of our ancestors] because there are no graves for our nearest and dearest with whose ashes the fields around the Hitleristic death camps were fertilized.

This memorial book for our *shtetl* was written by us alone. Each surviving Tarnogrod Jew brings a brick to the construction's account, to the gravestone to the memory of our martyrs. We tell about the life of our grandfathers and fathers, about the heroic struggle that they conducted for life and about their martyrs' deaths. We tell about the persecutions that were done both by the Germans and by the Ukrainians and Poles. We also tell about each noble act that was performed by the righteous of the nations, the individual Poles who risked their own lives and brought help to the pursued, tormented and persecuted Jews. There were such exceptional people everywhere and they were also in Tarnogrod and in the surrounding *shtetlekh* [villages].

We tell about the good-heartedness of our dear Tarnogrod Jews, who lived side by side for decades, became bound together as can only happen with good and sincere souls.

Tarnogrod Jews had an insight into the best Jewish character, for charity and for acts of loving kindness. In 1939, when the Hitler troops attacked Poland, thousands of refugees streamed through our town and all were taken in with open arms. A special committee was formed whose assignment it was to see that no refugee went hungry. Even the poorest people took their bread and shared it to the last bite. No refugee was left without a place to sleep at night.

In a far-off Russian town where I lived with several other Jews, there came to us some Jews who had been freed from a camp in Siberia. When we got to talking and they realized that I was from Tarnogrod, two of the Jews stood up and came over to me and greeted me with the greatest warmth.

"We will never forget," they said to the whole gathering, "the warm hearts of the Tarnogrod Jews, the goodness they showed us when we were fleeing the Hitler hell."

In their memories was etched the name of Yeshaya Leib Walfish in whose home they stayed four nights, not considering that they were not the only ones. Many others spent the nights there too and to everyone he showed the same hospitality and brotherly love.

These liberated Jews related that throughout their entire wandering they had not found such good-heartedness as they had been shown by the Tarnogrod Jews.

I later learned several facts from the Tarnogrod Jews who had met people in far-off Siberia who considered it an honor to speak with Tarnogrod Jews because they had not forgotten their touching impression of our town.

Such was the character of the Tarnogrod Jew. And we will also teach that spirit to our children, with reverence and love for those martyrs, for whom we bow our heads in deep and ongoing sadness.

[Page 466]

Yosef Fink

In Memory of My Parents

Yosef Fink

Translated by Chesky Wertman

**Dedicated to Joseph Fink Z"L who helped
me discover the treasures of Tarnogrod**

I see you, Tatte
In the early morning hours,
Wrapped in tallis and tefillin.
Also you, Mama,
The children to *heder*
You escort them with a prayer.

I see you, Mama,
Blessing the candles.
Fingers covering the eyes,
A sweet prayer
You whisper quietly,
Hovering over the candles.

I see you, Tatte,
By the Shabbes meal -
Children around the table,

Mama glistening
With adoring love
She serves the Shabbes fish.

Erev Yom Kippur,
When blessing the children,
I see you also then,
Heartfelt pleas,
Somberly expressed
Upon your face at that time.

How is it that you perished,
My precious and beloved?
I am reflecting on this now:
Also Shlomo, Hinde, Sara
And Dobtsche with her child.

Everlasting memories,
Are carried in my thoughts -
This is a holy mission.
Always and forever
You will dwell in my heart
Until my last step…

Brooklyn, 24 May 1963

Translator's note: Tatte is Yiddish for father

[Page 467]

V

<u>On the Ruins</u>

[Page 468]

I Walk Upon Ruins

by B. T. Boim

Translated by Irving Lumerman

Edited by Martin Jacobs

I walk upon fires, on eternal ruins,
And all the slain of my people follow me.
They rip up every paving stone,
And they count the tears in every brook and river.

I lift up a handful of earth in my hands –
Alas, how many eyes are peering at me!
Every pebble – a generation, every grain of sand – a grandfather.
The earth has been near to me these many years.

I walk upon ruins, I seek graves,
Only a lone tree lifts its head to me,
A fugitive tree, a survivor, broad in trunk and branch.
Once my poor grandfather sat in its shade.

The tree is struck dumb, its bark is cracked,
Bent over graves, with a broken spirit.
Its hide withers as my heart withers.
O tree, alas, O tree, you are to me as my father.

O tree, alas, O tree, before you is one who hears[1].
My heart is a flute, the deaf man refuses to listen.
Like birds from a cage my songs burst forth from my mouth,
But they do not give rest, they do not give quiet.

I stand upon ruins and carve a path through them.
Until a spring in the desert announces redemption.
Until my darkness changes to light seven times seven,
Until my angel[2] ascends to the highest heaven.

Editor's Notes:

1.   Literally "before you is an ear", but, by contrast with the next line ("the deaf man refuses to listen"), "one who hears" seems appropriate.
2.   "ayin-yud-resh-yud" generally means "city", but there is another, rarer word of the same spelling, which means "angel", more appropriate for the context.

[Page 469]

On the Ruins

Translated by Tina Lunson

Our *shtetl* [little town] is desolate as a cemetery and in this desolation still hangs the uproar of those for whom no one had any mercy. Each name – an open wound that tells of huge wonders, of fine, honest Jews who lived here warm, quiet and happy, and blessed with the power of simple speech, with the smell of fresh rye bread and with great belief in God the merciful and forgiving.

Oh, fine and strong Jews of our *shtetl*, with your virtues and demeanor were like bits of heaven over the Tarnogrod earth and so are you etched in the memory of the surviving Tarnogrod Jews. Your entire life in today's time is no more than a long-vanished story. But the longing for the fineness that you carried within yourselves and left as an inheritance for the survivors can never be stilled.

The soul of the *shtetl* has been taken away. It has been extinguished, has breathed its last. It looks like a throwback to its original condition hundreds of years ago, before the Jews had arrived and it was just a small peasant settlement. Now we come to the horrible, sticky filth of the horrendous crimes that were committed here which we will never forget.

[Pages 470-481]

Tarnogrod's Surviving Remnant

by Nachum Krymerkopf

Translated by Tina Lunson

The war had ended and the few Tarnogrod Jew left alive, who had saved themselves from the murderous hell, began to present themselves in the light of day. The Jews came out of the forests and from the bunkers and various hiding places provided for them by a few good-hearted Christians. The Jews turned back to Tarnogrod with the hope that the war was over and the Jews who had fled to Russia would return and they could begin a new life in Tarnogrod. They intended that the *shtetl* [little town] would once again become a Jewish settlement.

The Poles in Tarnogrod thought differently. One night they attacked the remnant of living Jews and beat them, robbed them and warned them to leave the town right away. The warning was accompanied by the threat that any Jew who remained in Tarnogrod would be killed.

For less than one year the surviving Jews lived in Tarnogrod and sought in several ways to find livelihoods to support a life and waited calmly, hoping, that other Jews would return and that life would be regularized. But their hopes were false. The danger of death still hung over their heads and they had to leave their homes and go away, some to Lublin, some to Wroc³aw, some to other German cities that belonged to Poland and where it was easier to rent an apartment, in place of the Germans who had been driven out and had returned to Germany.

It appeared that the Tarnogrod Jews' attachment to their town was so strong that even after the night of attack by bandits some families remained, thinking that the danger would pass. In 1946, when the last victims -- Ozer Wachnachter's wife and 6 month-old daughter and Chaim Weiner from Bilgoraj – were murdered by the Polish bandits, not one Jew dared to stay in Tarnogrod.

No more Jews in Tarnogrod. The Jewish houses, remaining empty places, went to ruin, vestiges of destruction, and the earth around them sprouted wild grasses.

A few houses remained around Lakhever Street, on Rozshinitzer Street and on the market square, on the side where Yentche Lemer had lived. Those houses were snatched up by the Poles, who lived in them and dealt in the shops and used the things that had been left there.

In the shop where the stately-looking Jew had stood and weighed out merchandise with his honest hands now stood Makhiek and did the same with his piggish hands. Instead of a mezuzah at the entryway, a cross was drawn.

In Tarnogrod not all the Jewish houses were burned, but were sold by the Germans once all the Jews lay in the mass graves. They sold them to the non-Jews from the burned-out and demolished villages. In 1945, when there was once again a Polish government, the Poles sold Jewish houses with the goal of cleaning them out and leaving empty places. A special committee was created by the authorities at the time to deal with this. Ninety percent of he Jewish houses in Tarnogrod were wooden so it was easy to dispose of them.

I was in Tarnogrod during those days and saw the Poles tearing apart the remaining Jewish houses that they had bought from the government and loading the lumber onto wagons and driving away with it. I went to the town hall and called on the Polish committee with a protest against the sale of the Jewish houses. I reproached them, that there were families of the killed Jews in Russia who would soon come back home and would want to live in the remaining houses. They answered me with derision and irony, that the town could not take it upon itself to protect the houses that were robbed and sacked by the peasants, who took off the doors and windows and also the wood siding. Thus it was better that the houses be sold and when a relative from Russia announced himself he could receive the money that had come from the sale.

The prices were negligible. But the true intentions of the city fathers were clear to me then. They were selling the houses just then when they had heard that Jews were beginning to return from Russia. They did not want the returning Tarnogrod Jews to come back to town and so were doing everything so that they would have no place to rest their heads and would be forced to leave Tarnogrod.

Such were the plans of our former neighbors in those days, and they carried their plans out. So they finished with the last Jews, with Azriel from Maydan Shinovski, with Shmuel from Borvits, with Rivka and Pesza from Bishtsh, with Mordechai Lipe Adler, with Itsik Egert.

Along the Streets of the Victims

Among the Jewish ruins, I saw straying in the empty places moldy pages from a prayer book, detached and decaying sheets imprinted with the Holy Name, stuck together with dust and mud. A child's summer cap rolled about someplace, and the wind played with a sack, chasing it to and fro in the empty space. Among the ruins lay a child's shirt, torn and molding. It was sad wandering through Tarnogrod streets, looking into the windows. The stones, the houses -- everything screamed with that scream of the most horrifyingly violent deaths that anyone can conceive of. The few passers-by looked at me strangely, with suspicion. In their eyes, faces, I could read the suspicion: What is he looking for here, this stranger? Has he come here to demand his due for an injustice that one of our current residents has done to him?

And I looked these people in the eye searchingly. Perhaps there would be a name, a familiar face, who could repeat for me the gruesome history of all that had happened on this soil. I felt so lonesome and needed to have someone with me who would help me shake off the horror of those days, help to demand justice, to cry out... I saw how non-Jews were wrapping their *treif* sausages in torn Talmud pages, to take to market. I was silent, mute, could not find words for my pain, and I thought: God, do You see how people are wrapping pig flesh in your Torah? Why are You silent?

I stood alone in the empty market square. A strange emptiness engulfed me. The same market and yet so strange as to be unrecognizable. It was the realization of the evil dream of the Polish anti-Semites who had fought even in the early days to have the Jewish shopkeepers thrown out of the market. But even they had not imagined back then that the realization of their dream would also remove all the Jewish householders from the Jewish homes. All those Jews, who had built up – from an empty piece of meadow – a bustling center of trade and craftsmanship that provided necessary supplies for the residents of the town and for the surrounding villages.

Here in Tarnogrod, at the Jewish blacksmiths, tailors and shoemakers, carpenters and harness-makers, the peasant repaired his plowing tools, his wagon or sled, had his clothes resewn or got a pair of boots or a coat for the winter. And they worked, those Jewish craftsmen, for bread and water.

How much life those Jews had brought to the whole area. The market was always full of them. Standing around in groups and chatting. Arguing with one another. Now not one of them. All is as though emptied out, asleep, dead.

Last Sparks Under the Ashes

I already knew then that among the surviving Jews from Tarnogrod and the surrounding villages who succeeded in evading the German hangman and hiding in the forests, in underground hide-outs at a peasant farm, some for money, some without, were Eliezer Wertman, Mordechai Lipe Adler, Chaim Adler and his wife, Lipiner, Shlomo Yehoshua Adler and his sister Tobtche, Malka Herbstman, Eliezer Lumerman, Avigdor Gut, Efraim Lumerman and his wife and children, Avraham Haler and his wife and children and also his sisters, Shmuel Borvitzer, Hersh Weltz, Teme Trinker, David Entner. All of these survived in the Józefów forest. David Entner was later murdered by Polish bandits outside Tarnogrod. Weltz killed a German in Frankfurt several years after the war. He tricked the German into coming to his home under the pretext of selling him gold, and he killed him there.

Also remaining alive were Sara Magram, Sini Groyer, Neche and Sara from the village Babitsh, Simcha Knochen, Teme and her two brothers, Krigsner from the village Bishtsh, Shlomo Shprung from Fatik, Azriel Korngold. They were all hidden by peasants who were well paid by them.

Also among the living were Rivka Lustrin, Mindel Klug, Rivka from Bishtsh, Itsik Egert, Ozer Wachnachter and his wife Pesza. They survived on Aryan papers.

Staying alive in camps were Yentche Melamed's grandson, Zelik Tryb, Sarale Fiter, Mendel Silberzweig. Simcha Statfeld and his son survived in the Lemberg (Lviv, Ukraine) ghetto and later in the forest.

All these survivors who thought that they could stay in Tarnogrod had to leave the town and settle in Lower Silesia, with the hope of emigrating from Poland later. The single dominating thought for everyone was *Eretz Yisroel* [land of Israel].

In Tarnogrod the big *shul* [synogogue] and the *Beit Midrash* [house of study] remained whole. But the Poles later built a coach house in the place of the *Beit Midrash* which they demolished. They turned the *shul* into a storehouse for various kinds of merchandise.

There is no trace of the old cemetery in the place where it had been. There are only unclean things there today. All the *matseyves* [gravestones] have been torn out. All the trees cut down. The Germans used the *matseyves* to pave the road to Rozanietz. The graves have become even with the earth, beaten down by paths and trails that the Poles have ground down as ways to the town. There is no sign of any grave.

The three fresh graves of the Wachnachters and Weiners are also effaced. The brick *ohel* [crypt] that held the remains of the Kreszówer Tzadik (see page 275) and Tarnogrod Rabbi has also been torn down. There is no evidence of the generations of holiness with which the Tarnogrod Jews encircled this place.

How terrible is the obtuseness of the remaining Poles. The holiness of that place is much greater and more fearful than that of an ordinary cemetery. This is the cemetery of a world that was murderously cut down. Everything that reminds us of that world must be held as holy and dear. There is no designation for those who desecrate it so brutally, so un-humanly, with animal boorishness.

We will never forget the murder of our shtetl, of our slaughtered people. We will carry eternally the debt that we owe our murdered Tarnogrod Jewish families, who with their last shout of "*Shema Yisrael!*" also demanded revenge for their innocent blood's out-pouring.

Honor all our dearest and best, who were so gruesomely slaughtered by the Hitleristic and Polish murderers!

Stones Along The Border

In 1946 Jewish refugees from Russia began coming home, including those from Tarnogrod. In their minds Tarnogrod remained their old home. With that word, home, they got by in far-off Russia. They who traveled home did not think that the home was already long gone, that the German devils had ripped up their homes roots and all.

Only with their arrival in the towns did they set their eyes on the destruction and perceive that the earth on which they trod was soaked with Jewish blood.

Already at the border their transports were attacked with stones and with Poles shouting "Jew, death awaits you!" All the refugee transports were turned toward the German cities that now belonged to Poland. The Jews felt somewhat safer there. More than 80 percent of the houses were vacant. The previous German residents had fled to the American zone. In those cities and towns, the Tarnogrod Jews who had lost their homes also set up their new homes temporarily. No matter who you spoke with then, there was always the call "How do we get to *Eretz Yisrael*?" But that promised Jewish land was closed and protected by the English military so that no Jew could sneak in illegally.

In those days the *Brikha* movement [organization that transported Holocaust survivors into Palestine] began to operate. Hundreds and thousands of young people, led by *Eretz-Yisrael Haganah* [volunteers protecting Jews] fighters, began to organize the refugees and help them to cross the borders to Germany, Austria and Italy where camps had been set up and from there they could take various routes – all very dangerous – to the borders of *Eretz*. But there were several reasons that Jews become chained to their new places. Some remembered later and wanted to travel out but it was too late, the *Brikha* was no longer working and the Polish borders were already closed.

The Tarnogrod residents learned, meanwhile, about the misfortune that had befallen the Jewish victims who were murdered by the Poles, and the refugees were afraid to travel into Tarnogrod. And the road back involved deadly dangers. The Polish underground army, the A. K., was set up in the forests and lay in wait for Jews passing through, whom they murdered in savage ways.

Only in the 1950s, when the Polish underground army was liquidated, did some of the Tarnogrod Jews who remained in Poland, decide to travel to Tarnogrod and there to sell their inherited properties, for which they had not received any payment. And later those same Jews, with the opening of the gates to free immigration, made *aliyah* [immigration] to Israel. And there are still some Tarnogrod Jews in Poland, working in various posts.

During the time when the Jews fleeing Poland found themselves in the specially-made camps in Germany and Italy, the Tarnogrod Relief Committee in America sent packages of food and clothing to the Tarnogrod Jews in the camps. The Committee was headed by Itche-Ber Adler as president and Berel Tryb, secretary.

When the Jewish state was proclaimed – a state located among nine Arab countries – there were Tarnogrod Jews among the volunteer fighters who came out of the camps: Moshe Rosenfeld, Shmuel Eliyahu Futer, Chaim Bornstein, Moshe Treger and Itche Weintraub, the last of whom fell in a battle with the Arabs. As soon as the stream of immigration began – after a cease-fire – many Tarnogrod Jews made *aliyah* to Israel. Unfortunately some could not arrange it and some of them went off to various American states, where they managed with help from the Joint Distribution Committee and the Hebrew Immigrant Aid Society, which also helped them to find livelihoods.

The help from our American *Landslayt* [countrymen]

The Tarnogrod Jews in America had founded the *Tarnogroder landsmanshaft* [organized society of countrymen] several decades before, according to the example of all the other Jews from various villages. They had their own *shul* and their own cemetery. These *landsmanshaften* met once a month and accepted new members, and at special meetings decided whom to give help to and how to help their *landsleit* on the other side of the sea.

The *Tarnogroder landsmanshaft* took in all the newly-arriving refugees from Tarnogrod without fees and helped them in every possible way to get on their feet.

The Relief Committee had been concerned even before the war with the poor Jews in Tarnogrod. They had sent aid, especially for Passover and other holidays. After the war, when the Committee was led by A. B. Adler and Secretary N. Krymperkopf, and later when the president was Lumerman and the secretary Fink, there was a regular stipend for poor Tarnogrod Jews in Israel. The Relief Committee in America also took upon itself the whole responsibility for publishing this Yizkor Book. A money stipend was promptly sent to Israel for the first expenses for the Yizkor Book by Yosef Schorer and Abraham Kramer.

My brother Avraham took me to a meeting of the society as soon as I arrived in New York. At the time the governance was composed of P. Rosengarten, President; Yakov Stiglitz, Financial Secretary; M. Baumfeld, Minutes Secretary; A. B. Adler, Chairman of the Relief Committee; Berel Tryb, Secretary.

The society took me in with heartfelt friendship and accepted me as a member without dues, and proposed to me to be secretary of the Relief Committee with a stipend of 50 dollars a year, which was considered a gift. I accepted the proposal and immediately took on the work of helping the Tarnogrod Jews in Israel.

The whole time that I was in America, I was occupied with the idea of creating a monument to our martyrs, the murdered Jews of Tarnogrod, and being Secretary of the Relief Committee and I often suggested that idea, mentioned and proposed, that we erect a *matseyve* to our martyrs. Everyone's reply was positive. Everyone understood the importance of that act, but the difficulties lay in gathering the financial help necessary for carrying out the project. Difficulties are presented so that we may overcome them, and I did not give up on the idea, and brought up the matter at a meeting with the administration of the society. Unfortunately there were those who did not want to deal with the matter as urgent, and they set it aside for a later time.

Time does not stand still. One administration dissolves and another takes its place. The positions were taken by the newcomers, the greenhorns. Yosel Schorer became President. A meeting was called, and only a few members attended, and I was called upon to present my proposal to erect a memorial in the cemetery for Tarnogroder Jews in New York, a special tombstone for the murdered martyrs.

The proposal was accepted with the condition that the erection of a *matseyve* be approved by a specially-called general meeting. That decision calmed me. We were certain that everyone at the general meeting would value the moral significance and not oppose the erection of such a memorial.

Among those attending the general meeting was former president of the Jewish Council in Tarnogrod, Sini Groyer. Along with him came his brother Zischa and a few other organized members of the society, Tarnogrod sons-in-law, and they opposed the decision to erect a memorial.

The proposal failed and that was a hard blow for me. I could not comprehend that Tarnogrod Jews, who had survived that horrible hell, would not understand the importance and the respectability of erecting a *matseyve* to the memory of our dear tormented families. I experienced a deep embitterment and disappointment and thought that something must be done for the memory of our martyrs. I decided to take on the project with my own strength and not to ask anyone for any help.

The Stone on Mount Zion

My disappointment caused me to renounce my duties as secretary of the relief committee. During that time I harbored the idea of going to Israel. In my plan it would be possible in a few years. But now the rejection of the idea of erecting a *matseyve*, made me quicken the pace for the plan and I hurried my trip to Israel.

Immediately upon my arrival in Israel I began with my own resources to erect a *matseyve* on Mount Zion in Jerusalem. Approaching the realization of this task called for assembling a meeting of Tarnogrod Jews in Israel. The meeting took place in Haifa, in the home of Yekhezkel Tofler. We discussed what the inscriptions should be on the *matseyve*. I also asked for the help of people who would travel to Jerusalem and decide which wall of the Holocaust House the *matseyve* should be mounted in.

I also met with the unexpected opposition of one person who maintained that there was no need for a *matseyve*, and who declared that the Tarnogrod Jews in Israel had never given such an idea any thought and were not in agreement about the importance of such a monument. Tzvi Rozenson stayed actively on my side and others also agreed. We went to Mount Zion together with Shmuel Fefer and wrote out the style of the inscription and showed the stone-carver which wall to place the *matseyve* into.

The unveiling of the *matseyve* was on May 1, 1960. Moshe Shprung sent out the invitations to all the Tarnogrod Jews and a fine audience attended. All were satisfied with immortalizing the memory of the martyrs from our shtetl.

Being in Israel for five months, I was in contact with many fellow *landsleit* and I could feel their satisfaction and understanding about the importance of the *matseyve* on Mount Zion. I was very touched by the evening gathering that the Tarnogrod *landsleit* organized at Golda Egert's home. We sat around two covered tables. People shared memories about life in Tarnogrod. People discussed questions having to do with the American Relief Committee, about the urgency of establishing a free-loan society and a committee charged with distributing the aid only to those in need.

At that same meeting we dealt with the issue of writing a scroll in which the names of all the martyrs from our *shtetl* would be written. Everyone accepted that proposal with great enthusiasm. Mr. Moshe Shprung sent out a letter to all the *landsleit* asking them to send in the names of their murdered relatives.

It was painful for me to convince myself of how few people responded to that initiative.

FROM A RUINED GARDEN

The Memorial Books of Polish Jewry

Edited and Translated by
Jack Kugelmass and Jonathan Bioyarin
With Geographical Index and Bibliography by
Zachary M. Baker
Published in association with the
United States Holocaust Memorial Museum
Washington, D.C.
INDIANA UNIVERSITY PRESS
<https://www.indiana.edu/~iupress/ >
Bloomington and Indianapolis

[Pages 481-482]

Searching for the Life That Was

Nachum Krymerkopf

Sefer Tarnogrod; le-zikaron ha-kehila ha-yehudit she-nehreva

Finding myself in Lublin when the war ended, I began to think about ways in which I, as a Jew, could travel to Tarnogrod, which entailed great dangers. At that time the Kelts pogrom also took place, costing the lives of forty Jews, and the anti-Semitic bands terrified every surviving Jew. Jews were warned not to ride trains until the hooliganism stopped.

But my heart was pained and would not let me rest. Seeing the great catastrophe that had befallen the Jewish people, my desire to live was lost; but at the same time the Jew felt within himself the mission of continuing the lives of his slaughtered parents and relatives. Despite the most gruesome nightmares, he knew that he must continue living. To ride from Lublin to Tarnogrod with a beard like mine meant risking my life.

After considering all of the risks involved, I went to a barber and wept over my beard as it was cut off. I left long mustaches like those of a Polish peasant, put on peasant boots and a peasant cap, and set off for Tarnogrod at the end of May 1945.

I took the train as far as Zamoshtsh, where I met a few surviving Jews, slept at the home of a Jew, and set off on the train in the morning to Zvyezhinyets. From there I took the local train to Bilgoray.

It was hard for me to tell whether there was another Jew on the train. Perhaps he was disguised as a gentile, as I was. But all of the passengers were positive that there wasn't a single Jew on the train. It was hard to believe that a Jew would dare to travel on that line in those times.

When I arrived at Bilgoray, Polish coachmen stood in front of the station. They fell upon me, asking me where I was headed; each one wanted to take me. I stood mute for a while, searching with my eyes: perhaps Mendl Roshe's would appear, or Mendl Avel, or another of the Jewish coachmen of Tarnogrod, who used to drive to Bilgoray and back each day.

But my search was fruitless. None of them was left. Gentile wagons had taken their place. Having no other choice, I approached one of the Polish coachmen, and we settled on a fare to Tarnogrod. For a short while we both sat silently. He was the first to speak; I tried to answer as little as possible, so that he wouldn't realize I was a Jew. Then he pointed in front of himself with his whip and said:

"See, on both sides of the road are buried Jews whom the Germans shot. Jews from Tarnogrod, Bilgoray, and the surrounding villages lie there. The Germans knew what they were doing when they shot all the Jews. It was a good thing they did, and we should be grateful to them for it."

The gentile sat talking with his back to me, and I sat as if petrified. As I looked around I saw that the entire road from Bilgoray to Tarnogrod was the same as before. Nothing had changed: the same houses, the same gentiles, the same women drawing water from their wells, just as before. Only the coachman wasn't the same. I no longer heard the rich Yiddish tongue and the Yiddish "Vyo, ferdelekh! Giddyap!" I no longer heard the melody of the prayer, "Let us give strength to the holiness of this day," which Yoysef Magid used to sing as he rode with his passengers to Bilgoray. Depressed, I thought to myself: Where am I going, and to whom? Is there really no one left? Is it possible that an entire city of Jews was slaughtered?

Frozen in these tragic thoughts I arrived in Tarnogrod. I didn't want to ride straight into town, and asked the coachman to let me off near the factory at the Bilgoray gate.

There I met Sore Magram. She stood on the porch of her house and looked at me without recognizing me. Seeing her, a Jewish woman of Tarnogrod, joy flooded through me for a moment. I approached her, told her who I was, and saw how she, too, was filled with the same joy.

[Pages 483-492]

Translated by Miriam Leberstein

We began to tell each other about our experiences during the war years.

She told me about the destruction of our town, describing the various ways in which Jews had unsuccessfully fought for their lives. She also told me about her own life, which had been fraught with danger. She enumerated for me the villages where she stayed and the peasants with whom she had hidden, living in fear of daylight, of strangers, of informers who swarmed everywhere. For a time, she had lived as a Christian, with Aryan papers, and watched as the Germans carried out their aksties against the Jews. After Tarnogrod had been emptied of Jews, someone denounced her, and the Gestapo came to get her one night. When she heard them knocking at her door, she immediately understood what she had to do, and jumped out a window and ran through the dark fields until she got to Lukow.

Among the Ruins

Fearful, ashamed, and in despair, I slipped into town by the backstreets, wending my way through the narrow alleys until I reached the market place, on the side where Shlomo Mantel once lived.

I stood there dejected, not knowing where to go next. After a while, I began to imagine that this wasn't Tarnogrod, that perhaps I had strayed into another town. Quickly I shook off that thought. After all, I recognized the shops the Jews had left behind. Nothing had changed except that instead of the Jewish merchants with their luminous, refined faces, there now stood Poles with their pitted, swinish mugs. No, I hadn't lost my bearings. This was truly Tarnogrod, the same town, but without Jews. With an aching heart I went to the left side of the market place and exited onto Razhenitser Street. Here was the house that Chaim Segalman had built for himself in 1940, already under German occupation. Here was the lot that belonged to Shabtai Sabel.

I proceeded along Razhenitser Street, not glimpsing a single Jewish face, not even a Jewish house. I soon reached the vacant lot where my father's house had stood. On this very spot I had taken leave of my parents and my sisters. Weeds were growing there and scattered around were remnants of the brick chimney and the oven where we used to bake matzo for Passover. I remembered where our house had once stood, where there was an alcove with two beds, the place near the window where my father had his weaving workshop. Here was the spot where my cradle had stood, where I and six more children were rocked to sleep. I envisioned the large, ragged basket in which the matzo maker delivered matzos to the householders. The mezuzah from our door lay muddied and broken on the ground. I picked it up and held it to my lips.

Standing on the ruins of my father's lot I looked across to my own house, which remained intact, because the Poles had turned it into a temporary school for their children. Although I thought it best not to go there, my feet took me there without thinking and I soon stood in front of my house on Lakhover Street. The entry was wide open; the doors had been removed by thieves. Some of the windows were missing their shutters and those that remained were hanging loose, like the limbs of cripples.

My eyes clouded; I wandered through the empty rooms with their peeling walls. What was I looking for? Who was I looking for? My ears were filled with noise and I sat down on the floor as I slowly began to grasp the scope of my own personal Holocaust, my own catastrophe.

I had left behind a loving wife and beautiful, sweet children and now...? Empty, deserted rooms, silent walls that could perhaps have told so much about the last hours of my family.

I looked at the peeling walls, as if waiting for them to answer me: Perhaps they knew where the bodies of my wife and children lay, where the soil had absorbed their blood? But the walls remained silent, as if angered and insulted by the horrific fate of the people who had lived within them so many years, who had painted and adorned them with pictures and drawings.

My gaze wandered over the piles of refuse and I lifted the torn briefcase in which my Peshe kept her school books. Then I saw a piece of my wife's Sabbath dress, a torn boot that had belonged to my son Kopel, a sleeve ripped from my Malkale's shirt. These were the only witnesses I found that my family once lived here, my dear good wife, my lovely, loving children.

With a broken heart I left my house and went out into the market place. The Christians didn't recognize me and looked at me as if I were a wild creature. Finally, they showed me where Wachnachter lived.

Someone added that he, too, would soon be driven away, that Jews were not needed here.

I went to visit Wachnachter, who was living in Guthertz's house. I found him at home with his wife Peshe and their little girl, who was lying in her cradle. They were very glad to see me and I again heard about their horrifying experiences.

The next day I went around to see my Polish acquaintances living in the area outside town and on the commons. I asked about my family and other Tarnogrod Jews, how had they lived under the German tyrants, when and how did they die.

I spent a week visiting the Poles, searching for information about the last days of our Jews. They told me the names of Jews whom they encountered after the aktsies, wandering around the fields, looking for a place to hide, something to eat, until they disappeared. Everyone knew the fate that awaited them.

A woman from the commons told me that my 13-year-old son Kopel had worked as a cowherd for Dekash. At dawn on the day of the *aktsie* he had driven the cows to the commons, where he was shot and killed by an S.S. officer near Avraham Ruer's unfinished mill. The woman showed me the field where he had been buried by two Christians from the commons. I tried to find out how I could remove his remains and rebury him in a Jewish cemetery. But it turned out that would have been impossible. Tall wheat was growing in the field and there was no one who was able to show me where exactly my child was buried.

Every day the Poles told me new details about those horrific years. Two days after the *aktsie* they found my wife Mindl wandering in the fields near Bartashik's mill. Two weeks after the *aktsie* my 15-year-old daughter Peshe was captured in the village of Korchow and brought to Tarnogrod, where she was held in Chaim Goldman's dark warehouse until they killed her.

For several days after the *aktsie* my 9-year-old Malkale wandered among the Christians who lived near the cemetery. Skura told me that he found her in his pig pen, eating from the trough. He took her home, fed her and let her sleep there overnight, but in the morning he sent her away because he was afraid of the Gestapo. Christian boys caught her and took her to the S.S., who killed her. That was how my own family perished.

Flickering Lights

The entire time of my 8 day stay in Tarnogrod, I slept at Wachnachter's house. At night we heard shooting. These were attacks by Ukrainians upon the Poles and Poles upon Ukrainians. There were only two other Jews besides Wachnachter living in Tarnogrod at that time – Ezriel from Majdan Sieniawski and Shmuel Barovitser. They lived in Rachel-Chaiake's house.

One Friday a Christian from Lezenski drove into town with a car carrying salt to sell. Baratshik wanted to buy the salt at half its value. It was already twilight when Wachnachter and the two other Jews bought two sacks of salt. When Baratshik found out, he denounced them to the militia and the three Jews were arrested.

At the jail, the three Jews were mercilessly beaten. Their money and watches were taken, as was the salt they had bought. They were threatened with death if they made a complaint. It took them three days to recover from the beating.

I urged them to leave Tarnogrod as soon as possible. The two single men followed my advice and left. Wachnachter, who had a family, stayed until the catastrophe occurred, about which I have already written [see page 470]. After having survived the hell of the Nazis, they were killed in a terrible way by the Polish beasts.

With each day it became more dangerous for me to stay in Tarnogrod. I returned to Lublin, coming back to Tarnogrod to complete the formalities for the sale of my house, for a negligible price. By that time, I had concluded that not a single Jew would return to Tarnogrod.

During the short time I was in Tarnogrod, Mordechai Lipe Adler would sometimes visit there from Bukovina, where he was living. Simche Shtatfeld would also visit Tarnogrod, from Lublin. He would buy butter and other foodstuffs, which were much more expensive in Lublin. After the tragedy with Wachnachter, not a single Jew came to Tarnogrod. Every day I spent there was a torture for me. The entire area became repugnant to me and I had the feeling I was moving through a horrible sticky filth of crime and decadence which could not be redeemed at any cost.

I stayed in Lublin for several more months and then escaped to Germany, and from there, with the help of the Joint Distribution Committee, left for America.

The Idea of the Yizkor Book for our Martyrs

At a meeting one evening the suggestion was made to write a Yizkor book, as other large and small towns in Poland were doing.

We weighed the difficulties entailed in such a project. In addition to the actual writing, and collecting memoirs, documents and historical material, there was the central issue of finding the necessary financial resources. The Tarnogrod *landslayt* in Israel placed a lot of hope in me. They saw me as the American, the former secretary of the Relief Committee, and thought that I would take care of the financial side. I promised to present the matter to the Relief Committee, that I would demand special meetings, would insist on the necessity to organize a broad effort to carry it out. But I objectively and truthfully told them that in America, too, we had to deal with people who didn't have the appropriate appreciation for such a Yizkor book. I described the circumstances under which the current secretary Mr. Yosef Fink had to operate.

Upon my return to America I immediately, at the first meetings, presented the suggestion made by the *landslayt* in Israel. But the Relief Committee did not display the appropriate understanding. The problem was discussed several times but the committee continued to send aid in the amount it deemed appropriate.

The entire time I corresponded by mail with the *landslayt* in Israel, especially with Mr. Meir Ringer and Mr. Moshe Shprung. I asked them to find out how much it would cost to publish the book. Meir Ringer put in a lot of effort to assemble the necessary information and after assessing the situation, I wrote him that he should begin to work more intensively to realize the Yizkor book, and I on my side, was ready to provide what was needed, including gathering the memoirs, documents and providing the financial aid.

The truth is that I placed hope for realizing the idea on the Tarnogrod Society in New York, thinking that it would be easier to gather the necessary funds with the help of the *landslayt* in America. I took every letter that I received from Messrs. Ringer and Shprung to meetings of the Society and pressed them to make every effort to collect or borrow the money necessary to put out the book.

I did not weary and I did not stop demanding that we fulfill the obligation we owed to our martyrs, until at a meeting, Mr. Max Levinger, from Lukow, son in law of Mendele Silberzweig, spoke up and demanded that the Yizkor book include everything that had been said about the last president of the *Judenrat*, Sinai Grauer.

In reply, I explained that it was not possible to do what Mr. Levinger suggested. I personally did not know anything about the deeds of the former president of the *Judenrat*, Mr. Sinai Grauer. Had I known anything, I wouldn't have needed his suggestion to write about it. In my drive to write the complete truth about what happened in the ghetto, I was not afraid of anyone, but I would have to bear sole responsibility for anything I wrote. I emphasized that writing about the conduct of the former president, as Levinger desired, would expose him to disgrace and condemn him in the eyes of history. Such a thing could only be done by a person who actually witnessed it. It would have to be thoroughly researched, and could only be based on precise and honest facts. It could not be based on rumors that had not yet been substantiated.

I sent a detailed report of these meetings to the *landslayt* in Israel. In return, Ringer wrote me that he was resigning from working on publishing the Yizkor book. I had no further correspondence with him. The work was resumed only after my visit to Israel for a longer stay.

Left All Alone

Nuchim Krymerkopf

Of all my family,
I alone remain
Without a home,
Hounded by strangers.

My life has been cut down
Everything I loved and cherished destroyed
Everything I owned is gone
And my home destroyed by fire.

No wife, no child
No father, no mother,
No sign of them remains
Oh, how bitter is my life.

I had a wife and three children
Each of them shot

By the Germans With their machine guns.

Peshe, my daughter,
Kopel, my son…
All I found of her was a bloodied dress
Where are their bodies buried?!

Malkale, the youngest
Mindl -- my wife.

If only one of them had lived,
Oh, woe is me.

When I remember the faces
Of my children and their mother
Buried in ditches along with thousands more
I am engulfed in horror and trembling.

How sad and terrible is this life,
As I have been left alone
How bitter and lonely is life
When one is alone like a stone.

Stay away from the murderers,
Have nothing to do with them
You must flee from the thorns [sic]
Have you so soon forgotten?
Oh, woe is me.

You must remember
The Nazi beast.
You must seek revenge
For your brothers and sisters.

Remember – Do Not Forget!

Nuchim Krymerkopf

Translated by Miriam Leberstein

Jews from Tarnogrod: I appeal to you, the heirs of Tarnogrod! Your inheritance is not a material one; it doesn't consist of houses or castles, or fields or gardens. You do not belong to that category of heirs who fear that they may need to fight over what was left by their deceased parents.

You are the heirs of a great and sacred commandment: You must remember and not forget.[1] You are the heirs of an exalted aspiration, that will overcome fire or water.

Until the end of time and generations we will cherish what remains written in fire and blood. We who have been saved from a horrific death will always have before us the words: "You must blot out the remembrance of Amalek" – now, the Amalek of the 20th century.

This is in fact the role and purpose of this very book, which is an expression of the obligation which we have assumed to perpetuate our inheritance, the golden chain of hundreds of years of Jewish life in Tarnogrod.

So hold dear and sacred this book of remembrance which reflects the spiritual life of our parents and ancestors, the special nobility and good heartedness of the simple Jews in our *shtetl*. May this book provide for future generations a deep appreciation of this destroyed beauty.

May this Yizkor book be an eternal reminder providing a portrait of a pure way of life which no longer exists.

May the cry that rises from this book never be silenced.

Footnote:

1.   This is a partial quote from Deuteronomy 25:17, which commands the Jews to "remember what Amalek did to you on your way out of Egypt," and "not to forget it", as well as "to blot out the remembrance of Amalek," which the author also cites in this section. The name of the Biblical Amalek is used as a synonym for any enemy of the Jewish people throughout history.

[Pages 493-500]

On the Ruins of My Hometown, Tarnogrod
From a visit in 1964

Yekhezkel Agiert

Translated by Miriam Leberstein

During the several decades that I lived in Brazil, I always dreamed of and strived to visit my hometown Tarnogrod, where I spent my childhood and youth, in good times and bad, hoping for better times, for a happy tomorrow.

And then came the day for which I had waited so long. My wife and I packed our bags, took leave of friends and comrades, and left Sao Paolo, Brazil, bound for Poland. On July 11, 1964 we sailed on the ship Augustus to Italy, where we took a train to Warsaw. We spent two weeks in Warsaw, where we met with acquaintances, visited various institutions and laid a wreath of flowers at the Warsaw Ghetto monument.

From there we went to Lublin, where we visited the Jewish Committee. Among the Committee activists I found many comrades [1] and acquaintances from my past. Since I was in Lublin, I decided to see the death camps where the German beasts killed our sisters and brothers. We took a car and within ten minutes we were at the Majdanek death camp.

There we encountered thousands of visitors from various parts of the country as well as many soldiers. I noticed that several soldiers wrote notes and placed them upon the graves. Curious to see what the notes said, I picked one up and read: "My dear people, I will never forget you, from me, Vasilevitsh."

Passing through the housing blocks I saw in some of them packs of hair and braids that the executioners had shorn from the heads of their victims before they gassed them. My heart bled at this horrifying sight. I thought about how much love and tenderness their mothers gave their children, their family and friends. Now all that remained of their memory was a museum.

I did not have the strength to visit the other blocks. I broke down and wept bitterly. When I had recovered somewhat from the pain, we continued on. One of our escorts pointed to a hill and told me that under that hill were buried 18,000 Jews killed by the Nazis two days before liberation.

I was devastated by what I had seen and wanted to leave. I parted with my companions and one of them took me to the bus that went to Tarnogrod. When I got on the bus, I decided not to take it directly to Tarnogrod; it was a Sunday and I didn't want to arrive on a Sunday. So I decided to stay overnight in Bilgoraj. On the way, we drove through many towns familiar to me. Unfortunately, no Jews remained there. My heart was aching. Could it be true? Where did they go, my beloved Jews, comrades and friends, the young people who had filled these towns with life and struggle?

We arrived in Bilgoraj in the evening. I didn't recognize it, but the bus driver convinced me that we were in fact in Bilgoraj.

One of the passengers who got off the bus with me saw that I was a foreigner and asked me where I wanted to go and what I wanted to see. I told him that I wanted to find a person who had lived on Tarnogrod Street. He took me there and found the person I was looking for. This was a close acquaintance and a former comrade. We had a short conversation. She asked if any of the comrades from Bilgoraj were still alive. I told her that sadly they had all died. I felt that this was very painful for her, and that she was suffering greatly. She asked me to forgive her for not being able to invite me to stay with her as her guest for at least a few days. She explained that her son, his wife and children had come from England to spend their vacation with her. We said goodbye, and I went back to the hotel, to wait for the next day's trip to Tarnogrod.

I waited a long time for a bus to Tarnogrod. There were no taxis or cars to rent, so I continued to wait. Suddenly a military vehicle with soldiers drove up. I asked them to stop and asked if they were driving to Tarnogrod and if so, if they would take me with them. They were going to Tarnogrod, and said I was very welcome to come with them.

When we arrived at Knishpoler Street I saw a sign. I asked the driver to stop for a moment so that I could take a closer look. I saw that it was the same sign that had been there several decades ago, just as I had left it. We drive on, and I started thinking: this little piece of tin had been luckier than a living person. The sign remained but the young people who frequented this spot, singing on this very street, no longer existed. The Nazi beasts destroyed their home and cut short the lives of the Jewish youth. From the car I could see peasants in the field harvesting grain, gathering the golden stalks. It seemed to me that the stalks were crying along with me over the misfortune that had befallen us.

We drove through a crossroads between Bilgoraj and the village of Bishte. I knew it well. The Jewish youth of the town would come here on the Sabbath to get together and enjoy themselves. How many wonderful songs were sung here, how much hope and yearning they experienced here.

At this same crossroads, on this very place, the crucifix with the figure of Christ still stood. Nothing had changed; he did not turn his head away from me, he did not feel guilty before me. The bridge was also the same. Under it there used to be a steady flow of cool water, but now it had dried up, even though it was raining. It appeared that no one came to swim in the waters of the stream. The church, too, stood in its place. It seemed to be asking, "To whom is he travelling, whom is he going to see?"

After travelling on for a while, we stopped and the driver announced that we were now in Tarnogrod. From what I saw, I didn't believe that I was already in my hometown. But this first impression changed as I gradually began to recognize the town. First, I recognized the small shops that had been built decades ago. I encountered a Christian and asked him where Lakhower Street was. He said I was standing on it, but that it was now called Kosciusko Street.

I still wanted to see the post office, which would help me better orient myself. Lost in thought, I suddenly realized that several Christians had approached and asked the man with whom I had been talking who this stranger was. In truth, I became a bit frightened and asked where the police station was. I soon arrived there, knocked on the door, and heard, "Enter." I introduced myself, said that I was from abroad, had been born here in Tarnogrod and wanted to be taken to see my former home, the synagogue, the *besmedresh* [house of study, also used for worship], and the rabbi's house.

They said that they were all too young to know these things, that I should go to the municipality, where I would find people from the older generation who could give me information about the things I was interested in. One of the young police officers accompanied me there.

Inside the municipal offices, when I saw the new leaders of the town government, I didn't need any introductions. I recognized all of them. I almost shouted, "Oh, are you here?" I encountered all the old Tarnogrod residents I knew so well: Bien, Karpol, Tzap and others. We chatted. They didn't immediately recognize me and I told them who I was, that my mother's name was Khane and what merchandise she dealt in. They immediately remembered and told me that she wasn't called Khane [by the Poles], but Yosvova. We argued about her name for a while, until I recalled that she was in fact known as Yosvova.

While we were talking a young man came in, greeted me, and said that his colleague had told him about my arrival, and that I had worked for Yekl Magran. Hearing this, I wanted to get more details and, excusing myself to the members of the municipality, asked the young man to join me for a glass of tea. We went to a bar–restaurant where all the tables were occupied by peasants drinking beer, many of them already quite drunk. I withdrew from the conversation, said goodbye to my acquaintance and set out to return to the municipality.

On the way, I encountered a lot of people. Each one introduced himself. I didn't want to call them by their names — that would have shown more respect than they deserved. Soon there were about ten people standing around me; they accompanied me to my former home.

When we got to the house a Christian woman emerged. She was living in the house formerly owned by Sakhile the tailor, which stood behind ours. My companions introduced me to the woman and told her that I was born and had lived in this house and had come from abroad to see the town of my birth. The woman asked, "What do they want, the crucifiers[i.e., the Jews]? There aren't any of them left here." I saw with whom I was dealing so I refrained from talking to her. One of my companions indicated to her, with a gesture, that she shouldn't say anything more.

From there I set off with my companions to look around the town. On the land where there had once stood the houses of Shaye–Leib, Shmayele the Tailor, my uncle Faiwel Bas, the cripple Yankl the tailor, where they used to bake matzo – that entire area was now an empty parcel overgrown with weeds.

We came to the place where the *besmedresh* had once stood; it had been converted into a hotel. The women's section had been completely dismantled by the Germans; a few stones were the sole remaining trace.

The Tailors' Synagogue was empty and desolate. Outside the synagogue, they had set up a green market where a Christian man was selling potatoes, cabbage, tomatoes and other fruit. I wanted to see the inside. One of my companions obtained a key and we went in. It was heartbreaking to see what the Fascists had done to our property. The *balemer* [desk from which Torah is read] was gone; the Torah ark was in pieces. The lonely wind whistled and wailed.

My thoughts brought me back to my town as it was years ago. I pictured the time of the high holidays Rosh Hashanah and Yom Kippur, how the Jews packed the synagogue, praying for health, livelihood a year of peace. I imagined the women in the gallery, standing and praying, reaching out their hands to me in greeting. I could not answer, my tongue froze. I leaned against the wall and wept.

A voice inside me called out to my *landslayt* [fellow townspeople] all over the world not to forget, not to forgive the Nazis, to take revenge on them for spilling the blood of our people and destroying our homes.

We left the synagogue and arrived at the rabbi's house, with its large courtyard and garden. The rabbi had a big family and in the house there had lived sons, daughters, sons–in–law, daughters–in–law and grandchildren. The house was always filled with visitors who came to the rabbi to consult on various matters. Now none of them was left. A Christian now lived there. Oh, what had become of it!

We continued on. A radio station had been built where there once stood Ite–Leibele's house. Not far away stood the house of Yankele the *Royfer* [a medical paraprofessional], now boarded up. The building that had belonged to Fishl Koniazh had been converted into a hospital. The large market square no longer existed. The entire area – once occupied by the municipality, the buildings owned by Yekl Magram, Hersh Shaye–Leib, all the way up to the Mantl family's house – all of it was under construction. I wasn't interested to know what was being built there.

We walked on. I encountered many people who asked me, "What is the gentleman doing here?" I asked them where I could find the mass grave [in which the Jews were buried]. They said they didn't know. I asked them to show me Leibish Koval's house. We arrived there, but no one was there. Near it stood the house of a village Jew named Leibish Flis; no one was there.

I continued with my companions toward Shaye Zeinwale's garden, where we encountered a Christian woman who said she knew where the mass grave was. I was introduced to the woman, and she recognized that I was truly Yosvove's son. We asked her to show us the location of the grave of my mother and other Jewish women murdered by the Fascists.

Leading us to the grave, she told us that once a teacher came to her and told her that the Nazis wanted to bury the murdered Jews in her garden, and he asked her to refuse. She promised to do so. Later, however, a Gestapo officer came to her and informed her that the murdered Jews would be buried in her garden.

When she told him that she didn't want that, he chuckled and said, "Why not? You can be sure that afterwards your garden will yield the best cabbage."

In that garden lay the mass grave of our mothers, fathers, sisters and brothers, all killed by the Nazi beasts. My companions gradually began to relate the atrocities committed by the Nazis, how they mercilessly killed their victims. A Nazi had thrown Yisroelke Pelts' daughter to the ground and placed his booted foot on her throat, strangling her. There were other such horrifying crimes which the murderers inflicted on the Jews.

I found several more houses that had belonged to Jews; these were Bromberger, the baker, and the Jew who manufactured oil. They were locked and nailed shut.

Walking on Lakhower Street, I saw that it had been completely reconstructed. It now had a children's school, which was closed for vacation. On the way I met a lot of women who, seeing a foreigner, wanted to talk to me. From their manner of speaking, I sensed that they wanted to provoke me, so I avoided conversing with them.

There were a lot of Christians who I knew still wanted to meet with me, but I didn't have the patience to stay any longer. I decided to leave my little town. I was tired, exhausted from my experience and I left Tarnogrod. I traveled to Lublin where my wife was waiting for me. From there we went to Wroclaw.

Let it be noted that I have written this in tears, let it be a reminder not to forget, not to forgive our deadly enemies who murdered one third of our people. Let it also be a consolation for all my *landslayt*, for all Jews, that we were fortunate enough to see Hitler's downfall and the regeneration of the Jewish land.

Footnote:

1.   The Yiddish word translated here and elsewhere in this article as "comrade" is khaver, and has several definitions, including friend, or a fellow member of a group or organization, among others. It bears no connotation, as it might in American English, of a particular political affiliation.

[Pages 501-503]

A Word and a Tear
In memory of my mother, who was killed by the Nazi murderers

by Yekhezkel Agiert

Translated by Miriam Leberstein

It has already been 35 years since I left my home for faraway Brazil. Each passing day, my thoughts were with my home and with the people with whom I spent my childhood and who remained there, in the hellfire of the Nazi extermination of the Jews.

Just five weeks ago I saw the crematoria of Majdanek and Auschwitz, and I still cannot free myself of the distress that I suffered there.

I had always longed and tried to meet someone from my town who had survived. You can imagine my joy when I met some surviving *landslayt* [fellow townspeople] for the first time 16 years ago in North America. In my talks with these survivors I learned about the catastrophe that befell our town, about what happened to my family, and my dear mother, whom the Nazis killed in a mass grave. The entire time I was tortured by the longing to visit her grave and recite the *Kaddish* [prayer for the dead], as every mother deserves from her children.

On August 15, 1964, I arrived in the ruined town of Tarnogrod, which had once held such love and charm and where each person was bound to another as true comrades. How forlorn had you become, my dear, warmhearted little Jewish town.

I was taken around by the town's current leaders, who during the war were almost as bad as the Germans.[1] I could have done without their help, but the Polish government wanted to honor me, as a native of the town. They – the holders of power – did not want to tell me where my mother's grave was. It was only when I pointed to the location that I had learned about from my surviving *landslayt* that they confirmed it by nodding their agreement.

I entered the garden of the house that had belonged to Shaye, the son of Zanvel the shoemaker. There among the gardens, lies the shared mass grave and within it, my mother's resting place. I wanted to cry out and tell her: Here stands before you your son Yekhezkel Berish, as you so lovingly called me. I wanted to tell her that she had become a grandmother. Listen, to how your grandchild calls you, *Bobeshi* [Granny], and pleads with you to cuddle him, to press him to your heart.

You did not live to see that happen. I went to look for you in your house; I found only grass. I went to look for you in the synagogue, where you had a permanent seat. It was empty and abandoned. I looked to see if you had perhaps accepted my invitation to my son's upcoming wedding. Why aren't you there, tossing nuts [at the bridegroom].[2] Aren't you rejoicing?

I looked around and saw nothing but cold stones, and a shudder shook my body. How alone you were. For the twenty years since your death, no one had lit candles at your grave.

Five weeks later, I met up with your son Avrom and we took comfort in the continuation of life, and in the thought that mothers will no longer suffer so. I am now in Israel, where your son Avrom came 40 years ago to build the land, so that Jews can be proud. Your *landslayt* are also here. They were fortunate to survive in a land where we finally feel at home.

So I wish my *landslayt* a happy and peaceful life in the secure and healthy Jewish state forever. Best wishes, my dear warmhearted *landslayt*, who have not been forgotten by us, survivors in far away Brazil.

Footnotes:

1.   The Yiddish term used by the author to describe the current Polish leaders of the town is "the former halbe-retsikhim [literally 'half-murderers'."]
2.   A probable reference to the pre-wedding aufruf ceremony where the bridegroom is called up to read the Torah and is showered with candy and nuts.

[Pages 503-504]

Surviving Auschwitz

Translated by Miriam Leberstein

In Tarnogrod, as in many towns, the Nazi murderers tortured the Jews and killed them on the spot, separately and in mass graves. All the roads leading out of Tarnogrod were soaked with Jewish blood. The few Jews who tried to escape were often betrayed to the Germans by their Polish neighbors. Some were killed on the spot; others were sent to the death camps.

In those years, Tarnogrod Jews were also living in other towns, including Lublin and Warsaw. There, too, they fell into the hands of the murderers. Eli Mantl was in Paris when the war broke out. But there, too, like thousands of other Jews, he wound up in the train transports to the camps.

Eli Mantl

***In the 1930's he was the secretary of the kehile [organized Jewish community] in
Tarnogrod, until he left for Paris, from which he was sent by the Germans to the death
camp at Auschwitz. He lives today in Paris, maintaining his ties to the Association
of Landslayt from Tarnogrod. From time to time he visits Israel, where the majority of
the survivors of the Tarnogrod Jewish community live.***

Every train car was crammed full of people, without food or drink, without a bit of air. Locked in the cars, they did not know where they were being taken, until the train stopped, the doors opened and the S.S. soldiers with whips in their hands drove them out of the wagons with shouts, curses and blows.

A selection was held on the spot. Some were sent directly to death, to the gas ovens, and others had to undergo all the sufferings of a horrific hell. Among the rare individuals who emerged alive was Eli Mantl. What he suffered was typical, perhaps with some variations, for hundreds of thousands. Some of them were able to write their memoirs, a tale written in blood, not ink. An entire folk died in horror and catastrophe. And sharing this fate were the Jews of Tarnogrod, from which all roads led to fearsome slaughter.

Max Levinger, after liberation from the Bergen Belsen
concentration camp, at the departure of a transport to Israel

[Pages 505-519]

In the Footsteps of the Town Which is No More

by Amnon Dror

Translated by Sara Mages

Before we left for Poland, a Jew asked us to go to a certain town and look there for a Pole who fifteen years ago received a sum of money from him to place, once a week, a bouquet of flowers on his father's grave. The Jew asked that we go to the cemetery, and if we find out that the Pole is keeping his promise, he would send him extra dollars so that he can continue laying the flowers on the grave.

We still did not know then that this request would bring us, after the tour of Poland, to an understanding of the significance of the Jewish problem, which does not let go of Poland and its Jews to this day.

We toyed then with the hope that we were about to meet the Jewish town, as we knew it in our childhood and adolescence from endless stories and descriptions. After all, in one way or another, we are all connected to the Jewish town in a bond of nostalgia. We travel to it, even if we have never seen it before, as we travel to a childhood friend. But, it did not work out. We did not find, although we searched and visited many towns, a starting point and a sufficient grip, from which we can recreate and rehabilitate in our imagination a Jewish town steeped in folklore and life, cramped with its rich and blessed with the joy of its poor. Because, as is well known, thousands of small and large towns have long since become cemeteries, and over time also the cemeteries were destroyed and no trace was left of most of them.

In Warsaw I knew an elderly couple, sick and poor, who were trying to maintain a kind of an archive of documents and photographs of cemeteries in the various stages of their destruction. But soon they would not be able to continue this activity, and there will be no one to register the destruction of the Jewish cemeteries.

I myself have experienced a very bleak testimony. I strolled the streets of the wonderful resort town of Kazimierz which was, and still is, a source of inspiration for artists and poets, among them some of the best Jewish artists. Kazimierz was once a typical Jewish town, and in the words of a Polish writer, it had shops where you could only find one large barrel of pickled cucumbers, and nothing else. In Kazimierz, at the end of the slope that rises from the town center, there is a Catholic monastery. A stone path leads to it, and when I climbed it I discovered that I was walking on Hebrew letters, on what were once gravestones in the local cemetery. I leaned over a tombstone, cleared with my fingers the sand that filled the carved letters and read: "Here lies buried the most honest man..." I later learned that someone approached the monastery's management and the local municipality and asked them to remove the gravestones from the sidewalk, and the answer was: "Please, just give us other paving stones." And there is no institution, organization or a Jewish person, who has the power in today's Poland to carry out this simple thing. The beautiful synagogue in Kazimierz has been renovated and is currently used as a cinema. In another town I entered to what was once a synagogue, and discovered that I was in the heart of the regional center for fruit and vegetable distribution. Some of the workers at this center, men and women, remembered the town's Jews by their first names. They stared at us and kept quiet, one of the town's veterans told us that the synagogue is a "historic place" and therefore it was not damaged. Synagogues, and cemeteries, in all the towns (and if we are not mistaken - except for Lublin, Krakow and Zamo, and maybe other half a dozen) had a similar fate. Many others were destroyed by the Germans and others by the locals and the rest are being destroyed and disappear in the absence of anyone to take care of them.

Typical is maybe the fate of the ancient Jewish cemetery in Lublin. A high wall surrounded it all around and only a lock was needed to protect it, to lock the gate that was preserved, but there was no one who could take care of that lock, and the cemetery was abandoned. In Praga, a suburb of Warsaw across the Vistula stood, for a long time, the famous local synagogue. There was a plan to turn it into a museum and Yosef Sandel and his wife collected, with great dedication, pictures and paintings with the intention of housing them in the museum. But in Jewish Poland - as it is today - there was no one to take care of it even though the Polish authorities showed a willingness to help with the establishment of the museum. The synagogue was demolished and eventually made way for practical and workable plans.

In the Streets and Alleys of Tarnogrod

We wandered from town to town, drove north and were close to Belz across the border. We were in Plock near Posk, in Bilgoraj - and we asked in vain what was kept in our hearts from the town. A kind-hearted farmer led us through the streets and alleys of Tarnogrod, between the wooden houses and thatched roofs, to the heart the same mixture of shops and animals and told us: "Malka'le Konigstein was imprisoned, before she was executed, together with my wife ... and on cold nights, on an empty stomach, Malka'le calmed her down and sang "The sun is setting in flames...""" Then, passed by us what was once an institution in the town - a water carrier who, as in those days, carried a yoke and buckets. The local farmer pointed at a roof of a house and said: "I live here. A Jewish family lived here before the war. Do you see on the roof a kind of square cover? The Jews removed it on the holiday of *Sukkot* and put the covering of the *sukkah* under it... For thirty-two years the cover was not taken off the roof and the overhanging branches turned the whole roof into one piece.

Not far away is the town of Gur (Góra). In the courtyard of the *Admor* [spiritual leader in the *Hasidic* movement], whose cleverness and wisdom went beyond the confines of the Jewish community and were famous throughout Poland, hundreds and thousands of Hassidim congregated from Friday to the end of Sabbath. Carriages and carts, which brought the Jews of the city and the surrounding towns, gathered around the courtyard. Around thirty to forty percent of the non-Jewish residents somehow integrated in the joy, helped and harnessed, sold and bought. Today, we cannot recognize the home of the Gerrer *Rebbe*, and not his famous *shtiebel*. In the first years after the war Polish citizens lived in houses, in the shadow of the Hebrew inscriptions that adorned the *shtiebel*, and in the end they were also removed. No name and trace of his past remained on the house.

The disappointment that accompanies the search for the remains of a town reminds me an excerpt from a book by the Polish-Jewish writer Adolf Rudnicki. He tells about a Polish-Jewish poet who during the war lives on the Aryan area and enters the ghetto to see everything with his own eyes, to live everything and to describe. But he was caught and cooperates. And so he explains himself: "I came to the ghetto to give evidence... as if humanity lacks evidence... if ever someone will wants to describe it all, he would be told: a small and awful Jewish nation, stop talking nonsense about your suffering... Your sufferings are natural and do not interest anyone..."

There is a real secret in the statement this literary figure, and not the truth in terms of justice, but the truth in terms of historical human experience. Poland itself is very busy. The authorities are intensively searching for the right socialist formula for the Polish people, and most of the people are preoccupied with the war of existence. The chapters of the Holocaust are integrated into the education system, and it seems that they are not hidden or skipped. But the Jewish people, among them thirty thousand Polish Jews, do not want, unable and do not believe, that they will influence Poland to devote much more attention, money and efforts to preserve the memory of Jews and Judaism, which have long been a living organ of the Polish body and state.

The authorities do not reject the initiative, and often show a great deal of understanding, but the few initiators, maybe naturally, are all Jewish survivors, weak and poor. When walking like this between the towns, there is no escape from the thought that only the State of Israel, and no other body apart from it can save, preserve and nurture what is left. And the matter is simple and technically easy, and it seems that the financial means will also be easily found. I have no doubt, that if there would be an address and financial means - there will also be a lock for the gates of the old cemetery in Lublin, gravestones will be collected, monuments will be erected, booklets and textbooks will be published. I do not think of a more vital and beneficial investment than this, because it is the one who will bring the mature Polish youth, him and his friends, along with relatives and the tourists. It will stop them before a gravestone, a monument and a chapter in a book. So that they may reflect, even for a moment and inadvertently, on what was once the Polish Jew.

The *Pinkas* [Registry]

A small handful of Jews, who also need a good opportunity and luck, still manage to save remnants and testimonies. We found a lonely and miserable man who collects prayer shawls and Torah scrolls and does not know what to do with them. We met an elderly couple who have been collecting photographs of Jewish ritual articles for several years. The Jewish Historical Institute Warsaw is working diligently on historical research and searching for evidence. Zero, in the absence of sufficient means and information they also depend on the grace of gentiles who decide, for whatever reason, to reveal, sell some assets or uncover a hidden chapter. It so happened that one day near the time of my visit to Poland, a Pole appeared holding in his hand a valuable historical asset that he had no idea what it was. He laid on the table "*Pinkas HaHevrah*" [the "Society Registry"] of the town of Nasielsk, took 1000 *zloty* in return, and left without anyone asking him how the *Pinkas* got into his hands and what motivated him to sell it right now. And so I, and others like me, who are exploring the remains of the Jewish town, had the opportunity to get to know the other side of the Jewish town, to peek into the depths of its structure, feel its continuity and uniqueness. For hundreds of years, Jewish craftsmen in hundreds of towns used to write in "*Pinkas HaHevrah*," the craftsmen's registry, the course of events, internal laws, the regulations requiring a Jewish craftsman towards his people, towards the landowner and the environment. The *Pinkas* was usually written in Hebrew rich in expression, and also incorporated words in Yiddish and the local language. Over the years the *Pinkasim* [pl. registries] were burnt together with the wooden synagogue and, from time to time, a new *Pinkas* was opened. The *Pinkas* handed over by the Pole was that of the tailors and furriers in Nasielsk, and written in sequels, mostly by the judge, in years1753 to 1841. It lists the reasons why a certain tailor was deprived of the right to vote for the society, and from another person - the permission to ascend to the Torah for three years, and it describes the act of a certain person who disobeyed the law. As in the rest of "*Pinkasi HaHevrah*," it was also noted in this one that a copy was also kept in the Polish language. And that the minister, that is to say, the owner of the local estate, approved its contents with his signature.

We browsed for a long time in this instructive *Pinkas*, which was 200 years old, and imagined that we - the natives of the State of Israel - are diving and delving into the intricacies of the complex concept called a town. "After all, it is known - the *Pinkas* opens - that the society of tailors, *kirznirs* (furriers) and *schmuklers* [traders for haberdashery products] was founded in the year 5513 by the abbreviated era [1753] and they've had a *Pinkas* since then, and this *Pinkas* was burnt and in the year 5527 [1767] we investigated and founded another *Pinkas* for the members of the society and we still have it, but we, the members of the society, saw with our own eyes that there is no beauty in this *Pinkas* and it is also not organized properly and correctly, and since we did not come to establish unseemly things, we, the members of society, young to old, we all agreed to fix a new *Pinkas* that would be nice an pleasant in the eyes of the seers..." And below: "all of us agree to accept the preacher, our teacher the rabbi R' Yakov, to be our leader, to judge us whenever we have a trial and to obey him in all..." The eighth regulation in the *Pinkas* says: "On every Sabbath *Kodesh* each and every member of the society, they and their workers, must come to the synagogue to hear a lesson, so that they would not walk idly in the streets and stroll in the markets, which brings the person into bad offenses, controversy and slander, and other bad things. And whoever is in his house on the Sabbath and does not come to hear the lesson, he is obliged to give a fine, half a golden [zloty] for the synagogue's candles."

And here is another regulation, which holds the answer to the many questions of those who wanted to know how Judaism was preserved in the Diaspora: "Every Sabbath eve every craftsman, his workers and apprentices, must stop their work, and no tool shall be seen on the table, and they have permission to do their work until the society's *shamash* comes to warn them that our *gabbai* needs to send the *shamash* to each and every one to stop them from their work. And if the *shamash* comes to warn them three hours after mid-daylight (noon), and if would happen that someone will say, I am desperate for this thing and he, or his workers and apprentice, will continue their work, then this man will be punished four golden by the court (of the minister-landowner), but if it appears that this work is needed and he forced to do his work three hours after mid-daylight, or more, then he is exempt from punishment..."

The society's *Pinkas* contains within it a whole world. It unfolds before you a complex tradition, customs and way of life which were handed down from generation to generation in the same town. And there were thousands of towns in Poland, and there was not a single town in which there was not at least one *minyan* of Jews.

The society's *Pinkas*, which was rescued and redeemed by chance, helped us, to some extent, to understand the town, grasp its greatness and feel the significance of its absence.

Conversations and Sights

The forest borders the extermination camp. Birkenau extends from it onwards. Human ash covers the roads, nourishes the weeds that grows on the same soil, as far as can be seen around.

The young Jew, who was once imprisoned in nearby Auschwitz, is today an American citizen. We followed him. From time to time he stopped walking and said as if he was talking to himself: "In this place I am sure that the soil is not saturated with ashes and bones. Here the soil is not so scorching. Here, I am at least sure that I am not stepping on my parents' ashes."

It rained in Birkenau, during my visit to the place, on the remains of the ruined crematorium, on the surviving barbed wire fence, on the mounds of ashes and the monuments. The drops were absorbed in the soil mixed with the ash. At the edge of the forest there is a small lake. It was deeper before hundreds of bodies and bones were thrown into it. We got down on our knees drew from the water a handful of thin human bones. The water flowed through our fingers, and the young Jew said that it was possible that he was now holding his father's bones in his palm.

Somewhere, about fifty meters from the lake, was once "Canada." "We called this place by that name because it was relatively safe there, the prisoners worked and received food," the young man recounted pointing at what had survived from that illusion. Hundreds of rusty dishes were scattered on the grass. For some reason they were not collected during the seventeen years that have passed. Soon the grass will cover them.

Before that I visited Auschwitz for a long time. Shortly after arriving at the camp's gate the young American introduced himself to me. He said that he was visiting this place for the second time and immediately led me to the "death block" where he was imprisoned. At the rear of the room was a reinforced concrete wall and thousands of people were executed next to it. The windows adjoining it were covered with wooden boards. The American Jew remembers every detail and explains that the windows were covered with wood boards so that the prisoners would not know the meaning of the frequent shots near their window. "Whenever the block commander asked us to move to the other side of the room, we knew that shots would be heard soon."

Then, we stood in front of the pile of suitcases. The young man pinned his head to the glass window and his eyes wandered from one suitcase to the other. From Gutman to Meirovitz, to Zuckerman, to Cohen and Goldman. He was looking for his suitcase. We continued up the hair pavilion, to the awful pile of pairs of shoes.

I spent a lot of time in the company of a former Auschwitz prisoner. We moved from one block to another, from exhibit to exhibit, and finally stopped to let the one who made his way here from faraway New York to present his claim.

Majdanek

I will open this article with a short description of my visit in Majdanek, although I do not ignore the danger that the reader will reach conclusions devoid of any justification and intent.

I searched for the death camp for a long time. Longer than it took to get to a nearby suburb of Lublin from which I had left. This may be due to the lack of proper signage and also the roads in this area were defective and, at the same time, were in the midst of repairs. When I finally got to the nearest residential area, which was certainly not a town or an independent neighborhood, I asked passers-by for the way to Majdanek. They looked very surprised and replied that I was in Majdanek itself. Meaning, once again the thought-determination was confirmed, that in Poland - both options are obvious: to the casual resident of the town of Majdanek, which is one of the thousands of towns in Poland, it is obvious that we ask about the town of Majdanek. The mental mechanism is constructed in such a way that it is not at all conceivable that a stranger, in a foreign car, who is arriving in this area, may be interested only in the Majdanek death camp which is adjacent to the town. While for a Jew and an Israeli it is obvious that a resident of the place immediately understands that the stranger can only be interested in the death camp (and it has happened before, that a local young man told me in good faith that he collected blueberries in the Auschwitz forests, and he did not, of course, imagine that it was simply impossible to collect blueberries in Auschwitz forests).

This situation, an encounter with "neutrality" of such a nature, is quite common in the journey of a Jewish and Israeli visitor, and this article will actually discuss that, because it is one of the components of the fact that there was not one Jew, especially a former resident of Poland, who did not ask us rhetorically, how a Jew can return, or visit, Poland. Not to mention the thousands who live there permanently.

In the Death camp

I needed a different wording and asked where the "*lager*" [camp] was, and only then I was shown the way. The camp is located on a wide plain, in an agricultural area, that on each side, to the edge of the fence and the guard towers, the farmers cultivate their fields. Several sheaves of grain were arranged within the boundaries of the camp itself, in the place where some of the hundreds of barracks once stood. A smooth concrete road, on which no vehicle or a person were seen, deviated from the main road and ran hundreds of meters along the barbed wire fence until it reached the memorial mound. I drove very slowly and looked at the camp to my right, at the huts that were similar to each other, at the dirt roads between them, at the thorns that had grown in the meantime. No living soul was seen in the area at this late afternoon hour and only beyond that smoke rose from the chimneys of the factories, and workers riding their bicycles passed as they do every day.

At the end of the road, next to the memorial mound, the road turned right and fifty meters later, on a low hill, next to a large wooden structure with a chimney extending from its center- I stopped. A wind blew and a soothing silence reigned all around, resting on the death camp.

I turned to the wooden structure whose nature was easy to guess and, suddenly, a man in his fifties came out of the doorway. He was wearing tattered uniform, carried a rifle on his shoulders and a pungent odor of alcohol wafted from his mouth. The drunken guard led me inside, to the crematoria. He pointed, swaying, at the six ovens that had been preserved intact. He held the stretchers that half of them were inside the oven and with a rough drunken hand began to drive the stretchers back and forth in a loud sound, in and out to demonstrate their action. Six times so and so corpses, twenty minutes each cycle - calculated the drunken guard and did not let go of the stretcher.

Darkness prevailed inside the crematorium and the guard volunteered to show me the second room. "Here hundreds of thousands got undressed, here they bathed, here - in this big hall, the strangled bodies were piled up and then dragged to the crematorium." And then, when the irrational vision which was reveled against the backdrop of loneliness, darkness and a lone guard, began to weigh, I saw through a dark opening leading to the gas chamber, behind an uprooted door which was leaning against the wall, human bones lying disorderly on the floor, limbs and skulls, as they were found in that gas chamber on the day of liberation. I "took advantage" of my guide's drunkenness and begged him to lift the door and let me peek inside. He hesitated a little, leaned his rifle against the wall and lifted the door. And inside the gloom, on the floor of the gas chamber, inside a large bathtub, piles of piles were placed what had once been the corpse, what the gas and time had left.

*

When I returned to the main road I met a worker who was leaning against the crematorium and painting the iron parts in fresh paint. The human bones were kept with the intention of storing them in a permanent museum. For some reason this has not been done so far. I later received a more detailed explanation from a group of people I met on my way back to the camp. I drove to them in my car on the bumpy dirt road. A cheerful young couple passed by and a peasant woman laden with a sheaf of grain on her back. One of the people who came out of the hut approached me and asked, for some reason, if he could speak Russian with me and said that he is the architect who oversees the renovation work of the museum. Majdanek - he explained - the huts, buildings, accessories and the ovens will become a large museum.

I returned to Lublin.

*

In the last years I visited several concentration camps. I was once in Theresienstadt in Czechoslovakia, Dachau and Bergen Belsen in Germany, Auschwitz in Poland, and the Gestapo's torture cellars in Warsaw. In most of these places the evidence was arranged for display, I saw them lying on shelves with explanatory notes next to them, behind glass or grille. Only in Majdanek, which is being restored, I found mounds of bones lying on the ground, piled in a bathtub, as they were found on the day of liberation. And maybe that's why the vision is so shocking and the response so complex. And between you and me, in disorder, you ask questions, why so far the authorities have not taken care of the establishment of the museum, and is it really possible to make do with one drunk policeman who wandered disrespectfully around the bones?! On the other hand - how can people isolate themselves from the camp they see in the morning, at noon, in the evening; from where does a normal person draw the strength to live so close to death; how did not a shred of Majdanek stick to the young couple who crossed the camp to its width! And who knows the human soul, maybe, after all, every local resident carries in his heart the desire to escape one day as far as possible to start anew on a different land, a new chapter of life.

*

The subjective impressions cannot obscure a single dry basic fact - that today the authorities are investing efforts in order to turn Majdanek into a museum, to an historic educational place for teens and adults.

And at this point the question arises - "How a Jew, born in Poland, can continue to live on Polish soil?"

We will try below to encompass the question from its various sides, but it is doubtful whether we will know how to answer it. In any event - despite the years that have passed, it is surprisingly relevant, just as the Holocaust, its reflection in literature, in people's conversation, in official policy, is the legacy of the present.

*

In this regard the town of Majdanek can symbolize "Polish" Poland, the daily life of the people, the obstacles facing the authorities in the realization of socialism and the fact that, after all, the problems of Poland are not Jewish but the problems of the Polish nation. The camp's drunken guard undoubtedly belongs to this area and he represents one of the problems. The "*lager*" and the death camps, on the other hand, maybe represent the central subject that preoccupies the Polish authorities, the intellectuals and the literature, and to a large extent the people themselves in the broad field called people's education. The extermination of the Jews on Polish soil, sometimes with the passive and active assistance of Polish citizens, and the fact that Judaism and the Jews have been an integral part of the way of life for centuries, constitute, without a doubt, the forefront of the problem in this field, both in terms of its sharpest and most extreme expression.

At first glance, the two domains are a kind of coexistence of situations that cannot be connected. Much like the existence of the camp with the human bones scattered in the gas chamber, right next to the town of Majdanek, with its problems and customs, which remind us of every other Polish town.

The Jew arriving in Poland immediately encounters this situation; he is hurt due to the lack of a "bridge" between the two areas; he does not understand how eighteen years have passed and not a single memorial plaque has been erected in Majdanek for the hundreds of thousands of Jews. Why the negotiations for the establishment of a Jewish pavilion in Auschwitz, in which two and a half million Jews were exterminated, is taking so long, and why are the roots of anti-Semitism so slowly being uprooted. This, it seems, is the background to the reluctance of so many to visit what was once their homeland, apart from, of course, the personal memories.

And this too: the Second World War, with its results and memory, has not ended here yet. During all my visits I felt that in this country it is still too early to open a new chapter, to move the page, as has already been done in some countries in Europe and perhaps also in Germany.

The Jew is not the only one who is sensitive to the daily whistle of a train traveling between a city and a town. It mentions the role of the trains, perhaps of all the trains in Poland, even those traveling today, in the extermination of the people. Very often the events of those days come to life and the attention is turned to what is being enjoyed here with great hatred- "Nazism" or "Fascism."

Those Who Rescued

One day a new museum was opened and it is announced that a certain site has been restored or renovated, and from time to time bouquets of flowers are placed on the graves of the fallen on street corners. And another example: a book written by two Jewish scholars will soon appear in Poland. It discusses the question of the extent to which the Polish people extended relief and aid to the Jews during the war. If I am not mistaken, the authors assume that about twenty Gentiles on average participated in the rescue of every Jew. Every child, or adult, who was hidden, passed from hand to hand, or his documents were forged and he was provided with food and clothing. All this involved the knowledge of twenty people. Since, with the liberation, between fifty and seventy thousand Jews were found in Poland, with the exception of the liberated from the concentration camps, at least one million Poles took an active part in rescuing the Jews.

I know that quite a few will say that this number is exaggerated especially from the fact that the book is funded and distributed by the government. It is also of great interest because the Polish authorities do not shy away from bringing this issue up for debate, and for bringing it into the consciousness of the citizens and perhaps as a matter for conscience and concern.

The Jewish Historical Institute can serve as an example to the good intentions of the authorities with regard to the rights of the Jews as a small minority, which was once large and influential. The diverse literature issued by the Institute, the annual budget amounting to 700,000 *zlotys*, the building, the permanent exhibition and the salaries provided by the state, all of these are a unique expression in this political area, of the recognition by the authorities of the cultural, and perhaps national, needs of the Jews, except that it is the fruit of a burdensome morality.

But those, who see the Jewish Institute as an expression of cultural activity and national awakening, are wrong. The Institute undoubtedly does immeasurably important work. Starting with a comprehensive research on the life of the Jews from the 17th century, systematic photography of Jewish sites throughout Poland, the printing of books and pamphlets, among them all of Emanuel Ringelblum's writings published this year and much more. But it lacks the same vitality that is only possible when there is a lively connection with an awakened community, with an interested readership and public. But since these are not and the approximately 30,000 Jews scattered throughout Poland do not coalesce into an organized minority with representation and an address, the Jewish Institute mentions a lonely island, from which the projections projected are not absorbed.

If we want, this is another side of the same unbridgeable coexistence that casts sadness on the stay of a Jewish visitor in Poland. He realizes that the integration of the Jews, in which the theorists were so confident at the time is, in this case, nothing more than an empty word. And what is easy to bring dozens of examples of Jews, whose souls are divided, and most of whom are loyal to the regime and believe in its future.

We have often been asked about the number of Jews in Poland, and it seems to me that even presenting this question, and the inability to answer it with certainty, illuminates another side of the problem. It is simply not technically possible to count the young. Many live to this day in small and remote towns, quite a few young people do not know about their Judaism, many choose to stay away from any Jewish institution, organization or newspaper. Only a small and insignificant number visits the few synagogues or participates in the educational effort of several communities, especially in Lodz. Things got to the point where a group of Jewish activists, to which I belonged, tried to count the number of Hebrew speakers in Warsaw and, in a joint effort, reached a number of nine.

In this situation it is not necessary to debate if there is a future for Jewish life in Poland, just as it is unnecessary to try to prove that a million Poles took part in rescuing Jews.

One meeting, like many others, might express our feelings on this issue. We stopped our car on Marszakowska Street and asked a passerby if he could guide us to the Jewish Historical Institute. Instead of replying, the man put his hand on the door handle, peeked inside, asked if he could enter and said: Drive! On the way he asked us if we were from Israel, what is the situation and his voice was excited and his eyes shone. Then we asked if he was Jewish, and to our surprise he said no. But only a hundred meters later, he asked to give his greetings to his sister who lives in Jaffa, and also to his cousin in Haifa.

The Treasures of the Lonely Jew in Leajsk

The town seemed to hold its breath for a moment. the barbers, the salesmen, the passers-by, those who rested on the benches of the municipal park - all stopped what they were doing and looked at us with curiosity, impudence and a slightest hint of provocation, but none in a look of kindness and understanding. Because, at that time, the only Jew of the city of Leajsk, Baruch Sapir, stood bent over our car and urged us in Yiddish to hurry away from there, from the cold and strange eyes of the townspeople who began to push from all sides. We started the car and left behind us 55 year old Baruch Sapir, with his long white-beard, awkward gait and refined virtues. To be precise - we left him with a heavy burden in our heart, as if we had left a wounded man on the battlefield.

*

We were about ten miles from Leajsk. In a small town named Tarnogrod, one of the many in which Jews lived. Sixty years ago our parents were born there, forty years ago they emigrated from there with the first *halutzim*, and twenty years ago all the

Jews were murdered in the town's streets. We went to the elders and asked where our relatives lived, where they traded, how they were murdered and where they were buried. We went to the synagogue, wandered, for no reason in the alleys, between the wooden houses and the thatched roofs, and stopped by a carrier of yoke and buckets next to loaded carts in the "*rynek*" [market] in the central square. Several townspeople wanted to help us, remembered a certain act and anonymous person, showed us where our grandfather's store stood and where the bodies were piled up, and while talking, we have been told that a Jew lives in the nearby city of Leajsk, maybe a rabbi named Sapir, and he knows the history of the Jews in all the towns in of eastern Poland. Therefore, we set out to look for the Jew. We drove through fields near busy farmers, got on a ferry that took us to the other bank of the San River and continued towards Leajsk. The first person who happened to be on our way to the entrances of the city knew immediately to reply that, indeed, they have a bearded Jew named Sapir and he lives on Main Street. And when we stopped there, one of the people pointed towards the entrance to an old building and said that this is where the Jew lives, but he likes to wander and it is possible that he is not at home. At that moment we saw a man with a white beard slipping into the entrance as he was holding two large silver Chanukah menorahs in his hand. We followed him into the building's dark entrance, climbed a wooden staircase and knocked on the door. And when it opened, the marvelous figure of Baruch Sapir stood before us, a man with large body, blue eyes, white beard that curled around his face and was dressed in tattered clothes. When he heard us saying "Shalom Aleichem he hurried inside, brought a chair from the neighbor's apartment, closed the windows, and turned on the radio in embarrassment. Only later he began to tell his fragmented story in Polish-Yiddish-Hebrew.

*

It seems that there is no place in the world where you can find a room like Baruch Sapir's room, with its treasures, atmosphere and meaning. It is impossible to have another room like this, because there is no one in the world who resembles its owner, Baruch Sapir. In a terrible mess, junk and neglect, were scattered in piles, inside boxes, on the tables and in every corner and crack - books, notes, utensils, Bibles and Torah scrolls, Chanukah menorahs and other accessories that served the Jews of the towns in the extensive area around Leajsk. For years, Baruch Sapir has been purchasing all of these from the farmers in the area. He leaves his house for one day, a week, a month, wanders from town to town and from city to city, searching and asking if anyone has any sacred vessels, any relic from a Jewish house, synagogue or cemetery. He pays with the best of his money and brings the object, the Torah scroll and the siddur, to his house until a piece of Jewish history was accumulated in this narrow apartment.

Baruch Sapir, who moves heavily across the room reminds us of the clumsy figure of "Arye Ba'al Guf" [short story by H.N. Bialik], says: "Here you have the ornate cane of the Rabbi of Tarnow, the Book of Psalms and Torah scrolls." At the same time he opens a box and in front of us are dozens of Torah scrolls, which were found at the peasants homes in the vicinity of the Jewish towns. "At one gentile - he says - there is box full of sacred books, in Krzeszów - he says - I tried to get them to build a fence around the graves of the murdered Jews, and yesterday I discovered two Chanukah menorahs in another place."

Baruch Sapir, excited and frightened by the meeting with us, reveals a little and hides- without special intention - twice as much. No one has imposed on him the work of gathering, these wanderings, and he does not try, even with the slightest hint, to act like one who fulfills a sacred mission. From his slightly wet eyes that wander over the treasures scattered in his room, you learn that he is worried about all the treasure he has collected. He pleads with us, begging us to take with us the cane of the Rabbi of Tarnow, bundles of Bibles, the surviving Shofar from a town in Poland or, at least, a few Torah scrolls.

*

We learned very little about him and his life. Only that he was born 55 years ago in Leajsk, grew and lived there in the small Jewish community, and when the war broke out he arrived in the Soviet Union and sat there in prison for 12 years. Five years ago, when he was released, he returned to his birthplace. There, he learned that he was the only Jew in this city, and in all the dozens of towns which stretch for hundreds of miles around. He is the only Jew who now travels on the roads connecting the towns on which thousands of Jews once traveled on their way to the fair and to the family for the holidays. Baruch Sapir has no idea what will be the fate of the treasure stored in his apartment. But this fact does not seem to detract from his eagerness to continue saving the remains, to continue to wander and coax the gentiles, to purchase and bring Torah scrolls and menorahs in trains, buses and on foot.

And while he recounts, with no continuous connection between matters, he combs his beard, again and again, and confesses: "I am persecuted, poor and sick, lonely here like a dog!"

*

All that time the townspeople gathered outside around our car, waiting curiously for the moment we leave. Baruch Sapir accompanied us outside. He straightened up, ignoring the looks of ridicule, the unconquered smiles and the bewilderment that gripped the town, as if he was protecting his friends from Eretz Yisrael who surprised him so much.

Baruch Sapir, who is worthy of a long life, may one day, as he puts it, walk away, and in his dark room, on the second floor of a dilapidated house, in a foreign town a great treasure will remain, an invaluable asset that may fall again into the hands of the local farmers. If any institution in Eretz Yisrael will undertake to transfer the collection, as soon as possible, to the realms of our archives, rest will have come to the soul of one holy Jew. And whoever gets to know Baruch Sapir will swear, because it was a great deed.

[Pages 520-523]

With the Souls of our Holy Martyrs

Zushe Fester

Translated by Helene Roumani

On the 1st of May, 1960, several Tarnogrod survivors living in Israel met on Mount Zion to dedicate a monument in memory of the Holy Martyrs of Tarnogrod.

With tearful eyes and grieving hearts, we greet one another when, right there and then our town Tarnogrod, Jewish Tarnogrod, reappears right in front of us, just as it was prior to the great disaster, the Holocaust. Suddenly, I'm a little boy, walking to the cemetery with my father on Tisha B'Av, clutching a little bag of garlic in my hand, as was the custom, to place on the graves of loved ones. Scenes flash in front of our faces, like in a nightmare, we are a strange assembly of acquaintances from the past.

Coming from all over the country, participants in the
Tarnogrod Memorial Dedication Ceremony on Mount Zion

Editor's Note: Although this photograph does not have a caption, Iser Stockman
also appears on page 11 and this appears to be the same person. Nuchim
Krymerkopf's relative has stated that this is not a picture of him.

Just then, a man with a camera slung over his shoulder arrives. Not everyone recognizes him. Turns out, it's Iser Stockman, a Jew with a warm heart and a generous hand, dedicated passionately to Tarnogrod and the Tarnogrod Fraternal Society. He approaches each and every one assembled with genuine brotherly concern and is most committed to the success of the memorial event in commemoration of the Holy Martyrs of Tarnogrod on Mount Zion. Coming all the way from London, he attends to every little detail and every concern, addressing each participant individually and as a group.

Here is Nuchim Krymerkopf, from America, the initiator of the memorial project, his face frozen in solemn tribute to the occasion.

Jews from Tanogrod after the Holocaust excavating mass graves
with remains of martyrs from Bilgoraj

Slowly, with heads bent low, we enter the dark chamber, illuminated only by candle light. A strange stillness accompanies the group. All deep in thought, we gather in a corner of the room where the monument is mounted on the wall, shrouded in a black veil. It is dark in the corner. We cannot see one another. We can only feel. We feel the souls of the martyrs, they are hovering above us. And we feel the cries of the children ringing in our ears.

Nuchim removes the black veil. For a moment, there is utter silence. Our throats choak with tears as the chamber is filled with the sound of heavy sighing. Rabbi Hershela's wife, the *Rebbetzin* Esther Teicher, accompanied by several older women, light memorial candles. Shmulik Stockman's son, Iser, recites the *El Malei Rachamim* [traditional Jewish memorial prayer] and addresses the group with a short speech.

Buried in a pile of ashes, our Jewish Tarnogrod is gone, devastated and forsaken. The destruction is too great to comprehend. How could we even try to imagine the Sabbath and the holidays in our Tarnogrod without a call to prayer? With not a soul in the street rushing to synagogue at sundown anymore? The truth is unbelievable, impossible to understand and too difficult to accept. Our beloved brethren have all been destroyed in the terrible catastrophe of the Holocaust.

With these thoughts we depart, leaving Mount Zion for our new homes and our newly established lives. Yes, Tarnogrod is dead and destroyed. We are the only survivors, rescued in some miraculous way from the great disaster that claimed the lives of our brethren in Poland.

We, the Jewish survivors of Tarnogrod, will never forget our devastated home, nor will we forget our holy martyrs whose lives were so dedicated to Jewish values. Our beloved fathers and grandfathers, our prominent community members and our simple folk, our beautiful people. Deeply entrenched in our hearts, we will cherish their memory forever and ever.

Godel Wetsher
His passion for great ideals resounded in everything he did and will never be silenced.

[Pages 524-527]

Potok – Gorny

(Potok Górny, Poland)

50023' 22034'

Moshe Shprung, Tel Aviv

Translated by Chesky Wertman

Mr. Wertman has dedicated this translation to
The Knochen and Wertman Families
who lived in Potok-Gorny until the end of the war and whose
members perished during the liquidation of Tarnogrod.

Potok-Gorny! I want to extol you and lament you. I want you to remain eternal, so that you will never be forgotten! May the future generations who read these words know, that once there were villagers, who provided for themselves as merchants and laborers, as honest and hard workers. Twenty Jewish families lived among thousands of Poles and Ukrainians and they did not loose their *Tzelem Elokim* [G-dly image], they maintained their Judaism transmitting it from parent to child. The life style of our homes in the village was infused with Judaism.

It was, and now, there is nothing that remains. *Reb* Shmuel Peretz Shprung, a Jew whose entire being was piety is no more. He is a "remnant", a sincere leader of prayer, and a reader of the Torah, who also served as the rabbi. He did not only rule on simple issues, but he also accepted the yolk of guiding the Jews of his village, advising them on how to improve and enhance their adherence to Jewish customs and traditions, and how to help themselves during a difficult time, and all followed his advice.

Yisrael Silberzweig, who clung to the tenets of his conviction, a pious Jew, who was vested with good character traits and integrity is gone. No more Aharon Brick, the only *Kohen* [a descendant of the biblical high priest Aaron] in our village, who blessed us when he recited the blessings of the *kohanim* [pl.], during the holidays.

Actually, the *minyan* [minimum gathering of 10 people necessary for a communal religious service] took place in our home. On *Shabbos* [Jewish Sabbath] and holidays all the Jews from Potok, and also from other close villages where some Jewish families lived would get together.

The *heder*, the school for the Jewish children from the village was also in our home. The teachers, who were brought in from Tarnogrod, would always stay with us in our home; they had a comfortable place and they ate with my parents. The teachers focused on the development of the students. The sound of *Reb* David Mantel, is engraved in the memories of the more advanced students. He had learned with us *Gemara* [Talmud] and told us beautiful stories, about G-d's kindness and wonders. He would tell us the wonderful tales from the *aggadah* [stories presented in the Talmud], and treat us with something from a *midrash*, or from the Bible. He taught us in a well explained manner, his words seemed to simply flow from his tongue.

At that time, I am not sure, that we completely understood everything, but the words alone, the Rabbi's exceptional countenance, the sweetness of his voice, warmed our hearts, providing us with much inner pleasure.

Our home was open to every wayfarer or traveler to distant lands, who would search for a place to comfort their heart and relax their weary legs. Summer and Winter, in pouring rain, and blizzards, they would always come to us, knowing that they would find a warm spot, something cooked, and lodging.

My darling dear mother! I see the softness of your clever eyes, your attentiveness warmed every entering guest, greeting him with a good word, a light meal. Your life was not easy, my poor mother, day and night you labored, washing and cleaning so that every corner sparkled with purity and perfection.

My father, *Reb* Yisrael Isser, was not only loved by the Jews of the village but also by those from Tarnogrod, and my father felt a bond and connection with them. His cleverness and integrity made him popular also among the peasants of the village. Our home was a model of a modest and pure life. Until today, my righteous mother and father, you stand before my eyes as a tower of light, shining with the pure, beautiful light of my childhood years, the image calming me during my turbulent bitter times.

The village Potok-Gorny was 12 kilometers from Tarnogrod and the 20 Jewish families that lived there, were connected to the Tarnogrod Jewish community. They shared each other's joys and sorrow, as one large family.

The people from Potok-Gorny were good, warm people. They were involved in trade and were laborers. Amongst them was a tailor, a shoemaker, and a miller, who provided their services to the rural dwellers.

Amongst them there were those who were the second and third generation in the village and they also maintained a connection with Tarnogrod. They learned from the Tarnogroders and their Tarnogroder teachers exalted and pleasant Jewish attributes and love for their fellow Jew.

Potok-Gorny was indeed a large village. Approximately 2,000 Poles and over 1,000 Ukrainians lived there. They had there own *Gmina* [Rural Administrative District] and even an independent *koza* [prison] where they kept the arrested. My mother and father would watch the prison, perhaps a Jew from a distant village was brought there. They were concerned that he should not remain there over *Shabbos* without the customary *Shabbos* food. My brother and I had the task to bring the food there -- the cholent, the kugel. I can still see that scene from the past, the thrill those Jews had when they would see us coming with the *Shabbos* food, which for them was as if they had just received a greeting from their *Shabbos* table at home.

Oh my father and mother, the memories of your lives, and of your magnificent deeds accompanied me through all my journeys.

As Hitler's onslaught began to descend, I was away from the house, and I was virtually deprived of your blessing. I did not want to consider the notion of separation, you, dear mother, did not know that I was arrested on the other side of the border, and during every meal time placed on the table a plate also for me.

So much longing, longing and sorrow, such incredible love which went beyond any country's border. After all of this I now come wordless, with memories of what once was. No words could adequately express my pain, and there is not a thing in the world that could be similar to your holy cry of distress from pain.

When that horrendous day in 1942 arrived, when the murderer took you away to Krasow, to be slaughtered. My beloved brother, Shimon Meir heard, that our other brother Shlomo, hid in the village and had returned. The Poles searched for him in the forest. They pursued him for a kilo of sugar, the reward the Germans gave to the Poles for the Jews that they caught and turned in. They caught him and brought him to the field in Potok, and from there they took him along with 27 other Jews that were caught, packed in a wagon, to the forest, towards Jedlinki and in a field near the forest they were all shot.

Later the peasants came, and tore off their clothing, and left them there. Many days later the corpses, continued to lay without a burial in the field.

My heart does not listen to the crying within me, saintly Mother and Father, Brother and Sister, good genuine Jews from the Polish village Potok-Gorny!

[Pages 528 - 530]

Olchowiec

(Olchowiec, Poland)

50°21' 22°59'

Rafael Wasserman

Translated by Martin Jacobs

The Wasserman family
Right to left: Elazar (lives in America), Moshe Naftali (father) and Beile (mother),
who were tortured by the Germans; daughter Chana (perished); Yosef and Rafael
(living in Israel)

[Pages 528 - 530]

My parents lived for years in Olchowiec, a village 18 km. from Tarnogrod. All five Jewish families living there belonged to the Tarnogrod Jewish community. Relations between the Jews and the peasant population were friendly, and no one foresaw that killers would come from there who would cooperate with the Nazi murderers.

The Jews in Olchowiec were pious and preserved the Jewish traditions. They eked out a difficult living trading with the peasants of the village, acquiring among them a reputation as honest people who worked hard for a little bit of bread but would never cheat anyone out of a penny.

The younger children were sent to Tarnogrod to study in the *heder*, where they absorbed Jewish ways for their journey through life.

*

Great was the weeping, and heart–rending the singing of the prayer leader. "On Rosh Hashana it is written, and on Yom Kippur sealed", and on that Yom Kippur the great Destruction was decreed for the Jewish people, which did not spare the simple honest Jews of Olchowiec.

Even in the most dangerous days the Jews of our village took care not to eat unkosher food (God forbid!). Avrahamtche, the ritual slaughterer, having walked a whole night from Józefów, came to our village to slaughter a cow. Jews came to my father to buy kosher meat from other nearby villages as well.

On that day two Jewish girls from Oleszyce came to us and bought two kilograms of kosher meat. As they were walking back home they were stopped by German SS personnel, who took the meat and forced them to show them where they had bought it. They arrested my father and also got to the slaughterer. I hid for about a week until they caught me too and arrested me. For three weeks straight they tortured us and beat us severely on our naked bodies. They wanted us to give them the names of other Jews involved in the kosher meat affair. When they were unsuccessful they freed us on two thousand *zloty* security.

Our peasant neighbors found out that we were given a brief period in which to bring the money and knew we were unable to raise such a large sum. Immediately one peasant after another came to us and in a few days the necessary amount was collected.

But the Germans didn't leave us alone for long. A decree was soon issued requiring us to leave our village and move to Józefów. They took my father away to Majanek, where he was among the first victims.

My brother Elazar was in Warsaw at that time. For a while he worked as a baker for the Germans, then did hard labor in the labor camps. The liberation found him in Germany, and he is now in America.

Yosl remained with us and also succeeded in being rescued, after experiencing all the horrors of that time, witnessing the death of our nearest and dearest. The three of us are the only ones left of our entire family, which so horribly perished along with all the other kind and sincere Jews from the village of Olchowiec.

****

Once, once, in Tarnogrod…

Right to left: Eli Han (lives in Bolivia), Eliezer Teicher (Israel), Yoske Goldman (died in exile in Russia), Faiwel Koenigsberg (Israel), Yehuda Leicher (Argentina), Baruch Gutherz, son of Chaim–Yechiel the slaughterer (perished)

[Pages 531-532]

The Tarnogrod Organization in Israel

Translated by Miriam Leberstein

Executive Committee of the Tarnogrod Landsmanshaft in Israel

Standing, from right: Shmuel-Eli Futer, Moshe-Efraim Shprung, Yehiel Hering, Chaim Bornshtein
Seated: Shmuel Fefer, Nuchim Krymerkopf and Meir Ringer

Very few Tarnogroders emigrated to *Eretz-Yisroel* before the end of the Second World War. During the war, several Tarnogroders came to Israel from Russia with the Polish Anders' Army, and remained there. The largest wave of immigration came after the war. Jews from Tarnogrod get together at memorials and other events. At such gatherings, we memorialize our martyrs, who met such horrendous deaths.

Executive Committee of the Tarnogrod Landsmanshaft in America
Standing, from right: Mikhl Levinger, Abraham Kramer, Gershon Herbstman
Seated: David Aksenhorn, Efraim Lumerman and Yosef Fink

[Pages 533-535]

And There Was ...

Shimon Kanc

Translated and Edited by Martin Jacobs

Translated by Irving Lumerman

"And there was ..." And there once was a city, Tarnogrod, which took pride in its truth rooted in Jewish concepts, in its Torah scholars and dreamers of Zion, in those who dreamt of a better world and in those who, day and night, sat with meager daylight, with the light of an oil lamp, or a tallow candle, studying, quietly absorbed for hours in a saying of the Sages; and in the fools, water carriers, and coachmen who loved the very noise and commotion – all these things, which were the stuff of our legends, gone, vanished.

But everything related here in our memorial book about their heroic life and martyrs' death is far from being legendary. So too the beauty for which they yearned and which they achieved was no dream, the earth on which their cradle stood, the heavens which filled their eyes with light, the air, the scenery, the shadows of the dark woods, the sound of the flowing Tanew, the gold of the open fields, the storms of shining spring and the sadness of weeping autumns, the silence of snows in winter, the pain of endless distances, the blessed labor of a whole week, and the welcoming lights of the Friday night table were no dream.

The friendly candlesticks and the blessing Mother said over them, full of mercy and unbounded love with which she shaped our world, our lives, from the cradle until we left home for distant lands.

"Greetings, angels of peace". This was the sound of father's singing, and as he sang angels from on high began to hover in the air and filled the house with song.

"By your leave, my masters" [1] – simple words pervaded with so much holiness.

"O King, the king of kings, return us to Zion" – Father's melody was full of inspiration and longing.

Everyone –

The simple Jews with the excited faces, having borne within themselves the pain of all sunsets and the plan for all sorts of business, of coaches traveling to fairs, with all Jewish aromas of weekday and holiday.

Those who have cleaved heavens with Torah and prayer, and lifted themselves up above grey actuality with songs, dances, and wondrous deeds.

Those who with songs, lessons, and lectures in the library and culture club have created and raised up a modern Judaism.

They all believed that there is an order in the world, until the dark night came and wiped it all out. Only the solitary few who survived weep by the rivers of the world over the great Destruction.

Every record which we have brought here, every picture of a Tarnogrod Jew, whether of individual figures or of whole families, is a brick for the tombstone of the former life in our old home, a reminder of the terrors, awakening, for us and for future generations, the lament for the third Destruction.

O, Jewish Tarnogrod, may our children, until the furthest generations, know how beautifully you have shone in our hearts and memories, how much we loved the heaven above you, which was like a prayer shawl woven from the prayers of our fathers and grandfathers. We loved your poor earth, the market place noisy with traders, with peasants on rustic carts, who bought less from the Jews than they sold, and looked forward to some Jewish fish, spiced with pepper, after a shot of brandy.

It was sad in the Jewish shops in the Tarnogrod market, but the Ten Commandments shone over them and ecstatic *hasidic* melodies were hummed forth from there.

And so the Divine Presence rested everywhere in that place, and now every wall there is like the ruin of the Western Wall.

O martyrs of the Tarnogrod Jewish community, only a few of your children survive, in various corners of the world, and wherever they are to be found, in Israel and in America, they carry with them not only the dark grief and woe, but also the desire that their children and children's children understand the spiritual elation of their grandfathers, read the simple words related in this book concerning that life and its dreadful destruction, and understand, feel, and suspect how many tears and how much weeping lie in these letters.

Translator's note:

1. The opening words of the Friday night Kiddush prayer.

[Page 536]

Do Not Sing

Translated by Martin Jacobs

Do not sing, do not play,
Please be silent, my lyre.
Do not sing, let no music be played,
For this day is an evil one for us.

This day is evil for us,
The days are days of mourning.
Be silent, lyre,
And thou too, O harp.

Days of mourning are these days,
The destruction of the people;
Do not play, do not sing
Let us place hand to mouth.

[Page 537]

[Pages 538-539]

These I shall remember

Shimon Kanc

Translated and Edited by Martin Jacobs

Translated by Irving Lumerman

Difficult, immensely difficult, was the task of collecting and putting together the materials from the great tragedy, from the Destruction without equal which came upon the Jews of our town.

It is possible that here and there an error slipped in, or a detail not precisely in agreement with the reality of that time, or was minimized or exaggerated. The passage of time is at fault, the distance we have traveled, which from time to time leads to a warped picture.

It is possible that here and there certain details are repeated, but we wished all the more strongly to show the great world which was annihilated by the greatest Satan of all time.

A world of holiness and heroism, a world which was so lofty even in the days of the most terrible destruction, a destruction which had no equal in all of human history and which therefore truly appears beyond belief.

But here is the list of the names, of the hundreds in our town, murdered by the Nazi killers and thrown, shot but not killed, into the graves while still alive. The names of those whose blood will never cease to cry out and demand: "'*Yisgadal*', may the revenge of blood innocently shed be great."

The great extended cemetery of their names, like the sanctity and bravery of their lives and their deaths, will be engraved in our memory for all eternity.

The names were collected by the editorial committee with great difficulty and it is not possible to take responsibility for errors and missing names. For every error and for every name left out we ask pardon.

The Editors

Note: 'W' after a name indicates a woman, 'C' indicates a child or children.

The names of the Tarnogrod martyrs were researched by N. Krymerkopf, M. Shprung, Chaim Bornstein, Fayvl Koenigsberg, Chaim Shmuel Lorber, and Yechiel Hering

Necrology

Transliterated by Lorraine Rosengarten

א Alef	ב Bet	ג Gimmel	ד Dalet	ה Hey	ו Vav	ז Zayin	ח Chet	ט Tet	י Yod	כ Kaf
ל Lamed	מ Mem	נ Nun	ס Samech	ע Ayin	פ Peh	צ Tzadik	ק Kof	ר Resh	ש Shin	ת Tav

Family name(s)	First name(s)	Sex	Marital status	Father's name	Mother's name	Name of spouse	Additional family & remarks	Page
Alef א								
ADLER	Moshe	M	Married	Yakov		Malie	Died together with children	540
ADLER	Malie	F	Married			Moshe	Died together with children	540
ACKERMAN	Leizer	M	Married	Moshe			Died together with children	540
ACKERMAN		F	Married			Leizer	Died together with children	540
APTEKER	Gershon	M		M. Yekhezkel			Died together with his daughter & son-in-law	540
ADLER	Zalman	M	Married			Chaia		540
ADLER	Chaia	F	Married			Zalman		540
ADLER	Male	F		Zalman	Chaia			540
ADLER	Tzvi	M		Zalman	Chaia			540
ADLER	Mordechai	M		Zalman	Chaia			540
ADLER	Yakov	M		Zalman	Chaia			540
ADLER	Leibtche	M	Married	Shamai		Feige	Died together with children	540

ADLER	Feige	F	Married			Leibtche	Died together with children	540
ADLER	Avraham	M	Married	Zev	Dobre		Died together with children	540
ADLER		F	Married			Avraham	Died together with children	540
ADLER	Dobre	F				Zev	Mother of Avraham	540
ACKERMAN	David	M	Married	Israel Tzvi	Kreindil		Died together with children	540
ACKERMAN		F	Married			David	Died together with children	540
ACKERMAN	Kreindl	F				Israel Tzvi	Mother of David	540
ACKERMAN	Moshe	M	Married		Feigale			540
ACKERMAN		F	Married			Moshe		540
ACKERMAN	Abish	M	Married	Eliezer		Rachel		540
ACKERMAN	Rachel	F	Married			Abish		540
ACKERMAN	Eliezer	M		Abish	Rachel			540
ACKERMAN	Etil	F		Abish	Rachel			540
ADLER	Avraham Hersh	M	Married	Chaim Zindl		Matil	Died together with children	540
ADLER	Matl	F	Married			Avraham Hersh	Died together with children	540
AKST	Kopel	M	Married	Sine		Dvora	Died together with children	540
AKST	Dvora	F	Married			Kopil	Died together with children	540
ACKERMAN	Leizer	M	Married		Sara Dvora			540
ACKERMAN		F	Married			Leizer		540
ACKERMAN	Yehezkel	M		Leizer				540
ACKERMAN	Rivka	F		Leizer				540
ACKERMAN	Hinde	F		Leizer				540
ACKERMAN	Yehoshua	M		Leizer				540
ACKERMAN	David	M	Married	Moshe		Rechil	Died together with children	540

ACKERMAN	Rechil	F	Married			David	Died together with children	540
ADLER	Weli	M	Married	Itche Ber			Died together with children	540
ADLER		F	Married			Weli	Died together with children	540
ARBESFELD	Moshe	M	Married	Motl		Mala		540
ARBESFELD	Mala	F	Married			Moshe		540
ARBESFELD	Yosef	M		Moshe	Mala			540
ARBESFELD	Shlomo	M		Moshe	Mala			540
ARBESFELD	Reizl	F		Moshe	Mala			540
EGERT	Chana	F		Joel				540
AKST	Avraham	M	Married	Yehoshua			Died together with children	540
AKST		F	Married			Avraham	Died together with children	540
AKST	Moshe	M	Married	Yehoshua			Died together with children Brother of Patl	540
AKST		F	Married			Moshe	Died together with children	540
AKST	Patl	M		Yehoshua			Brother of Moshe	540
AKST	Sine	M	Married	Natan		Serke		540
AKST	Serke	F	Married			Sine		540
AKST	Shlomo	M		Sine	Serke			540
ACKERMAN	Meir	M	Married	Eliezer		Nesha		540
ACKERMAN	Nesha	F	Married			Meir		540
ACKERMAN	Moshe	M		Meir	Nesha			540
ACKERMAN	Feige	F		Meir	Nesha			540
ACKERMAN	Yakov	M		Meir	Nesha			540
ACKERMAN	Bat-Sheva	F		Meir	Nesha			540
ACKERMAN	Daniel	M		Meir	Nesha			540
ACKERMAN	Itala	F		Meir	Nesha			540
ULRICH	Baruch	M	Married	Zev			Died together with children	540

ULRICH		F	Married			Baruch	Died together with children	540
ULRICH	Yitzhak	M	Married	Baruch			Died together with children	540
ULRICH		F	Married			Yitzhak	Died together with children	540
ULRICH	Mordechai	M	Married	Baruch			Died together with children	540
ULRICH		F	Married			Mordechai	Died together with children	540
ELBAUM	Dan	M	Married	Avraham Yitzhak		Rishe		541
ELBAUM	Rishe	F	Married			Dan		541
ELBAUM	Meir	M		Dan	Rishe			541
ELBAUM	Gitl	F		Dan	Rishe			541
ADLER	Gele	F					Died together with children	541
ADLER	Yeshaya Nate	M	Married	Shlomo		Rivka		541
ADLER	Rivka	F	Married			Yeshaya Nate		541
ACKERMAN	Zalke	M		Israel Tzvi				541
ACKERMAN	Yakov	M		Israel Tzvi				541
ADLER	Natanel	M	Married	Chaim Zindel		Rachel		541
ADLER	Rachel	F	Married			Natanel		541
ADLER	Fradl	F		Natanel	Rachel			541
ADLER	Etl	F		Natanel	Rachel			541
AKST	Yentche	M	Married	Pinkhas				541
AKST		F	Married			Yentche		541
AKST	Avraham	M	Married	Yentche			Died together with children	541
AKST		F	Married			Avraham	Died together with children	541
ADLER	Lipe	M	Married	Zev			Died together with children	541

ADLER		F	Married			Lipe	Died together with children	541
ALTFELD	Moshe Naftali	M	Married			Ite		541
ALTFELD	Ite	F	Married			Moshe Naftali		541
ALTFELD	Beila	F						541
REDL	Dikl	F	Married		Beila	Gedalja	Maiden name - ALTFELD	541
REDL	Gedalja	M	Married			Dikl		541
REDL	Rachel	F		Gedalia	Dikl			541
ADLER	Yitzhak	M	Married	Shamai			Died together with children	541
ADLER		F	Married			Yitzhak	Died together with children	541
ADLER	Aizik	M		Tzvi				541
AKST	Avraham	M	Married	Pinkhas			Died together with children	541
AKST		F	Married			Avraham	Died together with children	541
ACKERMAN	Leib Yosef	M	Married	Eliezer				541
ACKERMAN		F	Married			Leib Yosef		541
ACKERMAN	Roza	F		Leib Yosef				541
ACKERMAN	Dvora	F		Leib Yosef				541
ADLER	Chaia Miriam	F	Married			Meir	Died together with children	541
ADLER	Moshe	M	Married	Meir		Tova		541
ADLER	Tova	F	Married			Moshe		541
ADLER	Chana	F		Moshe	Tova			541
ADLER	Malia	F		Moshe	Tova			541
ACKERMAN	Shmuel	M	Married	Moshe			Died together with children	541
ACKERMAN		F	Married			Shmuel	Died together with children	541

ACKERMAN	Elimelech	M	Married	Moshe			Died together with children	541
ACKERMAN		F	Married			Elimelech	Died together with children	541
AKST	Malka	F	Married	Yehoshua			Died together with her husband & children	541
OPFER	Shamai	M	Married	Menachem		Freida		541
OPFER	Freida	F	Married			Shamai		541
	Chaia	F	Married	Shamai	Freida		Maiden name – OPFER Died together with her husband	541
ADLER	Aizik	M	Married	Chaim		Feige		541
ADLER	Feige	F	Married			Aizik		541
ADLER	Chaim	M		Aizik	Feige			541
ADLER	David Moshe	M						541
ADLER	Gitl	F		David Moshe				541
ADLER	Yeshaya	M		David Moshe				541
ADLER	Mordechai	M		David Moshe				541
AKST	Tauba Yeta	F						541
	Lea	F	Married		Tauba Yeta		Maiden name - AKST Died together with her husband	541
	Riva	F	Married		Tauba Yeta		Maiden name - AKST Died together with her husband	541
	Basha	F	Married		Tauba Yeta		Maiden name - AKST Died together with her husband	541
ADLER	Rachel	F			Malka			541
ADLER	Fradl	F			Rachel			541

ADLER	Moshe	M		Rachel				541
ADLER	Etel	F		Rachel				541
ADLER	Fishel	M	Married	Antch			Died together with children	541
ADLER		F	Married			Fishel	Died together with children	541
ADLER	Manish	M		Fishel				541
ADLER	Beinish	M	Married					541
ADLER		F	Married			Beinish		541
ADLER	Chaitche	F		Beinish				541
AKST	Leibish	M	Married			Male		541
AKST	Male	F	Married			Leibish		541
AKST	Beile	F		Leibish	Male			541
	Chana	F	Married	Leibish	Male	Fishel	Maiden name - AKST	541
	Fishel	M	Married			Chana		541
ADLER	Yosef	M	Married	Shamai		Pesil		542
ADLER	Pesil	F	Married			Yosef		542
ADLER	Chaim	M		Yosef	Pesil			542
ADLER	Etil	F		Yosef	Pesil			542
ADLER	Shamai	M		Yosef	Pesil			542
ADLER	Yitzhak	M	Married	Yakov		Necha		542
ADLER	Necha	F	Married			Yitzhak		542
ADLER	Hersh Avraham	M		Yitzhak	Necha			542
ADLER	Yetl	F		Yitzhak	Necha			542
ADLER	Yitzhak Dov	M	Married					542
ADLER		F	Married			Yitzhak Dov		542
ADLER	Male	F		Yitzhak Dov				542
ADLER	Etil	F		Yitzhak Dov				542
ADLER	Henia	F		Yitzhak Dov				542

AKST	Moshe	M	Married	Israel				542
AKST		F	Married			Moshe		542
AKST	Shmuel Yosef			Moshe				542
ADLER	Antch	M	Married			Necha		542
ADLER	Necha	F	Married			Antch		542
ADLER	Sara	F		Antch	Necha			542
ADLER	Yakov	M	Married	Aharon David		Feige	Died together with children	542
ADLER	Feige	F	Married			Yakov	Died together with children	542
ADLER	Aizik	M	Married	Meir			Died together with children	542
ADLER		F	Married			Aizik	Died together with children	542
ADLER	Aizik Yehoshua	M		Tzvi				542
ADLER	Yosef	M		Shimon	Mali			542
ADLER	Aharon David	M	Married			Chana		542
ADLER	Chana	F	Married			Aharon David		542
ADLER	Tsize	F		Aharon David	Chana			542
ADLER	Shlomo	M		Aharon David	Chana			542
ADLER	Shmuel	M		Chaim	Etil			542
ADLER	Henie	F		Shmuel				542
ADLER	Mali	F		Shmuel				542
AKST	David	M	Married	Chaim Leib			Died together with children	542
AKST		F	Married			David	Died together with children	542
ULRICH	Leibtche	M	Married			Rachel		542
ULRICH	Rachel	F	Married			Leibtche		542
ULRICH	Moshe Yakov	M		Leibtche	Rachel			542

ULRICH	Sara	F		Leibtche	Rachel			542
ULRICH	Genendl	F		Leibtche	Rachel			542
FEIGELIS	Leizer Sara	M	Married				Died together with his wife & children The son-in-law of Asher-Yosef	542
ELBAUM	David	M	Married					542
ELBAUM		F	Married			David		542
ELBAUM	Simcha	M						542
ELBAUM	Avraham	M						542
	Chana Miriam	F						542
ADLER	Leibtche	M						542
ADLER	Chaia Feige	F						542
ADLER	Shamai	M						542
ADLER	Hersh	M						542
ADLER	Yakov	M						542
ADLER	Mordechais	M						542
ADLER	Male	F						542
ADLER	Israel Tzvi	M						542
ACKERMAN	Dutshe	F						542
ACKERMAN	Shmuel	M						542
EGERT	Shmuel	M	Married			Rivka		542
EGERT	Rivka	F	Married			Shmuel		542
EGERT	Chaia	F		Shmuel	Rivka			542
EGERT	Lea	F		Shmuel	Rivka			542
EGERT	Chava	F		Shmuel	Rivka			542
EGERT	Yosef	M		Shmuel	Rivka			542
AKST	Shmuel Yosef	M	Married			Rela		542
AKST	Rela	F	Married			Shmuel Yosef		542

AKST	Gilda Bracha	F		Shmuel Yosef	Rela			542
AKST	Rechtche	F		Shmuel Yosef	Rela			542
AKST	Chaim Ozer	M		Shmuel Yosef	Rela			542
AKST	Rivka	F		Shmuel Yosef	Rela			542
AKST	Chaim Reuven	M	Married	Shmuel		Chana		542
AKST	Chana	F	Married			Chaim Reuven		542
AKST	Avraham	M		Chaim Reuven	Chana			542
AKST	David	M		Chaim Reuven	Chana			542
AKST	Bezalel	M		Chaim Reuven	Chana			542
AKST	Iser	M	Married	Pinkhas		Beila		542
AKST	Beila	F	Married			Iser		542
AKST	Pinkhas	M		Iser	Beila			542
AKST	Freida	F		Iser	Beila			542
AKST	Perl	F		Iser	Beila			542
AKST	Chaia	F		Iser	Beila			542
Obligenhertz	Masha	F	Married				Died together with her husband and child	543
ELBAUM	Shmuel	M	Married			Beile	Died together with children	543
ELBAUM	Beile	F	Married			Shmuel	Died together with children	543

Bet בּ

BRENER	Matityahu	M	Married	Efraim			Died together with children	543
BRENER		F	Married			Matityahu	Died together with children	543

BLINDERMAN	Yakov	M	Married				Died together with children	543
BLINDERMAN		F	Married			Yakov	Died together with children	543
BRAFMAN	Israel	M	Married				Died together with children	543
BRAFMAN		F	Married			Israel	Died together with children	543
BENDLER	Yakov	M	Married	David		Tzluve		543
BENDLER	Tzluve	F	Married			Yakov		543
BENDLER	Leizer	M		Yakov	Tzlave			543
BENDLER	Sima	F		Yakov	Tzlave			543
BENDLER	Yona	M		Yakov	Tzlave			543
BENDLER	Chaia	F	Married			David		543
BENDLER	David Leib	M					Grandson of Chaia	543
BENDLER	Manja	F					Granddaughter of Chaia	543
BENDLER	Sime	F					Granddaughter of Chaia	543
BENDLER	Hadas Gitl	F					Granddaughter of Chaia	543
BENDLER	Hersh Shimon	M					Grandson of Chaia	543
BLITMAN	Mordechai	M	Married			Teml	Died together with children	543
BLITMAN	Teml	F	Married			Mordechai	Died together with children	543
BZHITVE	Mordechai	M	Married			Teml	Died together with children	543
BZHITVE	Teml	F	Married			Mordechai	Died together with children	543
BZHITVE	Shmuel Yitzhak	M	Married	Yehoshua			Died together with children	543
BZHITVE		F	Married			Shmuel Yitzhak	Died together with children	543
BZHITVE	Shmuel	M	Married				Died together with children	543

BZHITVE		F	Married			Shmuel	Died together with children	543
BERGER	Meir Yehoshua	M	Married	Moshe	Sara	Gitl	Died together with children	543
BERGER	Gitl	F	Married			Meir Yehoshua	Died together with children	543
BERGER	Sara	F	Married			Moshe		543
BERGER	Chana	F		Moshe	Sara			543
BAS	Faiwel	M	Married	Yosef		Rechl		543
BAS	Rechl	F	Married			Faiwel		543
BAS	Yosef	M		Faiwel	Rechl			543
BAS	Simcha	M		Faiwel	Rechl			543
BAS	Zlate	F		Faiwel	Rechl			543
BAS	Azriel	M	Married	Faiwel	Rechl			543
BAS		F	Married			Azriel		543
BAS	Avraham	M	Married	Faiwel	Rechl			543
BAS	Fradl	F	Married			Avraham		543
BAS	Tzvi	M		Avraham	Fradl			543
BAS	Shoshana	F		Avraham	Fradl			543
BAS	Feige	F		Avraham	Fradl			543
BAS	Yukl	M		Avraham	Fradl			543
BERMACHER	Leibish	M	Married	Natanel			Died together with children	543
BERMACHER		F	Married			Leibish	Died together with children	543
BERMACHER	Chaim	M	Married	Natanel			Died together with children	543
BERMACHER		F	Married			Chaim	Died together with children	543
BROMBERG	Aharon	M	Married				Died together with children	543
BROMBERG		F	Married			Aharon	Died together with children	543
BAUMFELD	Baruch Meir	M	Married			Chana	Died together with children	543

BAUMFELD	Chana	F	Married			Baruch Meir	Died together with children	543
BRANDWEIN	Chaim	M	Married			Feige		543
BRANDWEIN	Feige	F	Married			Chaim		543
BRANDWEIN	Chava Ester	F		Chaim	Feige			543
BRANDWEIN	Tcherna	F		Chaim	Feige			543
BRANDWEIN	Perl	F		Chaim	Feige			543
BRANDWEIN	Freida	F		Chaim	Feige			543
BRANDWEIN	Zalman	M		Chaim	Feige			543
BERMACHER	Moshe	M	Married	Shalom		Shevi		543
BERMACHER	Shevi	F	Married			Moshe		543
BERMACHER	Etl	F		Moshe	Shevi			543
BERMACHER	Gitl	F		Moshe	Shevi			543
BERMACHER	Rekel	F		Moshe	Shevi			543
BERMACHER	Rachel	F		Moshe	Shevi			543
BERMACHER	Sheindel	F		Moshe	Shevi			543
BERMACHER	Freida	F		Moshe	Shevi			543
BRICK	Bentzion	M	Married				Died together with children	543
BRICK		F	Married			Bentzion	Died together with children	543
BAS	Yosl	M	Married	David			Died together with children	543
BAS		F	Married			Yosl	Died together with children	543
BLITMAN	Yehoshua	M	Married	Itche Meir		Bina	Died together with children	543
BLITMAN	Bina	F	Married			Yehoshua	Died together with children	543
BLUM	Moshe	M	Married	Henoch		Rachel	Died together with children	544
BLUM	Rachel	F	Married			Moshe	Died together with children	544
BAUMFELD	Moshe	M			Shevi			544
BAUMFELD	Shevi	F					Mother of Moshe	544

BLUM	Henoch	M	Married					544
BLUM		F	Married			Henoch		544
BLUM	Sara	F		Henoch				544
BLUM	Ester	F		Henoch				544
BORNSTEIN	Shalom	M		Yekhezkel				544
BORNSTEIN	Sheindel	F		Shalom				544
BORNSTEIN	Libe	F		Shalom				544
BORNSTEIN	Perl	F		Shalom				544
BRANDWEIN	Zalman	M	Married			Perele	Died together with children	544
BRANDWEIN	Perele	F	Married			Zalman	Died together with children	544
BRICK	Aharon	M	Married			Dvora		544
BRICK	Dvora	F	Married			Aharon		544
BRICK	Reuven	M		Aharon	Dvora			544
BRICK	Yakov	M		Aharon	Dvora			544
BRONER	Wolf	M	Married				Died together with children	544
BRONER		F	Married			Wolf	Died together with children	544
BRONER	Yitzhak	M						544
BRENER	Moshe	M	Married			Rechtche		544
BRENER	Rechtche	F	Married			Moshe		544
BRENER	Chaim	M		Moshe	Rechtche			544
BRENER	Efraim	M		Moshe	Rechtche			544
BRENER		F		Moshe	Rechtche			544
BRENER	Chaim	M	Married			Miriam		544
BRENER	Miriam	F	Married			Chaim		544
BRENER	Nechemia	M		Chaim	Miriam			544
BRENER	Yakov	M		Chaim	Miriam			544
BRENER	Pesil	F						544
BORIK	Avigdor	M	Married			Mindel	Died together with children Daughters	544

BORIK	Mindel	F	Married			Avigdor	Died together with children Daughters	544
BORIK	Avraham	M		Avigdor	Mindel			544
BLINDERMAN	Freida	F		Yakov				544
BLINDERMAN	Yudl	M			Freida			544
BRESIL	Yitzhak	M	Married				Died together with children	544
BRESIL		F	Married			Yitzhak	Died together with children	544
BLUTMAN	Mordechai	M	Married			Feige		544
BLUTMAN	Feige	F	Married			Mordechai		544
BLUTMAN	Yehoshua	M		Mordechai	Feige			544
BLUTMAN	Adela	F		Mordechai	Feige			544
BLUTMAN	Golda	F		Mordechai	Feige			544
BLUTMAN	Pesza	F		Mordechai	Feige			544
BLUTMAN	Yosef	M	Married			Beile	Died together with children	544
BLUTMAN	Beile	F	Married			Yosef	Died together with children	544
BLUTMAN	Hersh	M	Married			Dvora		544
BLUTMAN	Dvora	F	Married			Hersh		544
BLUTMAN	Natan	M		Hersh	Dvora			544
BLUTMAN	Yehoshua	M		Hersh	Dvora			544
BLUTMAN	Simcha	M		Hersh	Dvora			544
BLUTMAN	Nachman	M		Hersh	Dvora			544
BLUTMAN	Moshe	M		Hersh	Dvora			544
BLUTMAN	Gitl Elie	F		Hersh	Dvora			544
BLUTMAN	Sheindl	F						544
BERMACHER	Yitzhak	M	Married			Sara Rivka		544
BERMACHER	Sara Rivka	F	Married					544
BERMACHER	Chaim	M	Married	Yitzhak	Sara Rivka			544
BERMACHER	Rivka	F	Married			Chaim		544

Surname	Name	Sex	Status	Father	Mother	Spouse	Notes	Page
BERMACHER	Yosef	M		Yitzhak	Sara Rivka			544
BERMACHER	Manis	M		Yitzhak	Sara Rivka			544
BERMACHER	Ettel	F		Yitzhak	Sara Rivka			544
BERMACHER	Malka	F		Yitzhak	Sara Rivka			544
BERMACHER	David	M		Yitzhak	Sara Rivka			544
BERNER	Pinkhas	M	Married			Mindel	Died together with children Daughters	544
BERNER	Mindel	F	Married			Pinkhas	Died together with children Daughters	544
BERNER	Hersh	M		Pinkhas	Mindel			544
BLUM	Yakov Moshe	M	Married			Rachel	Died together with children	544
BLUM	Rachel	F	Married			Yakov Moshe	Died together with children	544

Gimmel ג

Surname	Name	Sex	Status	Father	Mother	Spouse	Notes	Page
GUTHERZ	Elimelech	M	Married	Natanel		Lea	Died together with children	544
GUTHERZ	Lea	F	Married			Elimelech	Died together with children	544
GOLDSTEIN	Elimelech	M						544
GOLDSTEIN	Azriel	M		Elimelech				544
GOLDSTEIN	Rachel	F		Elimelech				544
GOLDSTEIN	Lea	F		Elimelech				544
GOLDSTEIN	Mordechai	M	Married	Elimelech		Rivka	Died together with children	544
GOLDSTEIN	Rivka	F	Married			Mordechai	Died together with children	544
GOLDSTEIN	Berish	M		Mordechai				544
GOLDSTEIN	Malka	F		Berish				544
GOLDSTEIN	Zeiftl	M		Berish				544

GEIST	Yona	M	Married	Meir			Died together with children	544
GEIST		F	Married			Yona	Died together with children	544
GROISMAN	Moshe	M	Married	Nachman		Rivka		544
GROISMAN	Rivka	F	Married			Moshe		544
GROISMAN	Feige	F		Moshe	Rivka			544
GROISMAN	Rivka	F		Moshe	Rivka			544
GROISMAN	Aizik	M	Married	Leibish		Yeta		545
GROISMAN	Yeta	F	Married			Aizik		545
GROISMAN	Tzipa	F		Aizik	Yeta			545
GROISMAN	Miriam	F		Aizik	Yeta			545
GROISMAN	Tzvi	M		Aizik	Yeta			545
GLENZER	Mordechai	M	Married	Avraham			Died together with children	545
GLENZER		F	Married			Mordechai	Died together with children	545
GLENZER	Shlomo	M	Married	Avraham		Machla		545
GLENZER	Machla	F	Married			Shlomo		545
GLENZER	Rechtche	F		Shlomo	Machla			545
GLENZER	Avraham	M		Shlomo	Machla			545
GLENZER	Golda	F		Shlomo	Machla			545
GLENZER	Yekhezkel	M	Married	Moshe		Chaia Sara		545
GLENZER	Chaia Sara	F	Married			Yekhezkel		545
GUTHERZ	Natanel	M	Married					545
GUTHERZ		F	Married			Natanel		545
GUTHERZ		F		Natanel				545
GUTHERZ		F		Natanel				545
GISPENZ	Sara	F	Married			Yitzhak		545
GISPENZ	Moshe Aharon	M		Yitzhak	Sara			545
GISPENZ	Avraham	M		Yitzhak	Sara			545

GUTHERTZ	Chaim Yechiel	M	Married			Eigale	Ritual slaughterer.	545
GUTHERTZ	Eigale	F	Married			Chaim Yechiel		545
GOLDMAN	Yosef	M	Married			Sara		545
GOLDMAN	Sara	F	Married			Yosef		545
GOLDMAN	Moshe	M		Yosef	Sara			545
GOLDMAN	Miriam	F		Yosef	Sara			545
GOLDMAN	Shmuel	M		Yosef	Sara			545
GOLDMAN	Shmuel	M					Died together with children	545
GOLDMAN	Joel	M		Shmuel				545
GOLDMAN	Freidl	F		Shmuel				545
GOLDMAN	Moshe	M		Shmuel				545
GOLDMAN	Pasha	F		Shmuel				545
GOLDMAN	Chaim	M	Married			Matilda	Died together with children	545
GOLDMAN	Matilda	F	Married			Chaim	Died together with children	545
GOLDMAN	Avraham	M	Married			Henne		545
GOLDMAN	Henne	F	Married			Avraham		545
GOLDMAN	Miriam	F						545
GOLDMAN	Yosef	M	Married			Rachel	Died together with children	545
GOLDMAN	Rachel	F	Married			Yosef	Died together with children	545
GITERMAN	Nachman	M	Married			Perl		545
GITERMAN	Perl	F	Married			Nachman		545
GITERMAN	Peretz	M		Nachman	Perl			545
GITERMAN	Efraim	M		Nachman	Perl			545
GITERMAN	Chaim	M		Nachman	Perl			545
GRUER	Chava	F		Yakov				545
GRUER	Nachman Koppel	M		Mordechai				545
GROER	Ester	F						545

GROER	Fruma	F						545
GRINBERG	Rivka	F		Avraham				545
GLENZER	Ite	F						545
GLENZER	Tzipa	F			Ite			545
GLENZER	Miriam	F			Ite			545
GLENZER	Tzvi	M			Ite			545
GEITLER	Eliezer	M	Married		Szprintza	Bracha		545
GEITLER	Bracha	F	Married			Eliezer		545
GEITLER	Yakov	M					Son of?	545
GEITLER	Szprintza	F					Whose mother?	545
GEITLER	Masha	F			Szprintza		Whose sister?	545
GEIST	Yitzhak	M	Married			Feige	Died together with children	545
GEIST	Feige	F	Married			Yitzhak	Died together with children	545
GEIST	Avraham	M	Married				Died together with children	545
GEIST		F	Married			Avraham	Died together with children	545
GOLDSTEIN	Sara Hinde	F	Married	Berish			Died together with her husband & children	545
GOLDSTEIN	Pesil	F						545
GEIST	Peretz	M	Married			Feige		545
GEIST	Feige	F	Married			Peretz		545
GROISMAN	Nachman	M	Married			Rivka		545
GROISMAN	Rivka	F	Married			Nachman		545
GROISMAN	Feitl	F		Nachman	Rivka			545
GREE	Moshe Yitzhak	M	Married			Dvora		545
GREE	Dvora	F	Married			Moshe Yitzhak		545
GREE	Hersh Avraham	M		Moshe Yitzhak	Dvora			545

GREE	Chaim	M		Moshe Yitzhak	Dvora			545
GREE	Perl	F		Moshe Yitzhak	Dvora			545
GLENZER	Naftali Hertz	M	Married				Died together with children	545
GLENZER		F	Married			Naftali Hertz	Died together with children	545
GLENZER	Ite	F						545
GROISMAN	Kreindl	F						545
GROISMAN	David	M			Kreindil			545
GROISMAN	Avrahamtche	M			Kreindil			545
GROISMAN		F			Kreindil			545
GROISMAN	Rivka	F						546
GOLDBAUM	Shmuel	M	Married				Died together with children	546
GOLDBAUM		F	Married			Shmuel	Died together with children	546
GRAF	Zacharia	M	Married			Sheva Reizl		546
GRAF	Sheva Reizl	F	Married					546
GRAF	Moshe	M		Zacharia	Sheva Reizl			546
GRAF	Dvora	F		Zacharia	Sheva Reizl			546
GRAF	Nachum	M		Zacharia	Sheva Reizl			546
GRAF	Rashe	F		Zacharia	Sheva Reizl			546
GUTHERZ	Baruch	M	Married					546
GUTHERZ		F	Married			Baruch		546
GELERNTER	Avraham	M	Married			Chaia		546
GELERNTER	Chaia	F	Married			Avraham		546
GELERNTER	Sheindl	F		Avraham	Chaia			546
GELERNTER	Yosef	M		Avraham	Chaia			546
GELERNTER	Chaim	M		Avraham	Chaia			546

GELERNTER	Dvora	F		Avraham	Chaia			546
GELERNTER	Nechama	F		Avraham	Chaia			546
SPIELSINGER	Getzel	M	Married			Miriam		546
SPIELSINGER	Miriam	F	Married			Getsil		546
SPIELSINGER	Mekhle	F		Getzl	Miriam			546
SPIELSINGER	Mordechai	M		Getz	Miriam			546
GOLDSCHMID	Baruch	M						546
GOLDSCHMID	Aizik	M		Baruch				546
GOLDSCHMID	Sara	F		Baruch				546

Dalet ד

DAKMAZER	Avraham	M	Married	Leibish			Died together with children	546
DAKMAZER		F	Married			Avraham	Died together with children	546
DAKMAZER	Shlomo	M	Married	Leibish				546
DAKMAZER		F	Married			Shlomo		546
DUKMAZER	Malia	F						546
DUKMAZER	Hinde	F						546

Hey ה

HONIG	Yekutiel	M	Married			Teml	Died together with children	546
HONIG	Teml	F	Married			Yekutiel	Died together with children	546
HONIG	Avraham	M	Married	Leib Ari		Bracha		546
HONIG	Bracha	F	Married			Avraham		546
HONIG	Feige Bracha	F		Avraham	Bracha			546
HERBSTMAN	Motl	M	Married	Wolf		Sara		546
HERBSTMAN	Sara	F	Married			Motl		546
HERBSTMAN	Mali	F		Motl	Sara			546
HERBSTMAN	Yitzhak	M		Motl	Sara			546
HERBSTMAN	Rachel	F		Motl	Sara			546
HERBSTMAN	Shmuel	M		Motl	Sara			546

HERBSTMAN	Zisl	M		Motl	Sara			546
HERBSTMAN	Dvora	F		Motl	Sara			546
HERBSTMAN	Henne	F		Motl	Sara			546
HERBSTMAN	Rivka	F		Motl	Sara			546
HONIGMAN	Aharon David	M	Married			Sara		546
HONIGMAN	Sara	F	Married			Aharon David		546
HONIGMAN	Peretz	M		Aharon David	Sara			546
HONIGMAN	Yosl	M		Aharon David	Sara			546
HONIGMAN	Shalom	M		Aharon David	Sara			546
HONIGMAN	Gala	F		Aharon David	Sara			546
HALER	Hinde	F		Yehuda				546
HALER	Kresil	F			Hinde			546
HALER	Meir	M			Hinde			546
HONIG	Yitzhak	M	Married	Zev Ari		Beile Dvora		546
HONIG	Beile Dvora	F	Married			Yitzhak		546
HONIG	Tzvi	M		Yitzhak	Beile Dvora			546
HONIG	Dov	M		Yitzhak	Beile Dvora			546
HONIG	Moshe	M		Yitzhak	Beile Dvora			546
HONIG	Baruch	M		Yitzhak	Beile Dvora			546
HONIG	Fridl	F		Yitzhak	Beile Dvora			546
HERBSTMAN	Shamai	M	Married			Gitl		546
HERBSTMAN	Gitl	F	Married			Shamai		546
HOCHMAN	Yosef	M	Married	Joel			Died together with children	546
HOCHMAN		F	Married			Yosef	Died together with children	546

HOCHMAN	Eli	M	Married	Joel			Died together with children	546
HOCHMAN		F	Married			Eli	Died together with children	546
HERBSTMAN		F		Rivka Ester				546
HAUN	Zev	M	Married			Chana Bela		546
HAUN	Chana Bela	F	Married			Zev		546
HAUN	Matil Feige	F		Zev	Chana Bela			546
HONIG	Yekutiel	M	Married				Died together with children Maybe it's the same man - Yekutiel HONIG?	546
HONIG		F	Married			Yekutiel	Died together with children	546
HONIG	Meir Wolf	M		Yekutiel				546
HOCHMAN	Avraham	M						546
HOCHMAN	Joel	M	Married	Yechiel		Chana Frimet		547
HOCHMAN	Chana Frimet	F	Married			Joel		547
HOCHMAN	Feige	F		Joel	Chana Frimet			547
HOCHMAN	Tzirel	F		Joel	Chana Frimet			547
HOCHMAN	Miriam	F		Joel	Chana Frimet			547
HOCHMAN	Yeshayahu	M		Joel	Chana Frimet			547
HERBSTMAN	Tewel Nachum	M						547
HERBSTMAN	Yitzhak Leib	M		Tewel Nachum				547
HERBSTMAN	Meir	M		Tewel Nachum				547
HERBSTMAN	Rivka	F		Tewel Nachum				547

HERING	Efraim Yakov	M	Married			Sara		547
HERING	Sara	F	Married			Efraim Yakov		547
HERING	Chana Rachel	F		Efraim Yakov	Sara			547
HERING	Shalom	M		Efraim Yakov	Sara			547
HERING	Geula	F		Efraim Yakov	Sara			547
HERING	Peretz Yosef	M		Efraim Yakov	Sara			547
HAN	Mendl	M	Married			Lea		547
HAN	Lea	F	Married			Mendl		547
HAN	Sara	F		Mendl	Lea			547
HAN	Moshe	M		Mendl	Lea			547
HAN	Feige	F		Mendl	Lea			547
HAN	Moshe	M	Married				Died together with children	547
HAN		F	Married			Moshe	Died together with children	547
HUBERMAN	Yakov	M	Married	Antshel		Yehudit		547
HUBERMAN	Yehudit	F	Married			Yakov		547
HUBERMAN	Antshel	M		Yakov	Yehudit			547
HOLAND	Moshe	M	Married			Rachel		547
HOLAND	Rachel	F	Married			Moshe		547
HOLAND	David	M		Moshe	Rachel			547
HOLAND	Beinish	M						547
HOLAND	Malka	F						547
HOLAND	Yehoshua	M						547
HILF	Chaia	F						547
HILF	Lea	F						547
HILF	Benyamin	M						547
HILF	Yehudit	F						547
HILF	Fishel	M						547

Family name(s)	First name(s)	Sex	Marital status	Father's name	Mother's name	Name of spouse	Additional family & remarks	Page
HILF	Benyamin	M	Married			Chana	Died together with children	547
HILF	Chana	F	Married			Benyamin	Died together with children	547

Family name(s)	First name(s)	Sex	Marital status	Father's name	Mother's name	Name of spouse	Additional family & remarks	Page
Vav ו								
WACHSENFELD	Avraham Hersh	M	Married	Leib			Died together with children	547
WACHSENFELD		F	Married			Avraham Hersh	Died together with children	547
WEINTRAUB	Itche	M	Married	Berish		Rivka		547
WEINTRAUB	Rivka	F	Married			Itche		547
WEINTRAUB	Berish	M		Itche	Rivka			547
WEINTRAUB	Iser	M		Itche	Rivka			547
WEINTRAUB	Chaia	F		Itche	Rivka			547
WEINTRAUB	Blima	F		Itche	Rivka			547
WEINTRAUB	Yehoshua	M	Married	Berish		Tsharne		547
WEINTRAUB	Tcharne	F	Married			Yehoshua		547
WEINTRAUB	Tobe	F		Yehoshua	Tsharne			547
WEINTRAUB	Chana	F		Yehoshua	Tsharne			547
WEINRIB	Leibish	M	Married	Bentzion			Died together with children	547
WEINRIB		F	Married			Leibish	Died together with children	547
WEINTRAUB	Moshe	M	Married	Israel		Beile		547
WEINTRAUB	Beile	F	Married			Moshe		547
WEINTRAUB	Israel	M		Moshe	Beile			547
WEINTRAUB	Avraham	M		Moshe	Beile			547
WEINTRAUB	Zalman	M		Moshe	Beile			547
WEINTRAUB	Fela	F		Moshe	Beile			547

WALFISH	Yeshaya Leib	M	Married	David			Died together with children	547
WALFISH		F	Married			Yeshaya Leib	Died together with children	547
WERTMAN	Yekil	M	Married	Baruch		Breindl		547
WERTMAN	Breindl	F	Married			Yekil		547
WERTMAN	Chana Malia	F		Yekil	Breindl			547
WERTMAN	Pinkhas Yosef	M		Yekil	Breindl			547
WERTMAN	Ester Malka	F		Yekil	Breindl			547
WELTZ	Yekil	M	Married			Yekil	Died together with children	547
WELTZ	Golda	F	Married			Golda	Died together with children	547
WETSHER	Godl	M	Married	Moshe		Lea Teml		547
WETSHER	Lea Teml	F	Married			Godl	Died together with her mother	547
WETSHER	Chaim Pinkhas	M		Godl	Lea Teml			547
WETSHER	Bila	F		Godl	Lea Teml			547
WETSHER	Frimet	F		Godl	Lea Teml			547
WEINRIB	Bentzion	M	Married			Chava		547
WEINRIB	Chava	F	Married			Bentzion		547
WERTMAN	Leib	M	Married	Baruch		Sara	Died together with children	547
WERTMAN	Sara	F	Married			Leib	Died together with children	547
WIESEN	Moshe	M	Married			Chaia Beile		547
WIESEN	Chayeh Beile	F	Married			Moshe		547
WIESEN	Rechil	F		Moshe	Chaia Beile			547
WIESEN	Aba	M	Married	Moshe			Died together with children	547

WIESEN		F	Married			Aba	Died together with children	547
WEISS	Leibish	M	Married	Shachne			Died together with children	548
WEISS		F	Married			Leibish	Died together with children	548
WERTMAN	Rachel	F			Chaike			548
WERTMAN	Rivka	F			Chaike			548
WEISS	Leml	M	Married	Yavraham			Died together with children	548
WEISS		F	Married			Leml	Died together with children	548
WELTZ	Moshe	M	Married	Yekil			Died together with children	548
WELTZ		F	Married			Moshe	Died together with children	548
WACHNACHTER	Itamar	M	Married	Joel		Chana	Died together with children	548
WACHNACHTER	Chana	F	Married			Itamar	Died together with children	548
WACHNACHTER	Eliyahu	M	Married	Joel			Died together with children	548
WACHNACHTER		F	Married			Eliyahu	Died together with children	548
WACHNACHTER	David	M	Married	Joel			Died together with children	548
WACHNACHTER		F	Married			David	Died together with children	548
WALFISH	Yekil	M	Married	David			Died together with children	548
WALFISH		F	Married			Yekil	Died together with children	548
WACHSMAN	Yosef	M	Married			Tauba		548
WACHSMAN	Tauba	F	Married			Yosef		548
WACHSMAN	Bentzion Shmuel	M		Yosef	Tauba			548
WERTMAN	Leibish	M	Married	Chaim				548
WERTMAN		F	Married			Leibish		548

WERTMAN	Frimet	F		Leibish				548
WELTZ	David	M	Married				Died together with children	548
WELTZ		F	Married			David	Died together with children	548
WERTMAN	Israelke	M	Married	Leibish		Male	Died together with his daughters	548
WERTMAN	Male	F	Married			Israelke	Died together with her daughters	548
WERTMAN	Shmerl	M		Israelke	Male			548
WACHNACHTER	Pesza	F	Married			Ozer		548
WACHNACHTER		F		Ozer	Pesza			548
WERTMAN	Yosef	M	Married					548
WERTMAN		F	Married			Yosef		548
WEISSMAN	Yehoshua	M	Married	Pinie				548
WEISSMAN		F	Married			Yehoshua		548
WEISSMAN	Bentzion	M		Yehoshua				548
WEISSMAN	Chana	F		Yehoshua				548
WEISSMAN	David	M	Married	Abish		Rachel	Died together with children	548
WEISSMAN	Rachel	F	Married			David	Died together with children	548
WACHNACHTER	Ester	F	Married	Joel			Died together with her husband & children	548
WEISS	Moshe	M		Zacharia				548
WERTMAN	Ansch	M	Married	Baruch		Sara	Died together with children	548
WERTMAN	Sara	F	Married			Ansch	Died together with children	548
WEISSMAN	Falik	M	Married	Abish		Nesha	child	548
WEISSMAN	Nesha	F	Married			Falik	child	548
WASSERMAN	Moshe Naftali	M		Yakov				548
WASSERMAN	Beile	F						548

WASSERMAN	Arie	M					548
WASSERMAN	Libe	F					548
WASSERMAN	Chana	F					548
WASSERMAN	Sara	F					548
WASSERMAN	Eliezer	M	Married	Yakov		Rivka	548
WASSERMAN	Rivka	F	Married			Eliezer	548
WASSERMAN	Malka	F					548
WASSERMAN	Libe	F					548
WASSERMAN	Sara	F					548
WASSERMAN	Moshe	M					548
WEISSMAN	Moshe	M	Married	Fishel		Manja	548
WEISSMAN	Mania	F	Married			Moshe	548
WEISSMAN	Fishel	M		Moshe	Mania		548
WEISSMAN	Chaim Yona	M		Moshe	Mania		548
WEISSMAN	Ema	F		Moshe	Mania		548
WEISSMAN	Frimet	F		Moshe	Mania		548
WEINTRAUB	Itche	M	Married	Shimshon		Matil	548
WEINTRAUB	Matil	F	Married			Itche	548
WEINTRAUB	Rivka	M		Itche	Matil		548
WEINTRAUB	Hershl	F		Itche	Matil		548
WEINTRAUB	Berish	M		Leizer			Died together with children	548
WAKSLICHT	Yosef	M	Married				Died together with children	548
WACHSLICHT		F	Married			Yosef	Died together with children	548
WACHSLICHT	Chaim	M	Married				Died together with children	548
WACHSLICHT		F	Married			Chaim	Died together with children	548
WILDMAN	Chana	F		Naftali			549
WILDMAN	Chava	F			Chana		549
WILDMAN	Freida	F			Chana		549

WEINTRAUB	Liba	F		Israel				549
WEINRIB	Liba	F		Isaac			Yitzhak?	549
WEINRIB	Liftsha	F		Yitzhak				549
WEINTRAUB	Shmuelka	M	Married	Shimshon		Itta		549
WEINTRAUB	Itta	F	Married			Shmuelke		549
WEINTRAUB	Berish	M		Shmuelke	Itta			549
WEINTRAUB	Sheindel	F		Avraham				549
WEINTRAUB	Chana	F		Avraham				549
WEINTRAUB	Lea	F		Yekutiel				549
WEINTRAUB	Avraham	M	Married				Died together with children	549
WEINTRAUB		F	Married			Avraham	Died together with children	549
WEINTRAUB	Fishel	M	Married				Died together with children Baruch's	549
WEINTRAUB		F	Married			Fishel	Died together with children	549
WERTMAN	Meir	M	Married			Chaia	From Lukow	549
WERTMAN	Chaia	F	Married			Meir		549
WERTMAN	Mechl	M		Meir	Chaia			549
WERTMAN	Temale	F		Meir	Chaia			549
WEINRIB	Hadas	F	Married				Died together with her husband & children	549
WEISSMAN	Rechtche	F						549
WEISSMAN	Fradl	F		Rechtche				549
WEISSMAN	Itche	M		Rechtche				549
WEISSMAN	Avraham Leib	M		Rechtche				549
WASSERMAN	Leib	M	Married			Dvora	3 children	549
WASSERMAN	Dvora	F	Married			Leib	3 children	549
WASSERMAN	Libe	F					2 children The children were buried alive.	549

WASSERMAN	Chana	F	Married				Leib	549
	Leib	M	Married				Chana	549
WASSERMAN	Itche	M					Buried alive.	549
WEINBERG	Reizl	F						549
WEINBERG	Itta	F			Reizl			549
WEINBERG	Yosef	M			Reizl			549
WEINBERG	Getzl	M			Reizl			549
WERTMAN	Machla	F	Married				Yosef	549
WERTMAN	Chanina	F		Yosef	Machla			549
WERTMAN	Rivka	F		Yosef	Machla			549
WERTMAN	Roize	F		Yosef	Machla			549
WERTMAN	Hinda	F		Yosef	Machla			549
WETSCHER	Avraham	M	Married				Ester Malka	549
WETSCHER	Ester Malka	F	Married				Avraham	549
WETSCHER	Chana Male	F		Avraham	Ester Malka			549
WETSCHER	Pinkhas Yosef	M		Avraham	Ester Malka			549
WELTZ	Hersh	M	Married				Zelda	549
WELTZ	Zelda	F	Married				Hersh	549
WELTZ	Yosef	M						549
WELTZ	Zelda	F						549
WELTZ	Sara	F						549
WELTZ	Tobe	F						549
WELTZ	Ite	F			Tobe			549
WETSCHER	Zalman	M	Married				Reni	549
WETSCHER	Reni	F	Married				Zalman	549
WETSCHER	Avraham	M		Zalman	Reni			549
WEISS	Frimit	F						549
WEISS	Yosef	M			Frimit			549
WEISS	Beile	F			Frimit			549
WEISS	Rachel	F			Frimit			549

WISS	Shachna	M	Married			Rachel		549
WISS	Rachel	F	Married			Shachna		549
WISS	Yosef	M		Shachna	Rachel			549
WISS		F		Shachna	Rachel			549
WISS	Leml	M	Married				Died together with children	549
WISS		F	Married			Leml	Died together with children	549
WISS	Rivka	F						549
WISS	Asher	M						549
WISS	Leml	M						549
WISS	Sara	F						549
WISS	Chana	F						549
WERTMAN	Hershl	M		Yosef				549
WISS	Yakov	M	Married			Chaia		549
WISS	Chaia	F	Married			Yakov		549
WISS	Miriam	F		Yakov	Chaia			549
WISS	Yechiel	M						550
WISS	Mordechai	M	Married			Frimit		550
WISS	Frimit	F	Married			Mordechai		550
WISS	Moshe	M		Mordechai	Frimit			550
WISS	Yosef	M		Mordechai	Frimit			550
WISS	Ettel	F		Mordechai	Frimit			550
WISS	Dvora	F						550
WISS	Leibush	M						550
WISS	Mordechai	M	Married				Died together with children	550
WISS		F	Married			Mordechai	Died together with children	550
WISS	Chaia	F		Moshe	Teml			550
WEISSER	Berish	M	Married			Matil		550
WEISSER	Matil	F	Married			Berish		550
WEISSER	Mendel	M		Berish	Matil			550

WEISSER	Moshe	M		Berish	Matil			550
WEISSER		F		Berish	Matil			550
WEISSMAN	Natan David	M	Married			Chana	Died together with children	550
WEISSMAN	Chana	F	Married			Natan David	Died together with children	550
WELTZ	Frimet	F						550
WERTMAN	Aharon	M	Married			Sara		550
WERTMAN	Sara	F	Married			Aharon		550
WERTMAN	Moshe A.A.	M		Aharon	Sara			550
WEINTRAUB	Sara	F						550
WELTZ	Sara	F						550
VENK	Male	F						550

Zayin

SILBERZWEIG	Leizer	M	Married		Sara	Malie	Died together with children	550
SILBERZWEIG	Malie	F	Married			Leizer	Died together with children	550
SILBERZWEIG	Israel	M	Married	Shlomo Leib			some of his children	550
SILBERZWEIG		F	Married			Israel	some of her children	550
ZETZER	Simcha	M	Married	Leml		Tzippa		550
ZETZER	Tzippa	F	Married			Simcha		550
ZETZER	Feige	F		Simcha	Tzippa			550
ZETZER	Rivka	F		Simcha	Tzippa			550
SILBERZWEIG	Itche	M	Married	Moshe		Chaia		550
SILBERZWEIG	Chaia	F	Married			Itche		550
SILBERZWEIG	Leibish	M	Married	Itche		Hadas		550
SILBERZWEIG	Hadas	F	Married			Leibish		550
SILBERZWEIG	Sheindel	F		Leibish	Hadas			550
SILBERMAN	Avrahamtze	M	Married	Alter		Malka		550
SILBERMAN	Malka	F	Married			Avrahamtze		550

SILBERMAN	Levi	M		Avrahamtze	Malka			550
SILBERMAN	Bracha	F		Avrahamtze	Malka			550
ZAUBERMAN	Leibl	M	Married			Rivka		550
ZAUBERMAN	Rivka	F	Married			Leibl		550
ZAUBERMAN	Yekl	M		Leibl	Rivka			550
ZAUBERMAN	Yeshaya Hersh	M		Leibl	Rivka			550
ZAUBERMAN	Moshe	M		Leibl	Rivka			550
ZAUBERMAN	Koni	M		Leibl	Rivka			550
SILBERZWEIG	Mendel	M	Married	Gershon		Keila		550
SILBERZWEIG	Keila	F	Married			Mendel		550
SILBERZWEIG	Yeshaya	M	Married	Azriel			Died together with children	550
SILBERZWEIG		F	Married			Yeshaya	Died together with children	550
SILBERZWEIG	Moshe	M	Married	Azriel			Died together with children	550
SILBERZWEIG		F	Married			Moshe	Died together with children	550
SILBERZWEIG	Hudis	F						550
SILBERZWEIG	Itche	M	Married				Died together with children	550
SILBERZWEIG		F	Married			Itche	Died together with children	550
SILBERZWEIG	Baruch	M	Married					550
SILBERZWEIG		F	Married			Baruch		550
SALZMAN	Moshe	M	Married					550
SALZMAN		F	Married			Moshe		550
SALZMAN	Alter	M		Moshe				550
SALZMAN	Hersh	M		Moshe				550
SALZMAN	Sara	F		Moshe				550
SALZMAN	Leitche	F		Moshe				550
SALZMAN	Shlomo	M	Married	Moshe		Rivka		550
SALZMAN	Rivka	F	Married			Shlomo		550

SALZMAN	Drezl	M		Shlomo	Rivka			550
SILBERZWEIG	Welie	M	Married				child	550
SILBERZWEIG		F	Married			Welie	child	550
SILBERZWEIG	Ziskind	M	Married			Fradl		550
SILBERZWEIG	Fradl	F	Married			Ziskind		550
SUSSMILCH	Hersh	M	Married				some of his children	550
SUSSMILCH		F	Married			Hersh	some of her children	550
SUSSMILCH	Golda	F		David Yeshayahu				551
SUSSMILCH	Fishel	M			Golda			551
SUSSMILCH	Moshe	M			Golda			551
SUSSMILCH	Arie	M			Golda			551
SUSSMILCH	Beile	F			Golda			551
SUSSMILCH	Zisser	M	Married				Died together with children	551
SUSSMILCH		F	Married			Zyser	Died together with children	551
ZINDIL	Yosef	M	Married			Hadas		551
ZINDIL	Hadas	F	Married			Yosef		551
ZINDIL	Shlomo	M		Yosef	Hadas			551
ZYCHLER	Dvora Libe	F					Grandmother of Yakov	551
	Yakov	M					Grandson of ZYCHLER Dvora Libe	551
SILBERZWEIG	David	M	Married			Baltcha		551
SILBERZWEIG	Baltcha	F	Married			David		551
SILBERZWEIG	Rivka	F		David	Baltcha			551
SILBERZWEIG	Gitl	F		David	Baltcha			551
SILBERZWEIG	Adela	F		David	Baltcha			551
SILBERZWEIG	Shifra	F	Married				Died together with her husband & children	551

ZETZER	Yitzhak	M	Married				Died together with children	551
ZETZER		F	Married			Yitzhak	Died together with children	551
ZETZER	Leml	M	Married			Malka		551
ZETZER	Malka	F	Married			ZetSIL		551
ZETZER	Yeshaya	M		Leml	Malka			551
ZETZER	Moshe	M		Leml	Malka			551
ZETZER	Kresel	F		Leml	Malka			551
ZABERMAN	Natan	M	Married			Breindl		551
ZABERMAN	Breindl	F	Married			Natan		551
ZABERMAN	Gitl	F		Natan	Breindl			551
ZABERMAN	Dvora	F		Natan	Breindl			551
ZYCHLER	Yosef	M	Married			Malka		551
ZYCHLER	Malka	F	Married			Yosef		551
ZYCHLER	Bintche	M		Yosef	Malka			551
ZYCHLER		F		Yosef	Malka			551
ZYCHLER	Yitzhak	M	Married			Tobe	Died together with children	551
ZYCHLER	Tobe	F	Married			Yitzhak	Died together with children	551
SILBERZWEIG	Malka	F						551
SILBERZWEIG	Rachel	F						551
SALZMAN	Arie	M	Married			Sara	Died together with children	551
SALZMAN	Sara	F	Married			Arie	Died together with children	551

Tet ט

TEICHER	Moshe'le	M	Married			Malka'le	Died together with children	551
TEICHER	Malka'le	F	Married			Moshe'le	Died together with children	551
	Beile Sara	F	Married	Moshe'le	Malka'le	Kopel	Maiden name - TEICHER. I think that all the group are	551

						the children of Rabbi TEICHER.	
	Kopel	M	Married			Beila Sara	551
	Itche	M		Kopel	Beile Sara		551
	Chantche	F	Married	Moshe'le	Malka'le	Maiden name - TEICHER Died together with her family	551
	Eliezer Gershon	M	Married			Died together with children	551
		F	Married			Eliezer Gershon	Died together with children	551
HARMAN	Ite'la	F	Married	Moshe'le	Malka'le	Avraham'le	Maiden name - TEICHER. Died together withfamily	551
HARMAN	Avraham'le	M	Married			Ite'la	Died together with his family	551
	Roize	F	Married	Moshe'le	Malka'le		Maiden name - TEICHER Died together with her husband & children	551
TEICHER	Yekhezkel	M	Married				Died together with children	551
TEICHER		F	Married			Yekhezkel	Died together with children	551
TEICHER	Hersh	M	Married				Died together with children	551
TEICHER		F	Married			Hersh	Died together with children	551
TEICHER	Shaul Joel	M						551
TEICHER	Sosha	F						551
TEICHER	Tzivia	F						551
TEICHER	Yitzhak	M						551
TEUERSTEIN	Yehoshua	M	Married			Hentche		551
TEUERSTEIN	Hentche	F	Married			Yehoshua		551

	Male	F	Married	Yehoshua	Hentche		Maiden name - TEUERSTEIN. Died together with her husband	551
TEICHER	David	M	Married			Sheindl		552
TEICHER	Sheindl	F	Married			David		552
TEICHER	Bintche Rivka	F		David	Sheindl			552
TEICHER	Eliezer	M		David	Sheindl			552
TEICHER	Yosef Moshe	M	Married	Mordechai Tzvi		Ruchtche	Son of the Rabbi.	552
TEICHER	Ruchtche	F	Married			Yosef Moshe		552
TEICHER	Yitzhak	M		Yosef Moshe	Ruchtche			552
TEICHER	Asher	M		Yosef Moshe	Ruchtche			552
TEICHER	Zelke	M		Yosef Moshe	Ruchtche			552
	Gershon Henich	M						552
	Sara'le	F		Gershon Henich				552
TINTENFISCH	Moshe	M	Married			Sara		552
TINTENFISCH	Sara	F	Married			Moshe		552
TINTENFISCH	Shlomo	M		Moshe	Sara			552
TINTENFISCH	Zelda	F		Moshe	Sara			552
TINTENFISCH	Yakov	M		Moshe	Sara			552
TRYB	Yosef	M	Married	Aharon David		Rachel	Died together with children	552
TRYB	Rachel	F	Married			Yosef	Died together with children	552
TOFLER	Yosef	M	Married			Reizl		552
TOFLER	Reizl	F	Married			Yosef		552
TINTENFISCH	Avraham	M	Married	Asher Yosef		Sara		552
TINTENFISCH	Sara	F	Married			Avraham		552

TINTENFISCH	Chana	F		Avraham	Sara			552
TINTENFISCH	Moshe	M		Avraham	Sara			552
TINTENFISCH	Yehuda	M		Avraham	Sara			552
TINTENFISCH	Shmuel	M		Avraham	Sara			552
TINTENFISCH	Zalman	M		Avraham	Sara			552
TINTENFISCH	Sender	M		Avraham	Sara			552
TINTENFISCH	Shmuel Eliyahu	M	Married	Asher Yosef		Mirel		552
TINTENFISCH	Mirl	F	Married			Shmuel Eliyahu		552
TINTENFISCH	Fishel	M		Shmuel Eliyahu	Mirel			552
TINTENFISCH	Joel	M		Shmuel Eliyahu	Mirel			552
TINTENFISCH	Chaim Leib	M	Married			Elke		552
TINTENFISCH	Elke	F	Married			Chaim Leib		552
TINTENFISCH	Yokil	M		Chaim Leib	Elke			552
TINTENFISCH	Baruch	M		Chaim Leib	Elke			552
TINTENFISCH	Henia	F		Chaim Leib	Elke			552
TINTENFISCH	Avraham	M	Married	Chaim Leib		Freidl Malka	Died together with children	552
TINTENFISCH	Freidl Malka	F	Married			Avraham	Died together with children	552
TORBINER	Simcha	M	Married	Yosl		Basia	Died together with children	552
TORBINER	Basia	F	Married			Simcha	Died together with children	552
TRYB	Israel Leib	M	Married	Nachum		Lea		552
TRYB	Lea	F	Married			Israel Leib		552
TOFLER	Chana	F	Married			Kalman		552
TOFLER	Chaia Sara	F		Kalman	Chana			552
TOFLER	Reizl	F		Kalman	Chana			552

TOFLER	Yenti	F		Kalman	Chana			552
TOFLER	Simcha	F		Kalman	Chana			552
TOFLER	Golda	F		Kalman	Chana			552
TREGER	Mordechai	M	Married	Moshe Elchanan		Chaia Neche		552
TREGER	Chaia Neche	F	Married			Mordechai		552
TREGER	Eli	M		Mordechai	Chaia Neche			552
TREGER	Shmuel	M		Mordechai	Chaia Neche			552
TREGER	Eliezer	M		Mordechai	Chaia Neche			552
TREGER	Shimon	M		Mordechai	Chaia Neche			552
TRINKER	Leibl	M	Married	Yekutiel			Died together with children	552
TRINKER		F	Married			Leibl	Died together with children	552
TISHKEN	Avraham	M	Married				Died together with children	552
TISHKEN		F	Married			Avraham	Died together with children	552
TREGER	Chaia Sara	F	Married			Moshe Elchanan		552
		F	Married	Moshe Elchanan	Chaia Sara	Idil	Maiden name - TREGER	552
	Yidl	M	Married				Son-in-law of TREGER Chaia Sara	552
TRYB	Zalman	M	Married	Israel Leib		Pesza	Died together with children	552
TRYB	Pesza	F	Married			Zalman	Died together with children	552
TENENBAUM	Levi	M	Married	Moshe		Chaia		552
TENENBAUM	Chaia	F	Married			Levi		552
TENENBAUM	Mordechai	M		Levi	Chaia			552
TENENBAUM	Zelig	M		Levi	Chaia			552

TENENBAUM	Yakov	M		Levi	Chaia			552
TENENBAUM	Sara	F		Levi	Chaia			552
TINTENFISCH	Asher Yosef	M	Married			Sara		552
TINTENFISCH	Sara	F	Married			Asher Yosef		552
TURM	Breindl	F						552
TRINKER	Rachel	F						552
TRINKER	Chava	F		Azriel				552
TRINKER	Yakov	M					Died together with his family	552

Yod

JAHR	Moshe	M	Married			Roza		553
JAHR	Roza	F	Married			Moshe		553
JAHR	Perl	F		Moshe	Roza			553
JAHR	Tova	F		Moshe	Roza			553
JULI	Lea	F	Married				Died together with her husband & children	553

Kaf

KATZ	Golda	F	Married				Died together with her husband & children	553
KATZ	Yakov	M	Married			Malie		553
KATZ	Malie	F	Married			Yakov		553
KATZ	Tzvi	M		Yakov	Malie			553
KATZ	Meir	M		Yakov	Malie			553
KATZ	Galya	F		Yakov	Malie			553

Lamed

LEVINSON	Israel	M	Married			Miriam	ritual slaughterer	553
LEVINSON	Miriam	F	Married			Israel		553

LEVINSON	Shmuel	M		Israel	Miriam			553
	Yitzhak	M	Married				Died together with his wife & children Profession: Teacher	553
	Dudl	M	Married				Died together with his wife & children Son-in-law of Teacher	553
	Meir	M	Married				Died together with children	553
JULI	Golda	F	Married				Died together with her husband & children	553
LUSTRIN	Aharon	M	Married	Daniel		Serke		553
LUSTRIN	Serke	F	Married			Aharon		553
LUSTRIN	Meir	M	Married	Aharon			some of the children	553
LUSTRIN		F	Married			Meir	some of the children	553
LUSTRIN	Zelke	M	Married	Daniel		Blume		553
LUSTRIN	Blume	F	Married			Zelke		553
LUSTRIN	Miril	F		Zelke	Blume			553
LUSTRIN	Moshe	M		Zelke	Blume			553
LUSTRIN	Shlomo Leib	M		Zelke	Blume			553
LERMAN	Kalman	M	Married			Cipre		553
LERMAN	Zipre	F	Married			Kalman		553
LEICHER	Avraham David	M	Married	Kalman Moshe		Hinde		553
LEICHER	Hinde	F	Married			Avraham David		553
LIPINER	Yekil	M	Married	Moshe		Feige	Died together with children	553
LIPINER	Feige	F	Married			Yekil	Died together with children	553

LIPINER	Benyamin	M	Married	Moshe			Died together with children	553
LIPINER		F	Married			Benyamin	Died together with children	553
LIPINER	Shmuel Yosef	M	Married	Moshe				553
LIPINER	Dvora	F		Shmuel Yosef				553
LIPINER	Zelda	F		Shmuel Yosef				553
LIPINER	Golda	F		Shmuel Yosef				553
LIPINER	Neche	F		Shmuel Yosef				553
LIPINER	Azriel	M	Married	Moshe		Feige	Died together with children	553
LIPINER	Feige	F	Married			Azriel	Died together with children	553
LUMERMAN	Mordechai	M	Married	Iser		Sheindl	Died together with children	553
LUMERMAN	Sheindl	F	Married			Mordechai	Died together with children	553
LEITER	Avraham Daniel	M	Married	David			Died together with children	553
LEITER		F	Married			Avraham Daniel	Died together with children	553
LEMER	Yona	M	Married	Minyamin			Died together with children Perhaps Benyamin?	553
LEMER		F	Married			Yona	Died together with children	553
LUMERMAN	Pesach	M	Married	Iser			Died together with children	553
LUMERMAN		F	Married			Pesach	Died together with children	553
LIPINER	Mordechai	M	Married	Shmuel Yekil				553
LIPINER		F	Married			Mordechai		553
LIPINER	Shemaia	M	Married	Meir			Died together with children	554

LIPINER		F	Married			Shemaia	Died together with children	554
LUSTRIN	Hersh	M	Married	Zelke			Died together with children	554
LUSTRIN		F	Married			Hersh	Died together with children	554
LUSTRIN	Yehuda	M	Married	Aharon		Rivka'le	Died together with children	554
LUSTRIN	Rivka'le	F	Married			Yehuda	Died together with children	554
LEHRER	Hinde	F	Married			Chaim		554
LEHRER	Rachel	F		Chaim	Hinde			554
LIPINER	Leibtche	M	Married	Hersh		Chana		554
LIPINER	Chana	F	Married			Leibtche		554
LIPINER	Golda	F		Leibtche	Chana			554
LIPINER	Tzivia	F		Leibtche	Chana			554
LIPINER	Roize	F		Leibtche	Chana			554
LIPINER	Hersh	M		Leibtche	Chana			554
LIPINER	Ozer	M		Leibtche	Chana			554
LIPINER	Meir	M		Leibtche	Chana			554
LIPINER	Moshe	M		Leibtche	Chana			554
LORBER	Yakov	M	Married	Leizer Ber			Died together with children	554
LORBER		F	Married			Yakov	Died together with children	554
LEWINSON	Yehoshua	M	Married			Tauba	Died together with children	554
LEWINSON	Tauba	F	Married			Yehoshua	Died together with children	554
LEMER	Yakov Yehuda	M	Married	Bezalel		Sheindl Lea		554
LEMER	Sheindl Lea	F	Married			Yakov Yehuda		554
LERMAN	Simcha Binim	M	Married	Kalman		Basia		554
LERMAN	Bashi	F	Married			Simcha Binim		554

LERMAN	Peril	F		Simcha Binim	Basia			554
LEMER	Bluma	F						554
LEMER	Bezalel	M			Bluma			554
LEMER	Reuven	M			Bluma			554
FECHER	Sara'la	F	Married		Bluma	Avraham	Maiden name - LEMER	554
FECHER	Avraham	M	Married			Sara'la		554
FECHER	Amnon	M		Avraham	Sara'le			554
FECHER	David	M		Avraham	Sara'le			554
LIPINER	Bunim	M	Married	Tzvi				554
LIPINER		F	Married			Bunim		554
LIPINER	Gitl	F		Bunim				554
LIPINER	Yenta	F		Bunim				554
LIPINER	Meir	M		Bunim				554
LEICHER	Sara	F	Married			Moshe		554
LEICHER	Zlata	F		Moshe	Sara			554
LEICHER	Reichl	F		Moshe	Sara			554
LIPSCHITZ	Berish	M	Married			Neche		554
LIPSCHITZ	Neche	F	Married			Berish		554
LIPSCHITZ	Reuven	M		Berish	Neche			554
LIPSCHITZ	Shlomo	M		Berish	Neche			554
LIPSCHITZ	Avraham	M						554
LISTENBERG	Pinkhas	M	Married				Died together with children	554
LISTENBERG		F	Married			Pinkhas	Died together with children	554
LISTENBERG	Simcha	M		Pinkhas				554
LEHRER	Moshe	M		Yehoshua	Golda			554
LEHRER	Golda	F						554
LEMER	Shmuel	M	Married				Died together with children	554
LEMER		F	Married			Shmuel	Died together with children	554

LEWINSON	Hadassa	F					554
LEWINSON	Antshel	M			Hadassa		554
LEWINSON	Moshe	M			Hadassa		554
LEWINSON	Rivka	F			Hadassa		554
LEWINSON	Jonatan	M			Hadassa		554
LORBER	Masha	F				Died together with children	554
LORBER	Pesil	F					554
LODEN	Ite	F				Died together with children	554
LORBER	Lea	F					554
LORBER	Yakov	M	Married			Mani	Died together with children	554
LORBER	Mani	F	Married			Yakov	Died together with children	554

Mem מ

MARETIG	Shaul	M	Married			Peril		554
MARETIG	Peril	F	Married			Shaul		554
MARETIG	Berl	M		Shaul	Peril			554
MARETIG	Leibl	M		Shaul	Peril			554
MARETIG	Ptakhia	M		Shaul	Peril			554
MODEL	Shamai	M	Married	Shmuel Leib		Rekl	Died together with children	554
MODEL	Rekl	F	Married			Shamai	Died together with children	554
MODEL	Hersh	M	Married	Itche			Died together with children	554
MODEL		F	Married			Hersh	Died together with children	554
MAHLER	Rachel	F	Married			Chaim		554
MAHLER	Sheindel	F		Chaim	Rachel			554
MAHLER	Yosef	M	Married			Gitl		555
MAHLER	Gitl	F	Married			Yosef		555
MAHLER	Feige Lea	F		Yosef	Gitl			555

MAHLER	Chana	F		Yosef	Gitl			555
MAHLER	Jenta	F		Yosef	Gitl			555
MAHLER	Yekhezkel	M	Married	Yosef		Sara		555
MAHLER	Sara	F	Married			Yekhezkel		555
MAHLER	Perele	F		Yekhezkel	Sara			555
MAHLER	Tova	F		Yekhezkel	Sara			555
MANES	Pinkhas	M						555
MANTEL	Chaim Leib	M	Married	Yekil				555
MANTEL		F	Married			Chaim Leib		555
MANTEL	Mendl	M		Chaim Leib				555
MANTEL	Eli	M		Chaim Leib				555
MANTEL	Yafa	F		Chaim Leib				555
MANTEL	Berl Hersh	M	Married	Yekil		Beiltche		555
MANTEL	Beiltche	F	Married			Berl Hersh		555
MONTAG	Moshe Yosl	M	Married	Shlomo		Eidl		555
MONTAG	Eidl	F	Married			Moshe Yosl		555
MONTAG	Azriel	M	Married	Moshe Yosl			Died together with children	555
MONTAG		F	Married			Azriel	Died together with children	555
MODEL	Berl	M	Married	Shmuel Leib		Reizl		555
MODEL	Reizl	F	Married			Berl		555
MONTAG	Shmuel Pinkhas	M	Married	Moshe Yosl			Died together with children	555
MONTAG		F	Married			Shmuel Pinkhas	Died together with children	555
MARMAR	Hersh	M	Married			Lea		555
MARMAR	Lea	F	Married			Hersh		555
MARMAR	Israel Leib	M		Hersh	Lea			555

MENKIS	Avraham	M	Married				555
MENKIS		F	Married			Avraham	555
MENKIS	Shmuel	M		Avraham			555
MET	Eliyahu	M	Married	Kalman			Died together with children	555
MET		F	Married			Eliyahu	Died together with children	555
MET	Rachel	F		Avigdor			Died together with children	555
MERTSER	Malka	F					7 children	555
MONTEK	Naomi	F			Hinda			555
MAHLER	Feige	F						555
MAHLER	Chana	F						555
MAGRAM	Benyamin	M	Married			Beiltche		555
MAGRAM	Beiltche	F	Married			Benyamin		555
MAGRAM	Simcha	M		Benyamin	Beiltche			555
MEINZINGER	Chaia Libe	F					Died together with children	555
MAHLER	Alexander	M	Married	Yosef		Sima Feiga		555
MAHLER	Sima Feiga	F	Married			Alexander		555
MODEL	Rechl	F					? Appears after Rechl.	555
MANTEL	David	M		Mordechai				555
MANTEL	Chaim Leib	M		Mordechai				555

Nun ‫נ‬

NADEL	Yehoshua	M	Married	Leizer Shimon			Died together with children	555
NADEL		F	Married			Yehoshua Shimon	Died together with children	555
NADEL	Keila	F					Died together with children	555
NIRENSTEIN	Meir	M						555
NIRENSTEIN		F		Meir				555

Samech ס								
SOIBEL	Moshe	M	Married	Shabtai			Died together with children	555
SOIBEL		F	Married			Moshe	Died together with children	555
SEGELMAN	Chaim	M	Married	Yeshaya				555
SEGELMAN		F	Married			Chaim		555
SEGELMAN	Sara	F						556
SEGELMAN	Yeshayahu	M			Sara			556
Ayin ע								
ENTNER	David	M	Married	Shmuel			Died together with children	556
ENTNER		F	Married			David	Died together with children	556
ERDHOCH	Breintche	F						556

Family name(s)	First name(s)	Sex	Marital status	Father's name	Mother's name	Name of spouse	Additional family & remarks	Page
Peh פ								
FUTER	Chaim	M	Married	Leizer		Rivka		556
FUTER	Rivka	F	Married			Chaim		556
		F	Married	Chaim	Rivka		Maiden name - FUTER Died together with her husband	556
FEIFER	Wolf	M	Married	Elia				556
FEIFER		F	Married			Wolf		556
FEIFER	Leibl	M		Wolf				556
FEIFER	Dina	F		Wolf				556
FINK	Moshe	M	Married			Gitele		556
FINK	Gitele	F	Married			Moshe		556
FOLGER	Yitzhak	M	Married				Died together with children	556

FOLGER		F	Married			Yitzhak	Died together with children	556
FAIL	Tanchum	M	Married	Israel Hersh		Tema		556
FAIL	Tema	F	Married			Tanchum		556
FIRST	Frimet	F	Married			Itche		556
FIRST	Moshe	M		Itche	Frimet			556
FIRST	Chana	F		Itche	Frimet			556
FIRST	Mali	F		Itche	Frimet			556
FIRST	Rivka	F		Itche	Frimet			556
FLICK	Shimon	M	Married	Israel		Gitl	Died together with children	556
FLICK	Gitl	F	Married			Shimon	Died together with children	556
FLICK	Bentzion	M	Married	David Leib		Golda		556
FLICK	Golda	F	Married			Bentzion		556
FRIEDMAN	Yekhezkel	M	Married	Sine		Ester	Died together with children	556
FRIEDMAN	Ester	F	Married			Yekhezkel	Died together with children	556
FEINGOLD	Moshe	M	Married	Yona				556
FEINGOLD		F	Married			Moshe		556
FEINGOLD	Rechtse	F		Moshe				556
FEINGOLD	Beila	F		Moshe				556
FEINGOLD	Israel	M		Moshe				556
FEINGOLD	Yitzhak	M		Moshe				556
FINKELSTEIN	Yehoshua	M	Married	Shmuel David		Shifcha		556
FINKELSTEIN	Shifcha	F	Married			Yehoshua		556
FINKELSTEIN	Udel	M		Yehoshua	Shifcha			556
FINKELSTEIN	Azriel	M		Yehoshua	Shifcha			556
FEFER	Zacharia	M	Married			Sara Rachel		556
FEFER	Sara Rachel	F	Married			Zacharia		556

FISCHER	Mendl	M	Married	Yeshaya		Zisl		556
FISCHER	Zisl	F	Married			Mendl		556
FISCHER	Sosha	F		Mendl	Zisl			556
FISCHER	Chana	F		Mendl	Zisl			556
FISCHELSON	Yakov Meir	M	Married					556
FISCHELSON		F	Married			Yakov Meir		556
		F	Married	Yakov Meir			Maiden name - FISCHELSON. Died together with children	556
FISCHELSON	Berl	M	Married			Chana Rachel	Died together with children	556
FISCHELSON	Chana Rachel	F	Married			Berl	Died together with children	556
FUTER	Yehoshua Shimon	M	Married	Mendl		Chana	Died together with children	556
FUTER	Chana	F	Married			Yehoshua Shimon	Died together with children	556
FITER	Mendl	M	Married	Yosef		Heni Lea		556
FITER	Heni Lea	F	Married					556
FITER	Tzipora	F		Mendl	Heni Lea			556
FITER	Ite	F		Mendl	Heni Lea			556
FIKSMAN	Yosef	M	Married			Beile		556
FIKSMAN	Beile	F	Married			Yosef		556
FREIMAN	Moshe	M	Married	Efraim			Died together with children	556
FREIMAN		F	Married			Moshe	Died together with children	556
FREIMAN	Efraim	M						556
FRUCHT	Israel Mordechai	M	Married			Perl	Died together with children	556
FRUCHT	Perl	F	Married			Israel Mordechai	Died together with children	556
FRUCHT	Moshe	M		Israel Mordechai	Perl			556
FEFER	Itche	M	Married	Hersh Mates			Died together with children	556

FEFER		F	Married			Itche	Died together with children	556
FEFER	Chana	F	Married			Hersh Metot		556
FEFER	Malie Pesza	F		Hersh Mates	Chana			556
FISCHER	Itche	M	Married	Hersh			Died together with children	557
FISCHER		F	Married			Itche	Died together with children	557
PASINEK	Moshe	M	Married			Freidl		557
PASINEK	Freidl	F	Married			Moshe		557
FEIFER	Chaia Sara	F					Died together with children	557
FLICKER	Tzadok	M	Married			Chana	Died together with children	557
FLICKER	Chana	F	Married			Tzadok	Died together with children	557
FEFER	Moshe	M	Married				Died together with children	557
FEFER		F	Married			Moshe	Died together with children	557
FRUEHLINK	Kalman	M	Married			Pesza		557
FRUEHLINK	Pesza	F	Married			Kalman		557
FELDMAN	Tzirl	F	Married	Moshe			Died together with her husband & children	557
FESTER	Leibish	M	Married	Chaim Shmuel		Nechama	Died together with children	557
FESTER	Nechama	F	Married			Leibish	Died together with children	557
FEFER	Azriel	M	Married	Yehuda		Rachel		557
FEFER	Rachel	F	Married			Azriel		557
FEFER	Menachem	M		Azriel	Rachel			557
FEFER	Binim	M		Azriel	Rachel			557
FEFER	Chava	F		Bezalel	Chana			557

	Feiga	F	Married	Mendel		Avraham	Maiden name - FISCHER. Died together with her children	557
	Avraham	M	Married			Feiga	Died together with children	557
FISCHER	Sender	M	Married	Yeshayahu			Died together with children	557
FISCHER		F	Married			Sender	Died together with children	557
FISCHER	Aharon	M	Married	Yeshayahu				557
FISCHER		F	Married			Aharon		557
	Alka	F		Yeshayahu		Yakov	Maiden name - FISCHER. Died together with her children	557
	Yakov	M	Married			Alka	Died together with children	557
FINK	Zussman	M	Married	Moshe		Masha		557
FINK	Masha	F	Married			Zussman		557
FINK	Shlomo	M		Zussman	Masha			557
FINK	Hinda	F		Zussman	Masha			557
FINK	Sara	F		Zussman	Masha			557
	Dobtshe	F		Zussman	Masha		Maiden name - FINK	557
	Tobele	F			Dobtshe		Mother's maiden name FINK	557
FAIL	Yakov	M	Married			Rivka	Died together with children	557
FAIL	Rivka	F	Married			Yakov	Died together with children	557
FEFER	Chaia	F					From Chmelka	557
FISCHER	Nachman	M	Married				Died together with children	557
FISCHER		F	Married			Nachman	Died together with children	557

FISCHER	Meir Yehoshua	M	Married				Died together with children	557
FISCHER		F	Married			Meir Yehoshua	Died together with children	557
FISCHER	Ester Malka	F	Married			Yeshaya		557
	Yeshaya	M	Married			Ester Malka		557
FREUND	Shmuel Eli	M	Married	Alter		Yuta		557
FREUND	Yuta	F	Married			Shmuel Eli		557
FREUND	Mordechai	M		Shmuel Eli	Yuta			557
FREIMAN	Efraim	M						557
FRAMPOLER	Rachel	F						557
FRAMPOLER	Yosef	M			Rachel			557
FRAMPOLER	Moshe	M	Married		Rachel		Died together with children	557
FRAMPOLER		F	Married			Moshe	Died together with children	557
FISCHER	Yehoshua	M	Married			Maltsie	Died together with children	557
FISCHER	Maltsie	F	Married			Yehoshua	Died together with children	557
FEIFER	Mordechai	M	Married			Necha		557
FEIFER	Necha	F	Married			Mordechai		557
FEIFER	Leizer	M		Mordechai	Necha			557
FEIFER	Sara	F		Mordechai	Necha			557
FITER	Yosef	M	Married			Ester		557
FITER	Ester	F	Married			Yosef		557
FITER	Yona	M		Yosef	Ester			557
FITER	Israelke	M		Yosef	Ester			557
FITER	Gitele	F		Yosef	Ester			557
FISCHBEDEGEN	Aharon	M	Married			Masha Dov		557
FISCHBEDEGEN	Masha Dove	F	Married			Aharon		557

FISCHBEDEGEN	Shlomo	M		Aharon	Masha Dove			557
FISCHBEDEGEN	Hinde Sara	F		Aharon	Masha Dove			557
FLUK	Leib Gedaliahu	M	Married					557
FLUK		F	Married			Leib Gedaliahu		557
FLUK	Mordechai	M		Leib Gedaliahu				557
FEFER	Labish	M	Married			Rive	Profession: Teacher.	557
FEFER	Rive	F	Married			Labish		557
FEFER	Chaia	F		Lobish	Rive			557
FEFER	Leitche	F		Lobish	Rive			557
FISCHBAINDEGEN	Shmuel	M	Married				Died together with children	557
FISCHBAINDEGEN	Stefanie	F	Married			Shmuel	Died together with children	557
FISCHBAINDEGEN	Arish	M	Married			Dobra		558
FISCHBAINDEGEN	Dobra	F	Married			Arish		558
FISCHBAINDEGEN	Sheindel	F		Arish	Dobra			558
FISCHBAINDEGEN	Azriel	M		Arish	Dobra			558
FISCHBAINDEGEN	Hersh	M		Arish	Dobra			558
FISCHBAINDEGEN	Yakov	M		Arish	Dobra			558
FISCHBAINDEGEN	Moshe	M		Arish	Dobra			558
FISCHBAINDEGEN	Shimshon	M		Arish	Dobra			558
FISCHBAINDEGIN	Male	F						558
FISCHBAINDEGIN	Nechama	F			Male			558
FEFER	Wolf	M						558
FEFER	Avraham Lipa	M						558
FISCHER	Shlomo	M	Married			Gitl	Died together with children	558
FISCHER	Gitl	F	Married			Shlomo	Died together with children	558
FEFER	Lipa	M	Married			Male		558

FEFER	Male	F	Married			Lipa		558
FEFER	Ite	F						558
FIRST	Pinkhas	M	Married			Zisl		558
FIRST	Zisl	F	Married			Pinkhas		558
FIRST	Chaia	F		Pinkhas	Zisl			558
FIRST	Feige	F		Pinkhas	Zisl			558
FIRST	Breindl	F						558
FIRST	Tzvi	M						558
FUNT	Mendel	M						558
FUNT	Moshe	M						558
FLINDER	Henich	M						558
FLINDER	Gedaliahu	M		Henich				558
FLINDER	Freida	F		Henich				558
PELTZ	Israelke	M	Married			Beile		558
PELTZ	Beile	F	Married			Israelke		558
PELTZ	Zlata	F		Israelke	Beile			558
PELTZ	Moshe	M		Israelke	Beile			558
PELTZ	Simcha	M		Israelke	Beile			558
PELTZ	Yakov	M		Israelke	Beile			558
PELTZ	Chana	F		Israelke	Beile			558
PELTZ	Sheindl	F		Israelke	Beile			558
FEIFER	Avraham Daniel	M	Married				Died together with children	558
FEIFER		F	Married			Avraham Daniel	Died together with children	558

Tzadik צ

ZUKER	Yekil	M	Married	Chaim Yona		Sonia		558
ZUKER	Sonia	F	Married			Yekil		558
ZEIS	Shaul	M	Married	Shmuel		Malka	Died together with children	558
ZEIS	Malka	F	Married			Shaul	Died together with children	558

ZEIS	Hersh	M	Married	Shmuel			Died together with children	558
ZEIS		F	Married			Hersh	Died together with children	558
ZUKER	Israel	M	Married	Chaim Yona		Sara		558
ZUKER	Sara	F	Married			Israel		558
ZUKER	Tauba	F		Israel	Sara			558
ZUKER	Chaim Yona	M		Israel	Sara			558
ZUKER	Yosef	M		Israel	Sara			558
ZEIS	Chava	F						558
ZUKER	Shmuel Eli	M	Married			Lea		558
ZUKER	Lea	F	Married			Shmuel Eli		558
ZUKER	Yakov	M		Shmuel Eli	Lea			558
ZUKER	Moshe	M		Shmuel Eli	Lea			558
ZUKERMAN	Yakov	M	Married			Kreindil		558
ZUKERMAN	Kreindil	F	Married			Yakov		558
ZUKERMAN	Rivka	F		Yakov	Kreindil			558
	Feige	F	Married	Yakov	Kreindil		Maiden name - ZUKERMAN	558
	Yosef	M	Married			Feige	ZUKERMAN	558

Kof ק

KREITNER	Moshe	M	Married	Antch			Died together with children	558
KREITNER		F	Married			Moshe	Died together with children	558
KALIGSTEIN	Benyamin	M	Married	Yosef	Henne		Died together with children	559
KALIGSTEIN		F	Married			Benyamin	Died together with children	559
KALIGSTEIN	Henne	F				Yosef		559
KALIGSTEIN	Yekhezkel	M	Married	Yosef	Henne	Miriam	Died together with children	559

KALIGSTEIN	Miriam	F	Married			Yekhezkel	Died together with children	559
KREITNER	Eliyahu Meir	M	Married	Chaim		Sara		559
KREITNER	Sara	F	Married			Eliyahu Meir		559
KREITNER	Chaim	M		Eliyahu Meir	Sara			559
KRYMERKOPF	Chaim	M	Married	Nachum		Chana Lea		559
KRYMERKOPF	Chana Lea	F	Married			Chaim		559
KRYMERKOPF	Malie			Chaim	Chana Lea			559
KERER	Leibish	M	Married			Frimet		559
KERER	Frimet	F	Married			Leibish		559
KERER	Meir	M	Married	Leibish			Died together with children	559
KERER		F	Married			Leibish	Died together with children	559
KLEINER	Aharon	M	Married					559
KLEINER		F	Married			Aharon		559
KLEINER	Chana	F		Aharon				559
KLEINER	Shlomo	M		Aharon				559
KLEINER	Hinda	F		Aharon				559
KLEINER	Leml	M	Married					559
KLEINER		F	Married			Leml		559
KLEINER		F		Leml				559
KLEINER	Aharon	M		Leml				559
KLUG	Chaia Libe	F	Married			Hersh Artche	daughter and grandchildren	559
KRIMPENHOLZ	Mendl	M		Israel				559
KRIMPENHOLZ	Malie	F		Mendl				559
KRIMPENHOLZ	Mindel	F		Mendl				559
KRIMPENHOLZ	Chana	F		Mendl				559
KRIMPENHOLZ	Feige	F		Mendl				559
KRIMPENHOLZ	Nesha	F		Mendl				559

KRIMPENHOLZ	Ester	F		Mendl			559
KANTOR	Chana Rachel	F	Married			Avraham Moshe	559
KANTOR	Yakov	M		Avraham Moshe	Chana Rachel		559
KANTOR	Perl	F		Avraham Moshe	Chana Rachel		559
KANTOR	Menashe	M		Avraham Moshe	Chana Rachel		559
KANTOR	Yekhezkel	M		Avraham Moshe	Chana Rachel		559
KROIN	Mordechai	M	Married	Yentche			Died together with children	559
KROIN		F	Married			Mordechai	Died together with children	559
KRYMERKOPF	Leibish	M	Married	Benyamin		Feige	Died together with children	559
KRYMERKOPF	Feige	F	Married			Leibish	Died together with children	559
KRYMERKOPF	Mindel	F	Married			Nachum		559
KRYMERKOPF	Pesza	F		Nachum	Mindel		559
KRYMERKOPF	Kopel	M		Nachum	Mindel		559
KRYMERKOPF	Malka	F		Nachum	Mindel		559
KESLER	Sara	F	Married			Yakov	559
KESLER	Hersh	M		Yakov	Sara		559
KESLER	Shepsl	M		Yakov	Sara		559
KESLER	Reize Beila	F		Yakov	Sara		559
KESLER	Chana Yenta	F		Yakov	Sara		559
KLIG	Yeta	F					Died together with children	559
KROIN	Shmuel	M	Married	Yentche			Died together with children	559
KROIN		F	Married			Shmuel	Died together with children	559
KROIN	Meir Yehoshua	M	Married	Yentche			Died together with children	559
KROIN		F	Married			Meir Yehoshua	Died together with children	559

KESLER	Chaia	F	Married			Zalman	some of her children	559
KORNSGOLD	Yehoshua	M	Married	Shlomo		Tove		559
KORNSGOLD	Tove	F	Married			Yehoshua		559
KORNSGOLD	Moshe	M		Yehoshua	Tove			559
KREITNER	Eliyahu Michael	M	Married				Died together with children	559
KREITNER		F	Married			Eliyahu Michael	Died together with children	559
KESLER	Miriam	F	Married			Meir	some of her children	559
KENIGSTEIN	Eliezer	M	Married	Tzvi				559
KENIGSTEIN		F	Married			Eliezer		559
KENIGSTEIN	Rafael	M		Eliezer				559
KENIGSTEIN	Matyas	M	Married	Yeshaya Leib		Beiltche		559
KENIGSTEIN	Beiltche	F	Married			Matyas		559
KENIGSTEIN	Moshe	M		Matyas	Beiltche			559
KENIGSTEIN	Feiga	F		Matyas	Beiltche			559
KNOCHEN	Chaim Shmuel	M	Married	Moshe		Rachel		559
KNOCHEN	Rachel	F	Married			Chaim Shmuel		559
KNOCHEN	Leibish	M		Chaim Shmuel	Rachel			559
KNOCHEN	Tobe	F		Chaim Shmuel	Rachel			559
KESLER	Moshe	M	Married			Malka		559
KESLER	Malka	F	Married			Moshe		559
KESLER	Tzippa	F					Died together with children	559
KRIMPENHOLZ	Israel	M	Married	Avraham Itche				560
KRIMPENHOLZ		F	Married			Israel		560
KROIN	Shlomo	M	Married	Yentche			Died together with children	560
KROIN		F	Married			Shlomo	Died together with children	560

KRIMPENHOLZ	Chaim Leib	M	Married	Yosef			Died together with children	560
KRIMPENHOLZ		F	Married			Chaim Leib	Died together with children	560
KAMER	Pinie	M	Married			Rachel		560
KAMER	Rachel	F	Married			Pinie		560
KAMER	Yechiel	M		Pinie	Rachel			560
KAMER	Tova	F		Pinie	Rachel			560
KAMER	Chaia	F		Pinie	Rachel			560
KAMER	Yosef	M		Pinie	Rachel			560
KNOBLICH	Meir	M	Married					560
KNOBLICH		F	Married			Meir		560
KNOBLICH	Simcha	M		Meir				560
KNOCHEN	Yakov	M	Married			Roize		560
KNOCHEN	Roize	F	Married			Yakov		560
KNOCHEN	Yakov	M		Yakov	Roize			560
KNOCHEN	Yitzhak	M		Yakov	Roize			560
KNOCHEN	Yenta	F		Yakov	Roize			560
KNOCHEN	Riva	F		Yakov	Roize			560
KROIN	Tema	F	Married	Moshe		Yitzhak		560
KROIN	Yitzhak	M	Married			Tema		560
KROIN	Moshe	M		Yitzhak	Tema			560
KROIN	Chaia	F		Yitzhak	Tema			560
KRYMERKOPF	Todris Meir	F	Married	Chaim		Ester		560
KRYMERKOPF	Ester	M	Married			Todris Meir		560
KRYMERKOPF	Zelig	M		Todris Meir	Ester			560
KENIGSTEIN	Lipe	F	Married	Elchanan		Golda		560
KENIGSTEIN	Golda	M	Married			Lipe		560
KENIGSTEIN	Sheindel	F		Lipe	Golda			560
KENIGSTEIN	Elchanan	M		Lipe	Golda			560
KENIGSTEIN	Chaim	M		Lipe	Golda			560

KENIGSTEIN	Chaim	M	Married	Elchanan		Miriam Lea		560
KENIGSTEIN	Miriam Lea	F	Married			Chaim		560
KENIGSTEIN	Yakov	M		Chaim	Miriam Lea			560
KENIGSTEIN	Sheindel	F		Chaim	Miriam Lea			560
KENIGSTEIN	Tema	F		Chaim	Miriam Lea			560
KENIGSTEIN	Moshe	M		Chaim	Miriam Lea			560
KENIGSTEIN	Eliezer	M		Chaim	Miriam Lea			560
KESLOVITZ	Eliezer	M	Married	Yitzhak		Gitl	Died together with children	560
KESLOVITZ	Gitl	F	Married			Eliezer	Died together with children	560
KEIL	Zischa	M	Married			Itta		560
KEIL	Itta	F	Married			Zischa		560
KEIL	Zlata	F		Zischa	Itta			560
KEIL	Mordechai	M		Zischa	Itta			560
KEIL	Yitzhak	M		Zischa	Itta			560
KEIL	Yosef	M		Zischa	Itta			560
	Rivka	F	Married	Zischa	Itta	Kalman	Maiden name - KEIL	560
	Kalman	M	Married			Rivka	KEIL	560
	Gila	F		Kalman	Rivka			560
KENIGSTEIN	Hirsh	M						560
	Tzvia Masha	F		Hirsh			Maiden name – KENIGSTEIN Died together with her children	560
KENIGSTEIN	Matil	F		Wolf				560
KENIGSTEIN	Hillel	M		Yekhezkel	Matil			560
KENIGSTEIN	Feiga	F		Yekhezkel	Matil			560
KNOCHMAN	Feivel	M						560

KNOCHMAN	Itta	F						560
KNOCHMAN	Itchele	M						560
KLEIN	Matil	F	Married			Leibish		560
KLEIN	Katriel	M		Leibish	Matil			560
KLEIN	Yekutiel	M		Leibish	Matil			560
KLEIN	Margolis	M		Leibish	Matil			560
KORN	Chana Lea	F						560
KORN	Shmuel	M	Married			Chaitche		560
KORN	Chaitche	F	Married			Shmuel		560
KORN	Tauba	F		Shmuel	Chaitche			560
KORN	Mordechai	M	Married			Lea	Died together with children	560
KORN	Lea	F	Married			Mordechai	Died together with children	560
KENIGSBERG	Rivka	F						560
KENIGSBERG	Tzipora	F			Rivka			560
KNOCHIN	Chana Dvora	F						560
KNOCHIN	Antch	M			Chana Dvora			560
KNOCHIN	Avraham	M			Chana Dvora			560
KNOCHIN	Baruch	M			Chana Dvora			560
KNOCHIN	Moshe	M	Married			Feiga		560
KNOCHIN	Feiga	F	Married			Moshe		560
KNOCHIN	Chaia	F		Moshe	Feiga			560
KNOCHIN	Brucha	F		Moshe	Feiga			560
KNOCHIN	Yakov Tzvi	M		Moshe	Feiga			560
KNOCHIN	Hersh	M	Married				some of the children	560
KNOCHIN		F	Married			Hersh	some of the children	560
KROIN	Tuvia	M	Married			Chaia Lea		560
KROIN	Chaia Lea	F	Married			Tuvia		560

KROIN	Feivl	M		Tuvia	Chaia Lea			560
KROIN	Ben-Tzion	M		Tuvia	Chaia Lea			560
KROIN	Zev	M		Tuvia	Chaia Lea			560
KLEINER	Getzl	M	Married			Hinde		560
KLEINER	Hinde	F	Married			GetSIL		560
KLEINER	Yakov	M		GetSIL	Hinde			560
KESLER	Sheindl	F						560
KESLER	Dvora	F						561
KORENSGOLD	Antch	M	Married					561
KORENSGOLD		F	Married			Antch		561
KORENSGOLD	Male	F		Antch				561
KORENSGOLD	David	F		Antch				561
KORENSGOLD	Chaim	M		Antch				561
KRUMPENHOLZ	Shmuel Yosef	M	Married			Mani		561
KRUMPENHOLZ	Mani	M	Married			Shmuel Yosef		561
KRUMPENHOLZ	Feige	F		Shmuel Yosef	Mani			561
KRUMPENHOLZ	Bracha	F		Shmuel Yosef	Mani			561
KRUMPENHOLZ	Chaia	F		Shmuel Yosef	Mani			561
KRUMPENHOLZ	Rivka	F		Shmuel Yosef	Mani			561
KRUMPENHOLZ	Gitl	F		Shmuel Yosef	Mani			561
KRUMPENHOLZ	Yehoshua Tzvi	M		Shmuel Yosef	Mani			561
KRUMPENHOLZ	Moshe Meir	M		Shmuel Yosef	Mani			561
KNOCHEN	David	M						561
KOREN	Kalman	M						561
KATZENELENBOGEN	Yakov	M						561

KUPERSTOCK WEINTRAUB	Reizl	F						561
KROIN	Hinda	F						561
KROIN	Shlomo	M	Married			Hena		561
KROIN	Hena	F	Married			Shlomo		561
KROIN	Moshe	M		Shlomo	Hena			561
KROIN	Avraham	M		Shlomo	Hena			561
KROIN	Roize	F		Shlomo	Hena			561
Resh ר								
RICHTER	Shmuel	M	Married	Yentche		Tova	Died together with children	561
RICHTER	Tova	F	Married			Shmuel	Died together with children	561
RICHTER	Shmuel Joel	M	Married	Avraham			Died together with children	561
RICHTER		F	Married			Shmuel Joel	Died together with children	561
RICHTER	Itche	M	Married	Avraham			Died together with children	561
RICHTER		F	Married			Itche	Died together with children	561
ROSENGARTEN	Gedaliahu	M	Married	Aharon		Chana		561
ROSENGARTEN	Chana	F	Married			Gedaliahu		561
ROSENGARTEN	Mechl	M		Gedaliahu	Chana			561
ROSENGARTEN	Tobe	F		Gedaliahu	Chana			561
ROSENGARTEN	Henne	F		Gedaliahu	Chana			561
ROSENGARTEN	Chaia Dvora	F		Gedaliahu	Chana			561
ROSENGARTEN	Leizer	M		Gedaliahu	Chana			561
RINGER	Berish	M	Married			Rivka		561
RINGER	Rivka	F	Married			Berish		561
	Golda	F	Married	Berish	Rivka		Maiden name - RINGER Died together with her husband and children	561
RINGER	Etele	F		Berish	Rivka			561

RINGER	Sheindel	F		Berish	Rivka			561
ROISENFELD	Leibish	M	Married			Rachel	Died together with children	561
ROISENFELD	Rachel	F	Married			Leibish	Died together with children	561
ROSENGARTEN	Meir	M	Married			Tova		561
ROSENGARTEN	Tova	F	Married			Meir		561
ROSENGARTEN	Ben-Tzion	M		Meir	Tova			561
RICHTER	Reuven	M	Married	Avraham		Hena Lea		561
RICHTER	Hena Lea	F	Married			Reuven		561
RICHTER	Shmuel	M		Reuven	Hena Lea			561
RITZER	Shmuelke	M	Married					561
RITZER		F	Married			Shmuelke		561
RITZER	Yehoshua	M		Shmuelke				561
RITZER	Avraham Yitzhak	M		Shmuelke				561
RITZER	Chaia	F		Shmuelke				561
RITZER	Shalom	M		Shmuelke				561
RITZER	Mendel	M		Shmuelke				561
RITZER	Ester	F		Shmuelke				561
RITZER	Reizl	F		Shmuelke				561
RITZER	Moshe	M		Shmuelke				561
RITZER	Chana	F					daughter-in-law & children	561
ROSENGARTEN	Yitzhak	M	Married			Mali		561
ROSENGARTEN	Mali	F	Married			Yitzhak		561
RICHTER	Meir	M	Married	Avraham		Motl		561
RICHTER	Motl	F	Married			Meir		561
ROISENFELD	Yosef	M	Married	Yekil				561
ROISENFELD		F	Married			Yosef		561
ROISENFELD	Meir Wolf	M		Yosef				561
REIZ	Rachel	F						561
REIZ	Feige	F			Rachel			561

REIZ	MordechaiTzvi	M					561
REIZ	Yitzhak	M	Married	Aharon		Beila	561
REIZ	Beila	F	Married	Mordechai Tzvi		Yitzhak	Daughter of the Rabbi	561
REIZ	Rivkale	F		Yitzhak	Beila			561
ROSENBLAT	Yosef	M	Married				Died together with his grandchildren	562
ROSENBLAT		F	Married			Yosef	Died together with her grandchildren	562
RICHTER	Hentche	F						562
RICHTER	Frumet	F			Hentche			562
RICHTER	Ruchtche	F			Hentche			562
RICHTER	Yakov	M			Hentche			562
RINGER	Itsik Leib	M	Married			Libe		562
RINGER	Libe	F	Married			Itsik Leib		562
RINGER	Sara Minl	F		Itsik Leib	Libe			562
RINGER	Moshe	M		Itsik Leib	Libe			562
RINGER	Kopel	M		Itsik Leib	Libe			562
RINGER	Nachum	M		Itsik Leib	Libe			562
RICHTER	Chana Rachel	F						562
RICHTER	Miriam	F						562
RICHTER	Mordechai	M						562
RICHTER	Sheindl	F						562
RICHTER	Feivl	M						562
RICHTER	Shmuel	M	Married				Died together with children	562
RICHTER		F	Married			Shmuel	Died together with children	562
RICHTER	Frimit	F						562
RICHTER	Sima	F						562
RICHTER	Shmuel	M			Sima			562
RICHTER	Yona	M						562

Surname	Given name	Sex	Status	Father	Mother	Spouse		Page
ROISENZON	Malka	F						562
REITER	Feiga	F						562
REITER	Miriam	F						562
REITER	Yenta	F						562
REITER	Peril	F						562
RICHTER	Menachem Mendil	M	Married					562
RICHTER		F	Married			Menachem Mendil		562
RICHTER	Shlomo	M						562

Shin ש

Surname	Given name	Sex	Status	Father	Mother	Spouse		Page
STARK	Leibl	M	Married			Reizl		562
STARK	Reizl	F	Married			Leibl		562
STARK	Yekhezkel	M		Leibl	Reizl			562
STARK	Yona	M		Leibl	Reizl			562
STARK	Susha	F		Leibl	Reizl			562
STARK	Dvora	F		Leibl	Reizl			562
STARK	Joel	M		Leibl	Reizl			562
SCHORER	Shmuel	M	Married	Avraham		Ginendl		562
SCHORER	Genendl	F	Married			Shmuel		562
SCHORER	Chaim	M		Shmuel	Genendl			562
SCHORER	Yekil	M		Shmuel	Genendl			562
SCHORER	Shimon	M		Shmuel	Genendl			562
SPIEGLER	Wolf	M	Married	Benyamin		Peshe		562
SPIEGLER	Peshe	F	Married			Wolf		562
STRUZER	Chanka	F	Married			Tzvi		562
STRUZER	Dvora	F		Tzvi	Chanka			562
STRUZER	Yute	F		Tzvi	Chanka			562
STRUZER	Frimet	F		Tzvi	Chanka			562
STRUZER	Rachel	F		Tzvi	Chanka			562
STRUZER	Chaia	F		Tzvi	Chanka			562
STRUZER	Akiva	M		Tzvi	Chanka			562

STRUZER	Yakov	M	Married	Yosef			Brother of Miriam	562
STRUZER		F	Married			Yakov		562
STRUZER	Moshe	M		Yakov				562
STRUZER	Miriam	F		Yosef			Sister of Yakov	562
STATFELD	Eliyahu	M	Married	Leizer		Chanale	Died together with children	562
STATFELD	Chanale	F	Married			Eliyahu	Died together with children	562
STATFELD	Yeshaya Mendel	M		Eliyahu	Chanale			562
SCHORER	Israelik	M	Married	Yosef		Chaia		562
SCHORER	Chaia	F	Married			Israelik		562
SCHORER	Nate	M		Israelik	Chaia			562
SCHORER	Yosef	M	Married			Henne		562
SCHORER	Henne	F	Married			Yosef		562
SCHORER				Yosef	Henne			562
SHPRUNG	Yosef	M	Married	Shlomo Yitzhak		Feige		563
SHPRUNG	Feige	F	Married			Yosef		563
SHPRUNG	Rivka	F		Yosef	Feige			563
SHPRUNG	Beile	F		Yosef	Feige			563
SCHORER	Meir	M	Married	Israel Tzvi		Libe		563
SCHORER	Libe	F	Married			Meir		563
SCHORER	Azriel	M		Meir	Libe			563
SCHORER	Anshl	M		Meir	Libe			563
SCHORER	Ester	F		Meir	Libe			563
SCHORER	Israelik Tzvi	M		Meir	Libe			563
STOCKMAN	Avraham	M	Married			Dobre	Died together with children	563
STOCKMAN	Dobre	F	Married			Avraham	Died together with children	563
SCHLEISER	Shmuel	M	Married	Benyamin Leib		Chele	Some of the children?	563

SCHLEISER	Chele	F	Married			Shmuel	Some of the children?	563
SCHLEISER	Yosef	M		Shmuel	Chele			563
SCHLEISER	Lea	F		Shmuel	Chele			563
SCHLEISER	Bila	F		Shmuel	Chele			563
SCHLEISER	Yitzhak	M	Married	Benyamin Leib		Etl		563
SCHLEISER	Etl	F	Married			Yitzhak		563
SCHLEISER	Yakov Leib	M		Yitzhak	Etl			563
SCHWECER	Yekil	M	Married	Shimon		Miriam		563
SCHWECER	Miriam	F	Married			Yekil		563
SCHWECER	Saul	M		Yekil	Miriam			563
SCHWECER	Moshe	M	Married	Shimon		Miriam	Died together with children	563
SCHWECER	Miriam	F	Married			Moshe	Died together with children	563
SHPRUNG	Nachum	M	Married	Mordechai			Died together with children	563
SHPRUNG		F	Married			Nachum	Died together with children	563
SHPRUNG	Meir	M	Married	Mordechai			Died together with children	563
SHPRUNG		F	Married			Meir	Died together with children	563
SHPRUNG	Naftali	M	Married	Mordechai			Died together with children	563
SHPRUNG		F	Married			Naftali	Died together with children	563
SHPRUNG	Mordechai	M	Married	Mordechai			Died together with children	563
SHPRUNG		F	Married			Mordechai	Died together with children	563
STOCKMAN	Leib Joel	M	Married			Tova		563
STOCKMAN	Tova	F	Married			Leib Joel		563
STOCKMAN	Kopel	M		Leib Joel	Tova			563
STOCKMAN	Mendl	M		Leib Joel	Tova			563
STOCKMAN	Chaia	F		Leib Joel	Tova			563

STATFELD	Shamai	M	Married	Leizer		Chaia		563
STATFELD	Chaia	F	Married			Shamai		563
STATFELD	Rivka	F		Shamai	Chaia			563
STOCKMAN	Shimon David	M	Married	Avraham			Died together with children	563
STOCKMAN		F	Married			Shimon David	Died together with children	563
STOCKMAN	Wolf	M	Married	Yeshaya			Died together with children	563
STOCKMAN		F	Married			Wolf	Died together with children	563
SCHWETZER	Yakov Meir	M	Married	Shmerl		Henke		563
SCHWETZER	Henke	F	Married			Yakov Meir		563
SCHWETZER	Yitzhak	M		Yakov Meir	Henke			563
SCHWETZER	Moshe	M	Married	Yakov Meir		Pesil		563
SCHWETZER	Pesil	F	Married			Moshe		563
SCHWETZER	Ester	F		Moshe	Pesil			563
SCHWETZER	Zisser	M	Married	Yakov Meir			Died together with children	563
SCHWETZER		F	Married			Zyser	Died together with children	563
STATFELD	Mordechai	M	Married					563
STATFELD		F	Married			Mordechai		563
STATFELD	Manish	M	Married	Wolf		Zisl		563
STATFELD	Zisl	F	Married			Manish		563
STATFELD	Geula	F		Manish	Zisl			563
STATFELD	Miriam	F		Manish	Zisl			563
STATFELD	Avraham	M	Married	Wolf			Died together with children	563
STATFELD		F	Married			Avraham	Died together with children	563
STATFELD	Simcha	M	Married	Wolf			Died together with children	563

STATFELD		F	Married			Simcha	Died together with children	563
STOCKMAN	Mendl	M	Married	Kopil		Malka	Died together with children	563
STOCKMAN	Malka	F	Married			Mendl	Died together with children	563
STOCKMAN	Rachel	F	Married			Moshe		563
SPIELSINGER	Yekil Getzel	M	Married	Aharon Itsik		Mirtche		563
SPIELSINGER	Mirtche	F	Married			Yekil Getzl		563
SPIELSINGER	Machla	F		Yekil Getzl	Mirtche			563
STOCKMAN	Leibl	M	Married	Moshe		Sara		563
STOCKMAN	Sara	F	Married			Leibl		563
SCHUMACHER	Zalman	M	Married			Rachel		563
SCHUMACHER	Rachel	F	Married			Zalman		563
SCHORER	Elimelech	M	Married	Shmuel		Chantche	Died together with children	563
SCHORER	Chantche	F	Married			Elimelech	Died together with children	563
SHPRUNG	Brantcha	F	Married			Mordechai		564
SHPRUNG	Moshe	M			Breintche			564
SHPRUNG	Shamai	M			Breintche			564
	Blume	F	Married		Breintche		Maiden name - SHPRUNG Died together with her husband	564
SHPRUNG	Sheva	F			Breintche			564
STATFELD	Peretz	M	Married	Eliyahu		Rachel		564
STATFELD	Rachel	F	Married			Peretz		564
STATFELD	Chaia	F		Peretz	Rachel			564
STATFELD	Miriam	F		Peretz	Rachel			564
STOCKMAN	Rachmiel	M	Married				Died together with children Brother of Dvora	564

STOCKMAN		F	Married			Rachmiel	Died together with children	564
STOCKMAN	Dvora	F					Sister of Rachmiel	564
SCHLEIEN	Hadas	F	Married			Benyamin Leib	Died together with children	564
SCHWARTZ	Chanale	F		Arie			Daughter of the Rabbi	564
SCHWARTZ	Gitele	F						564
SCHWARTZ	Shalom	M			Gitele			564
SPIELEISEN	Yehoshua	M	Married	Shalom Kalman			Died together with children	564
SPIELEISEN		F	Married			Yehoshua	Died together with children	564
SHPRUNG	Israel Iser	M	Married	Shlomo Yitzhak		Reizl		564
SHPRUNG	Reizl	F	Married			Israel Iser		564
SHPRUNG	Shimon	M		Israel Iser	Reizl			564
SHPRUNG	Metot	M		Israel Iser	Reizl			564
SHPRUNG	Rivka	F		Israel Iser	Reizl			564
SHPRUNG	Drezl	F		Israel Iser	Reizl			564
SHPRUNG	Lea	F		Israel Iser	Reizl			564
SHPRUNG	Shmuel Peretz	M	Married		Sara	Rechil	Mother of Shmuel Peretz	564
SHPRUNG	Sara	F						564
SHPRUNG	Rechil	F	Married			Shmuel Peretz		564
	Rivka	F		Shmuel Peretz	Rechil		Maiden name - SHPRUNG	564
	Tova	F			Rivka			564
	Aizik	M			Rivka			564
SCHIFER	Tevl	M	Married	Joel		Tzuril		564
SCHIFER	Tzuril	F	Married			Tevl		564
SCHIFER	Sara	F		Tevl	Tzuril			564
SCHIFER	Moshe	M		Tevl	Tzuril			564
SCHIFER	Yitzhak	M		Tevl	Tzuril			564

STRASBERG	Pinkhas	M	Married	Aharon			Died together with children	564
STRASBERG		F	Married			Pinkhas	Died together with children	564
STATFELD	Peril	F		Avraham			Died together with children	564
STARKER	Israel	M	Married	Mordechai		Malka		564
STARKER	Malka	F	Married			Israel		564
STARKER	Mordechai	M		Israel	Malka			564
STARKER	Etl	F		Israel	Malka			564
STARKER	Roize	F		Israel	Malka			564
SCHAFRAN	Reizel	F		Yosef		Getzl		564
SCHAFRAN	Yosef	M		Getzl	Reizel			564
STRASBERG	Matilda	F		Avraham'le				564
STRASBERG	Felka	F		Avraham'le				564
STATFELD	Moshe	M	Married			Rivka		564
STATFELD	Rivka	F	Married			Moshe		564
SHEIER	Shmuel Eli	M	Married			Tobele		564
SHEIER	Tobele	F	Married			Shmuel Eli		564
SHEIER	Shlomo	M		Shmuel Eli	Tobele			564
SHEIER	Yitzhak	M		Shmuel Eli	Tobele			564
SHEIER	Frida	F		Shmuel Eli	Tobele			564
STOCKMAN	Shmuelke	M	Married			Chavale		564
STOCKMAN	Chavale	F	Married			Shmuelke		564
SCHAFRAN	Reizl	F		Leizer				564
SCHAFRAN	Reizl	F			Itta			564
STATFELD	Leib Yosef	M	Married			Rivka		564
STATFELD	Rivka	F	Married			Leib Yosef		564
STATFELD	Chana Rachel	F		Leib Yosef	Rivka			564

STATFELD	Yitzhak Meir	M		Leib Yosef	Rivka			564
STEIN	Dvora	F		Mendl	Rivka			564
STEIN	Yitzhak Meir	M		Mordechai	Nechama			564
STRINGLER	Yosef	M	Married			Reizl	Died together with children	564
STRINGLER	Reizl	F	Married			Yosef	Died together with children	564
SCHORER	Yitzhak	M	Married			Frimit		564
SCHORER	Frimit	F	Married			Yitzhak		564
		F	Married	Yitzhak	Frimit	Elimelech	Maiden name - SHORER	564
	Elimelech	M	Married				SHORER	564
SMUTZ	Yakov	M						564
SMUTZ	Reizl	F						564
SMUTZ	Fruma	F						564
SMUTZ	Etl	F						564
SMUTZ	Lipa	M						564
SMUTZ	Sheindel	F						564
STERNFELD	Rachel	F						564
STERNFELD	Sara	F						564
STERNFELD	Shimon	M						564
STERNFELD	Chana	F						564
SPIEGLER	Nachman	M						564
SPIEGLER	Rivka	F						565
SPIEGLER	Eliyahu	M	Married			Rachel		565
SPIEGLER	Rachel	F	Married	Avigdor		Eliyahu		565
SILBERZWEIG	Chaim Wolf	M	Married	Yona		Shontche		565
SILBERZWEIG	Shontche	F	Married			Chaim Wolf		565
SILBERZWEIG	Eliyahu	M		Chaim Wolf	Shivintche			565
SILBERZWEIG	Yona	M		Chaim Wolf	Shivintche			565

GOLDMAN	Chaim	M					565
GOLDMAN		F		Chaim			565
GOLDMAN		F		Chaim			565
GOLDMAN	Yoske	M		Chaim			565
SILBERZWEIG	Yekhezkel	M		Pinkhas			565
KENIGSTEIN	Moshe	M		Matyas			565
ADLER	Eliyahu	M		Yeshaya Nate			565
TEICHER	Tzvi	M		Ari		Son of the rabbi	565
SCHWEZER	Avraham	M		Lipe			565
FEFER	Lipe	M		Itsik Hersh			565
WEINTRAUB	Zalman	M		Leib Shimshon			565
HERBSTMAN	Breintche	M	Married		Tewl Nachum		565
WEINTRAUB	Sheindl	F					565
STRUZER	Matil	M					565
MODEL	Michael	M		Itche			565
KESLER	Wolf Leib	M		Zalman			565
EILBAUM	Aharon Shimon	M		David			565
WEINTRAUB	Yekutiel	M		Fishel			565
WEINMAN	Frimtche	F	Married		Itsik		565
MANTEL	Rochme	F		Shlomo			565
TRYB	Elimelech	M		Israel Leib			565
TENENBAUM	Yakov	M		Levi		Fell as a soldier on the Russian front	565
SETZER	Yakov Leib	M		Simcha			566
MOSHE	Reiz	M		Arie			566
STRUM	Wolf	M		Mordechai			566
FUCHSMAN	Wolf	M		Yosef			566

BAUMFELD	Tobele	F					566
WERTMAN	Chanina	M		Yosef			566
FEIFER	Niche	F					566
FEIFER		M			Niche		566
FEIFER		M			Niche		566
FEIFER		F			Niche		566
KATZ	Berish	M		Yakov			566
LEHRER	Chaim	M					566
ADLER	Gele	F		Pinkhas			566
ADLER	Itche	M			Gele		566
ADLER	Beile	F			Gele		566
ADLER	Malie	F			Gele		566

Obituaries

Translated by Lorraine Rosengarten and Zvika Welgreen

The memories of our loved ones stored forever in our hearts.

Pure saints, who perished, cut down by the wicked.

They shall shine as the brightness of the firmament...

Parents: Dov-Berish RINGER, wife Rivka

Brother: Wolf-Zev RINGER, wife Miriam and five children

Sisters: Golda, Etla, Sheindel

Their memory will never depart from us!
With eternal sorrow:
Families Meir and Aharon RINGER,
Rishon-LeZion

[Page 571]

WE SHALL NEVER FORGET THEM!

Parents: Rev Yakov Yehuda, Sheindel Lea LEMER

Blume, Bezalel, Rudy LEMER

Sarale and Avraham FECHER and children

Kreindil, Yakov ZUKERMAN, daughters, sons-in-law and children

LAND, COVER NOT THEIR BLOOD!

Forever:
LEMER FAMILY
in London

[Page 572]

TO SANCTIFY THE MEMORY OF OUR BELOVED

Shmuel LEMER, son of Yakov and Sheindel

with his wife and daughter

Shmuel LEMER was among the first halutzim [pioneer, specifically an early settler to Palestine before 1948], who made aliya [the act of immigrating to Israel] to Eretz Israel in the year 1925 and later on he went to Germany to heal from malaria and stayed there. He perished with his family in Hungary.

Forever:

LEMER Family

[Page 573]

TO SANCTIFY THE MEMORY OF

Grandfather
**Yisrael-Avraham-Yitzhak
KRIMPENHOLZ**

Grandmother **Sarale
KRIMPENHOLZ**

Father **Mendl-Chaim
KRIMPENHOLZ**

Mother **Mala-Mindel
KRIMPENHOLZ**

Sisters **Chana, Feige, Nesha, Ester
KRIMPENHOLZ**

Aunt **Tova BLUM, David HENEKH
and Family**

In deep sorrow:
**Chaia and Hersh WAJCHMAN,
Haifa, Kiryat Bialik**

May she rest in peace
Rivka LEWINSON

Perished in Tarnogrod

Forever: Feige MAHLER

[Page 574]

Exalted and hallowed be His Great Name...

To Sanctify the Memory of Our Beloved

Shmuel ben Avraham SCHORER

Genendl SCHORER bat Chaim LUMERMAN

Sara GISZPENC bat Shmuel SCHORER and her two children

Melech SCHORER bat Shmuel with his wife Chantche and two children

Chaim, Yakov and Shimon – sons of Shmuel SCHORER

Rivka BORAD bat Chaim LUMERMAN and children

Ratse FLIESSWASSER bat Chaim LUMERMAN with husband and child

Hersh-Sheyne ben Chaim LUMERMAN with wife and child

Lea LUMERMAN bat Tzvi KNOBL

Male FISCHBAINDEGEN bat Avraham SCHORER, husband and daughter Nechama

Mindel BORAD bat Avraham SCHORERwith husband and children

Israel ben Avraham Yehuda LUMERMAN with wife and children

Fruma Grossfeld bat Avraham Yehuda LUMERMAN husband and daughter

Godel ben Avraham Yehuda LUMERMAN with wife and children

We Shall Never Forget You!

Forever:
Avraham and Yosef SCHORER
Efraim LUMERMAN

[Page 575]

IN MEMORY

Mother:
Chaia Sara STOCKMAN
Who died in 1916 in Tarnogrod

Father:
Reb Shmuel son of Yosef Arie STOCKMAN
Put to death by the Nazi enemies in 1942 in Tarnogrod

Sister:
Beila Chava
and her husband
Menachem Mendl ECKSTEIN
and their two daughters
Killed by the Nazi enemies in Bialystok

Brother:
Yosef Arie STOCKMAN
Who died during the war
in wanderings in Russia

Shmuel STOCKMAN

WE SHALL NEVER FORGET THEM
In Commemoration:

Isser STOCKMAN and Wife, London
Rachel and Meir ZUCKERMAN, Afula

[Page 576]

For Eternal Memory

Her name will endure forever

Tsharne MANTEL

daughter of Reb Zacharia FEFER

Taken in the prime of her life, 1921 in Tarnogrod

May Her Memory Be Blessed

In commemoration:

Her husband **Moshe**
Naftali MANTEL
Tel-Aviv

[Page 577]

In Eternal Memory

My father:	**Aharon Hillel**, son of **Avraham Mordechai MANTEL** Who died in 1928 in the United States
My mother:	**Rochma Bina MANTEL**, daughter of **Reb Saul Yoel KATZENELENBOGEN** Granddaughter of the **Rabbi Rev Moshe Naftali KATZENELENBOGEN** known as Kreshover-Tzadik. Granddaughter of the **Rabbi Reb Tzvi TAUMIM,** President of the Rabbinic Court in the community of Wlodowa, who was murdered brutally by the Nazi enemies in the city Szczebrzeszyn (Poland) in 1941.
My sister:	**Beila** and her son **Aharon**, son of **Moshe TAJER** Killed brutally by the Nazi enemies in 1942, the city Zbarazh, Poland, now in the Ukraine.

Perpetually:

Son and
Brother: **Moshe
Naftali MANTEL,**   s
Tel Aviv

[Page 578]

THOSE ARE OUR LOVED ONES WHO FELL BY THE MURDERERS OF OUR PEOPLE

For His Eternal Remembrance

My Father

Matyas KENIGSTEIN

and My Mother

Beiltche

their son **Moshe**

and daughter **Feige**

Forever: **Golda AGERT-KENIGSTEIN**

Chana AGERT

Mother of **Avraham Yitzhak**

Forever:

Yekhezkel AGERT

[Page 579]

FOR ETERNAL MEMORY

Head of Family

Meir ACKERMAN of blessed memory

and son **Yakov** (eldest)

Commemorator:

Shmuel FEFER (CHEFER)

Nesha ACKERMAN and her children

Avraham Yitzhak AGERT

Died in Israel, 11 Sivan 5725

Zionist from his young age, all his thoughts were devoted to the idea of reconstruction of Israel. Was among the first pioneers and made Aliya to Israel in 1926. The strong belief in the national goal gave him the moral power to overcome day-to-day troubles and with this moral he kept on till his last day.

His memory is kept in the hearts of the few Tarnogrod survivors

Mourning: his wife, brother and sons
Tzvi and Amnon DAVID
And their families

[Page 580]

IN ETERNAL MEMORY

Bunim-Menachem-Mendl Zev-Arie HON

Wife:
Rachel-Lea, daughter of Eli LICHT from Krzeszow

Daughter:
Sara-Libe and her husband Leibl STOCKMAN

Son:
Baruch-Moshe HON

Daughter:
Feige-Sosha HON

Their Song Of Life Ended Too Soon

With Profound Grief:

Eli HON
Bolivia

[Page 581]

IN MEMORY OF OUR LOVED ONES

All perished except Tzvi (between his father and mother) who lives in Israel

My Parents:
Chana and David-Yeshaya SUSSMILCH

Brothers:
Mordechai, Leibel, and Fishel

Sister:
Golda

Golda SUSSMILCH
Perished in Lukow

Fishel SUSSMILCH
Perished in Lukow

In Mourning: Their Daughter and Sister

Bluma SUSSMILCH-WASSERMAN
with her husband

[Page 582]

My tears have been my bread day and night…
(Psalms 42)

MAY THEY REST IN PEACE

Shamai OPFER

Chaia OPFER

Zelda and her husband Tzvi WELTCH

and their two children

For Those That Are Gone And Cannot Be Replaced

May Their Souls Be Bound Up In The Bond Of Eternal Life

Bitterly Mourning:

OPFER Family
Bnei Brak

[Page 583]

IN PERPETUAL MEMORY

Our Precious and Saintly

Daughter

Reizel SCHAFRAN

Forever In Our Hearts:
Parents **Miriam and Leizer SCHAFRAN**

My Heart Is About To Burst In Tears

My mother **Ite SCHAFRAN**
Died In Israel

In Everlasting Memory:
Leizer SCHAFRAN and Family

To
Remember
Forever

**Yoske
GOLDMAN**

The whole GOLDMAN
family perished, some
in White Russia and
some in Tarnogrod.
Not one of them
remained alive.

[Page 584]

Eternal Monument Of Our Most Precious and Unforgettable

Zelik TENENBAUM
and wife Zelda

Children: Meir,
        Rachel,
        Avraham

In Everlasting Memory:
The Sister
Fride SHERMAN (TENENBAUM)

[Page 585]

Rivka STATFELD

Daughter of likever residents Yakov-Joseph

Forever: Simcha STATFELD

Remember

Reizl SCHAFRAN-WEINBERG
Rivka STATFELD

The child remained alive, is
living in Poland

Forever: Ettel NABBOR

Perele MAHLER
Perished during the action
in the Tarnogrod ghetto

Forever: Feige MAHLER

In Perpetual Memory

My Unforgettable Parents

Zissman and Masha FINK

In Memory of my Precious
Brother and Sisters

Shlomo, Hinda, and Sara

May their souls be bound up in
the bond of eternal life.

Victor:
Zev FINK

[Page 586]

IN REMEMBRANCE

The souls of my parents, brothers and sisters went up in flames along with the millions of pure saints of Israel.

Reb Yisrael-Iser and Reizl SHPRUNG

My dear and honored father **Reb Iser** son of **Shlomo Yitzhak** of blessed memory

My dear and honored mother **Reizl** daughter of **Reb Matityahu** of blessed memory

My sister **Rivka** and husband **Shlomo** and daughter **Drezl ZALTZMAN**

My brother **Shimon.Meir**

My sister **Leah**

My brother **Matityahu**

Perished 22-25 *Cheshvan* 1942 by the German Nazi soldiers (may their names be erased).

[Page 587]

Rivka SHPRUNG ZALTZMAN   **Shimon Meir**

The souls of all my relatives on my father's and mother's side whose date of death and burial place are not known.

Their resting place shall be in the Garden of Eden with the rest of all righteous souls. God will avenge their spilled blood and they will rest in peace and will stand up for their trial at the end of time.

Sons and brothers praying for their souls to rise up.

Shlomo SHPRUNG

Moshe SHPRUNG and Family

[Page 588]

My Parents:
Rachel and Avraham KIELICH

My Brothers:
Hersh, Eliakim with his wife Rivka

Moshe, Lived in Chmielnik

**With bowed head, in grief and anger:
Baruch KIELICH**, Bat-Yam

Yosef SPRUNG

FOR ETERNAL MEMORY

My Parents:
Feige and Yosef SPRUNG

My Sisters:
Rivka and Beile

We weep for them:

Daughter and Sister

Gitl and Moshe STERNFELD

[Page 589]

FOR THOSE WE WEEP

My mother:

Brantche

SPRUNG

My brothers: **Moshe and Shamai**

My sister: **Blume with her husband and Bat-Sheva**

In Eternal Sorrow:

Malka SPRUNG- ZUCKER, Paris

[Page 590]

We Shall Never Forget Them

Godl and Lea-Teml WETSHER

Son

Son

Pinkhas

Daughter

Beiltche

Chaim WETSHER

May their souls be bound up in the bond of eternal life

[Page 591]

May their memory remain with us forever

Our dear and saintly brother **Zalman WETSHER**
with his wife and their child

Bitterly mourning:

Moshe, Yeshayahu and Rachel WETSHER
and their familes

[Page 592]

MAY HIS GREAT NAME GROW EXHAULTED AND SANCTIFIED....

With sorrow and rage we weep bitterly for the holy, murdered by the cruel Nazi hangmen, our beloved, which we will never forget.

Grandfather **Mendel-Yoshes**

Father **Yoske**

Mother **Ester-Miriam**

Brothers **Yona-Chaim, Israelke**

Sister **Gitl**

Forever:

Yakov, Sinai, Sara and Shmuel-Eli

[Page 593]

IN EVERLASTING MEMORY

Grandfather
Mendel Yoshes

Father
Yosef

Mother
Ester-Miriam

Brothers
Yona-Chaim, Israel

Sister
Gitl

Marble relief made by Shmuel-Eli Puter

NAME INDEX

APPENDIX

<u>Appendix</u>

<u>Additional Reading:</u>

Tarnogrod Entry in the Encyclopedia of Jewish Communities in Poland
https://www.jewishgen.org/Yizkor/pinkas_poland/pol7_00250.html

A Dream Fulfilled: Return to Tarnogrod
By Joseph Schorer as told to Sheldon Schorer; 1989
Includes pictures and documents in English, Polish and Hebrew

Alone in the Forest (Re-published as Mala's Cat – May 29, 2023)
By Mala Kacenberg; 1995
https://www.nytimes.com/2022/01/12/books/review/malas-cat-mala-kacenberg.html

A Surge of Sympathy for Jews is Sensed in Poland
New York Times – June 24, 1985
https://timesmachine.nytimes.com/timesmachine/1985/06/24/073560.html?pageNumber=2

Tarnogrod Facebook Page – Tarnohotzkies
https://www.facebook.com/groups/2583360719/media

JRI-Poland
https://www.jri-poland.org/town/tarnogrod/

Tarnogrod Library – Located in the former Synagogue. Website includes interior photographs
https://bibliotekatarnogrod.lbl.pl/biblioteka/o-bibliotece

The story of a fragment of the Torah Scroll – Located in the Former Synagogue
https://blogs.timesofisrael.com/the-torah-scroll-in-tarnogrod/

Mt. Zion Cemetery, Queens, NY – First Tarnogroder Society, 123 Burials from 1904-1974
http://www.mountzioncemetery.com/search.asp
Search on Tarnogrod in the Society Tab

United Hebrew Cemetery, Staten Island, NY – First Tarnogroder Society, Burials Not Searchable
https://www.jewishmonuments.com/cemeteryguide_unitedhebrew.html

Helen Lipiner Adler Audio Interview – USHMM May 17, 2008 Interviewed by Brad Zarlin
Helen Lipiner was born in Tarnogrod in 1923. Her parents and two sisters died in the Holocaust
Helen describes growing up in Tarnogrod, life during WWII, and escaping to Russia
https://collections.ushmm.org/search/catalog/irn700371

434

Szukaj w Archiwach   How to search   About the service   News   Contact   Q   Sign in

⌂ / ARCHIWUM / PRADZIAD   ← Back to Search

Akta stanu cywilnego Okręgu Bożniczego w Tarnogrodzie

Reference code	Archives
88/782/0	Archiwum Państwowe w Zamościu

Name	Dates	Confession/Rite	Type of act	Summoning/Determination
Akta stanu cywilnego Okręgu Bożniczego w Tarnogrodzie	1877 - 1881	mojżeszowe	zgony	
	1883 - 1892			
	1895 - 1902			
	1904 - 1905			
	1907 - 1913			
	1915 - 1922			

Birth Record of Leib Sztrazberger. Leib emigrated to the United States and lived in New York as Louis Strassberg. From the Polish State Archives, Zamosc

This happened in the city of Tarnogrod. On the 22nd of December 1877, at 9am appeared in person a Jew Moses Strassberg, manufacturer of 36 years of age living in this city of Tarnogrod. In the city of Tarnogrod in the presence of witnesses Smul Klucz, about 60 years old and also Mordechai Mantel, 31 years of age, salesman living in the city of Tarnogrod and presented to me a male baby announcing that he was born in the city of Tarnogrod on the 3rd/15th of this month of this year at 2pm from his legal wife Gena Klucz of 33 years of age. The baby, after circumcision was given the name of Leiba....."

The Tarnogrod Synagogue, currently the town library, photographed by Jadwiga Zmuda in 2023. The building was stabilized in the 1980s, and repaired over time with the project completed in 2022. Pictures from 1989 during refurbishment from "A Dream Fulfilled" by Joseph Schorer.

Interior photographs of the library, former Synagogue, courtesy of Kamil Kopera, from 2023. Shown are the remains of the Synagogue ark, stone floor and recreated women's mezzanine. Used with permission from the Tarnogrod Library.

Photographs of street scenes in Tarnogrod taken by Marcel Weise, a German soldier in 1939/1940 used with permission from his family.

Keeping Warm

The Water Carrier

1939

Paintings by Mendel Muterperel born in 1891 in Szczebrzeszyn. Married Gena Mantel in 1911 in Tarnogrod. Gena was born in Tarnogrod. Used with permission from Sheldon Schorer.

JRI-Poland 1929 Business Directory Project - Tarnogrod Entries
From the Polish National Library in Warsaw
https://www.jri-poland.org/blog/the-1929-polish-business-directory-project/
Extracted by Tom Merolla and Nancy Rosenbloom

Name	Occupation	Name	Occupation	Name	Occupation
Francisek Kraczek	Doctor	G. Zylberman	Fabrics	J. Adler	Tailors
Berko Rozenberg	Doctor	T. Zylberman	Fabrics	A. Bas	Tailors
Krejndel Rozenberg	Doctor	A. Weczer	Cattle Dealer	F. Bas	Tailors
Jan Kuzminski	Lawyer	P. Juliz	Caps	H. Blutman	Tailors
Joz. Chadajewski	Property Owner	S. Sztarkier	Caps	M. Blutman	Tailors
Mauryey Zamoyski	Property Owner	J. Wertman	Caps	Ab. Daw. Fajfer	Tailors
E. Wagenfeld	Midwife	E. Mendel	Cement Tiles	C. Feldman	Tailors
D. Malicki	Drugs	J. Struzer	Medical Assistant	B. Firer	Tailors
W. Bartnikowski	Chemist	J. Koba	Photograph Studio	J. Fuksman	Tailors
Sz. Lesniak	Cooper	F. Akst	Fancy Goods	M. Margam	Tailors
Ch. Fridman	Brazier	K. Grossman	Fancy Goods	Waksman	Tailors
G. Apotekier	Fabrics	H. Kenigsztajn	Fancy Goods	M. Lederman	Kitchen Utensils
E. Cukierman	Fabrics	H. Rosengarten	Fancy Goods	R. Lewinfus	Kitchen Utensils
J. Cukierman	Fabrics	S. Wertman	Fancy Goods	S. Rosochasz	Painters
M. Cukierman	Fabrics	I. Zylbercwajg	Fancy Goods	D. Zaluzny	Painters
I. Fefer	Fabrics	P. Wajnreb	Fancy Goods	J. Rylko Rolniczo	Agricultural Machines
Z. Fefer	Fabrics	M. Baumfeld	Eggs	L. Herbstman	Agricultural Machines
H. Flinder	Fabrics	J. Szorer	Eggs	Rolniczy Syndykat	Agricultural Machines
M. Frajtag	Fabrics	J. Walc	Eggs	I. Zylbercwajg	Mills
K. Grinapel	Fabrics	S.M. Zylbercwajg	Eggs	I. Wajnryb	Mills
Ch. Kenigsztajn	Fabrics	H. Cajs	Shaft or Handle Maker	G. Weczer	Soaps
S. Lajcher	Fabrics	M. Krojn	Shaft or Handle Maker	F. Broner	Milk Products
M. Magram	Fabrics	A. Lacher	Shaft or Handle Maker	B. Goldsztajn	Milk Products
Chaim Maler	Fabrics	L. Rycer	Shaft or Handle Maker	L. Wertman	Milk Products
Chaskiel Maler	Fabrics	B. Apotekier	Shaft or Handle Maker	M. Wertman	Milk Products
H. Marmer	Fabrics	P. Sztadfeld	Shaft or Handle Maker	M. Zustryn	Milk Products
L. Opfer	Fabrics	Kredytowa Spoldzielma	Savings and Lending Bank	P. Zylbercwajg	Milk Products
Sz. Szorer	Fabrics	H. Rozensohn	Groats Manufacturers	D. Malicki	Seeds
J.Tafler	Fabrics	A. Banach	Wheelwright	C. Ulrich	Seeds - Warsaw
Sz. Tojersztajn	Fabrics	Sz. Akst	Horse Dealer	Ch. Fajngold	Footwear
H. Lewenson	Fabrics	Spozyweze Stow	Cooperative Society	G. Sztadfeld	Footwear
Rynek	Fabrics	Wyzwolenie	Cooperative Society	D. Zychler	Footwear
Sz. L. Zylberlicht	Fabrics	J. Glinianowicz	Smith	Ch. Zylbercwajg	Footwear

Name	Occupation	Name	Occupation	Name	Occupation
D. Elbaum	Oils	L. Adler	Butchers	J. Sztrum	Articles of Food
M. Gri	Oils	J. Zaluzny	Butchers	F. Szwecer	Articles of Food
I. Honig	Oils	W. Zaluzny	Butchers	N. Wakslicht	Articles of Food
A. Rychter	Oils	A. Adler	Leather	M. Wank	Articles of Food
M. Wajntraub	Oils	D. Adler	Leather	S. Zecer	Articles of Food
L. Akierman	Bakers	M. Fajngold	Leather	N. Zoberman	Articles of Food
Andrz Bien	Bakers	M. Fink	Leather	B. Apotekier	Articles of Food
P. Berner	Bakers	R. Frucht	Leather	J. Gatarz	Articles of Food
A. Bromberg	Bakers	I. Goldman	Leather	S. Liszyk	Articles of Food
W. Kesler	Bakers	F. Hering	Leather	M. Majzels	Articles of Food
B. Ryngier	Bakers	M. Lemer	Leather	M. Rychter	Articles of Food
Sz. Sztokman	Bakers	N. Manes	Leather	I. Tajcher	Articles of Food
Sz. Wajs	Bakers	J. Rofer	Leather	Sz. Wajnryb	Articles of Food
M. Wajs	Bakers	L. Zylbercwajg	Leather	Sz. Zylbercwaig	Articles of Food
A. Bogdanowicz	Beer Restaurants	F. Wnuk	Spirits	J. Blutman	Carpentry
Ch. Herbstman	Beer Restaurants	M. Akst	Articles of Food	W. Borek	Carpentry
M. Hochlest	Beer Restaurants	A. Apotekier	Articles of Food	M. Falanczyk	Carpentry
R. Hoendel	Beer Restaurants	F. Bartosik	Articles of Food	E. Korniak	Carpentry
R. Kandel	Beer Restaurants	Ch. Borensztajn	Articles of Food	W. Korniak	Carpentry
Sz. Korengold	Beer Restaurants	F. Brandsztajn	Articles of Food	W. Kukielka	Carpentry
J. Pszczola	Beer Restaurants	B. Bronsztajn	Articles of Food	Ch. Akst	Shoe Requisits
M. Rychter	Beer Restaurants	R. Fremer	Articles of Food	J. Akst	Shoe Makers
D. Sobol	Beer Restaurants	Ch. Glencer	Articles of Food	Z. Klejne	Shoe Makers
A. Stasiewicz	Beer Restaurants	T. Goldborjm	Articles of Food	S. Pele	Shoe Makers
I. Szarfman	Beer Restaurants	J. Goldman	Articles of Food	M. Rogala	Shoe Makers
S. Wajsman	Beer Restaurants	K. Grinapel	Articles of Food	Sz. Grynberg	Blacksmith
R. Lipiner	Beer Restaurants	A. Grusza	Articles of Food	M. Bien	Tobacco
D. Szafran	Beer Restaurants	Kamer	Articles of Food	W. Chmieleski	Tobacco
R. Kandel	Beer Wholesale	B. Mantel	Articles of Food	M. Falanczyk	Tobacco
M. Fajngold	Wire	H. Mantel	Articles of Food	F. Hulas	Tobacco
S. Gutherc	Wire	H. Margel	Articles of Food	L. Zoberman	Tobacco
A. Lustrym	Wire	R. Metler	Articles of Food	P. Borek	Tobacco
J. Rozenblatt	Wire	Sz. Nirensztajn	Articles of Food	M. Szuper	Tobacco
J. Chodacznik	Restaurants	R. Puter	Articles of Food	I. Wajnryb	Tobacco
F. Sochman	Restaurants	M. Rozengarten	Articles of Food	M. Kac	Popular Clothing
I. Giszpanc	Leather and Saddlery	P. Sztokman	Articles of Food	H. Mulawa	Pork Butcher Shop
F. Rutyna	Pork Butcher Shop				
M. Lemer	Aerated Water				
J. Sztrum	Aerated Water				
S. Zilberliecht	Aerated Water				
L. Klajner	Corn				
M. Krimpenhole	Corn				
M. Sztadtfeld	Corn				
J. Cukier	Iron				
S. Cukier	Iron				
J. Hochman	Iron				
I. Nirensztajn	Iron				
B. Ulrich	Iron				
M. Wajsman	Iron				
F. Zylbercwajg	Iron				

The following pages are reproduced from "A Dream Fulfilled" by Joseph Schorer. Joseph returned to Tarnogrod in the 1980s in part to find out where family members, including his parents were buried after being murdered by the Nazis. With the help of local Tarnogroders, two locations were identified. The following is the proclamation from the Mayor's Office and statements made by Joseph and an excerpt from Sheldon Schorer in 1985 and 1986.

Of the   : Mayor Community Tarnogrod, 12 May 1986

This is to inform you that two places in Tarnogrod — the scene of the mass murder of Polish Jews by the Nazis in November 1942, have been memorialized.

One site, on T. Kosciuszko Street was memorialized in the month of June 1985, and the second place on the Tarnogrod-Biscza road, in May 1986.

In these two places repose the remains of about 2,000 Jews — men, women, children and the elderly.

The places marked have been noted in the register of places of national commemoration under positions 12 and 13.

The patrons of these places of national commemoration are the youth of Tarnogrod.

Comments at the Dedication of the Memorial in Tarnogrod — June 4, 1985

By Sheldon Schorer

On the very Saturday immediately preceding the killing of the Jews of Tarnogrod by the Nazis, of cursed memory, the Jews read the regular weekly portion from the Bible in Genesis, Chapter 23. I wonder how many of the unfortunate souls listening to the story of Abraham upon the death of his wife Sarah had realized that this would be the last Sabbath of their lives. I wonder too how many of them could have guessed how relevant the opening few verses of the Bible reading would apply to them.

Abraham, after mourning for Sarah, faced the problem of burying her. So Abraham went to the people of Heth saying:

"I am a resident but a stranger among you. Give me a gravesite so that I might bury my dead. And the children of Heth replied to him saying: Select the choicest grave. None will deny you a grave so that so that you may bury your dead. And Abraham rose up and bowed down to the people of the land, to the children of Heth."

Proper burial of the dead is an important principle of Judaism, as it is the final means of showing dignity and respect to the dead and to the lives they had previously led. I thank God and I thank you good people for all your help in finally bringing my family and the Jewish citizens of Tarnogrod to a proper grave.

Remarks made by Joseph Schorer at the dedication of
the monument at the seven graves on May 13, 1986

REMARKS ON DEDICATION OF MEMORIALS – 13 MAY 1986
BY JOSEPH SCHORER

It is now nearly a year since we dedicated the first memorial in Tarnogrod. And now our task is done. Nearly a year has passed and I must confess that I still tremble when I consider what has been accomplished. I still tremble when I consider what these memorials represent.

Who among those living here before World War II could have possibly imagined the terrible catastrophe that would follow. Certainly not I. Not in my worst nightmares did I conceive that I would lose nearly my entire family, and that the thriving Jewish life that existed here in Tarnogrod would be destroyed.

We all know – only too well – what happened to Tarnogrod, in this place, and indeed in all of Poland – to Jews and to non-Jews.

We have accomplished much here today and last year. We have restored dignity to the memory of those whose lives were so cruelly destroyed. And more than that – we have denied the Nazis what would have been their final victory. Their plan was not only to murder the innocents, but also to utterly erase their memories as well – by abandoning their victims in unmarked graves. These monuments will forever preserve their memories. These monuments show that we the survivors will always remember the lives they led and will draw lessons from the terrible way in which they died.

I am grateful beyond words to my many friends who worked so diligently and so hard to help me realize my lifetime dream of erecting these memorials. I think you all know exactly how I feel at this moment.

It is impossible at this time to mention each and every inidividual who contributed to the erection of the monuments and who attended these ceremonies. At the risk of leaving out important people, I nevertheless wish to acknowledge the special contributions of the representatives of the Federal Government of Poland, from the Zamosc district and local officials of Tarnogrod who were so helpful in every way in carrying out these projects.

Last, but certainly not least, I wish to thank all of those people who attended the dedication of the memorial in Tarnogrod last year for their warm feelings. I especially wish to acknowledge the children and youth of Tarnogrod. I was so overcome with emotion last year, that to my regret, I failed to take sufficient notice of them. Later, on viewing the movies and the photographs of the ceremony I again saw the faces of the children. Their caring and their concern remains for me one of the most vivid images of the event.

To the children and to all of you – thank you very much.

The Monument of the Seven Graves in June 1989.

Sign at the monument entrance stating the site is under the supervision of the youth of Tarnogrod

Tarnogrod cemetery

Jewish cemetery in Tarnogród
Founded in the 17th century,
destroyed during World War II by
the Nazis.
Restored by
Charles Schreiber
The Schorer family
Courtesy of Sheldon Schorer

The common grave commissioned by
Joseph Schorer in 1984 and was the
resting place of the Jews who were
murdered on November 2, 1942, and
most likely included his father's
parents, his sister and her children
and three of his brothers.

Courtesy of Jadwiga Zmuda

446

United Hebrew Cemetery, Staten Island, NY. Ceremonial posts erected by the First Tarnogroder Society. Pictures courtesy of Tom Merolla

Printed in the USA
CPSIA information can be obtained
at www.ICGtesting.com
LVHW051933280923
758962LV00017B/22

9 781954 176720